T0288267

PREVENT CANCER

and

FIX WHAT AGING AILS YOU

David ZJ Chu, MD

PREVENT CANCER AND FIX WHAT AGING AILS YOU

David ZJ Chu, MD

ISBN (Print Edition): 978-1-09833-134-4

ISBN (eBook Edition): 978-1-09833-135-1

Dedicated to inspiration provided by family, wife Beini, kids Vincente, Toby, Alex and Olivia, and encouragement from the fortitude and hopes of my patients.

TABLE OF CONTENTS

INTRODUCTION

MOLECULAR MEDICINE NEW INSIGHT INTO CANCER SOLUTIONS, AGING AND YOUR HEALTH.

LEARNING ABOUT CANCER
is knowing the inner workings of our bodies.

THE ROAD TO CANCER PREVENTION
leads to good health, especially in older age.

Cancer is the most important disease of the 21st century, responsible for more deaths than any other illnesses, and recently surpassing cardiovascular diseases. History has recorded, in the past centuries, plagues, wars, pneumonic infections and more recently cardiovascular sclerosis, in the form of heart and cerebral infarctions, as the main killers of humankind. In this century, the toll on the human population will be taken by malignant diseases. The control of diseases carried by rodents and mosquitos, improvements in hygiene, availability of clean water, vaccines and the discovery of antibiotics eliminated most of the communicable disease epidemics. Ageing population and modern life-styles have seen a rise in cardiovascular diseases which are slowly surpassed by the rise in cancer. The major illnesses affecting humankind in the past reflect the changes in the environment, hygiene, nutrition, aging population and advances in medical care. Are the current major diseases the canary in the coal-mine? Are these illnesses telling us that something about our life-styles and changes around us? Is cancer a reflection of changes in our bodies and in the environment? The science in cancer prevention points to some intriguing ways that our body responds to our environment and how the lethal scourge of malignancies can be prevented, and moreover, it shows the link between the environment, our bodies, chronic diseases of old age, including cancer, and aging itself. Medical sciences advanced in tandem with the breakthroughs in technology, physical sciences and organic molecular chemistry, allowing the understanding of human health from the classical gross anatomy to the cellular dimensions and today to the molecular interactions which provide new paradigms to many unexplained aspects of cancer, chronic diseases and aging.

The recent projection by the World Health Organization, shows a 70% increase in cancer incidence in the next twenty years. This is in part due to an aging population, a changing environment, urbanization and increase in certain types of cancer. Improved detection and diagnosis have increased the recognition of the disease in instances that would have gone undiagnosed in the past. This means that most everyone of us will be affected by cancer in our lifetimes. Incidentally, most numbers of reported cancers do not include the common skin cancer, usually not lethal, however, does affect the integrity of our skin. Advances in the medical arts and sciences have provided dramatic cures, and yet, one would expect that the death rates would be abating. In few parts of the world, the death rates of colon, breast and lung cancer are slightly lower than couple of decades ago. In the global perspective and for most, both the incidence and mortality of several cancers are increasing. In the US, cancer is the leading cause of death for population over the age of 60, overtaking death from cardiovascular disease in the year 2,000. Managing and caring for cancer patients is daunting not only for the family, but also for entire society. Emotional distress, and disruption to daily living routine are common in families with a member afflicted with cancer. In addition, in most families, the burden is compounded by lost income, decreased quality of life, and enormous monetary expenses.

In the U.S., cancer will cost 130 billion dollars yearly, nearly 20% more than expenditures for the second killer disease, cardiovascular disease. The rate of increase of expenditures will exhaust the current economic outlays for health allocations in most countries. The dire outlook for the fight against cancer demands a new approach to control the disease.

The novel approach is prevention. Although an old and well recognized method as noted by prevention of scurvy using citrus fruits and smallpox eradication using attenuated cowpox, cancer prevention is a relatively young medical field. In the ensuing chapters, we will outline the nature of the disease, how achievements in science reveal the subcellular nuts and bolts of cancer development and indeed the inner workings of our bodies on a molecular level. The preventive approaches can alter the conditions in the cell that promote the molecular homeostasis and mechanisms that reverse, stop or slow the development of cancer. Medical and biological sciences has experienced a revolution in advances in knowledge, technology and a number of new diagnostics and therapies. A surge in technology, computational sciences, genomics, proteinomics and molecular biology have propelled our understanding of cancer at the molecular dimensions. The understanding of the cancer origins allows the identification of the early "pre-cancerous" lesions, thereby starting treatment strategies decades ahead, and adoption of preventive practices that are effective and easy to adopt. As we age, our cellular molecular environment is under greater stress and the need for prevention care becomes more important. Your quality of life will be improved in your senior years with regular housekeeping measures of avoiding carcinogens, by adopting appropriate dietary changes, and by taking up more physical activities. Prevention of cardiovascular diseases with blood pressure management, medications lowering cholesterol blood levels, smoking cessation, exercise and dietary changes have made significant impact in lowering cardiovascular deaths. Cardiac health has implemented these measures decades ahead of cancer prevention and have achieved remarkable results. Measures that prevent cancer include straight forward steps that include all the cardiovascular prevention guidelines, and others that address common chronic diseases such as diabetes, dementia, arthritis and autoimmune diseases. In addition, these steps incorporate physical activity and nutrition tips well accepted by health enthusiasts and now proven by studies based on molecular biology. The very underlying causes of cancer, starting with mutations in our DNA, are now been recognized as key reasons for aging and diseases of the aged. These causes are intertwined with changes in the environment and changes in our diet and life activities. Modern life style and urban environment have increased the stresses on our cellular molecular homeostasis, and these changes increase the rate of molecular gene damage and mutations, which then, accumulate in the somatic and stem cells, leading to cell dysfunction including malignant transformation.

Conventional understanding of cancer and other diseases have changed with scientific advances in molecular biology. Medieval physicians based their treatments on the balance of four humors: phlegm, black bile, yellow bile and blood. Although human anatomy was recognized several centuries BC, in Egypt and Greece, not until Vesalius, in 1676, anatomy was studied as a discipline. Microscopic and cellular anatomy, or histology, had to wait for the advances in optics, in the microscope, a century later. Molecular biology bloomed in the mid-twentieth century with description of the structure of insulin, DNA and hemoglobin. Thus, the evolution of medicine from framework of humors, to anatomy and physiology, then, to cellular and microbiology, and today to molecular biology has shown an acceleration in the pace of advances and understanding of body function and diseases. Current medical sciences have led to effective strategies in combating cancer. New paradigms are emerging, based on molecular genomics, genetic epidemiology, and environmental sciences that link our understanding of other major chronic illnesses to that of cancer. Hence, the unifying concept of cancer, chronic diseases, well-being and longevity is emerging in ways that can change our approaches to health care and daily living.

Our bodies are composed of trillions of cells, a marvel of a multicellular organism. However, from a cellular and molecular viewpoint, only a well-balanced eco-system, borrowing from well proven theories of environmental sciences, combined with knowledge of molecular medicine can lead us to well-designed approaches to the cancer problem. Each component, down to your organs, cells, genes and proteins, functions inextricably intertwined with each other and to organisms in and around us, the microbiome. Precise and personalized medicine, commonly referred to the present state of clinical practice, evolved from the paradigm of molecular biology that changed our view of cancer and other illnesses from organ-based malfunction, to a disruption in the homeostasis of our molecular ecology.

Our cells have a certain capacity to adapt to many changes such as growth, aging, trauma and infections. In our life-time, mutations and epigenetic changes can accumulate over decades and lead to malignant transformation. Current studies in molecular biology and cancer prevention shed light in the pertubations of the cellular eco-system conducive to tumorigenesis. Each cancer type and scientific advances have their own story to tell. The stories have protagonists, intrigues, villains and heroes, and happy endings as we are all beneficiaries of the new discoveries. Usually the scientist struggles with clues and riddles and sometimes serendipity reaches out with a helping hand. As Louis Pasteur, authored the germ theory of diseases, in 1864, said: "In the fields of observation, chance only favors the prepared mind." Our current approaches have fallen somewhat short of expectations. The cure of cancer campaign launched by President Nixon in 1971, and the Moon-Shot program proposed by Obama and Biden, in 2016, are focused on treating the established cancers. Despite several notable advances, we all agree that tragic cancer deaths continue. Greater attention needs to be focused on preventing cancer, as pointed out, being more effective and cost-effective. Using the new molecular medicine to confront and attack the disease years prior they are clinically diagnosed, PREVENTION should be the focus on the "war against cancer".

In the course of this book, we are covering the principles of cancer prevention and understanding the molecular machinery behind tumor growth and indeed the basic function of our cells. We will unravel fascinating stories behind the science and spare you the mundane and difficult minutia of the molecular biology. After describing the necessary background in the study of cancer, oncology, the molecular basis thereof, which also weave into the web of aging and chronic diseases. We will summarize the how to prevent illnesses of old age and maintain healthy living. You will realize that on the molecular level most illnesses of older age and cancer have a common basis, and by preventing cancer, you will reap the benefits of preventing other chronic illnesses of older age. Cancer prevention is a work in progress and despite the lack of exactness in health sciences we will outline specific easy steps one should follow along the road to well-being.

As this book was ready for publication, the coronavirus world 2020 pandemic virtually swept all continents within a few months after the alarm was sounded by WHO, affecting millions of people and causing havoc in healthcare resources, economic disruptions and significant numbers of deaths, in the hundreds of thousands. For a few years, this pandemic will easily surpass cancer and chronic diseases as the main health threat. As we learn more about this new SARS CoV-2 virus and the various aspects of the illness it is clear that to deal successfully with this pandemic requires the molecular tools and framework that the study of cancer, cancer prevention and molecular biology have developed in the last several decades. In addition, individuals with cancer, older age and illnesses associated with higher risks for cancer are considered more likely to have adverse outcome from the coronavirus infection. Thus, the narrative of the inherent intertwining of the molecular aspects of physiology and pathology underlying many of our ailments include this apparent foreign virus, that at closer examination, has been a part of our ecosystems, and our molecular ecology, since our origins and indeed since the origins of life, not millions but billions of years ago.

2

MAGNITUDE OF THE CANCER PROBLEM

Cancer is a conglomerate of different diseases with the common properties of uncontrolled cell growth and ability to skip and migrate into other body organs, called metastasis. Traditionally the classification of cancers is based on the organ of origin and cell morphology by microscopic exam, performed by pathologists, like breast or lung cancer, for example. By looking at the cell shape, size and staining characteristics, and arrangement of the cells relative to surrounding parenchymal cells, the pathologist can classify the cancer type in the majority of tumors. The classification by histology, cellular morphology, gives some predictability into the behavior of the tumor, along with its stage (extent the tumor has grown). Management and treatments can then be prescribed. There are a few tumors that cannot be classified by histology alone, such as metastatic tumors originating elsewhere and lodging in another organ without apparent presence of the primary tumor, known as cancer of unknown primary. The molecular characterization of tumors and tissue stains specific to some cellular proteins can reclassify cancers that may look alike. Molecular and genomic classification of tumors have advanced the field of cancer diagnosis, however, the histopathological classification of tumors, still serves the clinician well, since most diagnostic approaches, start with anatomical considerations. Newer techniques in identifying cellular and chromosomal changes, such as, receptor proteins identified by monoclonal antibodies, and tumor oncogenes, which can point to drugs active in certain tumors with specific gene mutations. The morphological and genetic classification of tumors are not mutually exclusive, but complimentary. What is important in the classification and ultimately the correct diagnosis of cancer sub-type, is to find the specific treatments that can reverse its growth potential and eventually eliminate all cancerous cells. In most instances, in medulloblastomas, for example, molecular techniques have contributed to sub-classification of tumors leading to more accurate, improved diagnosis, and more effective treatments. In the realm of cancer prevention, the sub-cellular changes corresponding to the cancerous behavior may give clues to molecular interactions that can be modified and prevent cells in becoming cancerous. In other words, as we understand the genetic changes and molecular steps that lead to tumorigenesis, transformation into cancerous cells, we will be able to diagnose the early changes and prescribe molecular tools to abort or delay the early steps of tumorigenesis.

Cancer is the major disease of this century. It is rapidly becoming the most common affliction capable of causing death and will have the unfortunate distinction of being the biggest killer. Presently, in the U.S., it has surpassed cardiovascular diseases as the most common cause of death in individuals over 60 years of age (CDC figures, 2016). Cancer as a disease, is a source of physical and psychological burden for patients and their families and not surprisingly also an immense economic burden, a costly set-back for families and communities alike.

The yearly expenditure for cancer care is 130 billion dollars, an estimate for the U.S., for year of 2010 (Mariatto, 2011), and is 20% higher than the second most common cause of death, namely, cardiovascular diseases. These estimates will rise dramatically for the future decades in US and worldwide as the incidence of cancer is expected to rise dramatically. There will also be more cancer survivors, as cancer management will cure more patients and prolong their survival, making cancer more like a chronic disease, such as diabetes, dementia and heart disease. These chronic diseases, more common in older age individuals, although diverse in character, such as diabetes and cancer, have common threads in their causation. Fortunately, the prevention measures, likewise, will decrease the risks for all chronic diseases in older age. Hence, by adopting cancer prevention strategies, you will also become healthier in your old age, and add to your longevity. As we will elaborate, the basic molecular mechanisms are shared by many of these illnesses.

The cancer burden can be felt not only as an economic loss but also as a struggle for the patient and the entire family, especially the caregivers for the cancer patient. This disease has been traditionally so feared, that many family members would ask the physician not to reveal the true diagnosis to their loved ones. Personal accounts of living and dying with cancer accentuates the degree of suffering, chronicity and severity of the disease. The financial costs of the entire ordeal will drain most families of their savings, and in many cases, will leave them heavily indebted. Options of radical treatments are difficult choices and are often presented by the medical team in the hopes for cure or prolonging life. It is not uncommon to find costly and morbid treatments accepted by patients very near the end of their fight against cancer. Some will call these efforts and treatments futile. Indeed, many hospitals have instituted panels of doctors (hospice team) to help achieve a realistic balance between quality and quantity of life and navigate some of these difficult choices, and in the process control the over-expenditures. Others will recall individuals that have launched a successful battle and survived the cancer after been assigned confort care by a competent team of physicians.

The future projections for this disease are simply alarming, a rise of 58% in the numbers of cancers, by year 2025. (Rahib, 2014). These projections may be on the conservative range and have been drawn by well-respected scientists and epidemiologists brought together by the World Health Organization (WHO) and the Surveillance, Epidemiology and End Results (SEER) in the U.S. These numbers are projections of published statistics on cancer around the different continents. One reason for the numbers of cancer rise, is due to the aging population in both developed and economically developing countries. Other factors include the rise in obesity, change in diets, sedentary life styles, pollution of the atmosphere and water sources.

Ozone thinning of the atmosphere allowing greater penetration of sun rays contribute to the increasing numbers of skin cancers. Other alarming signals are the increase in numbers of gastroesophageal junction tumors, colorectal cancers in the young and the world-wide findings of non-smoking related lung cancers. Not all these trends can be entirely explained. Global warming is an obvious environmental change rapidly affecting our lives, and its impact on cancer rates is unknown. Clearly, the stress imposed on all communities' budgets and social structures will necessarily impact negatively on health care resources. The global recession starting in 2008, was associated with an increase in cancer deaths in several countries. Though not far-fetched, the environmental links are inescapable; a fraction of degree temperature rise will correspond to significant sea level rise, and increase in frequency of destructive storms and droughts. Similarly, small levels of water and air contamination can over years increase cancers of the lung, leukemia and thyroid tumors. Tobacco use is increasing in several parts of the world, including areas of high population density such as in China and India. The incidence of lung cancer in China is estimated to overtake liver and colorectal cancers combined in the next decade due to tobacco use. Increased infections in low income populations, coupled with scarcity of clean water and clean air, are contributing factors for the rise in cancer rates.

These dire projections are met with unique opportunities, especially in identifying the potential causes in the context of disease prevention. The cancer statistics revealed in the last 10 years indicate some clues regarding rate increases and reassuringly some decreases in death rates. Among the most common 15 cancers, the majority show rising incidence, and only a few with decreasing trends, such as stomach and colorectal cancer, in the U.S. Elsewhere in the world, such as Korea, Mongolia, Guatemala, the incidence of stomach cancer still top 30 cases per 100,000 individuals. The key to these differences is the prevalence of stomach infections by H pylori worldwide. In the U.S., H pylori infections and the rate of stomach cancers are decreasing, due to the common use of antibiotics. Skin cancers, including melanoma has been rising at the rate of 5% yearly. The main cause is sun rays damage of the skin over decades, and the thining of atmospheric ozone layers, allowing higher dose of UVA and UVB sun rays, to reach the earth surface. Other significant increases noted recently are among the esophago-gastric and thyroid cancer incidence. Since many of these cancer stories vary by site, we will cover them individually in the following chapters.

Our current state of the art cancer therapies will yield unprecedented cures in many patients, however, even in an economically developed country as the U.S., we are ill prepared to tackle the increase of new cancer patients and maintain the health of cancer survivors, due to shortage of funds and trained cancer physicians. The quality of cancer care is unprecedented in some of the country's best cancer centers, and at the same time in stark contrast, severe shortages of cancer care specialists exist in many communities. Clearly, creative strategies are necessary to overcome some of these obstacles to combat cancer at every level of the population social strata, and cancer prevention is key to manage the projected magnitude of cancer as a world health problem. Cancer prevention has a robust background of scientific research and further on-going research is needed. The obvious issue is implementation, both in doctor's offices and as a planned public health issue. Only 2.7% of cancer care health expenditures have been earmarked for cancer prevention, according to one European study. Prevention of cancer is a simple concept and the strategies may employ some of the most up to date science, and clearly more research needs to be done. In the life span of an individual, prevention of cancer is not only cost-effective, and will in addition, save many the burden of the disease and lead to healthier and better quality of life. As will be clear in this discourse, the major preventive measures will also prevent other major chronic illnesses, diabetes, obesity, cardiovascular diseases, and others. Looking at the entire spectrum of health care needs for the elderly, a growing burden in this century, prevention of all chronic diseases, including cancer, will be one most important public health issue.

3

WHAT IS CANCER? WHAT IS CANCER PREVENTION?

Cancer is a commonly used word and often brings up personal impressions of this dreaded disease that hardly needs definition. Popular views are loaded with awful and fearful undertones coupled with images of a terminal illness. On the other hand, the scientific definition is so complex that many experts in the field disagree in the exact meaning of the word cancer. Most will agree on definition of cancer being a malignant tumor composed of cells that grow out of control destroying surrounding tissues and eventually spread or metastasize to other body organs. The complexity in the description of cancer, begin with the wide variety of cancer types and a wide variety of behaviors, from a slow growing mass to a life ending disease. Moreover, the many misconceptions of cancer originate in the dichotomy in its behavior. For example, common skin cancers, like the squamous and the basal cell carcinoma, grow slowly and invade locally only, and usually do not spread to lymph nodes or to other organs, and can be treated with simple surgery. Malignant melanoma, on the other hand, is a different type of skin cancer that can be lethal. When found in stages where the measured thickness is greater than 1 mm, melanoma can then potentially spread to lymph nodes and other tissues. Even within one class of cancers, such as breast cancer, there are notable disagreements amongst scientists regarding the definition of cancer. For example, many clinicians advocate that breast carcinoma in-situ (DCIS), non-invasive type, not be called a cancer. In their view, DCIS rarely cause deaths and by calling it, a cancer, an "over-diagnosis" defined by some, patients with DCIS will suffer over-treatments, such as major surgery or radiation therapy. Invasive breast cancers, originating from DCIS, can spread readily to chest wall and into other organs, bone, lungs and brain. Prostate cancer is common among elderly men, mostly in the occult form, asymptomatic and undiagnosed. Few cause symptoms and disseminate, causing death, while the majority, prostate cancers are indolent and often do not diminish quality of life nor cause death. Further details regarding the disparate behavior in breast and prostate cancers in Chapter 9.

A lump somewhere in the body can be benign or malignant and if the mass leads to death, then we are most likely dealing with cancer. Early description of cancer has been recorded in ancient Egypt in manuscripts dating to 1600 BC. Hippocrates (460-370 BC) referred to cancer as karkinos, a crab in Greek, and Celsius used the Latin term cancer. The compendium of herbal medicine, the Yellow Emperor Internal Classics (China, 100-200 BC), described remedies for ovaryan tumors and polyps. Publications in the late 1800's and early 1900's on cancer were mostly descriptive, outlining presentation, symptoms, findings and possible surgical treatments. Classification by cell type and systematic microscopic description of cancer was pioneered by Rudolf Virchow, a Viennese physician, credited to have started the field of modern pathology, by the publication of his book, Cellular Pathology, in 1858. Surgery for cancer has been referenced by Leonidas of Alexandria (200 AD) for breast cancer, and curative excisions described in the modern era by John Hunter in the latter half of XVIII century. Drug treatment for cancer started with the use of nitrogen mustard, when was noted to cause significant bone marrow changes in a World War II soldier exposed to this agent. It was then used to treat lymphoma, and thereafter, other similar alkylating agents were developed. Radiotherapy was used in breast cancer shortly after Roentgen, in 1896, generated X-rays, and was adopted in diagnostic imaging in therapy. Roentgen received the first Nobel Prize for physics in 1901. Subcellular description of cancer was led by the field of cytogenetics, and notable advances included the discovery of the Philadelphia chromosome in CML (chronic myeloid leukemia) in 1960, by Nowell and Hungerford. Mapping of diseases to the chromosome began with work in fruit fly, Drosophila, at the turn of the century. These studies with Drosophila chromosomes revealed the findings of aneuploidy in chromosomes associated with mutations, and Boveri (1929) proposed that cancer started in a single cell. Interestingly, around the time of the description of DNA double helix by Watson and Crick, 1951, there was still a debate in the cytogenetics field whether the human nucleus had 48 or 46 chromosomes. Undoubtedly, this period was the beginning of the remarkable advances in the molecular understanding of cancer, marked for example, by the sequencing of the human genome, in 2001, a world-wide collaborative effort that required nearly a decade to complete. Today, with several technological advances, such as gene sequencing machines, your entire genome can be deciphered in just one hour, at a thousand-fold lower cost. Surely, technological advances will eclipse even the current achievements and make precision and molecular medicine, terms used today, obsolete.

The molecular understanding of cancer and of other diseases has accelerated in the last two decades and will revolutionize the concept and the treatment of cancer. Asking again the definition of cancer, one needs to ask in what perspective or dimensions one is focusing on. In many patients with cancer the diagnosis and treatment are still based on anatomical and pathological features recognized for centuries. The pertinent clinical features of the disease in determining management decisions are still the gold standard. The type and stage of the tumor, i.e. organ of origin, size, and the extent of spread are paramount in determining treatment and management. The response to treatment and diagnostic follow-up will determine whether a change in treatment will be necessary. In the cases of early diagnosis and in the prevention of the pre-cancerous cluster of cells, the molecular paradigm of cancer is becoming more relevant. Immunohistochemistry staining of tumor tissues that target specific cellular proteins, can sub-classify carcinomas or leukemias that implicate a different type cell origin, entirely, and point to new classes of treatment targets and gene mutations with different prognostic significance. More sophisticated molecular tests are becoming used not only in the research laboratories, but more at bedside, in the patient care setting. Gene and biomarker profiling fit this category. Molecular information is becoming more commonly used, especially in situations where the tumor is uncommon or has not behaved in the usual manner. This is now referred to as personalized medicine, molecular, or precision medicine. Both names imply correlation between clinical behavior of cancer and other diseases to their molecular pathogenesis and that these diseases can be specific to one's individual genetic or molecular make-up. Each person has his or her unique genome, similarly every cancer has its unique set of cancer genes, known as oncogenes, which are mutated genes contributing to the oncogenesis, the process that transforms a cell into cancer. Today, the majority of the medical decisions at bed side and in the clinics are still mostly based on clinical findings, obtained by using the old tools, such as, history taking, stethoscope, basic laboratory tests and tissue examination under the microscope. One may ask if this is the proper progression of science slowed by the inertia of change, as in other fields such as sociology or economics. In medicine for example, there are no clear correlation or direct lines leading the anatomic and pathologic findings to the molecular make-up of the cell, as one finds in physics between the Newtonian and the sub-atomic description of matter using mathematical equations. Each clinical finding will most likely be associated with millions of molecular events. The challenge for the future of medicine is to find the link between a meaningful sum of several molecular events to the cellular changes, and then to the clinical findings. Medicine lacks the theoretical component that will speed up the experimental findings, as in theorectical physics. Clinical findings will need to be laboriously mapped to molecular changes through observed findings in large patient data banks. The shift of cancer management from the organ-based to the molecular or precision medicine seems to be slow, however with the benefit of hind-sight, some of these advances are coming at a lightning (or internet) speed.

The promise of precise medicine is greatest for cancer prevention. As the molecular changes occur in the pre-cancerous stage, and the fact that the molecular changes precede the actual diagnosis of cancer by a dozen years, then at this stage of cancer development, prevention measures will yield the greatest benefits. We all know that treating a late stage cancer will not necessarily end in a favorable result, even when the latest molecular based interventions are used. On the other hand, interventions in the pre-cancerous stage are effective and less taxing in costs and morbidities. We have essentially stated the rationale for cancer prevention.

3.1 WHAT IS CANCER PREVENTION?

A cure for cancer has eluded mankind since third century BC at the time of Hippocrates, who advocated that an ulcerated tumor, carcinos, was beyond the benefit of knife excision. Well after the launch of Nixon's War on Cancer in 1971, the cure still remains elusive. The field of cancer study, oncology, has benefited from the increased research budget, as we have seen numerous advances and better understanding of cancer and cell biology. Despite some successes in the management of lymphoma, testicular cancer and breast cancer, to mention a few, the real cure for cancer cannot be claimed. The notion of a miracle pill that will shrink cancers and keep them away for good, is entertained by the public and pursued by pharmacologists. The magic bullet has been discovered in the form of vaccines, for smallpox and polio, and found in the form of antibiotics such as penicillin, discovered by Alexander Fleming in 1928. He observed the common bread yeast had a serendipitous contamination upon an agar gel plated with streptococci, producing a halo effect. He astutely concluded that the yeast produced a compound inhibiting the bacterial growth. Technically a miracle cure is still possible, however a more realistic scenario is likely a series of smaller medical advances that will lead to significant treatment successes in the field of cancer.

The concept of prevention of repeated unwelcome events is very old and ingrained in many cultures. The well recognized quote "An ounce of prevention is worth more than a pound of cure" dates back to 1736, credited to Benjamin Franklin, in reference to fire prevention. We should also mention other early successes in illness prevention include the use of cow pox vaccination to prevent human pox disease, pioneered by Edward Jenner in 1796, and the use of lemons to prevent scurvy, a finding from a very first clinical controlled trial conducted by James Lind in 1747. Even though the sample size was relatively small, the results were overwhelmingly in favor of lemons. Modern study methodologies of statistical analysis, randomization of trial subjects, blinding the subjects and use of study coordinators were developed 200 years later.

Prevention is also wired into out brains. We learn from our past mistakes or unpleasant encounters and look for ways to avoid them. The principles of disease prevention are measures or interventions that can contribute to the reduction of risks of the disease, stopping the disease process in its track or delay the onset of the disease. This is classified as primary prevention. Secondary preventive measures deal with lessening the impact of the disease once it has taken hold, like early detection. And tertiary prevention decreases the symptoms, social or psychological consequences of the illness. Examples of primary cancer prevention are smoking cessation and adopting healthy living habits such as exercise and weight reduction. Secondary prevention includes cancer screening, early diagnosis in order to find the cancer in the early stages and achieve higher cure rates. Tertiary prevention covers the areas of palliative care and symptom management. Some measures such as screening colonoscopy can achieve both primary and secondary prevention. Colonoscopic removal of a non-cancerous polyp prior to becoming malignant, achieves primary prevention, and excising an early colon cancer, achieves secondary prevention.

Prevention measures work best when the development of the disease is protracted and involves multiple stepwise progressive phases. Understanding the science of cancer development and their molecular pathways are the keys to avoid, stop or delay cancer development. We will cover the science of cancer prevention in chapter 6. Today, even in cancers that apparently grow in a rapid fashion, such as pancreatic or brain cancers, there are steps that may avert these tragic tumors, since from a molecular standpoint, the conditions and pathways to these tumors have been brewing for years to establish a foot hold in the organ, not apparent to our traditional tools of observation. On the other hand, colorectal cancers grow slowly, however in few instances, even small cancers can invade into the bowel wall and spread. Small polypoid tumors are usually benign, adenomas, and as the polyp enlarges towards the lumen, at one centimeter in size, the risks of finding focal cancerous transformation increases. Flat growths in the large bowel and rectum, are characterized by a more villous appearance and have higher risks of frank cancers and can grow deeper into the bowel wall, associated with poorer prognosis. Endoscopic removal of these pre-cancerous lesions can prevent and lower the risks of colorectal cancer. There are more clues from molecular, genetic and clinical discoveries to be explored. Skin cancers, including the more aggressive types, melanoma and Merkel cell tumor, have long developmental stages and can also be readily recognized by visual examination. More details on skin cancer discussed in Chapter 9.1.

Table 3.1, below, provides a guide to the types of cancer prevention and methods:

	CANCER PREVENTION	
Category	Measures	Examples
	Chemoprevention	Aspirin, ibuprofen (NSAIDs) for colorectal neoplasms; tamoxifen (SERMs) for breast cancer
PRIMARY	Avoid cancer causing agents	Smoking cessation, sun protection
	Prophylatic surgery	Mastectomy for BRCA gene+, thyroidectomy for MEA RET gene 654 mutation
SECONDARY	Cancer screening	Colonoscopy; mammography
	Genetic Tests, Tumor markers	Breast cancer gene BRCA, P53 mutations; CEA, PSA
TERTIARY	Hospice Care	Pain management

Abreviations: NSAIDs non-steroidal anti-inflammatory drugs, SERMs selective estrogen receptor modulators, BRCA breast cancer oncogene, MEA multiple endocrine neoplasia; RET rearranged during transfection, proto-oncogene coding for a tyrosine kinase; P53 gene and protein involved in tumor suppression, CEA carcino-embryonic antigen, PSA prostatic specific antigen.

4

CANCER RISK ASSESSMENT

Cancer risks can be classified in three broad groups; sporadic, familial or genetic, and environmental / personal life style related. The life time risk for any one of us, in North America, to develop cancer is increasing and is nearing 50%. The general myth is that cancer is a hit and miss proposition, a random process, beyond our control or even beyond what doctors or scientists can do. This is reinforced by a recent scientific article authored by well-respected researchers (Tomasetti, Vogelstein, 2015) concluding that the major cause for cancer are genetic mutations and that these mutations occur randomly and essentially are due to "bad luck", an unfortunate roll of the dice, implying that we cannot alter the results. The truth is multi-facetted and multi-factorial, that come together in a confluence for a perfect storm resulting in a deleterious mutation. Only one of these factors is due to pure chance, the hit on the very DNA molecule that gets damaged. The hits come in the form of radiation energy, chemical radicals, or endogenous reactive oxygen species (ROS). Protecting the gene against mutations has been a struggle for multi-cellular organisms for millions of years. Our cells are constantly striving to keep a homeostatic environment, free from some of the outside agents that will alter the fine internal equilibrium, such as infectious microbes, chemical stresses, radiation, and from internal generation of reactive oxygen products and "worn-out molecules", thereby accumulating waste products. These stresses in the end and with passing years will cause DNA damage and gene mutations. For example, some of the reactive oxygen radicals will attach to DNA molecules, called DNA adducts, and lead to damage and malfunction. Not all gene mutations are deleterious, and some are refered to as single nucleotide polymorphism (SNP), however, taken altogether, additive effects result in functional deficiencies, contributing to chronic diseases, cancer and speed the aging process itself. The cumulative intracellular stresses on the genome and proteome go hand in hand with cellular accumulation of waste products that result in protein plaques such as amyloid deposits. These protein plaques are associated with Alzheimer's disease, chronic inflammatory conditions and cancer.

The stresses in the cellular nucleus and cytoplasm accumulate over many years starting well in the teenage years and their harmful consequences can present surprisingly at young age. For example, diet induced arterial plaques have been found in individuals in their teens and cholesterol plaques are indications of other conditions associated with higher oxidative stress and mutation rates (Cervelli, 2012). Cancer in the young has become a more frequent finding. These changes can be measured and constitute the cumulative risks for cellular dysfunction. The wear and tear of these stresses on the cell molecules, proteins and nucleic acids, as in the genes, can be measured as a totality called the exposome. Cardiovascular risk assessment and prevention have been developed in the last decades, with considerable success. High blood pressure, cholesterol levels, tobacco use and diabetes are well known risk factors and treatments lowering systolic pressure and blood cholesterol, avoidance of tobacco smoke will reduce the numbers of deleterious cardiovascular events. Cancer risk assessment can be calculated using family history, blood tests and few clinical findings. For each cancer, the risks may vary, and some of the blood tests are more complex such as genomic and oncogene testing. There are common risks factors for all cancers, and in common with cardiovascular risks for that matter, that can be altered for cancer prevention and benefiting health in general, especially in the older age. These are health dividends that can be gained by anyone after minor efforts in preventive housekeeping work. The majority of gene mutations and damaging hits are corrected and made whole by the DNA repair system. Cancer develops after multiple gene mutations and over decades.

Many factors can facilitate or inhibit mutational changes. Some ubiquitous ones are UV radiation causing skin cancer, tobacco smoke for lung cancer, and less well-known factors are by-products of industrialization making way into our foods and dissipated into the environment. Much of the cancer risks are driven by our daily activities, carcinogenic compounds ingested as part of our diet and exposures during our regular daily routines. Some of the technological advances will allow us to monitor our risks and our own microenvironment and create a personal risk scores that can be monitored. Can we then personalize the preventive measures to lessen the risks? The answer is yes, the mutagenic stresses can be diminished, and cancer can be prevented. If the risk scores reach a certain threshold, then screening tests can be performed and achieve primary and secondary prevention by intervening at the pre-cancerous or early cancer stages.

We are in the age of personalized medicine and precision medicine where your entire genome can be deciphered with several hundred billion nucleotides, in a matter of hours. This is truly amazing, considering that only a couple of decades ago, the human genome project took hundreds of scientists and 22 years to map the same genome. From this big data, known mutations or single nucleotide polymorphisms (SNP) can be identified that can modify your risks for certain diseases or characterize your metabolic clearance of certain compounds. This is an evolving field not only for cancer prevention, but also for all disciplines in medicine. Other gene profiles can give us information regarding diagnosis and treatment of other diseases, prognostication, and predicting drug efficacy and adverse reactions. Genetic analysis performed on tumor cells, for example, can identify certain mutated genes or oncogenes. There is a consensus that even more investments in scientific research will pay off in the end. In 2016, the "cancer moon-shot" program was launched, 45 years after the "war on cancer" and even though the "cure for cancer" was not delivered, we can outline numerous advances that was achieved and translated into treatments. These advances will broaden our knowledge of molecular biology and improve our efforts in cancer prevention.

Another basic reality in cancer, that needs to be repeated in this context, is that majority of cancers come to light and treated at late stages. Even stage I tumors, from the molecular view-point, is a late stage tumor. The transformation from a normal cell to a dysplastic, pre-cancerous cell, then to a cancer, requires accumulation of dozens of mutations, and chemical alterations (epigenetic) to the DNA. The molecular changes in the cells that will lead to cancer, called genetic instability, start at least a decade or more prior to the clinical diagnosis of the cancer. This is the very point in time when cancer prevention can intervene with high degree of sucess. Cancer prevention interventions at the molecular level can inhibit or reverse the biochemical progression into a clinically detectable tumor. Surveying the research activity and publications both in the scientific and lay media, the focus of molecular medicine is on treatment and cures, which at this time, is directed toward tumors found in the late stages. Late stage tumor is the popular image of what cancer conjures up, corroborated by everyday news stories about people with terminal cancer. Cancer prevention, dealing with tumors at their very nascent stages, is not considered as important subject, and rarely mentioned, even in the context of cancer news media or when advances in cancer are discussed. Related subjects on wellness, healthy diet, fitness and smoking cessation are more commonly heard and seen in print. It is time to integrate these related subjects into one: prevention of cancer, chronic diseases and healthy living. This singular paradigm, the molecular basis for wellness and illnesses, is not well recognized, and will be explained in this discourse to follow. The importance of diet and physical activity in our metabolic and energy balance as well as in the cellular waste clearance will be demonstrated on the molecular level. More importantly, paramount in the discussion of health and wellness is adhering to the science with as much experimental verification as available in the current research.

Despite the preciseness of molecular assays and the power to analyse genes from small amount of blood or tissue, clinical medicine itself is not an exact science. Medical diagnosis and treatment benefitted from advances in technology and the preciseness of science, however, is not yet as precise as rocket science, nor as accurate in estimating results as in physics or in engineering. It is not exactly predictable at many pertinent points in diagnosis, prognosis and response to therapy. When NASA launches a rocket or space probe, it will travel to its pre-planned destination, thousands of miles, and after months of travel away from earth with high degree of accuracy. When a physician makes a diagnosis and treatment plan employing the latest molecular tests, one would expect a high degree of certainty in the diagnosis and outcomes, however, there are always certain degrees of variation inherent in the heterogeneity of living organisms. First, the cancer diagnosis for the most part is assured. Occasionally the tissue of origin and its associated biological behavior are in doubt. Secondly, the treatment regimens have been developed over decades, and fine tuned by clinical trials, however treatment outcomes for the individual is extrapolated from previous clinical trials and experience. Surgical resection has evolved from radical removal of one or several organs, to more tailored excision due to greater effectiveness of chemotherapy and radiation. Chemotherapy has the problem of severe side effects, since the normal cells are also affected by their tumor toxicity. The elimination of all tumor cells is not a guarantee for cure. Cure rates in most instances can only be assured within 10% of the true estimate. Radiation will kill tumor cells in the area covered by the penetrating high energy beams. In the end, a favorable outcome can be predicted but the exact prognosis not guaranteed. Finally, the inherent aspect of biological systems bears some uncertainty of randomness as in the effector/receptor trigger. Translation: the reproducibility of tests, interpretation of genomics big data, and translation in to clinical usefulness can have a degree of variation. One could reproduce a rocket or a smart phone exactly as the previous one. And although one atom or molecule of a compound is the exact replica of the others, needless to say one person is not biologically the same as the neighbor nor the next family member, though genomically, there is 99.9 % identity. Illnesses in identical twins can differ by 50%. We are proudly unique and personalized. Hence, the clinical relevance of molecular medicine needs to be verified in controlled population studies. For example, the breast cancer genes BRCA 1 and BRCA2 are currently used to test women at high risk of genetic inheritance of breast cancer, i.e., the group of women with the following characteristics: younger age diagnosed with breast cancer or 2 or more first degree relatives with breast cancer. Under these criteria, the incidence of BRCA gene positivity is around 15%. With a positive BRCA mutation, the likelihood of developing breast and/or ovary cancers is high, but not greater than 75%, life-time risk. A BRCA carrier has increased risks for developing breast cancer, however, exactly when or even at all, is only predictable to within 20-30%.

The practical question in clinical medicine is how to proceed with the integration of the newly established scientific data into patient care. This new information can be related to a new molecule or gene that can be used as a tumor marker or a test revealing presence of tumor, its behavior related to treatment or growth and metastatic characteristics. This is also a key question for the medical biotechnology industry, in order to gain FDA approval, and to convince third party payors for reimbursement of the new medical service or therapy. From the patient point of view, how much information is needed and how many patient experiences are required to recommend a new treatment, molecular marker or a test? There are accepted statistical methods to show whether a result is reliably correct, calculated as p value of less than 0.05, meaning less than 5% possibility by chance encounter. There are also different qualities of clinical scientific evidence. Few patient case reports would be the lowest level of evidence, level III. Cohort studies with comparative groups without randomization or placebo controls, would be the next level of validation, level II, and the best validation studies would be the prospective randomized double-blind large patient population studies, level I. At the highest level of evidence, level I, there could still be some fallacies, such as lack of special populations within the cohort, differences in testing or drug manufacturing methodologies. A good example, is the extrapolations of adult data to the pediatric age group. Other factors of concern are the side effects or downsides of the intervention, the consequences of false positive or false negative results, and costs. Clearly, therapy interventions with serious side effects merit a higher degree of validation. On the other hand, a lower level of validation can be used for risk assessments. A final bar for clinical validation is the comparison to current standards of clinical practice. Will a new treatment improve on the results compared to current treatments? Will a new diagnostic tool be more accurate than the current set of tests used? Majority of new medical tools and therapies are stepwise additions to existing practices. A new cancer drug can be approved by the FDA with validated by phase II and III clinical trials, however the rate of tumor response can still be in 30% range. The duration of response can also vary from few months to a year. Only a third of patients with the particular type of tumor, melanoma for example, will have the tumor reduced in size by PD-L1 inhibitor. This is still a significant advance, since prior treatments, chemotherapy with DTIC or lymphokine interferon, achieved 15% response rates and no long-term control of tumor, only in the order of six months. The good news for melanoma patients, who respond to PD-L1 inhibitor, is that the long-term response rate, (greater than 2 years) in melanoma patients, were surprisingly around 50%.

Now that we have set the background for several relevant isssues, scientific methodology, and how to incorporate new molecular advances in clinical practice, we can delve into the subject of assessing cancer risks. Let us discuss why risk assessment is at the heart of cancer prevention. Polymorphism of cancer risk between individuals is the normal landscape in the population. Identifying the individuals with higher risk is necessary to utilize the prevention strategies to one's benefit. In addition, the risk for anyone type cancer varies in each individual. For example, your risk for colorectal cancer may be very low, while your risk for lung cancer could be high enough to participate in screening and primary prevention programs.

Molecular markers may indicate some common factors and risk across several cancer types in one individual. For example, tobacco related carcinogens can increase several DNA adducts that increases the risk of lung, head and neck, and esophageal cancers.

Risk assessment for cancer employs all the tools used in clinical oncology, including the new molecular tests. How the risks are calculated and used for preventing cancers will be discussed further. Genomic analysis is one of the new tools used for stratification of cancer risks, discussed in section 4.4 below.

Will the next generation genome sequencer revolutionize the way cancer is detected and treated? Scientists had accumulated quite formidable understanding of inherited diseases through studies of families with inherited syndromes and cancers, even prior to the new genomic data. Known inheritable patterns of cancers according to family history were better understood and expanded by the discoveries of germline mutations. These germ line mutations or oncogenes were also found in sporadic cancers. Clinical patterns associated with specific mutations were established, and the management of inherited diseases and cancer syndromes progressed beyond the "pre-genomic" era to the molecular omics era. Having the entire genome blueprint will help identify more cancer genes and will probably link some sporadic cancers to the interaction of a few or several gene mutations. The amount of molecular data available today is increased by more than hundred-fold, and the task to find clinical correlates to newly discovered oncogenes and their specific mutations has become the new challenge. Large databases studies will slowly reveal the multifaceted clinical aspects of oncogenes. Analysis of nearly 10,000 tumor samples in TCGA (the cancer genome atlas), showed some new information on established tumor oncogenes (Bailey 2018). The numbers varied from two to 55 oncogenes, among 33 types of cancers. The majority, 142 of 258 driver oncogenes (responsible for bulk of growth signals) were associated with a single cancer, while 87 driver oncogenes were associated with two or more cancer types. TP53 was the driver oncogene in 27 different types of cancer. Among the 300 driver oncogenes, thousands of mutations were found that all translate into approximately ten canonical cell pathways: cell cycle, Hippo, Myc, Notch, Nrf2, PI-3-Kinase/Akt, RTK-ras, TGFbeta signaling, p53 and Beta-catenin/Wnt (Sanchez-Vega 2018). These signaling pathways represent the basic functions of the cell, from growth and maintenance of tissue integrity, to down-stream signaling and production of specific protein factors. These ten signaling pathways may become a simpler way to understand the molecular ecology in and around cancer biology. The cancer gene story starts with different oncogenes and other players in the early chapters of oncogenesis, i.e., the factors pertinent for cancer prevention. The set of driver and passenger oncogenes changes in the growth history of the cancer, especially, in a hypermutable tumor and in different heterogenous clones of the same tumor. The oncogenes critical in the transformation stage between normal and cancer cells are likely different than cancer genes in well established and advanced tumors. Germline oncogenes associated with hereditary cancers, cancers derived from known carcinogens and chronic infections, and experimental murine stem cell tumors activated by certain oncogenes are examples of cancer genes associated with the very early stages of tumorigenesis and potential targets for cancer prevention. Epigenetic mechanisms, not affecting the gene nucleotide sequences, control the translation and phenotypic expression by silencing or activating specific genes. Methylation and histone components determine the DNA molecule folding and access to transposing (gene) elements, also know as "jumping genes". Epigenetic and genetic mutation interactions underlie the basis for biological evolution and from a pathological point of view, cancer, chronic diseases and aging. Barbara McClintock work on transposons in 1953, recognized by Nobel prize in 1984, illustrates some of the intrincacies of gene function and structure not fully understood. The "jumping genes" or transposons can account for some mutations especially in the intron regions. The tertiary structure of the DNA double helix allows the spatial proximity of gene segment transposition.

This powerful tool in revealing all genetic sequences gives us a pause in reflecting how much genetic information are still hidden in the very sequences we are able to identify yet not able to decipher their full function, especially in the intron segments, refered to as the genetic "dark matter". Hundreds of identified gene sequences, within exons, and their corresponding proteins translated around the ribosomes, have functions yet to be identified. Our genome can be the definitive guide to our risk to future cancers, however it is still a work in progress as to understanding all the information it holds (Nakagawa 2018). For the present, we rely on known oncogenes, protein tumor markers, clinical information, family history, and known risks for specific populations. Genetic testing reveal, in only 10-15% of the average population, the presence of known oncogenes, or inherited cancer genes. In a group of patients with presumed sporadic cancers, genomic analysis revealed up to 25% of individuals had a least one germline oncogene. Though the presence of gene mutations can be more common, many of these mutations are benign or a variant of unknown significance (VUS), meaning the mutation has not been well characterized and the disease or cancer implications are unknown. On the other hand, cancer tissue as opposed to non-diseased tissue or blood white cell DNA, carry dozens of oncogenes, as the cancer initiating oncogene leads to genetic instability and the accumulation of multiple oncogenes. For cancer prevention, we must identify the oncogenes in tissues in the early stages of tumor formation, when the anti-tumor interventions are effective and less likely to cause morbidity. Specific interventions can be tailored to screen individuals at the higher risk spectrum and in some cases aimed at the source of the tumor risk by countering the actions of the tumor inducing oncogene(s). Another confounding issue is that oncogenes has been found in normal tissues (Martincorena, 2018). Esophageal mucosa was studied from deceased transplant donors with anatomical and pathological normal esophagus. Clones of cells were found with hundreds to thousands of mutations per cell, greater numbers in older individuals. Several oncogenes were also found, including driver oncogenes, usually found in esophageal carcinomas. These findings show more complex role of oncogenes in tumorigenesis than a simple linear or binomial correlation. If oncogenes are used as criteria for cancer prevention, then the trigger point between the normal, pre-cancerous and cancerous cell will be more complex than a simple presence of oncogenes in the cell at risk. Clearly the molecular landscape for tumorigenesis and the successful navigation of this landscape for cancer prevention will need more clinical data and roadsigns.

Many recommendations and risk formulations are extracted from statistics drawn from population-based studies. While, the individual's risk of cancer can differ from an average number derived from population-based trials, the statistics provided by studies enrolling large numbers of volunteers is the best statistical method in calculating the average risk. The calculation of personal risks can be individualized by pooling the results of multiple clinical studies. The calculated risk helps in designing a surveillance strategy in monitoring and minimizing the individual's cancer risks.

4.1 PERSONALIZING THE CANCER RISK SCORES

The metrics for cancer risk, can be extrapolated from population incidence figures of cancer. The likelihood of finding a particular tumor in the years at risk, is calculated as the numbers of persons affected the particular cancer per 100,000 population count. For example, the incidence of female breast cancer in the U.S. is 68 cases /100,000 reported in the year 2010, which translates to a personal average risk of 0.49 % per year. These numbers are difficult to grasp, but are used by statistitians to compare incidences for population risk from region to region and from one year to another. A more personalized number is the life-time risk, which is 1 in 8, or 12% for breast cancer for the average risk woman in the U.S. With a first degree relative with breast cancer, the life-time risk doubles to 24%. Table 4.1 displays the average life-time risk of some common cancers.

Table 4.1 LIFETIME RISK OF COMMON CANCERS (U.S.A. rates)

All Sites	40%	22%
Breast #	12%	3%
Colorectal	4%	2%
Liver	1.5%	* 0.8%
Lung	7%	6%
	+ 18%	
Lymphoma	4%	1.8%
Leukemia		
Pancreas	1.6%	* 1.4%
Prostate	25%	5%
Stomach	1%	
	@10%	

** lifetime death rates of cancer (right column); # females only, + amongst smokers, @ among Japanese and Koreans*

Converting a population average risk to a more personal risk, requires family history information (or your genome), past medical history, dietary history, amount of regular physical activity, environmental exposure history and significant intermediate markers (blood tests, scans, tissue biopsies). Most Americans will have one or more family members who have been diagnosed or survived cancer. Family history may indicate likelihood of harboring a known cancer gene or other genes that may increase the risks of a particular cancer type. Cancer gene is basically a misnomer, since all genes have normal functions in the cell, a proto-oncogene. Once the gene is mutated and the cell, takes on properties of chromosomal instability or altered functions favoring oncogenesis, then the term oncogene or cancer gene is used. Mutations can occur in any genes in all our cells, some at higher rates, mutation "hot spots", resulting in altered function (or not, called non-deleterious mutations). Mutations in genes involved in cell growth, apoptosis, DNA repair or immune suppression, can lead to some oncogenes, as in the P53 gene. Inherited gene mutations are passed to new generations through the germ line, then, all cells in the offspring will carry the inherited mutated gene. Since we have paired genes in each chromosome, it takes two mutations, i.e. Knudson two hit theory of cancer transformation, to induce the process of oncogenesis (Knudson 2001). Consequently, cancer risk for inherited gene mutations are higher by the mere fact, that more cells are at risk of cancer transformation. And only one hit is needed to activate the mutated gene. Not all cancer genes have been identified, however the pattern of family involvement with cancer, alone, is a clue to inherent gene changes pertinent to oncogenesis. The new tools in molecular medicine bring new ways of identifying these genetic changes that represent information that can be incorporated into the calculation for personal cancer risk. Table 4.2 shows few of the inherited oncogenes and how their presence will alter cancer risks by themselves and in combination of other known risk factors, such as family history (Huang 2018). Clearly, we have no control over our family history, nor our gene make-up. However, we can alter the environment that surrounds our genes. This is another way of illustrating nature/nurture argument, where studies have shown environmental factors affecting cancer risks nearly as much as genetic factors.

TABLE 4.2 - COMMON INHERITED ONCOGENES

SYNDROME	ONCOGENE	Proto-oncogene function *	Cancer risk (life-time)	Second Cancers
Breast/Ovary #	BRCA1	DNA repair	Breast (65%) Ovary (50%)	
	BRCA2		Breast (50%) Ovary (23%)	
Lynch / HNPCC	MLH1	DNA repair	CRC	
	MSH2			
	MSH6			
	PMS2			
Familial Polyposis	APC	Suppress hyperplasia	CRC (100% by 4th decade)	Duodenal Desmoid
MEN (Multiple Endocrine Neoplasia)	RET	Neurotrophic factor	Thyroid	
Neurofibromatosis type I	NF1	neurofibromin	neurofibrosarcoma	
Retinoblastoma	RB1	Regulate cell growth	Retinoblastoma	
Von Hippel-Lindau	VHL	Protein degradation	Renal cell CA	
Li-Fraumeni	TP53	Cell growth	Sarcoma, Breast	Brain Leukemia

**not all functions listed; # BRCA gene in males increase risks of breast cancer, primary peritoneal CA, and prostate cancer.*

Single nucleotide polymorphisms (SNP) are common single base mutations that are passed on in the germ line and also occur continuously in all cells. They are not associated with deleterious results although when occurring in certain genes, they can alter the gene function in a partial quantitative rather than qualitative manner. Even as a single hit, without alteration in the opposing paired gene segment, the function could be slightly altered. Usually SNP occur randomly at a constant rate and their pattern has been used to trace ethnicity and migration patterns of certain populations. The accumulation of SNP and other more deleterious mutations with ageing contributes to cellular dysfunction leading to chronic diseases as well as cancer. Certain SNPs have been associated with increased risk of cancer (Fagny 2020).

Aside from known oncogenes, genes with known propensities for cancer induction, and SNPs, there are molecules, pathways and actual lesions that can be monitored as biomarkers, i.e., prostate specific antigen, as an example, or as biological intermediate endpoints, such as adenomas in the large bowel. Intermediate endpoints in the progression to cancer can be a clinical finding (colon adenoma, dysplastic nevus) or a molecular byproduct (CEA for medullary thyroid or colon cancer) that indicate predictable risks of developing clinical cancers. These biomarkers and intermediate endpoints can then be used to refine the risk estimates and used to monitor the risks in real time. Since, the molecular machinery can be modulated by several environmental factors including the very ones we adopt in our daily habits, these risks can be changed and assessed on a regular basis.

The scientific complexity on cancer risks, gene mutations, and the intra-cellular microenvironment favoring mutagens, can be daunting, even to a cancer specialist. In addition, we need a risk figure that is meaningful, reproducible and reflecting in real time how our bodies are adapting to environmental stresses. A good example is blood pressure, BMI and lipid profile as predictors of cardiovascular health. Are there biomarkers for cancer prevention with these user-friendly properties? The answer is yes. First, there are independent risks for each type of cancer. The risks should be assessed for each common cancer, as in the risks for breast, lung, prostate and colorectal cancers. Secondly, the individual genetic and exposure factors are calculated risks that can be personalized. The risk for each cancer can be reported in a simple binary fashion; a relatively safe, low risk level and a higher risk level that is actionable to trigger a set of screening and surveillace tests and diet and physical activity modification can be drawn up and personalized. We will assess the progress of risk-reduction measures and give early warning for the presence of pre-cancerous or early cancerous lesions. Some cancers can be detected in a straight forward manner, as in skin cancers, with a visual exam. Other cancers may require some minimally invasive tests, as in colonoscopy for colon cancer screening and prevention. The deleterious impact of skin cancer, some prostate cancers and thyroid cancers are low due to their indolent behavior. For most skin cancers, the treatment is also a simple local excision, cryotherapy, radiation or Moh's treatment. The exceptions are melanoma and Merkle cell tumor where the treatment may require wider surgery and lymph node dissection. Then, there are cancers that are more aggressive, and with greater consequences, such as GI, breast, pancreas, kidney and lung cancers. The screening tests for these cancers can be costly and associated with significant false negative and positive results. Fortunately, there are biomarkers and genetic tests that can complement imaging tests for other more "serious" cancers. From a global perspective, the risk for cardiovascular disease and other chronic diseases tract in the same direction as cancer risks. In order to reduce the risks for all these chronic diseases and cancer, there are relatively low cost and accessible therapies as in reducing animal fats and proteins in our diet, exercise, avoid carcinogens such as tobacco, as a few examples. By doing so, one reduces your internal reactive oxygen radicals (ROS) and conditions which decrease the risks for DNA damage and mutations. In addition, the accumulated intracellular wastes increase with internal balance towards excess ROS. Intracellular wastes and damaged (old) molecules are cleared by autophagy, and autophagy itself, is modulated by diet and physical activity. Higher cancer risk scores can motivate the individual to become more compliant in strategies to reduce cancer risks by undergoing periodic surveillance and prevention assessments and adoption of healthy diet and physical activity that at the same time reduces the risk of cardiovascular disease and other illnesses associated with older age.

4.1.2 GENE TESTING, PERSONALIZED MEDICINE AND CANCER RISK ASSESSMENT

Technology and advances in molecular genetics have changed our approaches to clinical medicine and launched an era of precision or personalized medicine. Our entire genome can be sequenced over a few hours from a small sample of saliva or blood, and now at affordable costs. The amount of data and information would be overwhelming without the aid of computerized analysis. The gene responsible for one's red hair color can be identified, as are many other traits we can see in ourselves, called phenotype. Thus, each mutation or SNP can be correlated to a clinical entity, or more likely, each clinical entity may be correlated to multiple genes. This a simple way to understand our genetic landscape, where each trait, organ, cellular or molecular feature can be linked to a particular gene function or protein expression. In order to validate the significance of detectable mutations, large number of individuals need to be studied with known clinical histories and banked tissue and serum for comprehensive molecular studies. With this note of caution on the potential false positive association of mutations, known in the trade as non-deleterious mutations, or as a VUS (variant mutation of unknown significance), we can expand on the enormous potential of molecular risk assessment and diagnosis of cancer. Currently there are dozens of studies correlating SNPs, non-deleterious mutations and oncogenes to future risks of cancer. There are commercially available tests for a panel of SNPs in determining prostate cancer risk, for example. Incidentally, there is a pitfall for prostate cancer risk. For males that pass their 60th birthday, the risk of prostate cancer rises to over 60%. Fortunately, the majority of these prostate cancers are indolent, not causing death nor disrupting quality of life. Some are occult and mostly diagnosed in autopsy series. The more aggressive cancers mandate a more urgent approach to screening, promotion of early detection and prevention of the early steps of molecular tumorigenesis. The progress in this area is rapid and we will soon need to revisit and revise our views regarding the usefulness and validity of multiple molecular risk assessment tools.

There are gene tests, several commercially available, where part of your genome can be screened for some relevant genes, for example, for ancestry surveys, health assessment, and for common cancers genes as in BRCA and Lynch syndrome. The costs are affordable (under 200$) and not covered by most medical insurances, contrasted to the specific cancer gene tests that can be ordered by physicians from approved laboratories. The techniques and accuracy of genetic testing are still being improved, but there are limits on who should be undergoing these tests. Hopefully, only individuals with higher risks are getting genetic testing. Since testing individuals with low risks would result in situations where SNP or VUS can lead to a series of diagnostic tests for borderline indications. The likelihood of finding cancer genes in the general population, from a routine blood sample, is less than 5%, however in individuals with higher risks, this figure can be in the 20-30% range. For example, breast cancer gene can be found in 16% among the Ashkenazi women. Today, we recognize mutations, known as cancer genes, that increase the risks of certain cancers, however the entire genome carries, undoubtedly, much more information regarding other genes predictive of future health risks. Thus the 5% figure is bound to increase as we recognize newer significant mutations or variants in our genome. In 2019, the United Kingdom NHS (National Health Service) considered obtaining the whole genome sequence (WGS) for a large number of newborns. The benefits were not only the 5% and higher figures for germline oncogenes, but also over a dozen recognized other inheritable diseases such as diabetes, Marfan's, cystic fibrosis, and others. This undertaking would become a large research project as majority of mutations identified (over 1 million) among 6.4 billion nucleotide bases in our genome, are associated with unknown clinical significance or VUS. Currently, though the WGS is technically feasible, the big data analysis and the clinical significance are still undergoing active investigations (Suwinski, 2019). Other reasons for more targeted oncogene tests include contributions of the epigenome and non-coding segments of the genome to oncogenesis.

The epigenome, the molecular changes attached to the DNA, not altering the nucleic acid sequence, has a large amount of molecular information affecting the phenotypic expression of the genotype. These molecular changes consist of methylated groups, histones, transcriptional factors, small RNAs, that can alter the three-dimensional configuration of the chromosomes, and can also affect cancer risks. The indications for genetic testing for cancer are going through constant revisions, and the genomic data will increasingly yield more clues for cancer prevention.

Environmental exposures can alter the risk for cancer. Tobacco smoke increase the risk of lung cancer and others including bladder, throat and gastrointestinal cancers. Second hand smoke can result in similar cancer risks. Sun exposure increases the risk of skin cancers. In this instance the risk is manageable with periodic skin visual exam. Skin cancers diagnosed in the early stages are entirely curable with surgery and this is true for melanoma and merkle cell tumors. Patterns of diet and sedentary life style can significantly modulate cancer risks and some biomarkers will reflect these intracellular events and give real time measures of tendencies towards tumorigenesis. Genomic testing of specific tissue cells will be relevant. Oncogenes in hereditary cancers can be confirmed by blood white cell assays, however pertinent somatic mutations may not be reflected in bone marrow cells which can be isolated with ease, a blood sample drawn from arm vein (liquid biopsy). Sporadic cancers, about 90% of all cancers, arise in any cells in the body that undergo mutations transforming its DNA favoring mitotic activity, growth, and further genetic instability. Thus, searching for oncogenes in a liquid biopy, would not reflect acquisition of oncogenes in specific tissues, in the lung or colon, predictive of lung and colon cancer, respectively.

Nevertheless, blood sample or a liquid biopsy could harbor fragments of oncogenes originating from these tissues, lung or colon, for example, which are then released into the blood compartment by metastatic or apoptotic cancer cells (Yamashita 2018).

4.2 HOW TO MANAGE YOUR RISKS AND PREVENT CANCER

Knowing your risks is like knowing your strengths and weaknesses. You will play to your strengths and protect your weaknesses. The simple plan in managing your cancer risks is to take a yearly inventory, i.e., allow your doctor to check your risks for cancer and see if they are being minimized. The check list includes many items that we can do ourselves: dietary and daily activities management and negotiating around environmental carcinogenic hotspots. Some of these hotspots could be inside ourselves as sites of chronic infections, disturbances in our own microbiome (oral cavity, skin and gut). Though some gene mutations can increase the risk for a particular cancer, their full expression can be delayed or modified by gene supressors and several epigenetic pathways. For example, several studies show a delay or avoidance of cancer in individuals with known inherited cancer genes (Walcott 2016). In plain talk, there are several things one could do to lower your risks, even if the unfavorable odds are cast in your genes. And in addition, judicious screening can also detect early signs of tumor and give further clues about future risks. Good news! the risks can be modified and monitored.

Genomics and the latest research findings are used to assess cancer risks, and more reassuring, that current research also concludes that the time-tested health advices, like your "Mom knows best" on diet and exercise, are important modifiers to cancer risks. In addition, as we are immersed in our changing environment, exposed to harmful chemicals, i.e. tobacco smoke, air pollutants, and water contaminants, that can be tested retrospectively, as these exposures leave imprints in our cells in the form of exposome.

In brief, your personalized cancer prevention protocol would look like the following. First, your family medical history will yield information on possible inherited cancer genes. Genetic and molecular testing are triggered only for individuals with higher risks, i.e., positive family history (Weitzel 2011). Second, personal habits history may mask any increased risks as result of environmental exposure, diet and lack of physical activity. Third, physical exam and blood tests will investigate molecular changes in the gene, exposome and other biomarkers. Risk for the common cancers will be calculated, and any potential risk for uncommon cancers will be checked. Monitoring for the modulators of cancer risk is recommended at regular intervals, even for the younger age group, as these molecular changes occur one or two decades prior to clinical diagnosis, usually in the 5th and 6th decades of life. In other words, adopting healthy daily habits in your prime, twenties and thirties, will lower your cancer risks in your fifties and sixties, and moreover lower risks of other chronic diseases in older age.

An example of colorectal cancer patient will illustrate these concepts and lead into a more systematic discussion of the risk management approach.

A thirty-two year-old male has an uncle and older brother who had colorectal cancer and his mother survived uterine carcinoma. The family history indicates greater than 10% risk for HNPCC (hereditary non-polyposis colon cancer syndrome) or Lynch syndrome, according to the Bethesda criteria. Genetic testing for possible HNPCC should be done. In order to confirm the diagnosis of HNPCC, the tumor tissue belonging to his relatives' cancers can be tested for microsatellite instability or be stained for the DNA repair enzymes. This approach can narrow the cDNA segments to be tested for pertinent mutations. Unfortunately, the tumor samples are no longer available for these tests to benefit our patient. The question now is whether gene testing for HNPCC should be carried out. Besides the cost, one good reason not to test, is that a negative test will not necessarily reassure our patient of a significant lower risk. There is still the risk of VUS (gene variant of undertermined significance), and in addition there could be a false negative rate of 10%. A baseline colonoscopy would be a better alternative, even at his young age. If a polyp is found, the size and histology can be predictive of future risks and it can also be tested for microsatellite instability, which is also a predictor for HNPCC. Diminutive polyps on the endoscopic exam would mandate a repeat exam at 3 years. A normal large bowel and rectal mucosa without lesions would trigger another exam at 5 years. With a negative colonoscopy, one could reconsider gene testing for Lynch syndrome. If the tests for HNPCC is confirmed in the affirmative, one can consider prophylactic colectomy (which is recommended for APC gene carriers). In HNPCC individuals, the risks of developing CRC are variable, in the range of 30-50% and the risk of extra colonic neoplasm may be just as high. For a female HNPCC carrier, uterine cancers occur in about 50%, and other tumors, breast, non-colorectal GI, kidney and melanoma in 15% range. The risk for other cancers can be further refined with tumor markers, and genetic profiling. When the risk of extra-colonic cancers are significant, prophylactic colectomies will no longer be reccomended, since would not reduce the risk of cancer mortality significantly. Periodic colonoscopy can be an alternative to prophylactic colectomy. Screening for extra-colonic tumors in Lynch syndrome, for breast, uterine, renal and other GI cancers should also be considered. In addition, the affected individual can modify dietary intake to include more fresh products of fruits, vegetables, nuts and lower the intake of processed foods, and increase physical activities. Soon there will be other markers to assess colorectal cancer risks including the microbiome of the gut.

The individual without risks of inheritable cancer syndromes, can be tested for the common oncogenes and here one need to ask which cells to test. Blood testing, also referred as liquid biopsy, is the most convenient and ascessible, and one is limited to either germ line genes or new somatic gene mutations affecting the blood compartment. Cancer genes from germline, in an average risk individual found by testing, is uncommon, measured in 1-2 %. Somatic mutations are more common and increases with age and ranges around 5%. We have more experience in predicting cancer risks with the presence of known cancer genes, however most mutations found in the thousand or more genes with little information regarding association with clinical cancers, would fall into the category of gene variants of unknown significance (VUS). Databases of gene mutations and associated cancers are key in developing a footprint of gene mutations in somatic cells predictive of future cancers. For example, gene testing of blood in individuals at risk for lymphoid malignancies shows a predictive pattern of some gene mutations (Malcovati 2017). In order to develop relevant gene tests for solid malignancies, one would need to examine genes in those tissues. The starting place would be to employ clinical surrogate markers already in use. Surveillance colonoscopy biopsies for inflammatory bowel disease and cancer screening could be submitted for gene testing in addition to standard pathology.

Some investigators see promise in liquid biopsy testing for somatic gene mutations. Tumor genes can be shed into the blood as well as present in exosomes (Heitzer 2017). This would be a novel way in early dectection of cancers. These methodologies are still in development. Individuals with known inherited cancer genes are now candidates for genomic testing since more concurrent relevant oncogenes can be found (Price 2018).

We may well see a shift in medical indications for gene testing as the technology of gene sequencing will lower the cost of deciphering the entire genome. The list of deleterious mutations for each oncogene will grow as well as known variants with lesser oncogenic or disease contribution (each mutated gene, oncogene, can have hundreds of different molecular changes or types of mutations). Soon the list of oncogenes will grow and their phenotypic significance will require in depth clinical correlation, especially when interaction of several oncogenes may result in sporadic cancers, making up the majority of cancers found.

As the cancer field shifts from the organ-based anatomical framework to the molecular, risk assessment straddles both, with several areas where the transition into molecular markers that may have higher accuracy and reliability than the traditional clinical organ-based signs and findings. Cancer screening in most common cancers, with imaging tests in lung and breast cancers, or colonoscopies in colon cancers are solely based on old school cancer incidences. The individuals eligible for screening may be narrowed to a smaller subset based on biomarkers or molecular strategies, in whom the yield for significant findings would be higher, sparing many individuals of negative screening procedures or allow the screening tests intervals to be less frequent. For the present, the traditional organ-based findings have more robust clinical experience, and will continued to be applied. On the other hand, one can calculate cancer risks given several meaningful biomarkers or oncogenes, once molecular oncology is more fully developed (Li 2011). Clinical approaches and risk calculations for screening and early diagnosis are rooted in the past, as the newer methodologies will gain greater clinical use after proper validation in larger groups of individuals.

4.2.1 RISK MANAGEMENT FOR COMMON CANCERS

Screening for common cancers have been worked out by numerous trials and despite many controversies, cancer diagnosis at an earlier stage in its development, will uniformly result in higher cure rates. The skeptics of cancer screening bring up the point of lead time bias. This can be true in some aggressive cancers, which even when found in early stages, can still harbour metastasis. Thus, one observes longer survival amongst tumors diagnosed earlier, ergo, the lead time bias. The cancer screening advocates, on the other hand, correctly interpret the findings as true gains in lives saved and prolongation of survival, and not due to improvement in medical treatments or lead time bias alone. When looking at the entire population of screened individuals, there are cases of early cancers that lead to cures, more often than in non-screened populations. In the subset of individuals that an aggressive cancer is diagnosed "early" there is a better response to treatments and longer survival, despite an eventual death due cancer. Thus, there are true benefits to screening measures. If you are the individual with early diagnosis of cancer from screening tests, you are definitely 100% better off. The controversies, entertained by some investigators, are based on population data. This topic will be discussed in detail in Chapter 7: Cancer screening and early diagnosis. Most of the downsides of cancer screening concern costs, possible morbidities from invasive diagnostic tests and false positive screening results. These potential complications of screening tests can be minimized by judicious analysis of false positive or negative results, balancing benefits and risks and use of invasive tests. Often correct identification of a malignancy at early stages can be basically the difference between life and death.

Knowing how to manage your risks and be aware of its significance will empower the individual with a plan of action. This understanding will also give you a renewed sense of confidence, well-being and control over your own health. Prevention strategies for cardiovascular diseases have preceded cancer prevention and have yielded significant reduction in cardiovascular deaths. We will point out in detail, that many strategies for cardiovascular prevention overlap those for cancer prevention, and this is more than a fortunate coincidence (Eyer 2004). Cancer is a set of different diseases, and in general the risk scores are each associated with specific cancers. For example, a risk score for colorectal cancer will reflect the likelihood of being diagnosed with colorectal cancer, compared to 4% life-time risk which is the base-line population risk. The same person may have a 25% life-time risk for breast cancer. However, both risks for colon and breast cancers can be reduced by dietary and exercise modifications, and at time same time, by disease specific measures, such as screening measures. Concurrently, you are also at risk for breast, prostate, liver, gastric, renal or lung cancer, depending on your gender. These risk scores may be linked, by some inherited oncogenes or conditions that favor similar somatic mutations in individuals with obesity, diabetes and sedentary life-styles. Chances for an individual to develop more than one primary cancer (excluding skin cancers) concurrently is low, thus it is somewhat low priority to discuss linkage between different cancer risks. Survivors from one cancer may have justified concerns for a second cancer, and linkage in this scenario, depends heavily on the driver oncogene of the first cancer.

Colorectal cancer (CRC) risk, as in several other common cancers, is affected by family history, and the potential of harboring gene mutations contributing to these risks. Familial polyposis or adenomatous polyposis coli (APC) and hereditary non-polyposis colorectal cancer (HNPCC) syndromes are two examples of diseases with known responsible genes, the APC gene and the DNA repair genes, respectively, also Table 4.2. An individual known as a carrier of these genes, the CRC risk increases to 50-90%. Family history charted on a family pedigree diagram (3 generations) gives very helpful visual display for the likelihood of being a carrier. In HNPCC as in other inherited syndromes, the disease can skip one generation.

Both syndromes are associated with autosomal dominant genes and the phenotypic penetration is high. Clinical confirmation of APC syndrome is straight forward since by early teens, the individual would have already developed many rectal polyps that can be seen on endoscopy. HNPCC on the other hand, develop polyps, but at a lower frequency. Family history of CRC can skip the immediate family, i.e., parents or siblings, and the suspicion as a carrier is determined by a set of criteria called the Amsterdam and later modified to the Bethesda criteria. APC and HNPCC account for just under 10% of the CRC, while the remaining group are called sporadic CRC, with the rare exception of other polyposis syndromes. Family and personal history of colorectal adenomas and other benign tumors can also impact on the individual risks. Other less common hereditary syndromes that affect risks are Peutz-Jeghers syndrome (STK11 gene), and Juvenile Polyposis Syndrome (SMAD4 gene). There are short segment DNA sequences in certain genes, called SNP (single nucleotide polymorphism), which characterizes the inheritance of certain genes and a collection of SNP gives a guide to one's genetic background. Certain SNPs are also markers for disease risks of varied types, such as Multiple Sclerosis. Several SNPs are also associated with certain risks of specific cancers, for example, breast and prostate cancers. CASP8 D302H and TGFbeta1 L10P are two SNP associated with increased breast cancer risks (The Breast Cancer Association Consortium 2006).

Life-style, habits and environmental factors have significant roles. Diet, caloric intake, lipid and protein consumption, and types of lipid and protein source have strong implications on cancer risks. Daily activities, exercise, type of work, location of residence can figure prominently in the risk calculation. All these factors are elucidated in several chapters dedicated in the nutritional and life style impact in cancer risks.

The cancer risk is not static. It will be higher or lower according to timely health management. There are methods to assess one's score. The scores can be confirmed by tests done on blood samples on a yearly interval. The tests are a composite of inflammatory proteins, such as C-reactive protein, microRNA and expression of oncogenes depending on the specific cancer risk.

Prevention of cancer concerns everyone at all ages, since at any age, the risks for development of cancer can be reduced. The beginnings of the cancer and the growth process can occur over many years with the ground work laid into the surrounding supporting cells of the transformed cancer cells, often during younger years. This process starts earlier than expected and can be reversed starting decades prior to the actual diagnosis of cancer.

5

How does Cancer Prevention lead to Well-Being, Longevity and to Prevention of Common Chronic Illnesses?

Quotes: The greatest wealth is health. Virgil

Health and well-being are more than absence of illness.... WHO, 1948

Well-being is difficult to define and yet we can say without hesitation, whether we are feeling well or not. Good health, happiness, enjoyment of life, and quality of life, are terms we associate with well-being. A gut feeling without much rational input, is clearly associated with our sense of self, inner awareness and with our body's wholeness. The body in a good working condition, can be compared to a fine orchestra with multiple instruments playing in harmony, in symphonic bliss. The body and its functions can be analyzed in its many components, such as the circulatory, respiratory, digestive, musculo-skeletal and central nervous systems. These organ systems are inter-dependent and when working harmoniously, in symphonic homeostasis, one can say that it represents well-being. For all the system components to be in good working condition, and remain in a state of well-being, your body requires care and interval house-keeping activities.

Health maintenance and disease prevention are by nature, low priority concerns, and especially when we are feeling well. These self-care activities include physical work or exercise, nutrition, rest, sleep, hygiene, social interactions, mental vitality and avoidance of disease inducing conditions. These activities can minimize the risks for illnesses but not entirely avoid them. The human body, like many complex machines, can in many circumstances, fall prey to component breakdown and illnesses. Health maintenance check up with your physician should be scheduled on a regular basis, preferably including a focus on prevention. Prevention of illnesses, and in particular the prevention of cancer, is getting to know your body on a higher level. Narcissism in this case is healthy. One should love your own body as a temple, including its intricate parts, and understand how our internal organs are so special. Protect yourself from excessive wear and tear, including illnesses and participate in a proactive maintenance and prevention programs. Cancer prevention in a nutshell encompass many of these activities that optimize the conditions for function and maintenance the body's state of well-being, health and molecular homeostasis. These conditions lower the risks of mutagenic stresses to our genome. In addition, all the steps recommended for preventing cancer happens to be pretty much the same steps recommended for heart health, management of arthritis and preventing dementia and other chronic diseases. These extra benefits of cancer prevention seem too good to be true, and in the course of reading the ensueing chapters, you will understand that the fortuitous health benefits are derived from addressing the common insults to our cells and to our molecular micro-environment that result in cancer, chronic diseases and accelerated aging.

We are at the transition of the traditional organ and cell-based medicine to the new molecular medicine. Molecular medicine will sporn a myriad of new advances and solutions to the paradigm of health and disease. Today, cancer and chronic diseases are distinct illnesses from the traditional organ and cell-based medicine. However, there are common molecular pathways affected in both apparent disparate illnesses. Molecular ecology (more in chapter 22) will further unify these concepts and the understanding of apparent different diseases, cancer and diabetes, for example, linking the cellular environment to our global changes in climate, pollution and food production. Our physiological and multi-cellular functions are derived from organisms that evolved over billions of years, and nature developed coping mechanisms to many of the chronic diseases and cancer. In fact, there are current solutions to the prevention of these illnesses. The absence of these chronic diseases and cancer in centenarians (Pignolo 2019), is a case in point. Longevity illustrates nature's real solutions to chronic diseases and cancer. Individuals with exceptional longevity is the phenotypic expression of nature's molecular solutions in preventing cancer and chronic diseases. Molecular biology will allow us to understand these existing solutions that so far has evaded discovery or remained outside our realm of biological knowledge.

Even to a keenly self-aware and informed individual, minute stresses and injurious assaults to your body systems are not perceptible. These environmental and internally generated insults to your cells are slowly cumulative, and in the end, are reflected in increased reactive radicals, mutated genes and damaged proteins, cell dysfunction, increased cell senescense, accumulated cell waste products, resulting eventually in aging, diseases and cancer. Thus, the concept of prevention applies to all of these conditions of older age. When the preventive measures (synonomous to healthy practices) are carried out on a regular basis and prior to any symptoms or illnesses development, the rewards may seem imperceptible at first, but felt more clearly with time. Since the basic causes of all these illnesses share much in common, these preventive measures work in warding off cancer as well as preventing chronic diseases. These benefits are the real golden goose eggs, i.e., multiple rewards with same input and they keep on giving, year after year.

Like for millions of people, cancer and other disease prevention measures are very low on their to do list, not on your radar screen. At first glance, this is counter intuitive, since regular visits to your dentist for dental hygiene is an accepted practice, as are regular scheduled maintenance visits for a newly bought automobile. Looking beneath the surface, several explanations can be uncovered. Regular doctor's visits usually are not rewarded with immediate tangibles such as a cleaner feeling mouth and shining teeth from a dental care visits or a humming engine from a car maintenance visit. The doctor rewards you with a bill without really explaining the benefits of disease prevention, and moreover you do not usually feel better. And to be a bit more critical of our physician's work in prevention, a failing grade needs to be given to the current state of medical practice. The major attention in the doctor's office is paid to treating the presenting illnesses and not prevention of events leading to or that further aggravate the presenting illness, now and in the future. Moreover, the current state of cancer diagnosis and the increased prevalence of cancer, show that majority of cancers are found much too late, likely, 10-15 years too late. We are failing in the prevention of cancer. Most instances, in the current medical practice, we get care for the medical problem after it presents itself, i.e., when you are ill. There may be an exception in pediatrics, where, visits of the infant are usually scheduled for well-baby care. Child obesity, increasing rates of diabetes in the young, the increasing prevalence of asthma and hypertension are a few examples that speaks to lack of preventive care. Furthermore, these illnesses are signs that molecular and genomic balance in our bodies are being stressed to the point of imminent major illnesses. These afflictions affect our young and old. Just as our earth's environment is reaching saturation limits, in terms of pollution, CO2 emissions, and climate change, our own body's microenvironment is also stressed by new environmental agents, chemicals and food additives. Air and water pollution increase the rates of cancer, diabetes, cardiovascular and chronic lung diseases, (Preker 2016). Our own internal microenvironment has shown the limits of self-renewal, manifesting in the forms of chronic diseases and cancer. Health education is lacking, and the public does not understand the basics of disease prevention and the rewards for undertaking prevention measures. Furthermore, we should award a failing grade to the entire tiers of responsible organizations in our society. Even though health maintenance organizations (HMO) are mandated to prevent diseases and keep us in good health, the reality is that our clinics are barely keeping up with the care of current illnesses. On a positive note, a movement is afoot in seeking self-help information especially in healthy practices and in topics of healthy living. The informed health consumer will then take the time to request from their physicians more information in prevention measures. Molecular medicine will soon aid in understanding, supply effective prevention strategies and provide sensible monitoring tests in prevention of cancer.

First, we need to convince the public that the concepts, rationale and strategies of cancer prevention not only embrace the activities needed to attain the state of well-being, but also, are the essence behind the principles of self-caring, maintenance and defense against illnesses. Although many of these strategies appear to be laborious and work intensive, by refining the personal cancer risks one could eliminate many of the invasive screening tests. Secondly, prevention is cost effective, saves lives and improve our well-being. Lastly, even for the believers of prevention practices, currently there is a lack of awareness of cancer risks and how to measure and monitor in real time the impact of the prevention measures. In cardiovascular prevention, BMI (body mass index), blood pressure and lipid profile can identify risk groups. In well-baby check-ups, grow charts and physical findings are monitored, and vaccinations are kept up. Measures for individual cancer risks and their changes according to prevention interventions are still under development in the molecular medicine age and soon we will have a simpler unified set of criteria, reflective of most types of cancers.

Many of these strategies for cancer prevention are recommended by cancer centers and investigators in the field, and as new research results are adopted, the novel paradigms in molecular medicine are challenging our traditional concepts of cancer, chronic diseases and aging. These discussions will adhere to scientific evidence, render background relevance, and at the same time provide more clarity on these issues. The hope is to narrate these many interesting stories behind the discoveries and advances in biology in a way that reflects the excitement of life itself, the inner workings of our body and the biology of organic molecules displaying their fascinating interactions, that are captivating and dramatic to the scientist. Much of the scientific writings in peer-reviewed journals, would be too boring for the average reader, besides being full of medical jargon. The goal here is to break that spell, and make cancer prevention come alive with a more interesting rendition, not unlike a true story with aspirations and struggles, except here, the protagonists are living molecules and the scientists are the detectives that are able to uncover their peculiar and mundane behaviors that literally sustain life and unfortunately also causing the mischief of diseases.

The first paradigm is that DNA mutations in our genetic code form the basis for cancer. This concept is well established, however less recognized, is the fact that this molecular underpinning underlies aging and chronic diseases of aging. The molecular picture from a global viewpoint include all the pathways involved in maintaining intracellular homeostasis. We will expand on this concept further in several of the chapters. The key cells affected are the somatic stem cells that repopulate all our tissues with few exceptions, such as the brain neurons, and the heart myocytes. Our body is de facto an enclosed environment, and its ecological health impact on mutation rates, and the ability to fix deleterious mutations and repairing or recycling basic molecular and cellular decay. Our terrestrial environment has reached its limits in tolerating changes from human activities, its limits in self-renewal and the disruption of inter-dependency between different living species. Similarly, our intra-corporeal environment demonstrates strains and cracks in the homeostatic mechanisms especially in older age. The consequences are clear, with accumulation of mutations, and damaged cell building blocks, cellular debris builds up, which in turn increases the cellular reactive oxygen and nitrogenous radicals. The cumulative effects are manifestations of accelerated senescense and chronic illnesses. This unified theory for the pathogenesis of chronic diseases, cancer and aging is not quite appreciated by most physicians and the clinical practice continues to emphasize patchwork interventions with medications directed narrowly to one aspect of the problem such as diabetes or hypertension, without addressing to some basic issues of continued intra-cellular damage to our genes and proteins. For example, the average American in their sixties age group take approximately 10 separate prescribed medications. Most address the diagnoses of diabetes, hypertension, hypercholesterolemia, arthritis and other inflammatory conditions. We postulate that all these diseases are chronic conditions of advancing age, and if preventive measures are taken outlined by the ensueing chapters, all these conditions will be ameliorated, and medications for each separate disease, can be spared.

We will return to these themes repeatedly in the next several chapters, in order to illustrate the universality of prevention concepts. A large body of scientific work and research support these concepts, though many are obvious, self-evident and passed down through the ages in many diverse cultures. Healthy diet, physical activities, sufficient rest and sleep, avoiding unnecessary stresses and pollutants, having a good laugh with family and friends are common practices that promote well-being. Now in the age of molecular biology, the science continues to support these ancient cultural practices. In addition, these illnesses and underlying molecular changes are cumulative and accentuated in old age. These prevention measures will actually slow the process of cellular ageing.

The genetic blue print is made up of strands of double helix, approximately 20,000 genes in humans, and each one containing dozens to thousands of base pairs of DNA nucleotide, thymine (T), adenosine (A), cytosine (C) and guanine (G). These four base pairs are the alphabet of the entire genetic code. Any misplacement of these bases in the genetic sequence can cause changes in its corresponding protein and its function. These misplacements can be as result of transpositions, deletions, duplications, fusions and insertions. Some of these misplacements can be deleterious when translated to a change in amino acid in a protein, a missense mutation, or a nonsense mutation, translating into a truncated protein (Chakarov 2014). Other mutations can be non-deleterious, with few consequences, referred to as single nucleotide polymorphism (SNP) or a variant with unknown significance

(VUS). Other genetic changes can translate into defective proteins. Lou Gehrig's disease or ALS (amyotrophic lateral sclerosis) is group of diseases associated with several gene defects, the most common being C9ORF72 and the SOD1 (superoxide dismutase) resulting in membrane protein defects affecting myelin metabolism. More straight forward association of gene defects and disease is illustrated by HgB gene defect in sickle cell anemia, resulting in valine amino acid replaced by glycine. This single amino acid substitution affects the hemoglobin molecular shape and its packaging in red cells, causing sickling in hypoxic and acidic blood. The genetic code in each one of us differ by less than 1%, and the SNP essentially give each one of us the unique genes that make us different from other individuals. Our cells are equipped with a complex and efficient set of enzymes and molecules that detect any changes in the genetic code and quickly cut out the error and replace it with the correct nucleotide. Thus, through the generations, our forebearers have accumulated genetic alterations that have evaded the self-corrective repair system and resulted in most part negligible functional anomalies in our cells. These genetic alterations can be passed on through the germ line DNA, i.e., the DNA in the cells that become eggs in the female, and sperms in the male. In addition, our own tissue cells, somatic DNA, can in our own lifetime undergo mutations as well. The mutations usually occur when the cells undergo division, mitosis, as in our stem cells. The rate of mutations is increased by internal cellular environment affected by reactive oxygen species, exposure to radiation and reactive chemicals. Although some of the mutational pressures are beyond our control, there is much we can do to decrease stresses in the cellular microenvironment and strengthen the normal DNA repair mechanisms. The ideal microenvironment to minimize mutational pressures is the protection of our own homeostatic mechanisms, such as restoration of ROS balance, proper metabolic and autophagy activities. Some of the contributors for ROS excess are in our diet, in the air and water. We can avoid foods with chemical additives like emulsifiers, and advocate for clean air and water. Exercise is the great equalizer in terms of ridding of excess dietary and environmental intake of pollutants. The totality of these genetic alterations adds up over time and with aging, resulting in cellular changes contributing to cancer and other chronic illnesses.

Well, a dissenting view would say that diseases caused by infectious diseases occur independent of genetic alterations. Would the viral illness outcome be affected by our genes? The cell struggle against foreign invaders has lasted for millions of years since the beginning of life. For example, bacteria have developed ways to ward off viruses. Fungi have developed chemicals like antibiotics to fight off bacteria. The human body can be considered as a vessel constantly remodeled through millions of years of genetic "experimental" engineering. The genetic code changes through mutations, incorporation of viral DNA and subjected to survival selection. This adaptive genetic evolution has incorporated means to deal with infectious agents, such as activation of the immune system, production of immunoglobulins, interferon, cytokines and short RNAs. With the same exposure to a load of viruses, not all individuals become ill, and moreover the severity of the illness varies with your immune competence. All the components that make up the immune response, antibodies, complement, interferon are coordinated by your genes. Upregulation of the immune system starting with increased transcription at the gene level, ramps up the production of specific anti-viral antibodies, for example. Genetic alterations can hinder the immune reaction. The accumulation of genetic mutations in older age is acutely illustrated in death rates from common infections, as in the influenza epidemics and pneumonic illnesses in the elderly, in part due to decreased immune competence, known as immune senescense.

Now, returning to the topic of chronic illnesses such as diabetes. How do accumulated gene mutations lead to one of the most common chronic afflictions in our society today? Sugar metabolism is basic to generating energy that fuels our cells. The brain uses glucose exclusively for its fuel and is unable to use lipids, for energy production. The liver can convert fats and glycogen into glucose through a mechanism called gluconeogenesis. Type I diabetes occurs early in childhood and is due to a lower insulin production in the beta cells of the pancreas. Type II diabetes occurs later in life and is associated with a host of factors, including obesity, and is becoming more common, currently at 7% of the population. Type II diabetes is a form of chronic disease associated with gene alterations. Mutations affecting diabetes have been studied and found to affect the production of insulin, pro-insulin and insulin receptor function. Type I diabetes is associated with HLA genes DRB1 and DQA1. Dozens more have been found using the genome wide association study technique (Basile 2014). Type II diabetes occurs more commonly in obesity, and among individuals with dietary intake associated with higher fat and caloric consumption, which in turn change the gut flora. Both type I and II diabetes occur as result of mutation on dozens of genes responsible for glucose metabolism.

Molecular ecology is a good concept and framework to analyse our internal microenvironment and the homeostatic balance of its constituents. Our internal milieu is made up of innumerable constituents from different cells to blood and interstitial plasma, containing millions of different proteins, glycolipids, hormones and smaller molecular components. All these constituents are in a fine balance for normal metabolic and organ function. The homeostasis at the molecular level is a prerequisite for proper functioning of our organ systems starting at the cellular level, and depends on a fine balance, interdependence of different elements, proteins and lipids. The body fluids in the blood, in the interstitial spaces between cells and in the lymphatic system have an ideal range of concentration of different electrolytes such as sodium, potassium, chloride, carbonate and various proteins. An imbalance of these elements in time can result in organ dysfunction. Just as taking out or adding one organism in a defined habitat, can affect other members of the fauna or flora, and sometimes in some very unpredictable ways. Likewise, the impact of a few single nucleotide mutation amongst 20,000 genes and a total of nearly a couple hundred billion base pairs in our genome is miniscule, however after a period of time and with more cumulative mutations, a cascade of molecular changes can facilitate the development of cancer or other chronic diseases. (There are 15 SNP per gene, on average). The study of mutagenesis has been more robust in the oncology discipline, however, several of these molecular changes have downstream consequences beyond tumorigenesis, affecting aging and chronic diseases of older age. Further discussion of molecular ecology can be found in Chapter 22. Our body homeostatic and cellular micro-environment require periodic attention and interventions to maintain good health and prevent the accumulation of genetic changes, waste products and reactive oxygen radicals and accelerating cellular senescense. We have also enjoyed an unprecedented increase in longevity in the last two centuries, nearly doubling the average population age to 74 years. The dramatic increase in the numbers of older folks, has brought to our attention the results of the underlying changes in our molecular make-up, manifested by the increased rates of cancer and chronic diseases. Just as climate change is a wake-up call for the limits of our planet atmosphere, the rise in cancer and chronic diseases is the canary in the coal mine for our inner cellular environment.

The totality of these alterations constitutes our genetic history, changing according to our exposures. DNA gene strands as a depository of life information can be modified according to which gene is allowed to express itself and at which time sequence, according to accessory molecules attached to the backbone of the DNA strands. The genetic structure is guilded by other molecular components making up the epigenetics. For example, histones and methyl groups associated with the helical DNA structure, does not alter the base sequences, however determines its three-dimensional folding, exposing segments for protein transcription, or shielding others from mutational hits in the course of silencing its function. Some will look at gene mutations and risks for cancer as random events and not under our control (Tomasetti, 2012), however the degree of genetic instability, and the effectiveness of DNA repair mechanisms are dependent on the quality of our cellular micro-environment. How we live will affect the make-up of our cellular microenvironment, the genome and the epigenome. Twin studies, looking at how genes determine development of certain diseases and cancer, conclude that environmental factors have approximately 50% weight on the phenotypic expression of our genetic blue-print, (Lakhani 2019). These findings emphasize that despite the randomness of mutations, how we interact with our environment can alter the final expression of the oncogene or whether the proto-oncogene is susceptible to mutations over our lifetime. All cells contain the same genes and the epigenome controls the expression of the genomes to produce the 200 or more types of cells in our bodies. The epigenome controls the genome to provide the different phenotype expression. As our tissues get older, these accumulated mutations will also affect the epigenome histone proteins, thus increasing our risk for cancer and chronic diseases. The body ecosystem balance is battered by the forces of reactive radicals, chronic infections, accumulated intracellular wastes, ageing and the resulting imbalance can lead to higher rates of genetic instability.

The rise in cancer, obesity, dementia and other chronic disease rates indicate that the self-regulatory mechanisms, that maintains intracellular homeostasis, are failing. The aging of our bodies lend itself to many of these health problems that today we can understand and manage under the science of molecular biology. In the final analysis, our molecular ecology is subjected to similar environmental pollutants and the deleterious afflictions can occur at younger age, which we are painfully reminded in cases of cancers in the young. At some point, we need to pause and take care of ourselves. As we will illustrate, in the course of the book, like our world environment, our diet and activities can leave so called waste products around our cells that can impact mutational rates in our genetic blue print.

6

THE SCIENCE OF CANCER PREVENTION

As our understanding of cell function progressed from the anatomic frame of reference to the molecular, the concept of the cancer cell has shifted from the histological and pathological findings, meaning the shape of the cell and the appearance of its organelles, to the genomics, proteinomics and other molecular studies. Likewise, paradigm shifts have occurred in other disciplines, from Newtonian physics to the sub-atomic particles and wave quantum physics, for example. The gene and its molecular blue print are translated into effector proteins and organic compounds that form the cell structures and their intricate and coordinated functions. The changes in the genetic code that lead to cancer can be characterized by turning on and off, or speeding and slowing molecular pathways, epigenetic modulators and synthesis of some unique proteins that hinder tumor suppressor or enhance oncogenic functions in the cell. The end result favors cancer cell growth, disruption of local cell to cell interactions, including cell contact growth inhibition, acquisition of tissue invasiveness and the epithelial to mesenchymal transition (EMT), (Friedl 2011).

One important aspect of cellular physiology is the redundancy of molecular controls and pathways. This multiplicity and interdependency of molecular functions and pathways are the remarkable simple complexities of nature. Comparing the work cells have to perform to numerous computer hardware and software platforms, such as in the major systems for commercial airlines and air space coordination, we can appreciate the scope of the tasks at hand. We can all remember the recent major glitches that grounded air transportation for hours to days. In a physiological setting, these similar glitches in the function of the cells would mean severe illnesses or cellular death, in completely unexpected circumstances. Surprisingly, these glitches are rare in cells, unless the genetic system is bugged by mutations or overwhelming attack by infectious organism. The redundant and overlapping interdependent molecular pathways allow the smooth physiological performances in our cellular mechanisms. One of these molecular routing is illustrated by a membrane receptor that is targeted by a drug named Gleevec, imatinib. This molecule targets the receptor c-KIT, at the cell membrane, which then transmit the activation signal to the pathway of BCR-ABL and PDGF-RA, and selectively inhibits the tyrosine kinase signal transduction. In patients with CML (chronic myelogenous leukemia) and others with GIST (gastrointestinal stromal tumor) in whom the function of of tyrosine kinase is up-regulated, imatinib treatment has yielded remarkable tumor responses. We will review how modification of one molecular pathway can yield a major cellular change. Going back to the air control analogy, c-KIT receptor is akin to one air controller directing a single airplane to re-route to another destination. Although we can outline each molecular pathway, the exact way how dozens of these pathways function together is still hard to imagine. In the new targeted treatment, like imatinib or PDL1 immune inhibitors, normal cells do not appear suffer any deleterious effects of lower tyrosine kinase function or greater immune activation against self, such as auto-immune diseases. These targeted treatments do have side-effects, mostly limited and not permanent, and illustrate the potential harm to normal cells.

The cell was characterized as a wet and warm bag of organic molecules by physicists in contrasting the the lack of scientific precision of a biological system to a physical event. Mapping out the course of billions of molecules within a cell could determine a biological process with more precision. Current biological experiments are providing the desired results without the precision at the molecular level. However, further insights at the molecular level can be made with big data calculations, molecular modeling and artificial intelligence using more sophisticated probes. The universal principle of homeostasis bridges both anatomic and molecular biological worlds. Our cells, organs and body have complex molecular systems to keep our molecular environment stable under a narrow range, even though the external environment could change beyond life sustaining conditions. Homeostasis was recognized by Claude Bernard, in late XIX century, prior to the concept of molecular biology, as evolution was observed prior to knowledge of genes (Torday, 2015). Negative feedback loop in cell physiology is as universal as the Newton's 3rd law of motion, inertia. In engineering design systems, homeostasis is also known as the set point. The cell succeeds in maintaining homeostasis despite numerous external chemicals and forces that could alter the internal environment. Failure to maintain homeostasis has many consequences, experimentaly reproducible in the acute conditions, however in the chronic conditions, the effects are better recognized from the molecular viewpoint. Mutations are molecular changes to the cellular DNA, occurring at higher rates in disrupted homeostasis, that can alter specific pathways leading to cancer and other diseases of old age (Bruchner 2019).

The cell has developed mechanisms to solve the problem of mutations over a billion and half years, which is pertinent to understanding of cancer and how to prevent it. Some are quite direct as in the repair of DNA damages and mutations, or eliminating the cell with the damaged DNA in a programed cell death, known as apoptosis. Others involve softening the insults that result in molecular damage and DNA mutations. Many of the intruding agents alter the intra-cellular homeostasis by increasing free molecular radicals, the reactive oxygen and nitrogen species (ROS) which in turn oxidizes cell molecules, essentially rendering intra-cellular proteins or lipids less capable of performing their functions, the Harman theory of oxidative damage and aging. ROS damage to the nuclear DNA molecule is a common way of initiating mutational changes. Accumulated damaged or aged proteins in the cytoplasm can present as lipofuscin or amyloid plaques, and is cleared or prevented by cellular autophagy an integral mechanism in nutrient recycling, cellular waste clearance and cellular immunity. The highly developed web of mechanisms to maintain molecular homeostasis and the relatively low and tolerable level of mutations resemble the balance of other ecological systems.

The cancer growth is very much dependent on surrounding tissues and the scaffolding around it. The collective health of the cells, in a particular tissue, can prevent or promote cancer growth. Mammary ductal cells, for example, need the surrounding stromal cells for optimal growth, both in tissue culture and in vivo. When breast ductal cells are dispersed in tissue culture combined with stromal cells, nice circular and tubular gland arrangements are formed spontaneously, while if the stromal cells or basement membrane elements are not present, the cells arrange themselves into disordered or random spheres. Mammary cancer cells, in vitro, show similar dependence on the stromal cells. As metastasizing cancer cells gain access to the lymphatic or venous system and are dispersed to other organs, they grow only in certain receptive organs. Several authors propose the seed-soil concept, in order to explain this phenomenon. Some cancers have the propensity to spread only to the lungs and others only to the liver, and others to both. The seed-soil interaction depends on factors in both cancer cells and the recipient cellular environment. Indeed, other factors independent of either seed or soil, can also be at play, such as the immune system. The cancer cell in our body's confined molecular ecosystem, represents an invasive specie with growth advantage. The adaptive advantage includes the cancer ability to lack contact inhibition, hyaluronidase to allow invasivess, angiogenesis to stimulate greater blood-flow and facilitating food supply, and metabolic advantage, the Warburg effect (Liberti 2016).

Few of us need introduction to cancer since most of us have one or more family members afflicted or taken from us, by cancer. A tumor growth is often not obvious since may be deep in the body, and pictures by X-ray scans may not show a growth of the order of an 1/2 inch and smaller. Not surprisingly, most early cancers are asymptomatic, no signs nor symptoms.

And by the time symptoms appear, such as pain, pressure, a lump, or a queasy feeling in the gut, the cancer may already be spreading and more problematic to treat. Most cancers, when detected and diagnosed, have been growing for a decade or more since its transformation from a single cell. When we consider this cancer history time line, it is clear that many of our treatments would fail to effect cure, for the simple fact that the cancer had all this time to evade our own immune surveillance and other systems of checks on a "rogue cell". In this era of molecular medicine, small number of cancer cells or pre-cancerous cells can be detected. Thus, it is understandable that cancer prevention is the very means of dealing with this disease that is not only helpful, but necessary to decrease the burden and the impact of the most important health problem of the 21st century. It would be a very foolish behavior to drive a car without occasionally checking the tires and changing oil to prevent predictable minor breakdown that can result in catastrophic accidents. Yet this concept has not been applied to our health. Well baby care is routine for pediatricians, and as adults we consider health maintenance as a lesser priority. Hopefully with larger numbers of senior citizens in this century, cancer prevention practices will be adopted as a cornerstone in overall health maintenance and well-being promotion. In addition, the science of cancer prevention brings understanding to other health problems which unattended will result in more consequential illnesses in old age. Newer cars can go longer without oil change, and tires are now equipped with sensors that allow maintenance work with less effort. The science of cancer prevention has also come a long way to yield better results and involve less invasive procedures. Currently 50% of cancers can be prevented, and in colon cancer for example, nearly 100% can be avoided.

AN OUNCE OF PREVENTION IS WORTH A POUND OF CURE.

Cancer prevention is a collection of diverse strategies that inhibit or slow cell growth or the molecular pathways leading to malignant transformation. In turn, the incidence of new cancers will be lowered and the tumor growth rates would be slowed resulting in fewer cancer deaths. Cancer prevention covers multiple methodologies such as chemoprevention, changes in life-styles and dietary habits, cancer vaccines, cancer screening and early diagnosis. Primary prevention addresses the mechanisms prior to cancer formation. Secondary prevention includes cancer screening, inhibition of tumor recurrence, and methods that minimizes the impact of cancers. Tertiary prevention eliminates or alleviates symptoms caused by cancer and improves quality of life.

Prevention of disease is a simple concept and should be incorporated into our routine practices, such as, infant immunizations, dental care, smoking cessation, diet modification and physical activity. Most adults visit their doctors for complaints of ongoing medical problems and overlooking prevention of future illnesseses. On a community level, several organized medical organizations and government agencies have given mixed messages regarding the current policies, standard of practices of disease prevention and funding for cancer prevention. The controversy over screening mammography is a case in point.

The Canadian study (Miller 2014) compared two groups of women, ages 40-49 years, one group screened with mammograms and the second group followed with usual care. After 25 years of follow-up the result of survival was actually lower in the screened group, even though more cancers were detected in the screened group. The conclusions by the authors and highlighted by the news media, and several medical organizations were a notable lack of efficacy in breast screening, neglecting results of prior studies confirming the effectiveness of screening for breast cancer, such as the Breast Cancer Demonstration and Detection Project (BCDDP). The US Preventive Services Task Force (USPSTF 2009) recommended scaling back the frequency of mammograms. Survival in breast cancer patients has improved in the last few decades due to improved treatments, chemotherapy and radiotherapy. The proportion of mammographic detected cancers of the non-invasive types (DCIS) has increased, which should contribute to improved survival. The cancers found in the unscreened group, often found to have bigger tumors, were nevertheless, effectively treated by the modern advances in treatment. Hence, modern screening studies would not be expected to show any survival advantage. The conclusion and reccomendations against mammographic screening derived from this study is short sighted and plainly misguided since it does not consider the other benefits of screening and early diagnosis. Other benefits of screening mammography that were ignored, include: 1. How many were cured by early diagnosis and how many patients received multiple rounds of chemotherapy, and number of tumor recurrences due to late diagnosis. (survival measures include living with disease recurrence), 2. Quality of life differences in the two groups were not measured, especially in the group with late diagnosis, and 3. Costs of breast cancer care in screened and unscreened groups. 4. Diagnosis of DCIS may not contribute to improved survival, which will be discussed further under breast cancer screening. There were three well conducted studies in mammographic screening, published years earlier, showing survival benefits (Kobruner 2011). Today, in both Canada and U.S., many health institutions have already scaled back the frequency of screening, recommending mammograms every two years for women ages 45-60 years, instead of yearly. The first screening mammogram is done at age 45 instead of 40 years. The revised recommendations will delay the diagnosis of breast cancer in significant number of women.

Prevention techniques have better outcomes with a long pre-cancerous, so called incubation period. Inhibition of growth or elimination of the cancerous growth in this pre-cancerous or early cancerous stage prior to distant spread, will in the end lead to successful cancer prevention. The biological process of the cell transformation into cancer, called tumorigenesis, can start decades prior to the actual diagnosis of a full-grown malignant growth. In order to understand this process, we must start at the DNA molecule which makes up the chromosomes. We will challenge ourselves by discussing the molecular biology as a brief primer and keeping the subject simple, but captivating, and expand the molecular and genetic complexities as we tour the world of cancer prevention and understand what is at the core of good health and well-being.

6.1 CLINICAL RESEARCH IN CANCER PREVENTION

Early clinical studies, i.e., using human subjects to answer a question or a hypothesis, go as far back as circa 500 BC, described in the Book of Daniel. The King of Babylon designed a diet for his soldiers to become physically fit by recommending a diet high in animal protein. A dissenting member of his court preferred a diet based on fruits, vegetables and nuts. Hence, the King authorized a comparative diet regimen study, with measuring physical strength, as the deciding factor. Surprisinly, the study favored the vegetarian diet. The first controlled human trial is credited to James Lind, a navy medical officer who tried lemons and oranges for the treatment of scurvy in 1747. Later, clinical studies involved treatments with drug concoctions and the methodologies evolved with inclusion of randomization, double blinding the study subjects and coordinators, the use of statistical analysis and human subject protection. Placebo was first used by the American physician Austin Flint, in 1886, in the study of remedy for rheumatism. The Nuremberg Code, formulated in 1947, and the Helsinki Declaration of 1964, drew the general guidelines for the ethical conduct and protection of human subjects enrolled in trials. The first major trial employing the method of randomization was carried out in England, 1946, for the study of tuberculosis treatment. Current oversight by the Food and Drug Administration (FDA) did not begin until 1938, created by the Food, Drug and Cosmetic Act. The need for regulatory agency evolved over several decades, with notable examples to reduce cases of drug toxicities and injuries. The Pure Food and Drugs Act, 1906, gave the agency some authority, however enforcement, was first, carried out by the American Medical Association Council on Pharmacy and Chemistry, who tested many of the drugs and granted the AMA seal of approval.

Evidence based medicine progressed from the introduction of statistical analysis to clinical trials of today, incorporating advances in laboratory discoveries. Majority of the new discoveries that are incorporated into clinical practice undergo trials. The standard approach for new drug development, start with understanding of the biology and pharmacology of the study agent and testing the agent in the test tube with cultured cells or in experimental animals. Investigational new drug application (IND) is submitted to the FDA when human trial is planned. Three phases of human studies need to be completed, phase I, establishing the dose-response parameters, phase II, monitoring the toxicity profiles, and phase III, studying the efficacy of the drug.

Let us first address the agents that have been tested through phase III studies, specifically for the prevention of cancer. The term chemopreventive agents is commonly used for this group of drugs, consisting of newly discovered natural chemicals, such as vitamins or plant compounds, phytochemicals or laboratory synthesized molecules, and hormones purified from humans or animals or produced through genetic engineering. Major breakthroughs in the understanding of molecular mechanisms and promising results in the in vitro cellular and animal models eventually translate into valuable human interventions. Please see table 1, listing most agents that have been tested in phase III trials, for a diverse number of cancers.

TABLE 1: CHEMOPREVENTION Phase III TRIALS

	Agent	% reduction Cancer	Comments
Breast	Tamoxifen	38%	1.5% uterine cancer risk; risk reduction in BRCA2 not BRCA1
(Mocellin 2016)	Raloxifene	35%	Lower uterine cancer risk, fewer blood clots, improved bone health
	Aromatase Inhibitors	50%	Bone fractures, heart disease; no increased blood clots nor uterine cancer risk
Prostate	Finasteride	30%	Increase in high grade cancers

	Selenium + Vitamin E	No reduction	
Lung	Selenium + Vitamin E	Negative Study	(Keith 2013)
Esophagus	Aspirin + Esomeprazole		Barret's esophagus as study risk group
Colorectal			Please see Table 2

Selective estrogen receptor modulators (SERM) arrived on the market in 1975 with the approval of tamoxifen. It proved active against estrogen receptor positive breast cancer in women by the criteria of prolonging survival both without recurrences (disease-free) and with recurrences (over-all survival). Tamoxifen (TAM) taken as a pill, can replace intravenous chemotherapy for post-menopausal patients with early ER (estrogen receptor) responsive breast cancer. Women treated with TAM were also found to have lower rates of breast cancer in the contralateral breast. This finding was tested in women without breast cancer. In a large, 2,000 participant trial, TAM was found to be effective in preventing invasive and non-invasive breast cancers. Other related SERMs, such as raloxifine, toremifine, have also been found effective in lowering risks of breast cancer without some of the side-effects, (Riggs, 2003). These side effects include venous clotting, endometrial cancer, cardiovascular events, joint aches and mucous membrane dryness. For the last two decades since approval of SERM for breast cancer prevention, the actual use of this option has been low, with poor acceptance by the public and primary care physicians alike. The less than warm reception to a drug with potential large impact in breast cancer, is quite understandable. When you are well, there is caution in taking on any risks of side effects, even when the side effects are mild. By contrast, breast cancer patients would choose adjuvant chemotherapy, with known serious side-effects, even though, there is a low 1-2 percent gain in cure rates. A second reason, pointed out by Dr Gabriel Hortobagyi, oncologist at the MD Anderson Cancer Center, is that cancer prevention lacks a real-time monitoring test. For example, drugs such as statins that lowers serum cholesterol level in order to lessen risks of cardiovascular events, have comparable toxicities to TAM, yet, are taken commonly in the order of millions of patients. One can measure cholesterol levels on a periodic basis with a simple blood test.

This experience is repeated in men for the choice of proscar, finasteride, a drug used for hair growth and approved for chemoprevention of prostate cancer. Finasteride, 5-alpha reductase, that blocks the conversion of testosterone into DHT, dihydrotestosterone, was initially developed to shrink the prostate in BPH (benign prostatic hypertrophy). The development of the drug was given impetus by the observation in a small group of Caribean male children born with ambiguous genitalia that were carriers of a mutation in the 5-alpha reductase gene. In a large study, Prostate Cancer Prevention Trial (PCPT), 18,000 male volunteers starting in the 6th decade of age, were randomized to finasteride and placebo. After seven years on study, there was a clear reduction by 30% in prostate cancer in the study group. In addition, there was a minor, but statistically significant higher numbers of high-grade prostate cancers, in the finasteride group. The recommendation for adopting the results of the PCPT, was tempered by the risks of compromised survival for the high-grade carcinomas. Recently, a 20-year follow-up of the PCPT study was published, showing no survival differences among men enrolled in the finasteride or the placebo group. These later results assure that men on finasteride and found to have high grade prostate cancers were not injured by the treatment, even when subset analysis was performed. On the other hand, one asks what is the point of preventing prostate cancer? The disease behaves in an indolent fashion. However, in some high-risk individuals, the benefits in prevention with finasteride are clearer, such as men of African-American descent and men with a strong family history of prostate cancer.

Gastric cancer is the second most common cancer worldwide with noteworthy high incidence in China, Japan, Norway and Chile. In the U.S., the incidence has been dropping in the last five decades, probably due to the wide use of antibiotics. The explanation becomes clear when Helicobacter pylori, rod-shaped bacteria, was shown to be one causative factor for gastro-duodenal ulcers and stomach cancers. Marshall and Warren were awarded the Nobel Prize in 2005, for their pioneering work that was counter the prevailing theory, at the time, as the cause of gastric and duodenal ulcerations. H pylori is associated with stomach discomfort and dyspepsia and can be diagnosed by endoscopic biopsy, breath exam or a blood test for the IgM antibody response to the bacteria. It is treated by a combination of antibiotics and anti-acid treatment. It has been found that the treatment of H pylori can decrease the incidence of distal gastric cancers (Peek, 2008). The H pylori strain that carries the cagA gene secretes a glycoprotein that causes an inflammatory response in the mucosal layer of gastric cells, allowing anchoring of the Helicobacter onto the stomach lining. Long term infection leads to chronic gastritis, atrophy of the cells and thinning appearance called intestinal metaplasia and cancer formation. The inflammatory response also leads to an increase of B-cell lymphocyte infiltration that rarely can turn into a lymphoma, called mantle cell lymphoma. This lymphoma can regress with the eradication of H pylori. In the U.S., as the number of distal, non-cardia stomach cancers have been decreasing, the numbers of lower esophageal, gastro-esophageal (GE) junction cancers, have been increasing. These cancers are associated with acid reflux and replacement of the squamous cell lining with gland cells called Barrett's esophagus. Interestingly, presence of H pylori is associated with a decrease of GE junction and cardia location cancers. This has been attributed to the lowering of stomach acid by the H pylori infection.

North-Americans who have migrated from high-risk areas of H pylori infection and gastric cancers should undergo upper endoscopy screening between age 55 and 60 years, looking for H pylori and undergo gastric mucosal biopsy to rule out lesions that can predispose to cancer such intestinal metaplasia. If H pylori infection is diagnosed, then treatment should be started to eradicate the infection. A follow-up test to H pylori should be taken in 6 months to a year to rule out re-infection with H pylori. Tissue findings that predisposes to gastric cancer should be followed by repeat endoscopy in 2-3 years. A trial conducted in a high prevalence region of China, showed a lowering of gastric cancer risk, by treatment with a regimen of antibiotics and anti-acid drug in individuals with H pylori infection.

Chemoprevention of colorectal cancer advanced with completion of several phase III, randomized, double blind and placebo controlled, clinical studies. These studies are outlined on table 2. Aspirin was seen in the prospective cohorts of the Framingham and Physician Health Study to lower CRC death rates. Other NSAIDs (non-steroidal anti-inflammatory drugs) as seen in table 2 were also found to be active through COX-1 (cyclooxygenase) and COX-2 down-regulation. There is a reduction in prostacyclins, a mediator of inflammatory response, in tissues of the large bowel mucosa. These drugs reduce pain through a similar COX inhibition of the prostaglandin pathway. Calcium and vitamin D metabolism in the gut are closely associated with reduction of carcinogenesis. Worldwide rates of CRC varied according to geographic location, where distance from the equator was associated with higher rates of CRC, reflecting a lower average sun exposure. This also correlated with lower blood levels of calcium and vitamin D (Lappe 2007). Oral calcium with and without vitamin D has been studied in several trials which enrolled patients with sporadic adenomas. One study in particular enrolled patients after colorectal cancer resection and followed the rate of metachronous adenomas. The end results are mixed. The possible explanation is that higher doses of oral calcium is required (Chu, 2011). A recent review on vitamin D health benefits did not show a definite decrease in colorectal neoplasms (Baggerly, 2015).

The above examples of well-planned studies resulting in chemopreventive strategies for some of the common cancers, with relatively low toxicities, illustrate the complexities of cancer prevention. By and large, these strategies are not widely used, thus, and the overall effect in tumor control is small. Nevertheless, for a particular individual with known high risk for these cancers, taking some of these proven chemopreventive agents, may be the wise course of action. The phase III human trials require large number of subjects and several years of follow-up for the end-point development of the neoplasms. Secondary endpoints can be used to narrow the target population for chemoprevention and calculate more precisely the risk of certain cancers, with shorter times to reach the surrogate endpoints. Genomics and exposomes are potentially the ideal secondary endpoints that can narrow the risk profile and personalize the approach for prevention strategies, (Brennan 2015).

TABLE 2. COLORECTAL CHEMOPREVENTION TRIALS

	% Reduction of Adenomas	% Reduction of Cancer	Comments
Aspirin	40%	34%	81mg vs 325 mg, comparable efficacy, GI toxicities
Celecoxib	34%	35%	Effects extend to NSAIDs
Calcium	18%	+/-	Conflicting nutritional studies; higher dose 1500mg daily with greater reduction of adenomas
DFMO + Sulindac	70%	-	Minimal hearing loss
Folic Acid	None	None	
			Dulai PS: BMJ 355:doi6188m 2016

Among the chemopreventive agents studied, phytochemicals are of special interest. Diets rich in vegetables and fruits are associated with lower cancer risks (reviewed in chapter 19). Common natural foods as in tomatoes, oranges or celery contain dozens of active phytochemicals. Pharmacology of each phytochemical needs to be studied and verified. Several classes of phytochemicals, as in polyphenols, carotenoids, and thiols, have several pharmacokinetic effects in common; anti-oxidation, anti-inflammation, vitamins, and anti-microbial, for example. There are some specific molecular interactions leading to unique anti-tumor and chemopreventive properties. Several have similar structures as human steroid molecules, in particular, estrogen. Refered as phytoestrogens, including genistein and resveratrol, they can block sex hormone receptors and have SERM like functions. Others can also down-regulate the enzyme, aromatase, intermediate to production of estrogens. Morin, a pentahydroxy-flavone isolated from Moraceae plants, has apoptotic functions by the caspase-mitochondrial pathway and inhibition of Bcl-2, and found to inhibit leukemic HL-60, MCF-7 breast cancer and hepatoma cell lines grown in-vitro. Can chemoprevention, with the promising prospect of phytochemical interaction with anti-tumorigenesis pathways, become more specific in preventing some common cancers? The future of molecular pharmacology employing artificial intelligence, new findings in plant based organic compound pharmacokinetics and plant microRNA are promising new avenues for cancer prevention, diagnostics and therapy.

6.2 TUMORIGENESIS - THE PROCESS OF A CELL TURNING INTO CANCER

Tumorigenesis, or oncogenesis, is the study of the cellular process of tumor initiation, growth and transformation into cancer. The process of cell division, called mitosis, is basic to life and reproduction, preservation of the species, wound healing and immune reactions. Though the mechanisms of cell growth and division are well understood, many questions still remain, especially when the control is altered in tumorigenesis. The normal cell has a limited life span, approximately 30 mitotic cycles, thereafter undergoes apoptosis, or programmed cell death, and is replaced by a new cell generated by stem cells. The mitotic activity in the adult cell is enhanced by inflammation, immune-modulation, wounding and inhibited by contact with neighboring cells. In addition, there are molecular pathways triggered by negative switches to cell growth, initiating apoptotic cell death. Apoptosis can be thought of as a drastic step in the cell life cycle, but it occurs as a natural and routine mechanism in many life-forms. The natural process of withering leaves and seasonal deciduous fall of leaves, and the resorption of the tail segments in the human fetus are part of normal function of apoptosis. When proliferation continues unabated, a state of hyperplasia, results in accumulation of cells, a benign tumor, as in skin tags, colon polyps, keratotic skin lesions, lipomas, calluses, all non-malignant and often self-limited. Occasionaly, in the background of hyperplasia, dysplasia can develop and the tumorigenesis process can transition into a cancer. This change in the mist of hyperplasia to dysplasia is now thought to be instigated by acquisition of mutated genes, namely oncogenes.

In order to understand tumorigenesis, we need to understand cell division, or mitosis and cell growth. Tissue growth is a well coordinated process of cell division in the fabric of different cell types. The birth of a baby is truly a miracle, a beautiful gift of life, and is the perfect example of cell growth. Beginning with the fertilized egg, with one cell, it begins to divide into multiple cells arranged in a sphere, the morula. The embryonic cells at this stage can develop into any type of cells or even into a whole new embryo. As the embryo grows, the cells start differentiating into the notochord (nerve tissues), an inner layer, endoderm which forms the early gut; an outer layer, the ectoderm which eventually forms the skin, and in between the mesoderm, eventually differentiating into muscles, connective tissues and bones. The rate of growth and the timing of differentiation are under a well orchestrated schedule, and by nine months of gestation, the baby is ready to be born. The importance of precisely controlling cell division and differentiation can be seen in errors of fetal development. Many of these errors are corrected by intricate and complex mechanisms in the cell, that can arrest the cell cycle, allowing time for corrective mechanisms, or even discard the entire process by initiating apoptosis. Some of these errors can also initiate the first steps of cancer formation or tumorigenesis. Most of these errors occur as result of mutations, others are miss-arrangements or recombinations.

The machinery is elegantly packaged in the nucleus in strands of DNA double helix which contains as much information as the library of Congress, and at each mitotic event, the DNA double helix is separated into single file and copied into equal sequences yielding two equal copies of each chromosome, then carefully pulled apart to the poles of the dividing cell. The single strands of DNA are realigned in pairs and the 23 double helix chromosomes are reconstituted in the two daughter cells. During meiosis, the formation of four haploid daughter cells, there is a recombination of genes ending up in the gametes. The retinoblastoma (Rb) protein prepares the cell DNA to start the cell cycle from G1 to S phase which then leads to cell division at M phase. Mutation at the Rb gene is associated with the rare children's eye tumor retinoblastoma. Rb protein is central to several molecular pathways in cell growth. Rb functions as a tumor suppressor, binding to E2F complex, which then functions as a gene promotor. P53 gene, also known as the guardian of the genome, has multiple functions including preservation of the stem cells, interaction with angiogenesis and telomere pathways, and most importantly, turning on or off the cell cycle at S/G1 checkpoint together with RB and p21. Many cancer genes, oncogenes, up-regulates cell growth through the master switch Rb/E2F complex and its counterpart P53. This is a very abbreviated list of molecules involved in cell division, which are controlled by dozens of mechanisms reflecting the necessities of different growth conditions; fetal development, adolescent growth, mature tissue maintenance, or cell repair during wound healing. In cancer, the growth inhibition is lost, and uncontrolled growth takes place. Can the growth signals be turned off in cancer? Multiple points in the growth signaling pathway are targeted in cancer with some success as therapy. Similar targets can also be developed for cancer prevention, as in chemoprevention.

Historically, scientists have studied tumorigenesis by using chemical and radiation carcinogens in the animal model. Percival Pott, in 1775, proposed that coal dust was carcinogenic, noting that chimney sweepers were prone to developing scrotal carcinomas. More than a century later, the concept of carcinogenesis was proven in animals and the aromatic hydrocarbon, in coal soot, was isolated as the culprit. The three stages of chemical carcinogenesis, initiation, promotion and progression can be demonstrated in a murine model by painting a carcinogen on the skin, then adding a promoter in the feed and observe the development of skin cancers over time. On the molecular level, these three stages correspond to mutagenesis, clonal expansion through hyperplasia and genetic instability, and finally, malignant growth. The chemical properties of mutagenesis are initiated by formation of DNA adducts. The carcinogenic adduct attaches to the DNA helix, pertubating its structure and function, hence leading to mutations or translational mistakes. Other initiators of tumorigenesis are viruses and other agents generating inflammation. In addition, the associated chronic inflammation can function as promoter of carcinogenesis, acting through endogenous reactive compounds (ROS, reactive oxygen species). The genetic instability initiated by mutations are promoted by other factors that inhibit gene repair or perpetuate conditions leading to a cascade of genetic changes and facilitating further mutations. Promoters of tumorigenesis include oncogenes and altered tumor suppressor genes. On a cellular level, histological aspects that correspond to the stages of carcinogenesis are: hyperplasia, dysplasia and carcinoma.

In cancer prevention, changing the cellular molecular environment by moving the pendulum towards slower or normal growth, or increased apoptosis in the transformed pre-malignant cells, i.e., in the dysplastic stage, will in effect inhibit the growth of tumors and decrease the risks for malignancies.

Maintenance of the normal DNA is taken for granted, since conditions causing DNA damage or mutations become evident very gradually and not perceived by routine observations and not readily confirmed by routine blood tests. With passage of time, over hundreds of milenia, our DNA held its fidelity, changing only very slightly, corresponding with minor evolutionary changes. Like printed letters in a book that have been copied millions of times, it is miraculous that the letters in the book can remain pristine, and that the DNA in the cell functions so perfectly. The story becomes even more remarkable, as the events damaging the DNA can occur thousands of times in a single day. Our cells have, out of necessity, developed mechanisms, conserved over millenia through evolution, to repair errors in the DNA sequence.

The DNA repair system and other coping mechanisms are credited for this very important feat. The entire DNA repair system is composed of dozens of enzymes, that detect any changes in the DNA sequence, others that clip out the few DNA bases containing the injury or changes, and more protein units that replace the DNA bases with the original correct sequence, and return the DNA chain to its original state. Though the reproduction of 2000 genes and billions of base pairs through dozens of cell divisions is nearly perfect, there are changes in one or more base sequence in the genetic material that are passed on as mutations. The mutations can be beneficial, deleterious, or inconsequential. An example of a deleterious mutation is a change in the DNA that upon translation, one amino acid change can alter the protein 3-D configuration, or a receptor attachment site, rendering the protein function reduced or incapacitated. If this kind of deleterious mutation is serious, then signals are triggered activating mechanisms to halt the cell cycle, preventing mitosis, and allowing time for the DNA repair to take place. On the other hand, the novel DNA changes can trigger cellular self-destruction, or programmed cell death, called apoptosis. In this manner, the mutation is for ever deleted. The deleterious mutation can be passed onto other daughter cells and be more consequential, and cause cellular or hormonal dysfunction. The P53 gene and its protein perform the surveillance function on the genetic fidelity. A single base mutation will result in a bump on the DNA chain which will then trigger attachment of DNA repair enzymes. The DNA repair system activates and coordinates several downstream processes, such as the apoptosis pathway. In a simplistic description, and not mentioning dozens of other genes and proteins involved, cell cycle checkpoint proteins Chk 1,2 arrest the cell cycle in G1 and activates Rad51/BRCA 2 complex which in turn binds RB1 and P53. Key proteins both pro and anti-apoptotic are involved, such as NF-kB, BCL2 or MDM, BAX. DNA repair enzymes are recruited and reparation work is completed or cell death mechanisms are triggered (Jalal 2011). In 2015, the Nobel Prize in Chemistry was awarded to three separate investigators who identified three of the several mechanisms of DNA repair; nucleotide excision repair (Aziz Sancar), base excision repair (Tomas Lindahl) and mismatch repair (Paul Modrich). There has been another exciting development in this field of DNA repair, namely the discovery of a DNA editing system, CRISPR-CAS9. This mechanism is present in bacteria and it is used to defend against viral infections. It retains part of the invading viral RNA sequence and uses this copy to recognize and cut the new DNA or RNA viral strands. At this point scientist classify this mechanism as part of the adaptive immune system.

A single mutation will not necessarily lead to the definitive event that turns the switch for a cell to become cancerous. There are usually a series of mutations facilitated by the first oncogene that push the pendulum towards the oncogenic direction, increased growth pathway signals, known as hyperplasia. In this state of increased replication, combined with genetic instability (allowing greater numbers of mutations), clones of transformed cells will appear and some will eventually grow into cancer cells that divide uncontrollably until reaching a large enough collection of cells that can be seen or detected as a lump. Tumorigenesis is then a series of events, a cascade of molecular changes, over a period of time, that will result into cancer. Prevention measures will be most effective in the pre-cancerous stages that have long latency periods allowing time for intervention. Even in the very nascent stages, the cancer will leave a trail of clues and these cellular, molecular or DNA changes can be detectable by blood or tissue tests. In this early period, when the cells under carcinogenic pressure show pre-cancerous characteristics or actual early cancerous behavior, cellular machineries at play are involved in one role or another in a permissive or active manner in suppressing or encouraging the tumorigenesis to proceed. Here, chemo-preventive agents, or activation of tumor suppressor genes could potentially reverse the tumorigenesis process.

Understanding the molecular genetics of cell function provides the knowledge and some tools to control cancer at inception, long before it acquires the potential to invade, metastasize or become clinically evident.

In reversing tumorigenesis at the molecular level, can we manipulate the changes precisely, as a surgical (microsurgical) incision through myriad of oncogenes and tumor suppressor genes. And avoid any short term or long-term side effects. In fact, the molecular changes in cancer prevention interventions should return the cell back to homeostatic state. At this point, our patient feels well and not ill, and surely will not accept any medical intervention with potential ill effects. From a molecular view point, when is a cell cancerous? To answer this question, we have to return to the old proven criteria, using cell morphology and clinical experience. Pathologists have gathered more than century of scientific experience answering this question, and today, the diagnosis is only established when a portion of the cancerous tissue is examined by histological and pathological tests, which include H&E (hematoxylin and eosin) stains of fixed tissue slices mounted on glass slides. Molecular tests, IHC (immunohistochemical) stains, flow-cytometry, and genetic testing are corroborative exams at this stage in time and not diagnostic. Information obtained by serum molecular markers, protein electrophoresis, are also used. There are general cellular, cytoplasmic and nuclear morphology criteria that are used to classify a group of cells to be cancerous or pre-cancerous. There are exceptions. High grade DCIS cells can have morphology of aggressive cancer cells, however by their relationship to the basement membrane of the breast ducts, these cells would still be classified as non-invasive. On the other hand, several endocrine tumors, have cells that appear to have benign morphology, only to eventually prove to be malignant, by growth characteristics and spread to other organs. Fortunately, it is rare when we have the situation where the biological behavior of the cancer cell is unknown, i.e., not able to classify the cell as cancer. In the molecular age however, there will a number of situations where the molecular signatures of the cell will flash cancer and yet the histology of the cell will be classified as non-malignant. These two findings occur when the molecular events precede the morphologic tumorigenesis. Pre-cancerous cells such as leukoplakia in the oral cavity, or atypical hyperplasia in breast tissue carry a predictable risk in becoming invasive cancers. For each molecular oncogenic marker, there will be a finite risk and association of future diagnosis of a particular cancer, which will be established through well controlled clinical studies. Hence the molecular diagnosis of cancer can encompass several cellular stages, including the pre-cancerous stages (Srivastava, 2018). Cancer prevention measures based on molecular findings need to be free of side-effects for the individual, since some of the pre-cancerous stages will not lead to significant injuries to the patient. Once the molecular and clinical diagnosis confirm a progression to a more aggressive cancer, then measures with greater morbidities, like a surgical intervention, will be justified and acceptable to the patient.

In summary, tumorigenesis is a process involving multiple molecular pathways initiated by mutated genes, oncogenes, occurring over several years prior to the completed transformation into a cancer cell. The threshold of precancer to cancer can be defined pathologically, aided by molecular markers, however the molecular threshold is difficult to draw. Nevertheless, the period of tumorigenesis is ripe for molecular interventions and diagnostics, where prevention of the very cancer cell establishing into a lethal malignant tumor can be realized.

6.3 ONCOGENES, TUMOR SUPPRESSOR GENES AND THE PARADOX OF CANCER

Several genes are central to the pathways key to cell survival, such as growth, housekeeping functions, and stress responses. When these key genes are mutated or functionally impaired, the very survival of the cell is called into question. When the gene integrity is under attack, gene repair mechanisms are activated, and programed cell death proteins are called into a stand by or active mode. In a multicellular organism, some cells are channeled into sacrificial death for the benefit of the group of cells or the entire organism. Apoptosis or programmed cell death is part of the normal cell function as in recycling the old cell parts as the aging cells get replaced by younger cells, generated by stem cells. Other life events, as in injured cells, by infection or trauma, will also call into action the apoptotic mechanisms of cell death. Apoptosis, or cell death (pre-programmed) is as normal as living, a cliché fit for drama in our own lives. The struggle to survive is a strong instinct ingrained in the genes of multiple species. By design, natural selection promotes the fittest set of molecules enabling the organism to survive and thrive amongst multitude of competitors. The cancer cell, often thought as the villain, if a role needed to be assigned, is a paradox of life. The genetic mutations promoting oncogenesis negotiate a pathway that pauses at a fork in the road, apoptosis or continued enhanced replication mode. Unfortunately for the host, the cancer cell is able to survive and become immortal. Unlike normal cells where the steady dynamic state of life and death exists, cancer cells ignore their neighbors, eventually at the cost of the whole organism. This paradox has been repeated elsewhere in nature where one invasive specie replicates to the point of exhausting the habitat's resources, resulting in wide spread damage (also see Peto's Paradox, chapter 18).

Oncogenes and weakened cancer suppressor genes are central to the cancer paradox. How will a cell decide to live or die when the oncogene is activated by a deleterious mutation? To live, means that it will grow as a cancer and eventually kill its host, or die and sacrificing itself, thereby allowing the majority of cells to live. This is a philosophical question which is answered by the cellular molecular machinery in the early phases of cancer transformation, or oncogenesis. The mutation occurs after a hit, a molecular interaction with molecular radicals or surge of energy as a photon or high-energy particle in and around the DNA, followed by an error in transcription. These events are thought to occur randomly, however, the oncogene function is prescribed and dictated by a myriad of other genes and protein interactions. In addition, stromal tissue environment around the cell, modulates its oncogene behavior and whether the protooncogene transforms into oncogene. The cellular and molecular microenvironment determine the likelihood for mutations (not randomness) and whether the switch to oncogene from proto-oncogene will activate apoptosis, the very self-sacrifice, to preserve the fidelity of the genome. The tissue environment providing another mechanism for the preservation of homeostasis, is provided by the stroma and niche cells. Myc oncogene, for example, has dual functions, both permissive in growth and when over-expressed leads to apoptosis. It was first discovered as the avian mc29 cells transformed by the myelocytosis virus and found to have multiple functions and target genes including promoting angiogenesis, apoptosis, stress responses, BCL-2 and BAX. Approximately 70% of cancers of various origins have mutations in MYC and is usually leading to low expression. Another example is P53, also referred to as the guardian of the genome. P53 facilitates DNA repair and induces cell cycle arrest in G1. If the repair is unsuccessfull, then P53 along with BCl-2 and Bax initiates the steps of programmed cell death. Tumor suppressor genes, in their normal state would inhibit tumorigenesis, and in its mutated state, in the abscense of its full function, tumorigenesis would be promoted. By a recent review, there are thousands of known oncogenes and tumor suppressor genes, collectively referred as cancer genes. The Network of Cancer Genes (NCG) database is a good reference. As of 2017, over 1,500 oncogenes have been characterized. It is estimated that another thousand cancer genes will be discovered soon. Many of the cancer genes identified by genomic studies of cancer samples, are classified by criteria other than function, some by statistical analytical techniques, such as the ANN (Artificial Neural Network). Gene expression or presence of oncogenes in cancers can yield different clustering by emphasizing different clinical or molecular characteristics. For example, the current TNM classification of organ-based tumors can prognosticate survival, metastatic and recurrence risks. Genomic analysis by neural network can also predict risks of future cancer behavior in the patient and dictate treatment and surveillance. Acquisition of multiple oncogenes, over many years, is required to complete the cell transformation into a cancer cell. Multiple oncogenes play roles in the cascading process of genetic instability in the oncogenic transformation and continued accumulation of oncogenes that can determine the tumor biological behavior, i.e., growth rates, metastases, and heterogeneity. The mosaic of different oncogenes is generally divided into driver and passenger oncogenes. The driver oncogene determines the growth potential of the cancer. Genomic probing into the pre-cancerous or cancer cell gives a static picture, which changes in time. The driver oncogenes may change as the tumor grows. Medical sciences have accumulated a large body of knowledge correlating symptoms, physical and pathological findings to each cancer, and accordingly the treatment modalities vary. As the cancer evolves, appropriate monitors are used and management readjusted. In the molecular era, how do the changes in our genes, proteins and other organic moieties indicate certain hallmarks of disease and specifically cancer? These new molecular findings need to establish their own guide posts that map to pertinent clinical entities. The molecular map integration with the clinical picture is not a linear relationship, as several molecular points will trace to several diseases and vice-versa. Some of the first molecular maps were developed in the inherited syndromes, in which gene mutations were correlated to well defined sets of inherited clinical findings. In oncology, some of the key landmarks on the map are oncogenes. Several large oncogene data bases have been accumulating information expanding these new genomic maps. ICGC (International Cancer Genome Consortium), TCGA (The Cancer Genome Consortium), Sanger COSMIC and the CCGD (Candidate Cancer Gene Database) are examples of these large cancer genomic libraries. Some of our previous classification of clinical data and paradigms in cancer may be changed with the new set of molecular findings, i.e., in the new map old landmarks will gain new significance, and previously unrecognized locations will gain new meanings.

In the clinics, doctors trained in the current tools of diagnosis and treatment of cancer, will eventually need to learn an entire new set of molecular data points. Aside from oncogenes, new molecular tests, from tumor markers, immune histochemistry stains, to gene profiles will require new tools like a pocket computer with AI capability, in order to integrate the new data. Large scale genomic information is being routinely used in clinical research. Gene microarray profile is used to test samples of cancer tissue, breast cancer for example, and verify if certain genes are up or down regulated. This type of gene profile can reflect prognostic behavior of the tumor and provide further information in the cell type of origin, and help therapy decisions (Khan 2001). The knowledge of the entire genome for any particular cell, or for the tumor cell, will provide a greater degree of precision. The current technology can identify thousands of cancer genes, many with unknown significance. It is not recommended, at this point, to analyse your entire genome looking for oncogenes, as there are no clinical conditions that will meet the criteria to measure the entire genome. At this time most clinicians will employ targeted testing of the genome. In research, the search for all potentially significant oncogenes would benefit from testing the entire genome (also see Chapter 4.1.2, gene testing). Another point of clarification regarding gene tests, discussed commonly in the scientific and lay press, is that the tests can refer to two completely separate group of cells; those that are cancerous and separately those of normal cells or usually of blood white cells (liquid biopsy). Oncogenes found in cancer cells usually number in the dozens, contrasted to oncogenes in normal cells from none to a few. Gene test of normal cells are usually done for geneology or for identification of possible germ line mutations. Oncogenes identified in cancer cells are used to identify targets for therapy, to prognosticate the future behavior, and subclassify the type or origin of the cancer. The clinical significance of these oncogenes, in the context of established cancers, is an ongoing and evolving field of investigantion helped by the several large genome libraries and cooperative groups: the KEGG (Kyoto Encyclopedia of Gene and Genomes), the ICGC, TCGH, COSMIC, CCGD and others.

The oncogene interactions in cancer are in a dynamic flux, where the driver oncogene may be assumed by new ones during the life of the cancer which in itself is made up of heterogenous clones with different oncogene arrangements. How oncogenes drive the tumor behavior and growth rates will yield basic information needed to solve the cancer puzzle (Begum 2019,

Ding 2018). Currently, investigations are searching for oncogene downstream functions that can be modified as a therapeutic target for tumor inhitibion. There are multiple examples of pharmacologic successes based on tumor oncogene targets (Lou, 2019). Oncogene interactions are also studied in the hopes that combination of known gene modulators, PARP and BRAF inhibitors, for example, have higher response rates than using one agent alone (Tutuncuoglu 2019).

The cell reproductive activity stops at a few dozens of mitoses, the Hayflick effect, limiting its life span. The cancer has overcome this survival barrier creating its paradox, addressed further in Chapter 18. Although several aspects of cancer are still enigmatic and we cannot say we solved the cancer problem, nature itself has developed several solutions. There are individuals who have resisted cancer late into their 9th to 10th decades of life, though their cells have been subjected to numerous oncogenes. Cancer in animals is common as in humans, however a very few, as in naked mole rats or elephants develop cancers at much lower rates than predicted. Indeed, plants do not succumb malignant tumors, even though benign plant tumors can cause severe deformities, as in galls and burls (Chapter 16). Once these solutions to cancer resistance is understood, novel anti-oncogenesis strategies will be developed for our patients in the form of cancer prevention treatments.

6.4 CHEMOPREVENTION AND OTHER PRIMARY PREVENTION STRATEGIES.

The pre-cancerous stage is usually many years in the making. The pre-cancerous cells are characterized by hyperplasia and dysplasia, faster growth rate and misshapened cytoplasm and nucleus. The underlying genetic changes accumulate gradually until the mitotic process becomes independent and non-reversible. Though most of these molecular changes go undetected, some clues are surfacing that allow early detection. Some of these changes can be reversed or physically eliminated to prevent the cancerous growth. Chemoprevention is the reversal or slowing the process of cancer development by molecular or genetic modification using natural, synthetic or biologic chemical agents. This definition was first coined by Sporn in 1976. Several phase III studies have shown the effectiveness of chemoprevention and thereby its proof of principle. In breast cancer, the NSABP (National Surgical Adjuvant Breast Project) P-1 study showed that tamoxifen can prevent breast cancers after the anti-tumor potential was noted in prior studies associated with lower rates of contralateral breast neoplasms. These studies included tamoxifen in therapeutic investigations of the ipsilateral breast cancer. Other estrogen receptor inhibitors (SERMS) with different secondary effects, like lower uterine lining stimulation, were also found effective in prevention of breast cancers. Although these drugs have low toxicity, the general acceptance of SERMs in breast cancer prevention is poor and often not offered by family doctors or oncologists. In colorectal cancer, NSAIDs and calcium have been shown to lower polyp counts in the large bowel which is associated with lower risks of colorectal cancers. In wider population studies, persons who routinely take aspirin have lower rates of colorectal cancers. Treating H pylori infections in the stomach has lowered the incidence of gastric carcinoma. Discussion of chemoprevention research is elaborated in section 6.1.

Endoscopic removal of large bowel growths constitutes a form of primary prevention for colon and rectal cancers. Currently, chemoprevention and periodic endoscopic surveillance and removal of adenomas can effectively eliminate the risk of CRC. The situation is different for breast carcinoma. Surveillance with mammograms increased the rates of detection up until 1990 then the incidence of breast cancer in the U.S. has found a plateau of around 130 cases yearly/100,000 for Caucasian women. The death rates for breast cancer has decreased since the 1990's to lately of 20 deaths yearly/100,000 Caucasian women and 27 deaths yearly/100,000 African American women. Chemoprevention in breast cancer with SERMs has little acceptance and local excision of DCIS does not decrease the future risks of breast cancer.

Primary cancer prevention covers reduction of chronic infections, cancer vaccines, avoidance of carcinogens, tobacco for example, nutrition and exercise.

6.5 SECONDARY CANCER PREVENTION

Secondary cancer prevention covers methods that diminishes the consequences of cancer once the clinical entity establishes itself, even prior to causing symptoms. Screening and early diagnosis of cancer is a major category and will be elaborated further in the next chapter. The ideal endpoint to judge cancer screening is improvement of the overall survival. However, in practice other intermediate endpoints need to be considered, such as the rate of cancer detection and quality of life. This can be illustrated for mammographic breast cancer screening and for PSA (prostate specific antigen) blood test for prostate cancer screening. The early diagnosis of prostate cancer by PSA blood test screening have not shown to decrease prostate cancer deaths. On the other hand, death rates from prostate cancer is low, and some experts have advocated watchful waiting in low grade prostate cancers.

Attitudes toward mammography have shifted from the universal yearly screening mammograms starting at age 40, to a more relaxed schedule of every two years starting at age of 45. Recent studies (Miller 2014, Gotszche 2013) showed no survival benefits for mammogram screening. Since the early mammographic screening studies, BCDDP (Breast Cancer Detection Demonstration Project, Smart 1994), breast cancer therapy has improved to the point of prolonging and increasing the survival of women with breast cancer. The cure rate and life with recurrent breast cancer are increased. As a consequence, women in the non-screened group and likely to present with a more advanced breast cancers, would not demonstrate an inferior over-all survival compared to the screened women, who would more likely present with smaller and less advanced breast cancers. Other criticisms of screening tests are the the costs, potential cancers caused by radiation dose of breast X-rays, increased diagnosis of indolent DCIS (ductal carcinoma-in-situ) tumors and the numbers of complications due to invasive procedures for false positive findings (Helvie 2018). Secondary endpoints should be considered for screening methodologies, namely the accuracy of detecting the cancer, with the associated false positive and false negative rates. Detection rates can be improved with attempts to minimize false positive and false negative rates. The complication rate as an endpoint, can study methods to minimize use invasive diagnostic tests, as the false positives can be corroborated with other non-invasive tests. Thus, these issues should be incorporated into the study of cancer screening as secondary endpoints, emphasizing efforts to minimize the negative effects of the screening methodologies. In this evolving issue of cancer screening, some point-counter point discussions are presented in the next chapter. Screening mammograms have generated much controversies, and the misinterpretation of benefits of of breast cancer screening has initiated a trend that will discourage women in participating future cancer preventiont efforts. Unfortunately, misinformation or partial representation of screening issues are portrayed in the lay press (Nagler 2019). When indolent tumors are identified in the screening process, as in squamous or basal cell carcinoma of the skin, ductal carcinoma in-situ of the breast, or well differentiated prostate cancer, doctors should treat them proportionally to the potential harm to the patient, as in indolent compared to aggressive cancers. In other words, the risk and magnitude of diagnostic process or treatment (invasive techniques, surgery or radiation) should be proportionate to the severity of the disease. From the patient's view, the fear of cancer makes these distinctions difficult, and these issues are precisely where the experienced clinician can help with the appropriate decisions.

Surgical treatment of early stage tumors has a higher success rate of cure, i.e., extremely lower local or distant recurrences compared to intervention for advanced cancers, where additional multi-disciplinary approaches are required, chemotherapy and raditation treatments, either before or after surgery. In addition, in early tumors, a more limited resections will effect cures, allowing minimally invasive techniques. Thus, cancer screening will lead to secondary prevention, with higher cure rates and fewer morbidities. Moreover, screening and early detection will lead to discoveries of pre-cancerous lesions, where primary prevention techniques can be applied.

Secondary prevention will also address tumor recurrence after the first cancer has been successfully placed into remission by surgical, chemotherapy or radiotherapy means. In addition, it will also prevent second primary tumors due to the field effect of carcinogenesis. The residual tumor cells whether local, regional or systemic can escape the immune-surveillance, become dormant, or replicate in a microenvironment conducive to oncogene action, or genetic instability. Thus, surviving cancer, means becoming more aware in preventing a second cancer or a recurrence of the first cancer.

Tertiary prevention lessens the symptoms, morbidities and socio-economic effects of cancer, prevents the development of severe side-effects, improves the quality of life, manages palliative care and helps the family and caregivers with mutually satisfactory end of life care. Palliative care is discussed in Chapter 12.

6.6 LIFE STYLE AND CANCER PREVENTION

Environmental factors shaping our health have become, in the modern era, significantly more important, even taking into account, the advances of modern medicine. Hygiene, clean tap water, nutrition and medical care have been large contributors to the increase in longevity and the decrease in the impact of communicable diseases. Natural disasters, environmental pollution, climate change, car accidents, and drug addiction increasingly adds to population mortality. Chronic diseases in the older population, including cancer, are becoming the more important threats to our health in the XXI century. Today, we have greater choices in life-styles and management of our personal internal environment than ever before, even though the risks to our internal homeostasis rise from external environmental pollution, changes in climate and pathogens.

Beginning with fetal development, we are more aware of the importance of pre-natal care. Infectious diseases, like German measles and the latest epidemic of Zika virus, can cause birth defects. Tobacco smoke, alcohol, and lead contamination are agents that can harm developing tissues such as the nervous system. Adequate intake of minerals and vitamins are important, as the requirement of growing fetal tissues are higher than the normal adult. Deficiencies in niacin can lead to defects in the formation of the notochord resulting in spina-bifida.

In infancy, adolescence and adulthood, the diet, physical activity and exposure to critical environmental carcinogens will alter the rate of gene mutations, shape the epigenome and exposome. These predisposing factors are highlighted in the investigations into nurture versus nature and studies of cancer risks in twins, (Mucci, 2016). There was a 46% concordance in risk of cancer in identical twins (mono-zygotic), leading to the conclusion that environmental factors are equally responsible for cancer risks as the inherited genes. Thirty-five years after landmark paper by Doll and Peto (1981) outlining the environmental causes of cancer, exposure to carcinogens still constitute the major cause of malignancies. In addition, the formation of cellular wastes, increased by carcinogens, is increased in the state of reactive oxygen and nitrogen species (ROS) excess. Both cellular wastes and ROS generate greater number of mutations, the redox triangle. The clearance of intra-cellular wastes is stimulated by physical activity, enhancing autophagy, covered in Chapter 20.3. The sources of foods, in the modern era, has evolved away from the local farms and the hunter-gatherer life style which necessarily included a hefty dose of exercise, and periodic fasting due to variable food availability. Today, our menu includes more processed foods, far different from the usual diet just over a half century ago. The additives in process foods include emulsifiers, color agents, and preservatives that are added to increase shelf life and appeal. When processed foods are over-consumed, changes in lipid metabolism and alterations in the gut microbiome can lead to obesity.

Obesity, diabetes and conditions of chronic inflammation are some of the precursors for chronic diseases, ageing and cancer.

The science behind nutrition and exercise point to the importance of a healthy life-style, and once these principles are understood, we will realize how these elements contribute to the intracellular microenvironment and homeostasis in a seamless integral interwoven tapestry. The adoption of these practices would then be a voluntary action, but incorporated into our activities as a natural part of our well being like any involuntary function of our organs ingrained in our genes. Naturally, we are also part, and not alone in our earth's environment. Mother Earth's atmosphere and bodies of water tolerance to man made changes is reaching a limit and these lessons are pertinent to our own inner microenvironment, elaborated in chapter 20, Molecular Ecology. Molecular tools in the genomics, proteonomics, microbiome and exposome, can provide surveillance and monitoring, and in turn allowing a more meaningful and accurate assessment of cancer risks. Molecular ecology can link all these disciplines into a coherent overview of health to do list. It is estimated that 50% of cancers deaths can be prevented by current knowledge of life-style changes and other prevention strategies (Golemis 2018).

From a practical viewpoint, one often adopts a nihilistic attitude of what can be done when we are immersed in a polluted environment. On the other hand, studies show small changes in our daily activities can make a difference. Living near a park with plenty of trees or taking regular walks in wooded areas show a difference in lowering rates of chronic diseases. Avoiding tobacco smoke and excessive intake of alcoholic and sugary beverages are also steps, taken one at a time, makes small incremental improvements in our inner environment, to achieve our own molecular homeostasis. Moderate modifications to our diet may be sufficient in reducing cancer risks, such as increasing the consumption of fruits, nuts and vegetables and decreasing animal fats and processed meats. Further tips are included in chapters regarding physical activity and nutrition.

Molecular homeostasis is the nirvana of your inner self. Not just an ideal mental state, but a zone where the molecules are in their ideal concentrations in your life fluids and interacting in a seamless manner defying the laws of thermodynamics (Davies, 2016). On a happy and hopeful note, our external environment, potentially an extension of our cellular micro-environment, can revert to a pristine (homeostatic) condition when man-made external insults are suspended, in a protected habitat, for example.

7

Cancer Screening and Early Diagnosis

Screening for early cancers is a core activity of cancer prevention. When identified early, the cancer is uniformly treated with complete success with minimal risk for recurrence. Several studies showed effectiveness in lives saved and cost savings for screening of breast, colorectal and cervical cancers. Successful screening is based on several competing factors such as the screened population's risk for cancer, the detection methodology, the risk of harm by undergoing further diagnostic tests, and the cost. The accuracy of diagnostic and screening tests in the medical field are evaluated by its sensitivity and specificity, which gives a value for the false negative and false positive test results. For example, mammograms are accepted, today, as the standard test for screening women at risk for breast cancer. The false negative rates are 5-10%, and one should not disregard other clues for breast cancer in the presence of normal mammograms. In women with a palpable breast nodule, 15% of the mammograms do not show the lesion, either because it is isodense to the surrounding breast tissue or the lesion is on the very periphery of the breast where the lesion is outside the boundaries of the mammogram image.

Several large screening trials use survival as the only endpoint. In recent studies, the task in demonstrating survival differences between mammogram screened and unscreened women, has become more difficult. Non-screened patients are eventually found with more advanced breast cancers. Their survival, however, can match that of screened population, because of improvements in chemotherapy and in other means of prolonging patients' lives with cancer. This means that cancer patients live longer with disease and yet, are not necessarily cured. These patients may be living with lower quality of life mainly from cancer treatments and cancer symptoms. Thus, studies of cancer screening protocols may no longer demonstrate survival benefits and yet other benefits of screening have not been studied. Therefore, new studies on cancer screening should include secondary endpoints, besides survival. These secondary endpoints include quality of life, cancer care costs, and complication rates from confirmatory invasive tests. Another more meaningful end point, in evaluating screening methods would be the rate of cancer detection and their accuracy in detecting early stage tumors. Survival should not be used as the only criteria to determine the benefits of a screening methodology. This is especially true when no significant differences are demonstrated in the survival data due to advances in treatments. The evaluation of false positive and negative screening test results are also a very important part of the clinical evaluation into the efficacy of the screening process. In mammographic screening, complications are seen mainly from invasive procedures done for false positive findings. There are several non-invasive tests that can verify a borderline positive test or a false positive test without resorting to a biopsy. Criteria can be established to minimize the use of invasive tests that result in a wide spectrum of morbidities. In the case of the abnormal mammogram, for example, other non-invasive tests can be used, ultrasound, MRI, or a repeat mammogram in 3-6 months, in order to confirm a true or a false positive test. These measures will reduce the use of needle breast biopsies and the morbidities and costs associated with the biopsy procedures. Double reading (interpretation by two radiologists) or AI (artificial intelligence) techniques have also reduced the false positive and false negative rates.

Many of the recommendations for cancer screening are extrapolated from large population studies. The benefits and risks of the screening study are then assigned to the average risk person. The vast majority of individuals are screened according to the average risk guidelines, without taking the time to evaluate the actual cancer risk. Most guidelines do not include the definition of the average, high or low risk individuals. In fact, most studies do not set clear criteria for entry or exclusion to the study, for higher or lower risk individuals. It is assumed that a large group of individuals would include a fairly even distribution of high, low and average cancer risk individuals. In addition, the recommendations are inherently set for the population as a whole and in some instances may be at odds for the individual cancer screening benefits. For example, mammogram screening reccomendations are designed for the average risk woman, starting at age 45 and every two years thereafter. However, for the 49% of women with higher risk, i.e., family members with breast or ovary cancer, dense breasts or previous breast surgery, mammographic screening should start at age 40 and repeated on yearly intervals. As risk assessment for each cancer becomes more commonly used, individuals should be aware of their own risks, expressed in life-time risk of being diagnosed with a particular cancer, 12% for average breast cancer risk.

Since each cancer has its own screening criteria and tests, we will cover the screening strategies for each of the major cancers.

7.1 LUNG CANCER SCREENING

Lung cancer is the most common cause of death in US and China due to tobacco use. Smoking over 30 pack/years (i.e. smoking one pack of cigarette per day for 30 years, or 2 pack per day for 15 years) will increase the risk of lung cancer by 35-fold. This effect is seen in both men and women, and recently lung cancer deaths in women have surpassed deaths due to breast cancer, formerly the most common cause of cancer deaths in women. In addition, tobacco use increases the incidence of heart disease, strokes, loss of distal limb from vascular stenosis, and raises the rates of other cancers. Once tobacco use is abandoned, the risk of lung cancer returns to base line after 10 years. Early detection of lung cancer, by chest X-rays, has not shown to lower deaths from lung cancer. Low dose chest CT scans used for screening demonstrated projected improvement in survival in a subset of individuals; ages 50 to 65 who had smoked more than 15 pack years. This protocol has been recommended by the U.S. Preventive Services Task Force (Abeele 2011). Once a lung lesion is detected by the low-dose CT, several further tests need to be done to prove the lesion to be cancerous or not. A CT guided needle biopsy is the most definitive. PET scan, in most patients, is the preferred next step and avoids the need for diagnostic biopsy. A PET scan gives guidance to observe and repeat CT in 3-4 months if the SUV units are low which would indicate not to be a neoplasm, or indicates that the lung lesion is likely to be neoplastic then VATS (video assisted thoracoscopic surgery) is performed for diagnosis and treatment, i.e., the nodule is removed with a minimaly invasive approach, and if cancer is diagnosed by pathology, then, at the same procedure, lobectomy and node dissection can be performed.

Smoking cessation remains the most important preventive intervention. Persistent smoking will lead to higher recurrence rates even after successful surgical and adjuvant treatments for lung cancer.

Tumor markers may prove to be the cost-effective way to narrow the risk group of smokers with greater risks of cancer and best candidates for screening with CT scans. In a recent analysis of serum markers, archived in the CARET study looking at vitamin E intake in lung cancer prevention, which resulted in a negative study, by Omenn et al (1996). Diacetylspermine and pro-surfactant protein B were found to be predictive of non-small cell lung carcinoma (Wikoff 2015). MicroRNA profiles and bronchial cell genomics are been studied for their potential usefulness in early lung cancer detection.

Screening is recommended for individuals of Asian origin, exposed to passive smoke and environmental pollutants. The cancers found are usually of the non-small cell adenocarcinoma type, and have a different spectrum of gene mutations compared to the cancers found in smokers, which are of the squamous cell carcinoma type. The adenocarcinoma of the lung has mutations, like EGFR tyrosine kinase and ALK that can be targeted by drugs with significant treatment responses (Planchard 2015).

7.2 BREAST CANCER SCREENING

Breast cancer is diagnosed in one of eight women in their life time, in the U.S., and the rate in men is 100 times lower. Screening mammograms have been found effective in lowering deaths from breast cancer, however more recently, studies have shown no survival improvement in screened women, probably due to improvements in the treatment of advanced breast cancers in the non-screened group. After much effort in convincing the public of the benefits of mammographic screening, there has been a relaxation of the guidelines of yearly mammograms starting at the age of 40 years until the age of 70 years. The gains resulting from the screening programs in breast cancer, in earlier decades should be highlighed. The public awareness of early detection has increased, and as the result of increased use of mammogram screening, the average tumor size of breast cancer found in the general population has decreased from 2.5 cm in 1960 to 1.6 cm in the 3 decades since screening mammography was introduced, (Welch 2016). This translates into an improvement in survival rates by 30%. In addition, the detection rate on non-invasive breast cancers increased from 5% to nearly 20% of all the breast cancers found. The diagnosis of non-invasive breast cancers, DCIS (ductal carcinoma in-situ), has been labeled as "over-diagnosis" by some physicians, which is an unfortunate misnomer, to be elaborated in the next few paragraphs.

In the last few years, since the publications showing lack of survival improvement in cohorts of women screened by mammography, and analysis of potential harm resulting from screening programs, there has been a movement to scale back the frequency of mammographic screening exams. The American Cancer Society issued a set of much publicized guidelines in 2015, starting screening at age 45 instead of 40, and relaxing the frequency to every two years starting at age 55, instead of yearly. At age 75 the regular mammograms exams are no longer recommended or at an age where the estimated life expectancy is less than 10 years. These guidelines are for the average risk women, and can be modified according to risk factors, such as family history, breast density and parity. The controversies in breast cancer screening illustrate several inherent problems of early detection and screening in balancing benefits, risks and costs for the population as a whole, and then extrapolating the validated information for the benefit of the individual patient. In breast cancer screening, we will address the current points of controversy, which are the misnomer of "over-diagnosis", potential harm in breast biopsies for false positive findings, and lack of survival advantage in recent studies of screening mammography.

Breast cancer has benefited from robust research both in the basic and clinical sciences, in screening and in early diagnosis. Breast cancer research funding has received one of the highest funding for a particular cancer type, and as a result, much more is understood regarding the pathogenesis, diagnosis and treatment of this malignancy. Yet, much controversy surrounds the area of screening and prevention. The debate in the public and scientific literature, unfortunately enhances the misconceptions and confounds the basic principles of cancer prevention. One of the findings of mammographic screening is an increased diagnosis of non-invasive breast cancer (DCIS). Many of these cancers are associated with cluster of small calcium deposits, which are readily seen on X-ray mammography. DCIS has an excellent prognosis with only 1-2% risk of dying of breast cancer with the initial diagnosis of DCIS, as it can transform into invasive breast cancer. Critics of breast screening programs, point to the increase of DCIS, in some series up to 15% of all breast cancer found by mammograms, as an "over-diagnosis", meaning from their point of view, that DCIS, when not diagnosed and remain occult, would not result in cancer deaths. The original definition of "over-diagnosis" was the number of patients in the screened group diagnosed with breast cancer compared to the number of breast cancers diagnosed in the control group of women. Noted that in the study of concern, no increased deaths were found in the control group compared to the screened group. The excess numbers in the screened group, "over-diagnosis" of breast cancers included both invasive cancers and DCIS. These occult cancers are asymptomatic in the study time period, most likely DCIS type, however they are not inconsequential in the patient's life-time. Eventually, beyond the time observed in the study, these breast cancers will be deleterious, either becoming invasive or presenting as palpable mass. These critics would add that DCIS should not be classified as a cancer. The answer to these critics is simple. These arguments of leaving DCIS undiagnosed go against the concept of cancer progression and how it starts from a transformed cell and progress to invasive cancers capable of causing cancer deaths. Pathologists have no difficulty calling DCIS a cancer, even though it is the very nascent phase of breast cancer. There are many other examples of indolent cancers (skin and prostate cancers), which are not labelled a misdiagnosis or "over-diagnosis", and moreover, clinicians in general, do not recommend aggressive treatments for indolent cancers. The molecular changes in DCIS are also consistent with the progression of the cancer from a non-invasive behavior into an invasive cancerous cell capable of penetrating the basement membrane and travelling into blood capillaries and lymphatic channels. There are well recognized morphological characteristics of DCIS, associated with a spectrum of presentation that corresponds to risk of finding invasive cancers within a DCIS. Though DCIS can remain dormant and indolent for a period of 10-15 years, the risk of progression into invasive cancers is ever-present. Thus, the terminology of "over-diagnosis" is misused and should only apply to false positive diagnosis of cancers. One should not ignore the presence of indolent cancers, like DCIS, as it serves as guide for cancer prevention and management of future risks of cancer. Cancer specialists or oncologists, whether belonging to the surgical, medical, radiation, genetics or molecular sub-specialties, may differ on the approach to DCIS due to its indolent behavior. What is indisputable, is the potential to change into a more aggressive tumor, i.e., invasive cancer. The risk of DCIS to become invasive cancer is 5-10% per year for under 1 cm in size, and higher for larger volume of DCIS. There are other molecular markers that predict the risks of transforming into invasive disease. After surgical excision, there is a 10% risk of local recurrence with half of recurrences being of the invasive type, if breast conservation method is used. Most DCIS present in a multifocal manner in the ipsilateral breast. Despite the issues of local recurrence, the risk of distant spread and death from DCIS remain in the 1-2% range. The need to diagnose and identify DCIS should not stir much controversy, however, the management of this indolent disease can generate multiple recommendations. The most important issue is to separate indolent from aggressive cancers and customize the risk of treatment and diagnostic procedures to the risk of death and morbidity of the cancer. If the woman is willing to take a wait and watch approach to DCIS, it is quite reasonable. The surveillance imaging tests can be repeated periodically. Upon diagnosis, I would advise removal of the entire area at risk for DCIS to make sure there are no invasive components, and often breast conservation is feasible. In large studies of DCIS, about 10% can recur locally, and half of these recurrences have invasive cancer components. The invasive recurrences have good outcomes after re-resection.

Today, most DCIS are found on routine mammograms. The usual clues are microcalcifications and small densities. The majority of these suspicious findings will turn out to be benign on needle biopsy. This leads to the first decision. If the suspected result is going to be DCIS versus a benign calcium deposit, then we have the luxury of watching and waiting, repeat mammogram in 6 months, or further investigations with breast ultrasound and MRI. We are advocating caution on the biopsy step and not foregoing the mammogram exam or relaxing the screening mammogram intervals. Once the diagnosis of DCIS is made on biopsy results, then the next decision process is how extensive of a surgery to perform. Theoretically, removing the entire DCIS is curative with surgery alone. Practically, DCIS is often multifocal, making negative surgical margins difficult to achieve, and less meaningful, since the margin positive disease is not necessarily cured with wider margin resection nor re-resection. On another end of the spectrum, some young women elect to have mastectomy or even bilateral mastectomies and reconstruction for a focal DCIS. This may seem an extreme approach for a focal area of DCIS, however this option does guarantee freedom from future risks of breast cancer. Most doctors will also recommend radiation treatment to the breast if only part of the breast is removed for DCIS. A study found that radiation is indicated even for low risk lesions after excision, as the radiation treatment will decrease the risk for local recurrence in the breast. Others will argue for observation after surgery without irradiation, since the recurrences are usually localized disease, and amenable to further treatment and rarely lead to spread of disease elsewhere in the body. Another camp will argue for hormone suppression with SERMs, such as tamoxifen, especially in the older individual, thus even sparing surgery or radiation.

In summary, with respect to DCIS, there are many options for treatments with low morbidities, including observation. We do not advocate using the indolent nature of DCIS to advocate against breast cancer screening nor relaxing the intervals for screening tests. We will mention, later, instances where a personalized approach can lead to screening to 2-year intervals instead of yearly. Recommendations for breast cancer screening should start with proper risk assessment for breast cancer then individualize the approach for screening and other means of prevention. Despite the growing body of knowledge and research in breast cancer, we cannot predict which DCIS will change its behavior into an aggressive cancer, with high accuracy. A recent article, based on gene profiling of DCIS, showed that their local recurrence rates can be predicted independent of surgical or pathological parameters (Zambito 2014). Few critics of mammogram screening argue that treatment of DCIS does not prevent advanced cases of breast cancer, from a population wide analysis. This is counter-intuitive, since in the patient with DCIS when treated eliminates the possibility of progression into invasive cancer. These critics point to the data in studies where the incidence of advanced cancers (defined as node positive) has not decreased, though 15% of breast cancers treated are DCIS. Clearly the link between DCIS and advanced cancers, or the lack of, is intriguing. One would expect that by treating the early cancers, i.e. DCIS, the incidence of more advanced cancers would decrease. This expectation depends on several assumptions, one of which is that most breast cancers arise from DCIS. Quite possibly some breast cancer arises from de novo invasive cancers, or that some DCIS becomes invasive and metastasize in a very short interval. The increased number of node positive cancers can be accounted by the new surgical method of lymph node biopsy, namely the sentinel node technique, which up-stages some tumors to node positive breast cancers, due to higher accuracy in the identification of micro-metastases in lymph nodes.

Potential harm can result from screening mammograms or any medical tests that lead to invasive diagnostic tests that ultimately prove to be a false positive test for the intended diagnostic aim, the discovery of new and early breast cancer. On the other hand, false negative results from mammograms can occur leading to missed diagnosis. For example, palpable breast cancers can be missed if solely relying on mammography findings, with inherent 15% rate false negative results. Misreading of mammographic pictures can partly be corrected by double reading, where the films are examined by two radiographers. Among the new imaging techniques for the breast, such as thermography, ultrasonography, 3-d mammograms and magnetic resonance imaging (MRI), none have been found to be superior to mammography as a screening modality. MRI though more specific, fail from the cost standpoint and would increase the false positive rates. The false positive lesions found on mammography are blamed for increasing the cost, by leading to diagnostic biopsies and risking more complications. The medical community could refine the indications for biopsy in indeterminate findings such as obtaining ultrasound, repeat studies in 3-6 months, or studying the breast with an MRI when justified by risk assessment scores. Often the management path chosen are driven by the fear factor of potentially harboring a cancer and patients would more readily agree to an invasive biopsy, without thorough consideration of available options.

Let's examine some other criticisms of screening mammography. Recent studies have shown that screening mammography no longer demonstrate an advantage in breast cancer survival. Several other studies indicate otherwise, as seen in a comprehensive review of most mammographic screening studies completed. The results showed a 23% reduction in breast cancer deaths in the screened women (Seely 2018). Potential harm from the screening tests comes from the false positive and false negative results. Nearly 20% of screening tests will request a call back for additional views or ultrasound, and 12% will have a false positive result with approximately 3% of patients undergoing a needle biopsy. Women who had one false positive mammogram become less compliant in future screening mammograms. The false negative rates are 0.1-0.15% of mammograms and the tumors are usually discovered on basis of physical exam. However, among palpable breast lumps, about 15% of mammograms have a false negative reading.

A final argument raised against mammography is that the rate of advanced breast cancers has not decreased in the women screened with mammography, even though the rate of dectection of early cancers, including DCIS has increased. Advanced breast cancers are defined as cancers with associated lymph node metastasis, N1 nodal stage or higher. This finding of steady rates of N positive disease at diagnosis, among mammography screened women, is indeed unexplained, and one should not use it to argue against mammographic screening, as we shall explain. Nodal involvement increases with tumor size. One would expect the rate of node positive screened tumors to decrease with effectiveness of breast cancer screening. This expectation assumes, however, that the biological behavior and the diagnosis of nodal metastases stay constant over time. First, the technique of sentinel node identification and diagnosis of micrometastases, now well established in clinical practice in the last decade, has significantly increased the rate of nodal disease in tumors in the 1-2 cm size range. Secondly, breast cancer heterogeneity can influence the biological behavior in any individual. Tumor heterogeneity occurs in all types of cancers, due to the genetic instability, mutational differences and clonal growth. As the molecular determinants are discovered regarding each particular clone with specific patterns of oncogenes, the biological behavior of a breast cancer or a group of breast cancers can be predicted. One cannot assume that certain patterns of heterogeneity will remain constant over time, especially the propensity of nodal involvement in T1c breast cancers, between 1 and 2 cm in size.

Are yearly mammograms really necessary? Can the schedule be relaxed to every two years? For the population as a whole, greater numbers of early cancers will be diagnosed with yearly mammograms versus biannual mammograms. Even at this schedule, interval cancers will be picked up by physical exam, and not by mammography. These cancers are usually of higher growth rate and more aggressive in behavior, not likely to benefit from "early diagnosis". Quite possibly, "early diagnosis" by mammography technique will be insufficient for these fast-growing tumors. Are there studies comparing yearly versus every two-year screening schedule? There are two retrospective studies that found survival rates on yearly screening are superior by 5% at ten years compared to biannual screening and that 20% of cancers found were in the advanced category, in the two-year interval group (Wai 2005).

7.2.1 HOW TO PERSONALIZE THE BREAST SCREENING METHODOLOGY?

Breast screening guidelines are recommended for the average risk woman and most women think they fall into the average risk category, including their physicians. By definition, half of all women fall into the higher risk category, thus one needs to be careful to determine who is in the average risk category. Breast cancer risks are affected by family history, age, breast density, prior breast imaging results, prior breast surgeries, exposure history such as tobacco, radiation to the breast, especially around time of puberty, and alcohol intake. With the fast pace of developments in genomics, soon, gene testing will be included in the risk calculations. In the absence of known risk factors, the first screening mammogram should be obtained at age 40, even though revised recommendations say age 45. In the 2019 meeting of the American Society of Breast Surgeons, it was announced the new reccomendations regarding mammogram screening. Risk assessment of breast cancer is evaluated for all women after age 25, and obtain yearly mammograms starting at age 40. The agreed classification of mammogram interpretation among radiologists is the Bi-rads system: 0 – incomplete; 1-negative; 2-benign findings; 3-probably benign, need for follow-up studies; 4- suspicious for malignancy; 5- highly suspicious or probable malignant. Call back for additional mammogram views is also common, though anxiety producing, usually will not result in final interpretation of abnormal mammogram. A birads 3 result needs follow-up with more studies, physical exam or possibly repeat mammogram in 3-6 months, or further elucidation with breast ultrasound. Birads 4 usually leads to a recommendation for needle biopsy. An abnormal mammogram that leads to a request for breast biopsy, should also be a reason to initiate a consultation with a surgical oncologist or breast surgeon, who is the clinician of choice to recommend the next step in the diagnostic work-up. The surgical oncologist has the experience in putting together the given information of mammogram findings, breast exam and the patient's risk factors to arrive at the best and safest options: 1. observe and repeat the exam (in 3-6 months) if the likely diagnosis is benign. 2. Obtain MRI and/or ultrasound of the breast, helping to make a better distinction between benign or malignant lesions, 3. a needle biopsy or 4. a lumpectomy followed by immediate pathological exam with frozen section, and if pathology result is invasive, then proceed with sentinel lymph node biopsy and assurance that lumpectomy margins are negative, during the same surgical procedure. In some cases, the mass is highly suspicious for malignancy or even if benign and growing in size, it should be removed for assurance (some malignancies have substantial component of stromal tissue that can yield benign results on needle sampling). A needle biopsy in these cases would not change the surgical recommendations, only add an extra procedure. The needle biopsy can result in a local hematoma, which could result in difficulty in obtaining clear surgical margins, or worst, if the needle biopsy is a false negative and the patient is sent home without definitive treatment of the cancer. If the lesion is DCIS without any components of invasive disease, then a node dissection need not be performed.

Radiologists (American College of Radiology) advocate for image guided biopsy for all birads 4 and 5 lesions prior to surgical treatment. Most breast surgeons agree that needle biopsy is preferable over open diagnostic procedure. Today, breast imaging studies, breast cancer risk assessment and physical exam can narrow the pre-operative risks of a breast lesion being malignant or benign, at rates of accuracy in the 90% range. Thus, a breast mass with a risk of 90% or higher of being a malignancy, and the patient, with proper surgical assessment and counseling, prefers breast conservation then a pre-operative needle biopsy would not change planned surgical treatment in cases where the breast lesion mandates resection, even in cases of non-malignant diagnoses (growing benign tumors, recurrent complex cyst, phylloides tumor). If patient desires a mastectomy or if she chooses to have chemotherapy prior to surgical removal of the tumor, known as neo-adjuvant chemotherapy, then tissue diagnosis prior to surgery is required. For example, the tumor is large, and a lumpectomy may result in a positive margin despite carefull intra-operative pathological examinations. In the latter instance, a needle biopsy with tissue diagnosis of carcinoma, will expedite the option of mastectomy, and allow proper evaluation for neo-adjuvant chemotherapy.

Mammogram screening for breast cancer raises many controversies, however, the main message is that effective screening does detect breast cancers at earlier stages and improves the survival after treatment. Abnormal mammograms are common and lead to much anxiety. Despite these controversies, women should know their risks of breast cancer and continue prudent prevention practices and screening.

7.3 COLORECTAL CANCER SCREENING

Colorectal cancer causes the second highest numbers of cancer deaths and affects men and women nearly equally. There is a consensus on the effectiveness of screening using any three of the following methods: colonoscopy, sigmoidoscopy combined with barium enema radiography and stool occult blood tests. There is a preference for colonoscopy as a screening tool of choice even though the cost is higher and there is a 0.5% risk of perforation. It is the most effective option, in the sense that, when abnormality is found it can also be diagnosed and treated at the same time with excision or biopsy. The majority of colorectal cancers originate as a precursor adenoma which has a predictable behavior by its size, histology and numbers, translating into a known risk of carcinoma (Chu, 1986). In addition, the adenoma is present for several years prior to becoming carcinoma. In the course of the screening endoscopy, removal of adenomas will decrease the risk of developing colorectal cancer. Colonoscopy can miss up to 15% of small adenomas, especially the flat adenomas, sessile lesions and small carcinomas. In the last several decades, the distribution of colon and rectal cancers shifted more into the proximal colon. The majority of cancers were in the rectum and could have been reached with a short scope introduced from the anus. The recent shift to the right side of the large gut for majority of cancers mandates screening with a full colonoscopy, in order to visualize the mucosal surfaces from the rectum to the cecum. The shift to the right colon is still unexplained. The average risk of developing CRC is 5% life-time risk, translating to 45 cases per 100,000 individuals per year. The screening recommendations are first colonoscopy at age 50 and repeated every ten years up to age 70 or older if the estimated life expectancy is greater than 10 years. If the risks are increased, as in family history of colon cancer, history of inflammatory bowel disease, or findings at colonoscopy, the endoscopic schedule can start at younger age and repeated at more frequent intervals. By following these guidelines, which have been adopted by major cancer advocacy groups, the American

Cancer Society and the American Society of Gastroenterology, the rate of dying from CRC can be reduced by over 50%.

7.4 LIVER CANCER SCREENING

Primary liver cancer, distinct from liver tumors from metastatic disease, is one of the leading causes of cancer deaths in some parts of Asia and the Near-East. The etiology is the prevalence of hepatitis B resulting in chronic hepatitis, cirrhosis and hepatomas. Hepatitis C is also emerging as a common virus responsible for chronic liver infections, cirrhosis and hepatocellular cancers, especially in the U.S. Cholangiocarcinomas are made up of malignant bile ductal cells, also thought to be caused by chronic inflammation, and uncommonly by parasitic infections from Clonorchis sinensis. Screening for small liver tumors is not generally advocated since there is a lack of controlled studies supporting this practice. Liver ultrasound and tumor markers such as CEA, alfa-feto protein and CA 19-9 have low specificity, and may lead to false positive results. Knowing these shortcomings, liver ultrasound and blood tumor markers could still be used as the first line of screening, and positive results need to be confirmed with CT or MRI scans. Hepatitis B vaccine has been found to lower incidence of hepatomas if given early in infancy, first confirmed in a cohort controlled Taiwanese study. The prevention of chronic hepatitis and subsequent reduction of liver cancers is a form of primary prevention. The Center for Disease Control (CDC) has recommended Hepatitis B vaccination for all newborns in the hopes of reducing morbidity of the hepatitis and risk of cancer in the future. This will be discussed further under Chapter 8, Cancer Vaccines. Hepatitis C has increased in prevalence in the US and is becoming the dominant cause of hepatocellular carcinomas. Unfortunately, thus far, there is no effective vaccine against Hep C.

Current guidelines for liver screening (Sherman, 2012), recommend liver ultrasound for only candidates with higher risks: liver cirrhosis, chronic hepatitis, history of hepatitis viral infection and individuals originating from endemic areas. Alpha-feto protein (AFP), a tumor marker for hepatocellular cancers, and CA 19-9, a marker for cholangiocarcinoma can also be used in combination with liver ultrasonography. In addition, in individuals with chronic hepatitis, active surveillance and screening for hep B and C are recommended. Smaller liver tumors are more easily resected for cure and likely amenable to minimally invasive resections by laparoscopic techniques.

7.5 FEMALE REPRODUCTIVE ORGAN CANCER SCREENING: CERVIX, OVARY AND ENDOMETRIUM.

Screening and early diagnosis of cervical cancer has become another success story. The death rate from cervical cancer has fallen by half from 5.55 to 2.38 deaths per 100,000 women in three decades attributed to Papanicolau cytology screeening (Schlichte, 2015). Young women are still suffering and dying from this preventable disease, especially in countries like Mozambique, Bolivia and India. Screening with Papanicolau test had been effective in detecting early changes in the cervical cells leading to treatment of early cervical cancers and prevention by intervening in the precancerous, dysplastic stage. The Pap test is a cytology reading of the cervical smear, and the modern version of this test includes the DNA assay for the HPV virus which is the main culprit of this disease. Several strains of this virus are found in the cervix, penis and oral cavity which can be eliminated by vaccination or anti-viral treatment. Vaccine directed against several strain of the human papilloma virus (HPV), has been approved for adolescent girls and boys for the intention to prevent cervical and penile cancers. In the first report of the vaccine trial, cervical-intra epithelial neoplasia (CIN) were measured. Cervical cancers, which are the very endpoint that matters, would take 20 years to develop, on average, and did not have sufficient events to show significant differences in the first several studies on the HPV vaccine. The longterm effects of the vaccine are unknown. Test for HPV is recommended for women undergoing Pap test over the age of 30. Pap test is recommended for women starting at the age of 21. Risk factors for CIN and cervical cancer are: early age of coitus, multiple sexual partners, tobacco use and use of hormone contraceptives. CIN 1/2 (mild to moderate dysplasia) can be observed with repeat of Pap test within 6 months. CIN 3 (severe dysplasia) requires a colposcopy procedure and biopsy. If in situ disease is found, then a LEEP (loop electrosurgical excision procedure) can be performed. Invasive cervical cancers are treated with hysterectomies and regional node dissection. For women over 30 years of age, after negative Pap and HPV tests, the cervical smear tests can be extended to every three years. HPV interaction with the vaginal and cervical microbiota creates conditions of chronic inflammatory reactions that can lead to oncogenesis. Chronic inflammation or infection can be the basis of other cancers including hepatocellular carcinoma caused by hepatitis B and C, gastric cancer and mantle cell lymphoma by H. pylori. HPV infection, especially with strains 16 and 18, are necessary precursor for CIN and cervical cancer, however there are usually other promoting factors. HPV test is specific for cervical cancer, however with low sensitivity. For example, women with new HPV infection usually clear the virus in the cervical epithelium in 6 months. Repeat HPV tests are suggested to confirm that the infection is eliminated. CIN can develop and if cervical inflammatory response is sustained, from repeated HPV or other infections, then cervical cancer can develop over several years. Other co-factors are usually required, such as tobacco use, and co-infections, such as Chlamydia (Mitra 2016).

Ovarian and endometrial cancers take a large number of lives among young and middle- aged women. Ovary cancers is fifth most common cancer in women, being diagnosed in 22,000 females and causing 15,500 deaths in 2008 (U.S. data). With high proportion of women dying after the diagnosis, it is imperative to identify this disease at earlier stages. In the screening study by PLCO (The Prostate, Lung, Colorectal and Ovarian Cancer Screening Randomized Controlled Trial, 2011), 78,216 average risk women were enrolled, and randomized to observation and CA-125 blood test and trans-vaginal ultrasound screening. There were no significant differences in mortality in each group, after 13 years of follow-up and the ovary cancers found in each group did not differ in the proportion of advanced stages.

Despite these disappointing findings, several centers do recommend screening with both CA-125 and trans-vaginal ultrasound for higher risk women based on family history of ovarian and breast cancer, age, infertility, history of endometriosis, hormone replacement, heritage (Ashkenazi Jewish descent), or BRCA gene mutations.

Endometrial cancers have an overall risk of 18 cases per 100,000 women yearly, a slight rise from the last decade due to obesity and fall in fertility rates. Uterine cancers are the most common of the female reproductive organs, ranked 4th after breast, colorectal and lung cancers. Screening with trans-vaginal ultrasound has not been recommended for average risk women. For higher risk women and in women with Lynch syndrome, screening with trans-vaginal pelvic ultrasound, Pap smear and CA-125 should be considered. A thickened uterine stripe should be followed with repeat ultrasound or endometrial biopsy.

7.6 PROSTATE CANCER SCREENING

Prostate cancer is the most common cancer in males in the U.S. The true incidence is masked by the prevalence of occult disease and varies according to screening rates with PSA (prostate specific antigen) and digital rectal exam. Autopsy studies indicate higher rates due to lack of symptoms in occult prostate cancers. There is high variability in the incidence even within different regions in the world, and what remains a constant thread is the higher mortality in individuals of African descent and ones with higher incomes, possibly due to association of high fat and protein diets (Azgomi 2016). Occult prostate cancer in the aged is common, over 50% in men over the age of 65, however it is an uncommon cause of death. Currently, there is a debate whether to perform major surgery for prostate cancer since the indolent form often do not cause symptoms nor death. About a third of prostate cancers do progress and may need surgery, radiation or hormone therapies. Some younger men develop an aggressive form of the disease and leads to metastatic disease. In the light of the prevalence of indolent prostate cancers, early diagnosis and screening of these tumors will not alter the survival rates in prostate cancer. Two large screening studies with digital rectal exams and PSA (prostate specific antigen serum test) published in 2009 (Andreole et al, Schroder et al) showed no difference in survival in the American study, while the European study favored the screened group. The different outcomes are hard to explain, perhaps due to non-prostate cancer related deaths. A more recent re-analysis of the European study with 13-year follow-up showed a narrowing of the survival in both groups. These two screening tests are simple and low cost to administer and recommended for men from age 50 to 70. Abnormal tests can lead to further imaging tests such as MRI or PET scan and not necessarily to prostate needle biopsy if watching and waiting is the chosen approach. If watchful waiting is chosen over invasive biopsy or prostatectomy, then screening and monitoring for progression of tumor is the more prudent approach.

Primary prevention with finasteride is feasible, and can be considered for high risk individuals, such as family history of aggressive subtypes and African American males (Violette 2012).

8

CANCER VACCINES AND IMMUNOTHERAPY

Vaccine inoculation is a practical and effective preventive intervention for many of our infectious diseases, saving millions of lives and untold illnesses. It is one of the earliest clues into the workings of our immune system. Thucidides in 429 BC recorded that small pox survivors were resistant to future infections. As early as the 9th century, variolation, introducing small pox skin scabs either in skin wounds or inhaled in the powder form, was effective in preventing the active infection. In 1796, Edward Jenner formulated the vaccine using contents of a pustule from a milk maiden, infected by bovine pox. Since then many viral and bacterial infections threatening public health have been controlled by herd immunity established by vaccinating at least 80% of the community members for most infectious agents.

Tumor immunology is based on the premise that the cancer cell, with unique tumor antigens, is recognized as foreign invader and would undergo rejection through immune cytotoxic reactions. These concepts were put forth by Paul Erlich, 1909. As mutations occur constantly, and malignant transformation follows in a fraction of mutated cells, most cancer cells are being eliminated by the immune system and sparing the host of clinical evident cancers. This paradigm is called immune surveillance, and occurs at the cellular level, prior to any awareness of the cancer threat and presentation of a tumor mass. Tumor immunologists had long expected that by exploiting the natural immune defenses and immune surveillance, to find the ultimate cure to cancer, perhaps in a form of a tumor vaccine. The enthusiasm surrounding this goal has waxed and waned through the last several decades, mainly due to the lack of success in human trials, although the proof of principle, was seen in animal tumor vaccine experiments. Burnet, one of the leading tumor immunologists of his time, would predict that the cancer evasion of the immune surveillance would be overcome by interventions through the understanding of the cancer immune blockade or tolerance (Parish, 2003). Several strategies in immunotherapy have been used both in pre-clinical animal studies and human studies, such as, anti-tumor antigen antibodies, irradiated whole tumor cells, lymphokine activated killer cells (LAK), tumor infiltrating lymphocytes (TIL), attenuated cultured tumor cell lines, tumor antigen binding cofactors with various modifications and dendritic cell stimulation. Once again success has been limited in human studies, though findings in the animal or in-vitro models were very promising (Mellman, 2011). The last decade has ushered in some new therapies and strategies in boosting the immune system. Monoclonal antibodies blocking tumor cell membrane receptors such as Her2/neu, VEGF and EGFR showed significant clinical responses in breast and lung cancers with over-overexpressed receptors compared to normal cells.

Several serendipitous findings have pushed the field to probe new areas. Graft versus host effects in allogeneic bone marrow transplantation after high-dose tumor chemotherapy, initially treated as an undesirable complication, was soon found that the graft effected significant cytotoxicity towards the cancer cells, yielding more durable cures. The desirable cytotoxicity from allogeneic lymphocytes gave impetus to develop new cytotoxic lymphocyte epitopes and newly engineered receptors to attack the cancer cells more effectively. Hence, the modified cytotoxic T cells by the CAR (chimeric antigen receptors) methodology was developed (Eshhar, 2014), elaborated in next few paragraphs, section 8.2. Tumor surface antigens can be shed and new tumor surface antigens acquired, functioning as a shield to host complement, antibodies and cytotoxic lymphocytes, macrophages and N-K cells. In this manner, the tumor cell can be invisible to the circulating antibodies, complement and effector cells. Many vaccines using tumor antigens have been ineffective in phase III trials, probably due to immune blockade by the cancer.

Two vaccines for infectious agents are credited in preventing cancers, the hepatitis B and the HPV vaccines. Chronic infections, caused by bacteria, as in the case of H pylori for gastric cancer (read more, section 8.4), or by viruses, as in the case of Hepatitis B and C, can lead to local immune suppression, as well as mutagenic instability, both of which are conducive to tumors and malignant change. Chronic inflammation, seen often in the background of chronic infections, and also, in non-infectious conditions, such as auto-immune disorders, colitis, non-healing wounds, sets the stage for mutagenic activity and promotion of hyperplasia. HPV and Hepatitis B vaccines, referred to as cancer vaccines, could be a convenient misnomer for anti-infectious vaccine. Nevertheless, since preventing the chronic infections in both hepatitis B virus and HPV leads to reduced liver and cervical cancers, respectively. Vaccines against infectious agents are effective when given prior to the significant exposure to these microbes or prior to contracting the disease. Similarly, cancer vaccines would be more effective when given prior to developing the clinical evidence of tumor, in other words, as a truly preventive modality. This creates an investigative conundrum for the development of tumor vaccines. How can you test your tumor vaccine in healthy individuals? Even though the vaccine has promising results in the pre-clinical phase, i.e., animal subjects that are usually vaccinated prior to tumor inoculation. In human trials, we are actually testing in a different situation, anti-tumor activity in relatively established cancers. The human volunteers with advanced cancers are unable to develop a vigorous anti-tumor response, and the immune response is far lower than what is required to reject established tumors. In order to carry out the proper human study, it would require volunteer subjects with early tumors or pre-cancerous lesions, and it would be a formidable task to convince healthy individuals to volunteer for a vaccine study that has unknown consequences. If a study with healthy volunteers with no established tumors was completed, tens of thousands needed, the results would mature after 20-30 years, indeed a very long period required to observe any infrequent spontaneous development of tumors, plus a cohort requirement of thousands of subjects. In opinion surveys of the public, it was found that 30% would take a vaccine to prevent future cancers.

Are there other reasons for the lack of success in human tumor vaccines trials? Though immunity to tumor antigens can be readily demonstrated, and tumor shrinkage observed in some patients, success defined by statistically significant improvement in placebo-controlled trials, has been difficult to achieve. In the animal model, on the other hand, strong immune reactions can be initiated against these tumor antigens, and many vaccines found to render the animal free of established tumor and can also reject implantation of new experimental tumors. Several theories have been proposed to explain the success in experimental setting and yet insufficient activity against human tumors. Immune shielding, tolerance and tumor anergy have been proposed as mechanisms working against tumor immune activities and tumor vaccines. The tumor antigens are shed at a rate capable of thwarting an effective immune response and coupled with the ability of the tumor cell to modify its antigenic exterior or mask the antigens with non-specific mucins or glycolipids similar to the chorionic cell surface in the placental implantation onto the pregnant uterus. In other words, the placenta-fetus interface is another natural example of shielding or blocking the expected immune rejection of foreign antigens, the fetus in this case. Specific tumor immunity tolerance can be mediated through dendritic cell antigen presentation inhibition. T cell regulatory cells and several T cell inhibitory receptors including CTLA4, PD-L1, TIM-3 and others have been manipulated and re-directed the immune cells not to attack cancer cells. A different escape mechanism to the immune surveillance is developed by the malignant cell through its high rate of mitosis and genetic mutations supplying with surface antigen modifications and possible other novel strategies aided by survival pressures of Darwinian selection among rapidly dividing cancer cells. The vast majority of malignant cells are eliminated by the immune surveillance, and the selected survivor, by definition, has the characteristics capable of evading effective methods of rejection. This theme of molecular ecology is common to all biospheres including our bodies. Treatment of an infection with antibiotics can lead to opportunistic infection of a resistant bacteria and chemotherapy treatment leads inevitably to clonal resistance in the tumor. The cancer cell can suppress host immune anti-tumor activities, learned from trial and error over their evolutionary development, and in particular, manipulating key signals in immune reaction and inhibition. There has been progress in the clinics in using antibodies blocking the different receptors of immune inhibitory check-points, see Section 8.3. Viruses, through trials and errors like mutations, are also capable of selecting new ways of circumventing the immune rejection, Chapter 23.

8.1 PREVENTING LIVER AND CERVIX CANCERS WITH VACCINES

Hepatitis B vaccine lowers subsequent chronic HBV infections and in turn lowers the rates of hepatocellular carcinoma. This was found by a controlled, non-randomized study in Taiwan. Similar studies were done in Alaska, Korea and Qidong, China, looking retrospectively at groups of vaccinated and non-vaccinated cohorts, (Qu,2014). Though the studies had controlled cohorts, and not randomized, the results had significantly fewer events in the vaccinated cohort that would be difficult to justify a non-vaccination study group. Human papillomavirus link to cervical carcinoma was well established by Hausen (awarded the Nobel Prize 2008), and about 15 subtypes of HPV are associated with cervical cancer among the 40 types that infect the genital and oral tracts. The first HPV vaccine reacted against 4 HPV subtypes, and later a 9-valent vaccine was approved by FDA. HPV infections are clearly reduced as well as the cervical hyperplasias/dysplasias by cytological exam. No invasive cervical cancers were found in the vaccinated group and only a few in the control group (Garland, 2016). There is insufficient data to conclude that HPV vaccine prevents cervical cancer, as was expected, since the oncological process evolves over 10-20 years.

There are several benefits of the vaccines, in the anti-infectious realm, but the anti-cancer outcomes are more difficult to measure as there are several confounding issues. Hepatocellular carcinomas are more common in the subset of individuals with chronic active hepatitis in association with liver cirrhosis. Other factors include tobacco use, alcohol intake, HCV infection, steatosis and diabetes. In general, hepatitis infection raises the risk of hepatoma by 0.1%. Development of cervical cancer with HPV infection is a pre-requisite, however, not a sufficient cause. The prevalence of HPV infection in young sexually active women is as high as 70% in some series and falling significantly, as the women turn 30 years of age. The HPV infection is usually cleared spontaneously over several months. Re-infection is common, and cervix mucosal hyperplasia conversion from CIN (in situ neoplasia) to higher grade of dysplasia, is more common with persistent HPV infection. Other contributing factors are multiple sexual partners, co-infections with other STDs (sexually transmitted diseases). Hepatocellular carcinoma incidence is decreased by 70% in the vaccinated population, while HPV vaccine has a more recent history and it is still too early to observe a decrease in cervical cancers. It is hoped that a decrease in HPV infections will translate in fewer cervical cancers.

8.2 CAR (CHIMERIC ANTIGEN RECEPTOR) MODIFIED T CELLS

CAR modification of T-cell effectors against tumor cells has shown some promising early results, notably in B cell malignancies. It is a clever way to bypass the step of dendritic cell processing and presentation tumor antigens to cytotoxic T-cells, since one imports the antigen that directs the T-cell to attack the certain tumor cells. It was first engineered by cloned CD-3 delta-trans-membrane receptor proteins, coupled with an antigen binding moiety and a CD-28 co-stimulatory segment. The new receptor tricks the

T cell to attach to the tumor cell and perform its cytotoxic activity. CAR-T cell therapy is an example of persistence and risk-taking by immunologists, clinicians and brave patients, resulting in FDA approval of this cancer therapy (Rosenbaum, 2017).

In preparing this suspension of CAR engineered T lymphocytes, one starts with the patients' own cells by pheresing the blood and collecting the CD4+ and CD8+ lymphocytes, the subset of lymphocytes capable of killing tumors and secreting lymphokines necessary in the growth expansion process in culture. The remaining blood portions are returned back to the patient. The engineering maneuver occurs in-vitro by first inserting the CAR onto the cell membranes. The CD-28 will provide the signal for the lymphocytes to expand clonally in tissue culture and not die off, a normal process of in-vitro culture. The antigen moiety, most times a cloned product, provides the homing information for the target. In a few clinical trials, in patients with leukemia, the antigen homing unit was CD-19, a common antigen for many B cell malignancies. Surprising complete responses were obtained and found to be reproducible leading to FDA approval for this methodology. Newer engineered combinations are tried for other tumor types, *including solid tumors, for example using CEA antibody moiety for metastatic colorectal cancers. Tumor responses in solid tumors have not been as successful, thus far.*

In manipulating its internal mechanisms to fight against cancer, there are risks in misdirecting some of its effects and causing some unforeseen consequences. In the experience with administering LAK (lymphocyte activated killer) cells, where cytotoxic T lymphocytes are incubated with tumor antigens, some patients develop inflammatory responses out of proportion to the LAK activity. In some instances, this has been attributed to an excess IL-2 production. In many instances, there is no identifyable culprit and has been named "immunological storm", characterized by swelling of tissues in the lung, gut and skin, accompanied by hypotension and "leaky membrane" syndrome that can lead to death due to pulmonary failure and secondary sepsis. Infusions with CAR modified lymphocytes, though appearing to be specific to tumor cells, have also been found to release a cascade of lymphokines capable of causing immunological storm. In fact, one of the first human placed on trial of CAR modified donor lymphocytes, was a 5-year old girl with leukemia, failing several courses of chemotherapy, and developed life-threatening leaky membrane syndrome due to excess IL-6. She received experimental anti IL-6 monoclonal antibodies and survived the ordeal. The young patient has been free of disease for over 7 years, and her personal success and fortune, did not appear so in the beginning. She had been near death, a tragedy averted, and her miracle saved the experimental clinical protocol, and since thousands more patients.

8.3 SUPPRESSING THE IMMUNE SUPPRESSOR

Immune checkpoints are T and B cell receptors that when activated initiate lymphocyte cell death and decrease the immune activity and the proliferation of activated T cells. These are normal pathways that slow down and turn off normal immune reactions. In the early studies of PD-1, it was found lacking in mice with autoimmune disease. Tumor cells have taken adavantage of these checkpoint ligands to turn off the full activated T cell cytolytic activity. A ligand to PD-1 was identified, PD-L1, which tumor cells use effectively in suppressing anti-tumor immunity. Monoclonal antibodies developed to several of these checkpoint proteins have been introduced into clinical trials, called checkpoint inhibitors. Ipilimumab is an antibody which blocks CTLA-4, another checkpoint receptor which is one of the signals that initiate the suppression of immune response, often exploited in transplantation research. By blocking the CTLA-4, Ipilimumab allows greater T-cell effector cells to replicate and perform its cytotoxic roles against tumor cells. This treatment has had durable responses in patients with metastatic or recurrent melanoma that could not be resected. These treatment results are clearly superior to existing and prior treatments for stage IV advanced melanoma such as combination chemotherapy and forms of immunotherapy such as high dose interleukin-2, interferon, and adoptive T-cell therapies such as tumor infiltrating lymphocytes, LAK cells, for example. The few responses were tempered by the life-threatening toxicities and intensive care unit type of life supports. Another interesting aspect of the treatment is that the responses can be late, even months after initiation of treatment, indicating a possible new unrecognized mechanism of tumor death or inhibition. Most of these responses are durable, over several years. This was not the case with responses to chemotherapy or other biological therapies, that usually are met with recurrences within six months. Responses to the different checkpoint target inhibitors vary as well as their toxicities, such as colitis, which appears to be more common with PDL-1 compared to CTLA-4 inhibitors. When tried in other tumor types, investigators have also found some remarkable responses.

Durable responses are found in about a third of melanoma patients treated, and another third have minor responses, and benefits in over-all survivors have not been uniform in several series (Jenkins, 2018). There are several reasons for weaker responses, including the poor generation of effector cells, and up-regulation of other check-point receptors, on the cancer cell surface, on the host lymphocytes and on the peri-tumor supporting cells. One of the important take home lessons, is that although the significant responses are only a few, some patients respond dramatically and some are cured. The process of tumor growth and immunotherapy are not fully understood, or possibly, the process can be substantially different for different tumors, even amongst melanomas, or within different individuals. The latter is a strong argument for personalized therapies, and the genomic approach. Measurements of tumor PD-1 receptors, and various tumor gene mutations were predictors of which tumor would respond to the check point inhibitor therapy.

The Nobel Prize committee awarded the prize in medicine and physiology in 2018 to James Allison and Tasuku Honjo “for their discovery of cancer therapy by inhibition of negative immuneregulation”. Dr Allison has done pioneer work on T cell receptor CTLA-4, and Dr Honjo on PD-1.

8.4 GENE EDITING

Ever since the genetic code has been unraveled, scientists have strived to alter the genes to treat illnesses, produce better crops and even produce new organisms. Genetic engineering has achieved some notable successes. Bacterial genes were modified in 1972 by Boyer and Cohen, transgenic mice developed by Jaenish in 1974, and first human gene therapy completed in 1990 at the National Institute of Health. It is noted that for thousands of years, the genome has been indirectly manipulated in domestic animals and farmed plants by selecting the desired qualities, preserving naturally ocurring genetic changes and by cross-fertilization. Mandel noted the binary nature of genetic combinations in 1865. Darwin described the early concepts of evolution by noting the results of selection by humans in husbandry and horticulture compared to natural selection, and later included these postulates in his book, On the Origin of Species, 1859. Viruses have developed plasmids, circular segments of RNA or DNA, that when inserted into the host bacterial genes, viral products can be made within the host. Occasionally these plasmids have been preserved by the hosts for their own functional needs and some conserved through evolution. Bacteria and archea have also evolved defensive mechanisms that remove segments of invasive viral DNA, responsible for their virulence. One mechanism in particular, CRISPR-Cas 9, has been discovered in 2002, and few years later, its function in coupling onto double stranded DNA and cutting at specific locations was understood and now applied in vitro and in vivo for gene editing, a more precise and simpler way of introducing new genes into the genome. This new development is a significant advance over the former DNA engineering techniques using viral or bacterial vectors, electroporation or micro-injections. These latter methods were inneficient. The rate of incorporation of engineered DNA was low or the sites of the DNA incorporation were not reliable.

Gene modification or editing using the CRISPR method has been improving to the point that clinical applications have increased exponentially. In immunotherapy, The CAR modified lymphocytes has employed CRISPR to introduce new membrane proteins targeting tumor cells. A knock-out gene mouse has been a valuable experimental animal for the study of gene and protein product interaction in tumor biology and targeted therapy development. With CRISPR technology, one could develop entire cell arrays with specific gene mutations for study. These in-vitro techniques will allow narrowing the focus of particular gene locus in the process to tumorigenesis and in turn allow more targets for therapy (Zhan 2018).

8.5 A NEW DAWN IN CANCER IMMUNOTHERAPY?

After decades of clinical trials with cancer vaccines, activated lymphocytes, and various lymphokines, such as interferon, with limited success, the recent proliferation of new approaches, from antibodies targeting cancer membrane receptors, to check-point inhibitors and engineered CAR-T cells, has given renewed interest in immunotherapy.

William Coley is attributed to be the father of immunotherapy. In 1891, he treated his first patient with intratumoral injections of soft tissue sarcoma with culture medium of streptococcus bacteria. He had observed a spontaneous regression of tumor with erysipelas and gathered other reports of similar observations. Dr Coley as the head of Bone Tumor Unit of the Memorial Hospital in New York, treated over 1,000 patients with this method, known as Coley's toxin (McCarthy 2006). He reported many patients with tumor regression and long-term survivors. His work was continued until mid-twentieth century, when was abandoned due to the advent of chemotherapy and radiation. Immunotherapy research, at Memorial Sloan Kettering, was continued by Lloyd J. Old, with the use of BCG in bladder cancer and the isolation of TNF (tumor necrosis factor), among several other projects.

Several publications have reviewed the new advances in immunotherapy as the beginning of a new era, where wider range of tumors can be controlled by manipulating the immune system (Wirth 2017). Are we seeing a new era in oncology, cancer treatment and prospects for cancer prevention?

The progress in the science and understanding of cancer immunology have advanced gradually though at an increased pace, as seen in other fields in science and technology. Actual successful therapies may come at incremental bursts of advances between periods of apparent inactivity, and clearly the promise of genomics, tumor immunology and cancer prevention has yet to be realized. Scientific revolutions and their fruits in new therapies are usually a result of new discoveries and paradigms, wide application of new technologies or a cross pollination of different ideas and techniques from one field to another field of science.

8.6 CHRONIC INFECTIONS AND CANCER: A PERMISSIVE IMMUNE STATE?

The role of infectious agents in human illnesses has been suspected in conditions other than infections, like stomach ulcers, diabetes, and cancer. In 1926, the Nobel Prize in Medicine was awarded to Fibigner for his work linking stomach cancer to parasitic diseases, and later the findings were discredited by other investigators. The relationship between infectious agents and cancer can be observed in non-healing wounds colonized by multiple microbes. After several years, these wounds with copious granulation tissue can transform into ulcerating tumors, showing up as squamous carcinoma under microscopic examination. These tumors are called Marjolin ulcers, named after the French surgeon, Jean Nicholas Marjolin, reporting his findings in 1828. Further research observed multiple microbes, in the chronic phase of infection are associated with some specific cancers. Parasitic infections like schistosomiasis of the bladder are linked to squamous type cancers of the bladder. Stomach lining infection with the bacteria Helicobacter pylori can cause adenocarcinomas of the gastric mucosa and in some MALT (mucosa associated lymphoid tissue) lymphomas. Several viral infections such as hepatitis virus B and C are associated with cirrhosis and liver cancers, and human papilloma virus (HPV) are associated with cervical and oral cancers. In the large bowel, for example, there are well established set of microbials, as part of the microbiome, that are associated with inflammatory bowel diseases, Crohn's and ulcerative colitis. IBD (inflammatory bowel disease) increases the risks for colon and rectal cancers. The interesting and paradoxical aspect of the microbiome is that the normal resident gut flora protects the gut against infections due to invasive microbes as in inflammatory bowel disease or other gut infections. For example, in severe colitis, introduction of normal stool sample can repopulate the microbiome and help resolve the inflammatory condition. Chronic inflammation is a common feature in tissues subject to oncogenic transformation, hepatitis and cirrhosis in the liver, gastritis in stomach mucosa, colitis in the large gut. The immune response in the acute phase of infection, need to be sufficiently robust to overcome the invading organisms, to protect and rebuild normal tissues, while in the recovery phase, the immune system needs to attenuate the mobilized response to return to normal resting state. This special task of self-defense, tissue repair and return to normal homeostasis performed by the immune response can at times leave some residual foreign microbial agents to linger and contribute to a chronic infection. Not all infections have a complete clearance from the body. Some infectious agents can survive in our tissues well beyond the acute phase, reaching a state of coexistence with the immune system, usually at a low infectious burden, and become so called an attenuated infection, not causing much bodily harm and not eliciting a major immune reaction, a classical state of immune tolerance. From a population standpoint, epidemic infections become less lethal with passage of time partly due to an increase in herd immunity and also due to natural selective advantage of a more attenuated infectious agent.

The immune mechanisms facilitating chronic infections are refered to as immune tolerance. The corresponding signals in the antigen presenting dendritic cells, T regulatory lymphocytes, T helper, T4 activator, T8 suppressor cells and host of lymphokines are geared towards toning down the immune activity and returning to the resting state, after controlling the invading pathogens (Mantovani, 2010). The resting state and homeostasis are achieved in most of our organs, however, at the previous infectious epicenter, there can be some smoldering traces of low-level inflammatory response or chronic infection. Although, the body as a whole and the circulating immune factors have normalized, locally there is a background of low inflammatory activity. Leukocytic infiltrates are found around the portal triad of the liver in chronic hepatitis, found underlying the mucosal lining of the stomach in H pylori infection, and in the colonic crypts in inflammatory bowel diseases. Virchow, one of the early pioneer pathologists, observed the predilection of leukocytic infiltrates in tumors, around the mid nineteenth century. More than fifty years later, Ehrlich, Burnet and Medawar would build on these observations to propose the basis of tumor immunology, immunological surveillance and immune escape used by tumors. Analysis of tumor infiltrating lymphocytes will find a combination of T effector and suppressor cells, reflecting the immunological activity against the tumor and potential escape mechanisms, used by tumors. Immune tolerance, in several conditions, is beneficial to the neighboring tissues, as in auto-immune conditions, pregnancy, and recovery from pathogens. In dealing with the microbiome, immune tolerance allows a co-existence that yield several benefits, as in absorption of gut nutrients (Peterson, 2014). A stand-by mode of immune tolerance in cancers, however, permits the early cancer cells to grow and mutate, acquiring new tumor antigens and enhancing the immunological suppression. This explains the conditions in which the immune surveillance fails to eliminate the cancer cells in the early phases of tumorigenesis, under the veil of immune tolerance.

Immune tolerance can also be viewed as a cooperative mechanism between our bodies and life-forms, in and around us. Symbiosis, a co-existence in the same environment between two of separate species. Corals with Anthozoa and microbial alga, flowering plants and pollinating bees are couple of examples. These symbiotic relationships often are mutually beneficial. Human gut and the gut microbiota are not often considered in a mutually helpful relationship. Bacteria and fungi aid in the digestion by producing fermentation agents to breakdown some of the saccharides, and supplying needed short chain fatty acids and vitamins, such as biotin, riboflavin and ascorbate (Jandhyala 2015). The microbiome serves as a deterrent to invasive microbial species that can initiate infections. The microbiome barrier, made up of "normal microbes", are found in several interfaces in our bodies: on the skin, in the gut, in the upper aero-digestive tract, and to a lesser extent in the lungs. As we will see in Chapter 19, the gut microbiota can play important roles in obesity and in other health and disease conditions. The gut mucosa, along with its GALT (gut associated lymphoid tissue), and gut inner-surface mucus layer are important in nutrient absorption and barrier to pathogen translocation. Interestingly, the microbiome can affect brain function. The gut-brain axis participates in digestion, as in the cephalic phase of salivary, gastric and pancreatic juice secretion. The microbiome contributes to the autonomous nervous function as well as neurotransmitter production in the gut. Brain health and the gut interaction is now called the microbiome-gut-brain axis (Mohajeri 2018).

9

COMMON CANCERS

9.1 SKIN CANCER

Skin cancers are by far the most common malignant tumor. Except for malignant melanoma and merkel cell tumor, skin cancers hardly ever result in mortality. Nevertheless, it is a burden on the quality of life and health costs and moreover, there is a great opportunity for prevention (Call to action on skin cancer prevention, The Surgeon General, HHS.gov, 2004). The common skin cancers are referred to as basal cell and squamous cell carcinoma. They arise from the skin cells of the basal layer which are continuously growing and pushed to the surface of the skin. In the process, the more superficial cells differentiate into squamous cells, more flattened, and gives the protective and shielding effect of the skin to the outside world. In a more specialized differentiation, they become cells that generate hair, nails, and in animals, scales and feathers. Melanoma arise from melanocytes, which originate from neural crest cells. In the embryo, the neural tube grows into the central nervous system, and gives origin to the neural crest cells. Some neural crest cells at the periphery of the neural tube migrate into tissues, forming peripheral nerves, and populate the skin and mucosal surfaces as melanocytes. Melanocytes produce the melanin pigment of the skin. Merkel cell carcinoma arise from skin stem cells that have been infected with polyoma virus. Its name suggests it originates from the neuroendocrine Merkel cells, as was thought initially. The skin is a quite complex organ and by weight and surface area is the largest organ of the body.

Both basal and squamous cell cancers are induced by sun over-exposure as they present in the areas of the skin most affected by sun rays. Melanoma, however, does not always present in locations affected by the sun, as it can present on skin usually covered by clothing. Sun exposure in general increases the incidence of melanoma even in non- exposed areas. There are several susceptible genes, BRAF/RAS/MERK pathway being the most commonly affected, and one mutation, in particular, V600E, has been identified early in the tumorigenesis, as in dysplastic nevi, (Griewank 2014). Melanin comes in several forms, found in bacteria, in plants, and in human skin. In humans, melanin has two isoforms, eumelanin and pheomelanin. Melanomas can carry pigment of either type and also be amelanotic. Several skin conditions are associated with increased melanin production including benign skin tumors such as seborrheic keratosis, and with malignant tumors such as basal cell carcinoma. Melanin is the best protector against UV radiation damage and individuals, with heavy skin pigmentation, are less likely to develop skin cancer. UV radiation damage is the main culprit for skin cancer. Individuals with darker skin and hair can develop melanoma in the nail bed (ungual melanoma) and on palms of hands and soles of feet (acral lentiginous melanoma). These individuals have lower risks of squamous and basal cell carcinomas. There are other curious clinical association with melanin, i.e., melanin loss in hair with aging (graying with age), higher incidence of deafness with albinism (genetic lack of melanin production, also within the ear, cochlear body) and development of Parkinson's disease with CNS melanin defects. The non-cutaneous melanomas, as in the retina in the eye and mucosal melanomas (associated with mucous membranes in the nasopharynx and GI tract) have a different genetic pathway, even though, these malignancies involve the melanocytes in non-cutaneous sites. In contrast to BRAF changes found in cutaneous melanoma, NF1, KIT and RAS mutations were more common in mucosal melanomas.

The diagnosis can be made with a simple skin exam, and confirmed by biopsy in cases of suspicious lesions. In suspected cases of melanoma, the diagnostic biopsy should encompass enough tissue to adequately assess the depth of the tumor. For basal and squamous cell carcinoma, narrow margin excision is sufficient for cure, although local recurrence is common. Some of the recurrences are due to field gene abnormalities rather than from residual tumors. These recurrences are not problematic since re-excision can be achieved in most parts of the skin. Recurrences with deeper penetration can signal more aggressive behavior and the need for wider excision, Moh's surgery or for addition of radiotherapy. Spread to regional lymph nodes is unusual and can be treated with nodal dissection. Many local recurrences are actual multifocal disease and would argue against radical surgery. In indolent cancers such as skin squamous or basal cell carcinomas, radical surgery is usually not indicated, since repeated local surgical excisions are effective. Altogether a different story for melanomas and merkle cell tumors, potentially more aggressive tumors, to be covered later.

The issue of multifocal disease in cancers is conceptually intriguing, since theoretically all cells are subject to the same molecular insults and mutations, and as a result, why are multifocal cancers not found more frequently? Let us digress briefly, and expand on the question on multifocal cancers and field effects. The field effect gives the clinical and spatial analogy to the principle of genetic hits (mutations) that can occur in all cells in a certain anatomical region and thus there may be multiple cancers arising in one area, multifocal cancers, and also close in time scale, metachronous cancers. This is observed in cluster of cancers in colon polyps, in skin and breast cancers, and also explains the tendency for local recurrence after resection. However multiple clustered cancers are not as frequent as suggested by the events of the field effect. From the molecular viewpoint, a hit or molecular injury on the DNA resulting in a deleterious mutation, does not lead directly to cancer. As we know there are intermediary steps before malignant transformation is achieved, such as multiple mutations (genetic instability), apoptosis and the role of niche cells. Microscopic tumors could be eliminated by host immune surveillance prior to being detected. Thus, it is reasonable according to our knowledge of the molecular oncogenesis that field effect can occur with any primary tumors with varying degrees of frequency. Another form of secondary tumors, where the cells arise from a primary tumor, is the ability to metastasize to other organs, as in the regional lymph nodes, the liver or lung. Squamous and basal cell skin cancers rarely spread to lymph nodes or to distant organs. Clinical experience shows that each tumor type has different predilection to metastasize, and this behavior is also associated the ability to grow faster and cause death. Where the travelling tumor cell finally lodges and grows can also be predicted by original tumor type and growth pattern. From the molecular aspects of metastasizing tumors, several oncogenes are at play. Genetic instability leads to acquisition of multiple oncogenes in multiple heterogeneous clones allowing the properties of invasion, motility, surviving in the interstitial and intravascular environment, and in a distant host organ.

Another curious manifestation of molecular oncogenesis in clinical findings, also referred to as phenotypical gene expression, is the finding of cancers attributed to a particular oncogene derived from the germ line. As these inherited oncogenes are passed to every single cell in the offspring, cancers are only manifestated in specific organs, even though, other cells carry the same oncogene. For example, inherited mutation in BRCA 1 gene results in breast or ovaryan cancers and not in other organs such as skin or bowel cancers (frequency of other secondary cancers is extremely low). There may be yet unknown molecular events that protect other cells from cancer, a yet unknown anti-cancer mechanism? On the hand, the explanation could be as unexciting as the field effect. Even though breast tissue is embryologically similar to skin, both have different stromal and accessory cells, that are important in modulating molecular and physiological changes. The field effect can be seen in the cells around the index tumor by measuring the oncogenes. Few of the oncogenes in the index tumor can be found in the normal appearing cells in the vicinity of the index tumor. For example, the index cancer in the cecum will usually demonstrate a field effect extending to a 5 cm area into the ascending colon (and not into the ileum), or a nasal skin basal cell carcinoma will demonstrate a field effect in the bulbous nasal area. The field effect would also provide an appearance of effectiveness of radical surgery, as the local recurrence rate would be lower, however, it will have little effect on distant metastases. The higher incidence of local recurrence can also be explained by field effect rather than due to inadvertent positive or close margin surgery. Multifocal cancers in inherited cancers, as in BRCA breast cancers or Lynch syndrome colon cancers, are more common events than in sporadic cancers, however organ preservation is still clinically possible, i.e., mastectomy or total colectomy are not routinely required. Cure rates remain the same, since rates of metastases are not affected by organ preservation, as long as the primary cancer is removed entirely, and local recurrences due to field effect are resectable.

Returning to the discussion of skin cancer, we will now address malignant melanomas. They are classified into morphological groups such as superficial spreading, nodular, acral-lentiginous and lentigo-maligna. All cutaneous melanoma, behave according to their depth of invasion, measured in millimeters and used for tumor micro-staging, T stages. The deeper the melanoma penetrates the skin, the higher the risks for nodal spread, N staging, and the development of distant disease, M staging; coming together as the TNM staging, see table 1. The initial growth characteristics of melanoma are superficial and radial and then at some point in time, the growth pattern adds a vertical phase and reaches deeper into the dermis. When the melanoma cells grow deeper past the basement membrane, where the rich network of lymphatics are located, the risk of spread to lymph nodes and distant sites increases dramatically. This depth is 0.76 to 1 mm by Breslow criteria, or level III, by Clark's classification, or T1 (up to 1 mm) by TNM classification. This level also corresponds to the reticular dermis. If the melanoma is excised prior to reaching this critical depth, high cure rates are nearly universal. The early guidance of surgical excision of melanoma was based on a publication in 1907, by the British surgeon Handley who reported a case of lower extremety melanoma with satellitosis cleared with surgical resection with a radius of 5cm. This surgical practice continued until 1993, when a randomized trial, 2 cm versus 4cm margin resection, showed no advantage to the wider resection (Balch et al). The wider resection necessitated a skin graft, leaving an unsightly wound. Furthermore, for melanomas 1 mm and thicker, full node dissection was recommended. This practice was replaced by selective node identification and excision (sentinel node mapping and excision), which carried much lower rates of limb swelling (lymphedema), regional numbness and stiffness. Sentinel node mapping in cancer surgery and selective lymph node dissection was developed by surgeon Donald Morton (Balch 2018), who advanced the concept of tumor spread and precision oncologic surgery.

Table 1 TNM staging of Malignant Melanoma

T - tumor depth	N – node mets	M – distant mets	Stage
T0 in-situ	N0 none	M0	IA T1A N0M0
T1 < 1 mm	N1 1 node	M1 skin mets	IB T1B,T2A N0M0
T2 1.01-2.00 mm	N2 2-3 nodes	M2 lung mets	IIA T2B,T3A N0M0
T3 2.01-4.0 mm	N3 4 or more	M3 any other	IIB T3B,T4A N0M0
T4 >4.01 mm			IIC T4B N0M0
			III any T any N, M0
			IV any T any N, M1-3

Adapted from AJCC Cancer Staging Manual, 8th edition, 2018.
T: A – Clark's level 1-3 no ulceration, B Clark's level 4-5 or with ulceration
Node: A micrometastasis, B macrometastasis, C satellitosis or in-transit skin lesions

Once nodal metastasis is identified either clinically or by the sentinel node mapping and biopsy technique, node dissection is recommended for local control of tumor (avoid recurrence in the nodal area) and decrease the risk of distant metastasis. In the breast cancer model for example, the effectiveness of node dissection is only limited to local control benefits (i.e. prevent recurrence in the lymph node basin), and full node dissection is not recommended for nodal spread in sentinel nodes when the spread is limited to a single node. In melanoma, however, nodal basin recurrence is more common in the absence of anatomical nodal dissection. This concept was challenged by MSLT-II trial where survival was comparable in the observed versus full nodal dissection group, (Thompson 2018). Nodal recurrence in melanoma is associated with poor prognosis and development of distant metastases.

The different types of skin cancer illustrate some of the basic principles in approaching and preventing cancer progression or recurrence with varying degrees of virulence, morbidity and incidence. The growth rate and the capability to spread to vital organs characterize the more aggressive biological behavior, demonstrated dramatically between the squamous and basal cell histologies from that of the melanoma and Merkel cell types.

Basal and squamous cell carcinoma are common, affecting over 50% of adults sixty years and older, and are slow growing with a very low propensity to spread to regional lymph nodes or to distant organs. Local surgical excision has high success rates, and local recurrences, often due field effect tumorigenesis or occult residual disease, can be addressed by additional surgery without risking distal disease spread. The few exceptions are second recurrences and naso-palpebral junction in the midface, where the skin cancer can have deeper penetration (Batra 2002). On the other hand, melanoma and Merkel cell tumors, are less common, but with more aggressive behavior, especially when diagnosed with depth greater 1 mm, as re-growth at local sites and to distant organs can lead to fatalities.

There has been a rise in the incidence of skin cancers, including melanoma and Merkel cell carcinoma, approximately 5% per year (Saraya, 2004), and the estimates put melanoma as the fourth most common cancer by 2020, behind lung, breast, prostate and ahead of colorectal cancers.

All types of skin cancers can be prevented by avoiding prolonged sun exposure. In childhood and adolescense sun exposures should be limited to intermittent short spans, 1-2 hours, as to avoid sun burns and blistering. A spaced recuperative period in shady areas, allows the skin to tolerate the UV damaging effects, thereby lowering the risks of future skin cancer. Sun-screen creams and sun-proof protective clothing and hats should be used. With age, the skin can tolerate shorter periods of exposure, and the effect of sun ray damage are cumulative over the years. The sun-light spectrum which damage skin are in the ultra-violet range of UV A and B. There is no definitive proof that sun screens prevent skin cancers, however, there are no proven harmful effects from the use of sun screens, except that, its use may lead to greater sun exposure. Environmental run-off of benzylidene chemicals in the sun screens have been implicated in the depletion of micro-algae in corals. Sun screens do prevent sun burns when used properly. Use of sun screens was found by one study to decrease age related wrinkles to the skin as measured by number, length and depth of wrinkles. Darkened skin from sun tan is an effective screen against UVA and UVB, thus on a vacation to sunny locations, it is wise to limit the sun exposure to graduated doses until a good tan is developed. Individuals with dark skin have lower incidence of skin cancer compared to fair skin and light hair individuals, although acral lentigionous melanoma do occur in people with darker skin. Melanomas can grow in the palms of hands, soles of feet and nail beds. Non-cutaneous melanoma can occur in mucosal surfaces of the nasopharynx, gastrointestinal tract, genital tract, choroid and iris in the eye. Mucosal melanomas are not associated with sun exposure. Though melanoma in all those sites originate in melanocytes, mucosal surface melanoma differs from cutaneous melanoma in several features; sensitivity to radiation treatment and greater c-KIT and NF-1 mutations versus BRAF alterations in cutaneous melanoma.

Vitamin D role in cancer prevention has been studied extensively by Garland (2006) and has a special link to skin cancer since it is produced in the skin during sun exposure (Reichrat 2009). In children for example, the outdoor play time is important for maintaining adequate vitamin D levels, and also found to prevent skin cancers compared to kids with lower exposure to sunlight. We must also add that sun exposure in the young years of life also leads to lower rates of myopia, near sightedness. Clearly, excessive exposure at one time, is harmful, since we all had the experience of blistered and sore skin after too much sun. Graduated sun exposure and protecting skin of the scalp and face with hats and other skin surfaces with clothing, make a whole lot of sense for kids and adults.

Screening for skin cancer is effective relative to other cancers, since skin exam is very straight forward and the incubation period of the skin cancer from time that can be recognized to invasive behavior is relative long, even for melanoma. If the melanoma skin lesion is recognized and removed with a tumor thickness less than 1 mm, the cure rate is very high.

As an aggressive tumor, melanoma demonstrates some of the key issues of how cancer becomes lethal and yet, initially grows slowly, before acquiring the aggressive features, at some point in time. This point in time and the mechanism of transformation, from an indolent to a more aggressive biology, are also key opportunities for prevention and understanding of the molecular process. Melanoma grows first in a radial phase, as in the superficial spreading type and in the Hutchinson freckles, not uncommon in older individuals. In the latter, the radial phase can be quite prolonged, giving the behavior a very benign outlook, as opposed to superficial spreading melanoma, which is capable of becoming nodular at several sites within the radial growth, looking as dark spots embedded in the flat thin brownish area, as in a blueberry pancake. The morphological change and the ability to penetrate the basement membrane and interstitial tissues, is associated with the initiation of the metastatic progression. These steps can be correlated to genetic acquisition of key gene mutations.

Uncommon skin cancer types, the Kaposi's sarcoma and cutaneous lymphoma are discussed in the chapter of Unusual Cancers, section 10.6.

9.2 LUNG CANCER

Lung cancer is the most common cause of cancer deaths world-wide. The numbers are staggering, reaching more than a million deaths per year. Air pollutants and tobacco smoke are contributing factors, and more importantly these factors can be reduced by personal and societal choices in the prevention of lung cancer. The awareness of the dangers in smoking is high, and its continued use, speaks volume to nicotine addiction and the effectiveness of advertisement. Second hand smoke, i.e., breathing tobacco smoke generated by smokers or lit cigarettes, is also a significant risk factor for lung cancer. Spouses of smokers have a 25% risk increase for lung cancer. In addition, lung cancer among non-smokers are 3/1 predominantly females, pointing to other significant contributors like air pollutants, especially indoors, from the process of cooking and from second-hand smoke.

The projected incidence of lung cancer by 2030, will demonstrate an increase of 30%, with a preponderance increase in death rates of lung cancer in the non-Western hemisphere. The rise of lung cancer in nonsmoking populations, brings up the importance of other atmospheric pollutants. Several studies delineate the association of industrial and traffic air pollutants to lung cancer independent of tobacco use. The global rise in air pollutants nearly parallel the rise of atmospheric CO2. On a better note, lung cancer rates in the USA has decreased in the last decade mainly due to efforts in smoking cessation.

Lung cancer behaves aggressively with spread to other segments of the lung, pleura, lymph nodes and distant organs. The lethality of lung cancer is aggravated by the relatively late diagnosis, since lung cancer has few symptoms, until reaching a growth large enough to be seen on chest X-ray, around 2 cm in size, at which time, the lung cancer cells have already populated tissues beyond the original tumor site. Persistent cough, hemoptysis (coughing up blood) and chest discomfort are some of symptoms of lung cancer. Chest X-rays may miss a small cancer, 1 cm or less, and chest CT scan can delineate a smaller or more amorphous lesion. Bronchoscopy can diagnose endobronchial lesions missed on imaging tests. The common cell types of lung cancer are small or oat cell cancer, non-small cell cancer in the form of squamous or adeno carcinoma. Tobacco use is associated with small cell and squamous carcinoma types and adenocarcinoma type is predominant in non-smokers. The response to epidermal growth receptor antagonists is dramatic. Squamous cell carcinoma in smokers being poorly responsive and the adenocarcinomas in non-smokers responding well with many complete responders. Unfortunately, even in good responders, relapse is common.

The window for early diagnosis is short, thus the success for screening and early diagnosis is limited. Limited resources can be spent on screening, such as CT scans of the chest or on education efforts and legislations limiting the use of tobacco products and the generation of air pollutants. Lung cancer screening with CT scan is discussed in section 7.4.

Needle biopsy of lung nodules suspected for cancer was the method of choice until PET (positron emission tomography) scans proved effective in distinguishing benign versus malignant nodules. In addition, PET provided information regarding spread of disease, or staging of the disease, for example, whether lymph nodes are involved, or distant metastases have already occurred. If lung cancer has extended beyond the primary tumor, chemotherapy can be the initial treatment. For localized disease, video assisted thoracotomy (VATS), a minimally invasive technique compared to the traditional thoracotomy and resection, can be used for segmental or lobe resection and node dissections. Survival rates for lung cancer varies by stage and the overall survival is less than 40% at five-years. Better survival can be reached when the tumor is diagnosed at earlier stages, I or II (3 cm or smaller tumor size and no lymph node spread). Immunotherapy with check-point inhibitors have been used with significant responses. In the final analysis, prevention strategies in decreasing the use of tobacco products and lowering the concentration of ambient air pollutants may have greater impact on overall decrease in lung cancer death rates.

9.3 BREAST CANCER

One in 8 women in the U.S. will develop breast cancer in her lifetime. Even among women of Asian descent, in whom the risk is lower, the incidence of breast cancer is rising which has intrigued investigators. Soybean products, green tea, increased caloric consumption, including fats and red meat, and alcohol intake have been studied as potential factors for breast cancer. The rapid change in incidence among the Asian women population, presents unique opportunity to link environmental influences and breast cancer. Asian women who had migrated to the California, for example, have a higher incidence of breast cancer than their counterparts living in Asia. More recently, women living in metropolitan centers in Asia, such as in Shanghai, Singapore and Peking, have also seen a rise in breast cancers. The explanation for this dramatic change is in the change of diet and personal habits. Consumption of alcohol, low parity and work during night hours have been linked to increased incidence of breast cancer.

The increased use of screening mammography has been associated with an increase in diagnosis of non-invasive breast cancer, ductal carcinoma in-situ (DCIS). Several investigators have raised the issue of over-diagnosis and over-treatment of DCIS since this type of breast cancer rarely causes death. DCIS constitutes the earliest form of breast malignancy that progresses slowly into the invasive form. When DCIS is diagnosed, and treated, lower incidence of invasive breast cancers and lower the death rates from breast cancer should ensue. Currently, studies are not conclusive on these issues, and some investigators claim that DCIS should be watched and not treated. Some claim that the rate of advanced breast cancers has not decreased proving their point of "over-treatment" of DCIS. This controversy is addressed in the chapter of tumor biology and mammographic screening, section 7.2.

Greater acceptance of breast cancer screening and greater awareness of treatment alternatives, like breast preservation instead of mastectomy, for a newly found breast cancer led a shift in attitudes towards this disease resulting with higher rates of screening mammogram and visits to the doctor for smaller breast lumps. The average size of breast tumors at diagnosis has decreased in size in the last three decades, mainly attributed to mammographic screening and increased awareness. The overall survival rates have improved (Welch, 2016).

Breast cancer rates are reaching near epidemic proportions. Life time risk of one in eight women is alarming, especially when our women from one or two generations ago had risk at the least 50% lower. Multi-parity, breast feeding, later menarche, dietary changes, environmental breast gland stimulatory compounds, aging women population, alcohol consumption are all risk factors of breast cancer. Immigrants from low risk geographic regions, who are now living in major Western cities, also acquire a significant rise in breast cancer risk and in a rather short period of time. The change in breast cancer risk is independent of ethnicity. Investigators have examined different dietary components as potential culprits. Tea and soy products have potentially preventive activity for breast cancer. Alcohol consumption and life styles associated with obesity, tobacco use, hormone replacement therapy are a few factors associated with higher breast cancer risks (Momenimovahed, 2019).

9.3.1 BILATERAL MASTECTOMIES, THE CASE FOR AND AGAINST.

The radical Halsted mastectomy has long been abandoned for the most part and only reserved for advanced local tumors invading the pectoralis muscle. The operation was popularized by William S. Halsted, the head surgeon at John Hopkins University, circa 1892. The procedure removed breast and underlying pectoral muscles, large part of the skin around the breast, often requiring skin graft for closure. Full nodal dissection in the arm pit, often resulted in arm swelling, lymphedema. The radical extent of the procedure was relatively appropriate to that era. The common presentation of the breast cancer was advanced, near 10 cm in size and accompanied by satellite tumors, requiring a wide resection. Today, mastectomies remove less skin, are performed with smaller incisions and spare the pectoral muscles. The current surgical approach is usually refered as a total mastectomy. Reference to the radical connotation of mastectomy has been dropped.

Bilateral mastectomies have become more common recently for treatment of early tumors and DCIS cancers, and this approach can be considered radical for the early stage disease. The potential advantages include: cure of the ipsilateral tumor, cancer risk elimination in the contra-lateral breast and opportunity for breast reconstruction.

We should examine, more closely, the benefits depending on the tumor type and stage, patient's personal preferences, and morbidities for this form of surgical treatment.

The arguments for double mastectomy can be convincing and the procedure has improved dramatically in the last several decades. This choice, among ipsilateral mastectomy or partial mastectomy, has become more popular. The mastectomy, today, will spare muscles and most of the skin of the breast and occasionaly the nipple. Lymph nodes are checked by sentinel node mapping and biopsy, a technique associated with fewer arm and shoulder complications. Only a few nodes are removed, resulting in fewer symptoms in terms of arm lymphedema, shoulder stiffness and upper arm numbness. When more than a single sentinel lymph node is found with cancer cells spread from the breast location, then a full lymph node dissection is indicated.

Breast cancer survivors have a higher risk of contralateral breast cancer compared to other women with average risks. If this risk is higher than that of recurrent breast cancer, then a double mastectomy will lower overall mortality rates. For example, younger women with breast cancer will carry a higher life-time risk for contralateral breast cancer, and in the event of ipsilateral low-risk breast cancer, including DCIS, one could argue for the advantages of bilateral mastectomies.

Techniques of breast reconstructive surgery have also improved. New procedures include use of implants and microsurgery allowing transfer of tissues such as muscle flaps with overlying skin with their own vascular supply. Reconstructive surgery allows several choices in unilateral or bilateral breast surgery that enhances the emotional recovery of the breast cancer patient, when done concurrently with mastectomy. In other words, the woman undergoes one operation for both the cancer treatment and reconstruction. Thus, the choice of surgery in breast cancer has an element of personal preference, where, the advising oncologist needs to defer to the patient, and yet not compromise on the curative aspects of the treatment. Whenever the choice can impact on survival, tumor recurrence or morbidity rates, then, these differences of choosing mastectomy or breast conservation need to be clarified.

In order to illustrate how the benefits of these choices as well as how some of these risks are balanced, we will begin to make some points against the choice of bilateral mastectomy. When the breast cancer is invasive and will need adjuvant chemotherapy to reduce the risk of distant metastasis, then bilateral mastectomy can add a distraction and a real delay in the treatment to maximize cure rates. Chemotherapy administered prior to surgery, known as neo-adjuvant chemotherapy, can circumvent the issue of delay of systemic treatment, however, it creates new potential disavantages, such as delay of surgery and increase in surgical morbidity. Tumor response to chemotherapy is the best guide to the timing of surgery. A complete response can be seen with shrinkage of tumor after the second cycle of chemotherapy, with disappearance of the mass, and in these instances, surgery can be postponed to the end of the entire drug regimen, usually around 6 months. A weak partial response with less than 30-40% shrinkage, leaves a significant portion of the tumor at risk for drug resistance and potential development of metastasis. In this case, earlier surgical treatment can eliminate the risk for clonal escape and metastasis. Bilateral mastectomy following full 6 cycles of chemotherapy can encounter increased surgical morbidities such as infection, healing delays and seroma formation. Starting with unilateral mastectomy, completing chemotherapy, and then electively perform the contralateral mastectomy with reconstruction on both sides, can lessen the rate of morbidities and allow timely completion of chemotherapy.

9.3.2 MASTECTOMY OR BREAST PRESERVATION (LUMPECTOMY OR PARTIAL MASTECTOMY), SOMETIMES A DIFFICULT DECISION.

There are several misconceptions regarding the indications for breast cancer surgery, namely the choice of mastectomy or removal of lesser portions of the breast, as in partial mastectomies. Many patients are told that breast conservation surgery is not possible for small breast, multiple tumors, node positive tumors or breast cancers with aggressive cell types. For example, women diagnosed with tripple negative breast cancers, potentially carrying a worse prognosis, are candidates for breast preservation. Some surgeons inform patients that it is safer to have mastectomy compared to lumpectomy, without much scientific evidence. The cure rate for breast cancer is determined by stage and not by the surgical procedure, mastectomy or lumpectomy, assuming that is done correctly (margin negative excision of tumor and involved lymph nodes removed). There is a higher local recurrence rate, around 5-10%, for most cases of lumpectomy, which can be salvaged by mastectomy. Radiation treatment to the remaining breast tissue and possibly to lymphatic drainage areas, is recommended, post-operatively. Patients 70 years and older with hormone receptor positive tumors could forgo radiation therapy, according to few studies. For stage II breast cancers, chemotherapy prior to surgery (neo-adjuvant chemotherapy) can be given to "down-stage" or shrink the tumor. Thus, decreasing the risk of margin positive surgery. Pathological examination is used during surgery, and sometimes even with these precautions, the final pathology on permanent sections can still return with positive margins. For most tumors, post operative cosmesis for lumpectomy or partial mastectomy are acceptable to the patients. In addition, most women respond with better quality of life after breast conservation surgery. The rate of distant metastases is equivalent for mastectomy and lumpectomy.

Deciding on which procedure to undergo, mastectomy or breast preservation, can be difficult. The increased risk of local recurrence and cosmetic results are the general concerns. When the patients ask for my advice as to the choice of mastectomy or lumpectomy (I prefer segmentectomy), I emphasize that it is a personal choice, and if the risk of local recurrence is a paramount concern, then mastectomy may give them a better peace of mind. In addition, they should consult women who underwent the same experience, and these advisory groups can be found in the community sponsored by the American Cancer Society, or by the Wellness Community. The eventual survival rates for mastectomy or breast conservation are equivalent, even though the local recurrence is slightly higher for breast conservation. The main cause of death is due to distant metastases and not to local disease that is impacted by the choice of mastectomy or lumpectomy. Often refered as lumpectomy, removal the entire segment of the breast involving the same lactiferous duct drainage areas in the breast is the procedure of choice. Multifocal occult tumors usually occur in the same segment, and thus by removing the entire segment leads to better local control of tumor and lower local recurrence rates. This was demonstrated by a comparison study done by Veronesi et al, comparing lumpectomy and quadrantectomy. Local recurrences after breast preservation can become life-threatening in patients with poor compliance, in whom the local recurrences become advanced due to delayed treatment. Local and regional recurrences can occur after mastectomy at rates dependent on tumor stage and usually these rates are several-fold lower compared to breast conservation.

9.3.3 ADJUVANT CHEMOTHERAPY VERSUS NEO-ADJUVANT THERAPY

Small breast cancers under 1 cm and DCIS have high cure rates with surgery alone. Invasive cancers acquire the metastatic potential when continues to grow and undergo de-differentiation into more aggressive clones. Hence these tumors benefit from systemic chemotherapy treatment to eliminate remaining clones of cells apart from the surgically excised tissues enveloping the tumor. Several regimens of chemotherapy have been refined for breast cancer treatment. Women with stage II and higher breast cancers (T2 or N1), i.e., tumors greater than 2 cm or node positive, where the recurrent disease risk exceeds 30%, will benefit from systemic chemotherapy, with increase in survival rates (Anampa 2015). T1 size tumors (between 1-2 cm) with negative nodes also benefited from chemotherapy, showing the potential presence of metastasis even for smaller tumors. In the past, therapeutic chemotherapy did not cure the patients with low recurrent breast cancer burden, and eventual tumor growth progressed even after initial tumor response. Today, complete salvage is possible with improved chemotherapy regimens, however, the decision to forego adjuvant chemotherapy needs careful evaluation. In node negative breast cancers, additional prognosticators for subclinical metastatic disease has been used, such as the tumor gene profiling, and in low-risk patients, adjuvant chemotherapy can be withheld (Karagiamis 2016).

In patients benefitting from adjuvant chemotherapy, starting the regimen prior to surgery have several advantages (neo-adjuvant chemotherapy). One will get an in-vivo response information, in observing a near term decrease in tumor size, and allow breast conservation. Improvement in survival was not observed in a phase III trial, though most patients in the trial had rather small size tumors, under 2 cm. In patients with inflammatory breast cancer (IBC), T3B classification, a presentation with skin redness, edema, and ridging, a characteristic that signals tumor spread into skin dermal lymphatics, surgery alone has proven futile, since tumor recurrence was rapid. Not until effective chemotherapy was developed, surgery was used as a palliative measure by decreasing the tumor burden. The role of chemotherapy in IBC, in a neo-adjuvant fashion, followed by surgery has extended the disease-free survival by several years.

Neoadjuvant chemotherapy has gained wider use not only for conversion of a larger tumor into a candidate suitable for breast preservation, but also for "down-staging" the tumor prior to mastectomy and node dissection.

In a significant number of these patients, pathology showed a complete response (CR), which is associated with longer survival.

9.3.4 PRIMARY PREVENTION OF BREAST CANCER: NEW STRATEGIES?

SERMS and aromatase inhibitors have been shown to decrease the risks of breast cancer and despite elegant phase III studies proving their efficacy, these drugs currently available in your local pharmacy, have low acceptance and are uncommonly used for prevention of breast cancer. Secondary prevention with mammographic screening has provided some confort in dealing with this disease. Several oncologists have contrasted and compared the use of SERMS with the statins recommended for lowering cholesterol. Both classes of drugs have minimal side effects, however the adherence to statins use is much higher than that of SERMS, even though the reduction of risk for adverse health effects are comparable. The difference is that lowering cholesterol levels is verifiable with a blood test, while the risk reduction of breast cancer risk is not verifiable with simple tests. There may be other barriers to taking SERMS for prevention, one of which may be the fact that SERMS were developed to treat breast cancer. Nevertheless, breast cancer prevention will only become more acceptable to women and physicians, with the development of simple ways to assess and monitor risks of breast cancer. This is probably true for other types of cancer as well.

Are there any other promising agents for breast cancer primary prevention? Women in low breast cancer regions that migrate into environment with higher risk, eventually acquire a higher risk profile. The most plausible explanation is the change in diet and physical activity. Lower breast cancer risk areas usually correspond to more rural life-styles, with lower caloric, protein and animal fat consumption coupled with more vigorous physical activity. Lower BMI (body mass index) and higher physical activity are also associated with delayed presentation of breast cancer in women with BRCA gene mutations and with lower recurrence rates in treated breast cancer patients. These life-style choices are also associated with healthier states as measured by the absence of chronic diseases, and longevity. Are there biomarkers of breast cancer risk that at the same time reflect the changes in cancer risk from dietary and exercise regimens? Current advances in molecular biology present several new markers that likely reflect breast cancer risks in real time. Clinical studies to confirm these biological realities are underway.

9.4 COLORECTAL CANCER (CRC)

The large bowel and rectum function as the reservoir for ingested foods after undergoing digestion and traversing through the small intestines. Very few nutrients are extracted from the digested food in the colon, although some micronutrients are produced by the microbiome. The small intestine dumps between 1.5 to 2.5 liters of the liquefied and digested food contents into the large bowel and 90% of water is then extracted. The colon also contains 100-fold more bacteria, viruses and fungi compared to the rest of the GI tract. Adenocarcinoma of the colon and rectum is 100 times more common than cancers in the small bowel, though the surface and cell volume in the small bowel far surpass those of the large bowel. In addition, the most common cancer of the small bowel is lymphoma, neuroendocrine and GIST rather than adenocarcinoma. Taking into account all the types of malignancy in the small bowel, cancer of the large bowel is by far more prevalent. These large differences between cancers of the large and small intestines, with seemingly comparable cell types, are unexplained. One possible explanation is the interaction of bacteria in the colon, generating the state of chronic inflammation. Findings that would support this concept are: 1. Patients with inflammatory bowel disease have a higher risk for CRC, especially ones that has active disease for over 10 years. 2. Most CRC are found in the distal segment, rectum and recto-sigmoid, where the action of bacteria and the effects of their associated toxins have their greatest effect. This latter finding has been confounded by another fact that in the last three decades, the incidence of CRC has been shifting to the more proximal segments. 3. Adenocarcinoma is nearly absent in the distal small bowel as mentioned, and the clustering of this type of cancer around the duodenum is probably due to factors associated with peri-ampullary carcinoma (covered in the section of pancreatic cancers). 4. Early malignant change is also associated with inflammatory reactive changes in the submucosa around the affected mucosa crypts.

The association of polypoid growths as a pre-neoplasia and clinical marker indicator for CRC risk is well established (Chu, 1984). The genetic basis of these clinical changes can also be found in familial polyposis, due to APC gene, and in HNPCC (hereditary non-polyposis colon cancer syndrome) associated with mutations in the family of DNA repair enzymes MSH2, MLH1, MSH6, PMS2. The intermediate lesion of the polypoid adenoma serves as focal point in the screening and prevention of CRC. By identifying early polyps, diminutive polyps (3mm in size) and larger ones, such as advanced adenomas (1 cm and larger in size or any size with dysplasia), and removing these growths endoscopically, the risks for CRC are reduced. The numbers and size of adenomas indicate likelihood for developing future adenomas and cancer, and are markers for chemoprevention interventions. The caveat is that the precursors of CRC can be missed on endoscopy, unlike the polypoid adenomas, these lesions are flat, serrated adenomas or small carcinomas, whose physical characteristics are more difficult to discern from normal large bowel surfaces. These constitute approximately 15% of early CRC. There is also an interesting association of polyps, right sided cancers and microsatellite instability (a marker for DNA repair gene mutations and Lynch syndrome) and biological behavior of CRC (Mattar 2005, Stingzing 2018). Microsatellite unstable tumors (MSI-H) due to the frame shift mutations develop new epitope proteins that give these tumors their added immunogenicity, lymphocytic infiltration on histology, improved prognosis and sensitive to check-point inhibitor immunotherapy.

Once symptoms develop, such as change in bowel habits and rectal bleeding, the CRC detected will usually be in more advanced stage. The staging of CRC is dictated by the depth of penetration by tumor cells into the bowel wall and lymph node metastases. For example, stage I CRC, T1,2 (tumor penetration to muscle layers and not to serosa) and N0 (negative lymph nodes) patients have a 5-year survival over 90% while a stage III, any T, N1 (involved lymph nodes) survival rates drop to less than 50%.

Surgical resection is usually the first order of the treatment process, except in rectal cancers and metastatic CRC. T3 and N1 rectal tumors, with penetration to the wall into perirectal fat or positive lymph nodes with metastasis, can benefit from radiation treatment and chemotherapy prior to surgery, in order to shrink the tumor. The neo-adjuvant treatment has been found to benefit the patient by lowering the local recurrence rates and by allowing higher anal sphincter preservation rates. When the tumor is very close to the anal muscles, and when the pre-operative treatment is not successful in shrinking it away from these sphincter muscles, then a resection of rectum including anus and anal sphincter muscles with permanent colostomy will be necessary. Under these conditions, anal sphincter preservation surgery will result in tumor recurrence in the anal area, resulting in incontinence and rectal pain (Matsuda 2018). In patients with metastatic disease, chemotherapy will take precedence, in order to reduce tumor bulk in all metastatic sites and the primary tumor. Occasionally CRC will present with obstruction, bleeding or perforation which will require surgical intervention first then followed by chemotherapy and radiation. FOLFOX (Folinic acid, Fluoro-uracil, and Oxaliplatin) has become a standard regimen for CRC and is given for 6-12 months duration on 3-weekly cycles. Response rates have improved, compared to previous chemotherapy combinations, and some complete tumor shrinkage have been observed. Radiation combined with chemotherapy is used in the pre-operative treatment for rectal cancer. For colon cancer, there is no role for radiation in the initial treatment, since the gains in local tumor control is lost in the downside of the toxicities on other nearby organs such as the small bowel, liver and kidneys.

The treatment of CRC precursor, the adenoma, or a limited stage I CRC, would be a lot more desirable, with either endoscopic or minimally invasive laparoscopic methods, yielding nearly universal cures. Chemoprevention and screening can increase the opportunities of finding the tumor in the polypoid stages or inhibit its growth altogether. NSAIDs or calcium prescription for individuals with repeated findings of colorectal adenomas on endoscopy, could potentially reduce rates of recurrent adenoma and the required frequency of endoscopies.

9.5 GYNECOLOGICAL CANCERS

The female reproductive organs can be sites to three common malignancies in the female; uterine cervix, corpus uterus and bilateral tubes and ovaries. Although these cancers originate in organs in close vicinity in the pelvis, their pathogenesis and clinical behavior differ from each other as well their presentation, diagnosis, treatment and prevention.

9.5.1 CERVICAL CARCINOMA

Women in the 3rd and 4th decades have the highest risk of cervical cancer and is associated with HPV infection. HPV genotypes 16, 18, 31,33, 45,52,66, and 70, are the most common strains of HPV in the cervical mucosa found in association with cervical carcinoma. The tissues at risk are the columnar cells located at the junction of the squamous cells of the cervix and the mucosal cells of the uterus, called the endocervix. This is called the transformation zone, starting at the ectocervix. The pathogenesis is the chronic inflammatory process generated by the viral infection. Why this narrow strip of tissue, the transitional or transformational zone, bears the brunt of the malignant transforming process? The transitional zones in the anorectal canal and in the esophagogastric junction are also at risk for SCC and Barrett's adenocarcinoma respectively. HPV are involved in the oral, nasopharyngeal cavities and well as in anal cancers. The pathogenic genotype for cancers in these three different locations are similar. One should also consider that HPV distribution of genotypes also include commensal strains that do not cause disease, and there are other factors associated with the pre-malignant transformation. It is noted that some HPV strains can cause the verrucous changes and not strongly associated with cervical cancers. In addition, not all infections with the pathogenic genotypes will result in malignant change since the majority of infections are eventually cleared. Re-infections and co-infections, with other viruses, CMV and herpes, are associated with higher rates of cervical cancer. Anogenital warts are associated with different strains of HPV (6,11) and have low incidence of malignant transformation, however they are associated with higher risks of cervical carcinoma, probably due to increased risks of infection with higher risk strains of HPV (16, 18). A recent discovery of residual embryonic rest cells in the transition between two epithelial zones may shed some light in this narrow transitional zone cuboidal cells susceptibility to cancer. The role of HPV in all three anatomical locations of transitional zone (cervix, anus and esophagus) is an important clue.

In the early phase of the disease there are no symptoms and bleeding can occur in late phase of disease. The diagnosis should be made on basis of routine Papanicolau (PAP) smears of the cervix and now HPV DNA tests can also be obtained, with the same smear. An abnormal test should be repeated until either a normal test is returned or if suspicious smear is persistent, then a direct visualization of the cervix is done by colposcopy and biopsy. Some clinicians do not submit the smear for HPV test unless abnormal cells are visualized.

The most common cancer is that of the squamous carcinoma type and when localized, a local procedure called conization or trachelization is performed. If the disease spreads into the uterine body, hysterectomy should be performed with lymph node dissection. Radiation therapy can be done in the form of brachytherapy with tandem and ovoids or with external beam therapy. Chemotherapy with platinum-based regimens are reserved for advanced disease.

HPV vaccine, against nine genotypes, should lead to lower infection rates and expected lower rates of cervical carcinomas, though long term results are not available to confirm these expectations. Pap's smear has already lowered the rates of cervical carcinoma in populations in the U.S., and should continue to be used as a preventive measure. Pap smear should be obtained every three years starting at age 21.

9.5.2 UTERINE CARCINOMA

Uterine adenocarcinoma, also known as endometrial carcinoma, arises in the glands lining the uterine cavity, the endometrium, and is the same tissue that provides for the implantation of the egg and for the nourishment of the growing embryo through the placenta. Malignant transformation can rise in the background of hyperplasia from hormonal stimulation, such as estrogen use in the post-menopausal period or drugs that affect the hormone receptors such as tamoxifen. Birth control pills will lower the risk due to lack of menstrual cycling of the mucosal growth. Other risk factors include obesity, nulliparity, and inherited mutations as in HNPCC (Hereditary Non-Polyposis Colon Cancer or Lynch syndrome). A thickened mucosa, seen on ultrasound as a thickened stripe at the uterine cavity lining, can alert the clinician of the early hyperplastic changes in the endometrium. Both uterine and cervical carcinoma can present with vaginal bleeding. The diagnostic test is first a pap smear done at time of vaginal exam and then a D&C (dilatation and curettage) if the smears show atypical cells. Both of these minimally invasive procedures can obtain cells that can be diagnostic. High risk women should undergo screening ultrasound.

The treatment of invasive uterine carcinoma starts with hysterectomy and bilateral salpingo-oophorectomy (TAHBSO), coupled with lymph node drainage removal for proper staging. Uterine carcinoma has propensity to travel to regional nodes, peritoneal surfaces and bones, the lumbar spine.

Post-operative chemoradiation or radiation alone are the adjuvant treatments of choice for node positive or locally advanced tumors (penetration of tumor to the uterine surface or beyond), the large controlled trial PORTEC-3 comparing adjuvant chemotherapy and radiation versus radiation (RT) alone is currently being analysed for 4- year follow-up of 674 patient accrual.

Uterine sarcoma can also present with vaginal bleeding. It is much less common than the adenocarcinoma type and usually presents as a mixture of glandular cell tumor and spindle cells which originate from the stromal cells, appearing as carcinosarcoma. Leiomyomas originate from the smooth muscle cells of the uterus and are by far the most common tumor of the uterus with low propensity to malignant transformation. The occasional leiomyosarcoma is encountered, approximately 1 among 1,000 uterine fibroids. Uterine sarcomas are treated with surgery. Radiation and chemotherapy are used in the advanced cases.

9.5.3 OVARIAN CARCINOMA

The more common adenocarcinoma type occurs in older post-menopausal women while the less common sarcoma occurs in young women. It is also associated with BRCA gene mutations which is found in familial breast cancers. Other risk factors include low parity, and environmental factors such as the use of talc and exposure to asbestos (Cramer, 2016). The fallopian tube and fimbria can be the site of origin for ovarian carcinomas (George, 2016). Thus, prophylactic surgery for ovary cancers should include the fallopian tubes. Symptoms are few and are usually non-specific such as abdominal discomfort. Late presentation include spread to peritoneal surfaces with ascitic fluid production and increase in abdominal girth.

Screening is best performed by trans-vaginal ultrasound and prophylactic salpingo-oophorectomy is controversial except in the patients with BRCA mutations and who carry nearly a 70-80% life time risk, (Schenberg

2014). The downsides of oophorectomy are increased cardiovascular risks, and rates of dementia, arthritis and Parkinsons' disease. The timing of prophylactic surgery can usually be delayed until after starting a family with the desired number of offsprings.

The fallopian tubes can be the source of ovaryan cancers as determined by histological examination and the prevalence of serous tubal intraepithelian carcinoma. Tubal ligation renders a decreased risk for ovary cancers, probably from a decreased reflux of endometrial material that can stimulate chronic inflammation. Prophylactic oophorectomy can deprive women of beneficial hormonal production in the ovary, that helps ward off cardiovascular disease, osteoporosis and cognitive impairment, while prophylactic salpingectomy can reduce the risks of ovary cancer without sacrificing the ovaries themselves (ACOG, 2015).

Ovaryan carcinoma is treated by hysterectomy, bilateral salpingo-oophorectomy, omentectomy and node dissection. Peritoneal surfaces should be checked for drop metastases, and peritoneal washings for cytology should be performed. Neo-adjuvant chemotherapy can be started if disease is found beyond the ovary and salpinx followed by surgery. Intraperitoneal chemotherapy, also called belly-bath chemotherapy, has been found to improve results in conjunction with systemic chemotherapy and cyto-reductive surgery in advanced stage disease.

There is no consensus on screening for sporadic ovaryan cancers. Screening protocols are recommended for tumors associated with BRACA 1,2 and secondary ovaryan cancers associated with Lynch syndrome, with transvaginal ultrasound and CA-125. Ovary cyst and tumors are common findings after pelvic ultrasound or CT scans for other indications. When incidental ovary cancers can be found and resected, prognosis is good due to the early stage of diagnosis. What is the investigative work up for an incidental finding of ovary cyst or tumor? A solid tumor 2cm or greater in a postmenaupasal woman should be investigated with laparoscopic techniques.

In a pre-menaupausal woman, it should be followed and hormone work-up obtained. A cystic lesion, without evidence of solid components, can be followed with CA-125.

9.6 PROSTATE CANCER

Prostate cancer is the most common malignancy in the elderly male. In the sixth decade over 50% of males have occult prostate carcinoma and fortunately majority of these sub-clinical cancers behave in an indolent fashion, i.e., causes no symptoms, nor physiological problems, and lead to deaths in only a fraction of patients. Benign prostatic hyperplasia (BPH) which commonly causes gland enlargement and urinary retention is not a precursor for prostate cancer. Co-existence of both conditions in older men is common, BPH usually involve the transition zone, centrally around the urethra. On the other hand, cancers usually involve the prostatic glands in the peripheral zones (Miah 2014). The rate of occult prostate cancer increases with age. Most cancers are found in the posterior lobe of the prostate gland and can be felt by the examining finger on rectal exam. Digital exam and PSA (prostate specific antigen blood assay) performed yearly are the screening regimen of choice.

Surgical resection of the prostate gland, whether with open or robotic approaches, is recommended for localized disease. Since significant numbers of prostate cancers in the elderly are indolent, observation has been proposed as an alternative. Why do some tumors behave more aggressively and how do you distinguish them from the more indolent type? A classical method has been based on Gleason score, according to the appearance of cells on microscopic exam. The survival rates according to these classifications have not been consistent, and most localized and regional disease, stage I-III, behave in an indolent fashion with over 90% of patients surviving at 5 years. Are there newer molecular markers that can help to differentiate biological behavior in these tumors? Much of the research on the molecular aspects implicate PTEN, MYC, SMAD, and others genes (Irshad 2013). Presently, no single or combination of markers are predictive to the point of being clinically applicable. The older age of onset, over age 65, is predictive of indolent behavior. There is no doubt that once the disease is metastatic, stage IV, life-span is compromised and symptoms develop such as bone pain from metastases, invasion into pelvic organs with recurrent or persistent disease. At stage IV, 5-year survival drops to 50%. What is the rate of progression to stage IV? And more importantly, how can we predict or prevent it? These questions will be studied at greater length, once watchful waiting, becomes a more common approach.

Prostate gland provides alkaline mucous secretions rich in zinc and sugars promoting sperm motility in the ejaculate and converts testosterone produced in the testis into dihydrotestosterone (DHT). Male androgen hormones are positive contributors for the growth of prostate glands. Gland hyperplasia is not a precursor for prostate cancer and occurs more commonly in the central zones, while cancers develop in the peripheral zones. Androgen hormone levels are not predictive of gland hyperplasia. PIN, in-situ neoplasia of the prostate, is predictive for the development of frank carcinoma. Finasteride, a competitive inhibitor of testosterone conversion into DHT, have been shown to reduce the risks of prostate cancer in patients with PIN by 30% in a phase III study. The presence of associated stromal and neuroendocrine cell changes in the prostate parenchyma, are also correlated with development of prostate carcinoma in presence of PIN. All of these findings give interesting association of ageing prostate tissue and PIN. Obesity, high fat diet, low fruit and vegetable intake are associated with increased incidence of prostate cancer.

A study conducted in the U.S., PCLO (Prostate, Colon, Lung, Ovary Study Group), found over 8 years, that screened prostate cancer patients did not have lower prostate cancer specific survival compared to unscreened individuals. The screening was carried out based on blood PSA level. A Swedish Study, on the other hand, concluded with a marginal benefit in the screened population. The lack of benefit in screening was accounted by the biological behavior of most prostate cancer found, being extremely indolent in their growth pattern. The more aggressive type, occur in younger men and usually does not express PSA. Using Gleason's score, 30% of screened prostate cancer on basis of PSA, are over grade 7, implying potential for growth and spread beyond the prostate gland.

With the current information and study results, how do we best approach the diagnosis and treatment of prostate cancer. First, yearly PSA, starting at age 50 and rectal exam starting at age 45 should be employed until the age of 65. Will an abnormal finding trigger a prostate biopsy? Most urologist and other experts would recommend so. Considering that a positive biopsy with Gleason score 7 or higher would also qualify for criteria for prostatectomy, one could propose close observation instead. The risk of harboring an indolent cancer is balanced by the potential risks of invasive procedures of biopsy, radical resection and possibly radiation treatment. Let us digress and review the information on watchful waiting. Two large studies of early prostate cancer, randomized to radical prostatectomy and watchful waiting have long follow-up, 18 years. The PIVOT study showed no difference in survival between the the two groups, and the Scandinavian (SPCG-4) study yielded small difference in survival favoring the surgical arm. In the SPCG-4 study, the sub-group of men over 65 years and low risk tumors, showed essentially no benefit from surgical treatment. Thus, until we have a straight forward manner in determining indolent tumors amongst others that can behave more aggressively, a degree of uncertainty is inherent, and to err on the side of safety one can risk side effects of the more invasive treatments. These two studies would also support watchful waiting, in older men with co-morbidities that will result in higher surgical risks.

9.7 LIVER CANCERS

The liver is the largest solid organ in the digestive system weighing on the average 1.2 kilograms, approximately 4% of the body mass. It has two sources of blood supply, arterial and portal, one with oxygenated blood and the second with gut nutrients. The liver cells are arranged in hexagonal collumns with the central portal vein and peripheral arterioles and venules. The nutrients crossing the gut membrane into the portal vein are delivered to the liver for metabolic processing. Some lipids are transported from the gut through the lymphatics. The nutrients transported from the gut to the liver are in form of chylomicrons for lipids, or conjugated with transport proteins for aminoacids and vitamins and free in the serum for glygogen, fructose and glucose. The hepatocytes re-assemble the gut nutrients into ready energy substrates, protein globulins, and other important blood and bile products.

The liver is the metabolic center for our body, providing much of our building material and fuel, thus main keeper of homeostasis on glucose level, the important fuel for our cells, especially in the brain. Liver is surprisingly an immunological organ, as well, capturing the gut blood flow and clearing the unwanted inflow of microbes and toxins that crossed the gut barrier. The reticulo-endothelial system in the liver provide the filtering and the phagocytic activity in processing of antigens and of foreign or native breakdown materials.

Primary liver cancers arise from the hepatocytes, called hepatocellular carcinoma or hepatoma, and from cells of the bile ducts, cholangiocarcinoma. Worldwide, hepatocellular cancer is one of the most common cancers, many caused by chronic infections, like hepatitis virus. In the US, hepatocellular cancers are the tenth most common cancer, mainly in the context of alcoholic cirrhosis. Hepatitis C is becoming more prevalent and a contributor for hepatocellular cancers, 2.5 times higher, compared to persons without hepatitis. Cholangiocarcinoma are associated with chronic inflammation in and around the bile ducts, in conditions such as parasites, anatomical anomalies such as Caroli's disease, with multiple bile duct cavernous dilatation, and sclerosing cholangitis.

Secondary liver cancers are metastatic tumors, where the primary tumor originate from cancers of the lung, colon and rectum, breast, kidney, melanoma, and other gastrointestinal organs, such as pancreas and stomach.

An isolated metastatic tumor in the liver may be difficult to differentiate from a primary liver cancer, especially when the primary tumor has not been identified. Prior history of cancer, tumor markers, imaging tests as CT, MRI and PET scans can be helpful.

Prevention of primary liver cancers can take several fronts, first preventing the chronic liver viral infections using vaccines, and treating chronic active hepatitis with anti-viral medications (Westbook 2014). Since these drugs are relatively new, more data is needed to confirm this premise. Alcoholic cirrhosis can also be treated and prevented with early diagnosis of the cirrhotic inflammatory component and vigorous education and treatment of alcohol addiction. Screening for early hepatic cancers can be performed with tumor marker AFP (alpha feto protein) and CA 19-9, combined with liver ultrasound or CT/MRI scans. Screening a high-risk group, like individuals with chronic hepatitis, has proven to be cost-effective and life-saving (Singal, 2014). Molecular medicine may identify individuals with yet higher risk of developing liver cancers. For example, newer markers, have in some studies, able to indicate the presence of early HCC (hepatocellular carcinoma). These markers can be measured from peripheral blood in form of proteins (DKK1, GP73) and microRNA (miR 122, miR 192, miR 22), (Zhu, 2013).

` Surgical removal of liver tumors can lead to cures. Depending on the number, location and size of the tumors, pre-operative chemotherapy or embolization of the feeding blood supply can lead to more successful resections with clear margins. In the cases of unresectable liver tumors, or concurrent disease beyond the liver, systemic treatment is applied. Liver transplantation can be used in selected cases and is limited by the availability of donor livers. Some advocate transplantation as the first surgical treatment of choice, especially in advanced stages. There are no ramdomized comparative study, however, a meta-analysis favored transplantation, (Menahen 2017). The evolving technology and understanding of hepatic tumor biology can change the treatment of choice, such as use of segments liver for transplants, thus allowing a cadaver liver to help more than one recipient or allowing living donors to participate.

9.8 BLOOD CELL CANCERS, LEUKEMIA, LYMPHOMA AND MYELOMA

Fascination with blood can be traced to ancient history and has been described as the basis for life, energy for the intellect, and ties to inheritance. Blood letting could cure illnesses by releasing "spirits" or humors. Scientific examination of this life sustaining fluid dates back to 1628, with William Harvey's description of circulation and with the discovery of blood corpuscles, in 1674 by Leeuwenhoek. Progress in hematology was advanced by microscopic identification of the corpuscular elements of leukocytes and platelets, by identification of the proteins in coagulation, and by the recognition of the blood types needed for proper blood transfusions. Erlich from Germany and Osler from America are recognized as early contributors to the field of Hematology.

Hodgkin's lymphoma was first recognized as enlarged lymph nodes, in 1832, and Virchow first described leukemic cells, in 1845, often associated with splenomegaly (Coller, 2015). Early classification of leukemias followed the understanding of developmental lineage of leukocytes. As differentiation of leukocytes from stem cells to fully functional immunocytes were better understood as well as their molecular developmental pathways, the corresponding leukemic and lymphoma cellular classifications were revised (Arber, 2016).

Treatment of Hodgkin's lymphoma reached some success with X-rays starting the turn of the 20th century, couple of decades after Wilhelm Roentgen discovery of these high energy electromagnetic radiation. He was awarded the Nobel prize in 1901. Nitrogen mustard was found effective in 1946, which then spurred the development of other alkylating agents. Folic acid antagonists were developed for childhood leukemias and in next two decades, thereafter, dozens of new chemotherapy agents were developed. Multiple agents, used in combination, were found to have higher response rates and longer remission periods than single agents. Genetic characterization of leukemias and lymphomas were first studied by chromosome karyotypic analysis. Philadelphia chromosome was the first identified chromosomal abnormality in chronic myelogenous leukemia (CML), caused by a translocation of chromosome 9 to chromosome 22, t (9;22) (q34; q11), which contributes to the fusion gene of ABL-BCR, upregulating tyrosine kinase function, (Nowell, 2017). Chromosome aberrations, as translocations, deletions, and fusions, were found in solid tumors as well. These seminal studies in hematologic malignancies gave further impetus into the identification of new oncogenes. These gene markers served as useful characterization of subsets hematopoetic cancers, as well as becoming molecular targets for therapy. Molecular markers identify subsets of leukemias with higher chemotherapy refractory rates. Treatment alternatives have been developed to decrease toxicities of chemotherapy and also to salvage chemotherapy treatment failures. Bone marrow transplant, both autologous and allogeneic, did achieve some cures. Monoclonal antibody targeting tumor proteins and receptors and chimeric modified T cells have been more recent therapeutic advances.

The spectra of oncogenes in hematological and solid tumors differ by a range of driver and non-driver genes. For example, CML are noted by the ABL oncogene, while lung cancer, by k-RAS, and these cancers can be treated by different targeted inhibitors. Risks factors include excess benzene, radiation exposure and tobacco use. MicroRNAs interact closely with gene activity in protein translation, and in hematopoiesis, there is a fine distinction between normal leukocyte production and leukemogenesis of leukemia. In prevention, mirna in the early process of leukemogenesis are of interest. Mirna profiles are unique in ALL (acute lymphocytic leukemia) and AML (acute myelogenous leukemia) and have prognostic and therapeutic significance. Current research is asking the questions whether modifying certain miRNA can change the course of these malignancies and whether the miRNA profiles can be used to select certain individuals for prevention interventions (Pandita 2019). HIV, the human immune-deficiency virus has been linked to several cancers, especially lymphomas, increasing its risk by over 100-fold. The treatment with anti-retroviral drugs has decreased the risks of lymphoma, limited to the subtypes of Burkitt's and lymphoblastoid (DLBCL). Viral activation of oncogenes and the role of virus in the pathogenesis in cancer has been investigated since Peyton Rous experiment in 1911, in which he claimed that cancer was caused by virus. From a cellular point of view, lymphomas and leukemias are related hematological malignancies. Notch pathway is closely associated with stem cell differentiation and the Notch oncogene spectrum are associated with multiple solid and blood leukocyte tumors, including both leukemia and lymphoma. In leukemias, for example, Notch 1 mutation can act as a tumor suppressor, and when activated, the leukemic cells actually regress (Mao 2015).

9.9 KIDNEY AND BLADDER CANCERS

All living organisms maintain their own intra-cellular environment with a remarkable degree of homeostasis. In simple terms, that means excreting excess water, salts or other waste products to achieve the necessary state of balance. The excretory function for unicellular organisms is achieved by a saccular organelle that gathers waste and empties to the outer environment by fusing with the outer-cell membrane. Multicellular organisms have a primitive nephron and excretory tubules that can empty to the skin as in invertebrates. In humans, the renal excretory system has developed into a complex cooperation of mesodermal and endodermal cells, forming glomeruli, a convoluted system of tubules and collecting system which allow the exchange of molecules from the circulatory system into the urinary excretory system. In addition, there are endocrine cells in close association responsible for cardiovascular flow, pressure controls and for erythropoeisis. Different cells and structures are responsible for filtration, resorption of key molecules, production of renin-angiotensin, erythropoietin, and conversion of vitamin

D. It is curious how the homeostatic regulation is achieved by what appears to be a round-about manner: for example, several molecules like sodium, are filtered out of the glomeruli in excess then re-absorbed by the proximal tubules. The hormone secreting cells in the renal interstitium (fibroblasts with special functions) are intimately associated with this filtration/resorption process, rather than situated in a separate self-contained organ, as for example, the thyroid or the adrenal hormone producing glands.

Kidney cancers can present with the triad of signs and symptoms: blood cells in the urine (hematuria), flank pain and mass. However, the majority of kidney cancers are now found incidentally on imaging tests, such as ultrasound and CT scans. They are the 6th most common cancer, approximately 300,000 new cases yearly, around the world, and clear cell carcinoma is the most common cell type. Both clear cell and papillary carcinomas arise from the epithelium of the proximal tubules, while chromophobe, oncocytomas and other rare tumors arise from the distal tubules. Genomic studies of both normal nephrons and renal cell cancers provide one the more complete molecular genetic maps of cellular components of the kidney and subsequent subtypes of cancers, which also support the hereditary phenotypes of these cancers. Von Hippel Landau (VHL) is the most common hereditary syndrome manifesting with kidney cancers, clear cell type, and to a lesser extent pheochromocytomas, retinal angiomas, and pancreatic cysts. The autosomal dominant inheritance of the VHL gene mutation, interferes with its normal tumor suppressor activities, leads to activation of angiogenesis (VEGF) and HIF (hypoxia inducing factor), all of which have their own down stream regulation of growth factors. Hereditary papillary renal cell cancer syndrome carries a MET gene mutation leading to upregulation of tyrosine kinase to a cell membrane ligand for HGF/SF, hepatocyte growth factor. A second type of familial papillary renal cancers is associated with FH (fumarate hydrate) gene, and also present with leiomyomatosis of skin and uterus. Chromophobe carcinomas (including hybrid histology/mixed oncocytomas) can be found in patients with familial syndrome of BHD, Birt-Hogg-Dube, involving the folliculin gene (FLCL), a tumor suppressor gene. In cases of folliculin deficiency, BHD can lead to activation of mTOR (mammalian target of rapamycin). These hereditary kidney cancer syndromes account for only 5% of all kidney malignancies, where sporadic forms compose the overwhelming majority of tumors. The underlying mutations often involve VHL, and to a lesser degree P53, PTEN, MYC and RB. Male predominance 2:1 over female is found, possibly due to tobacco use, and a third presents with advanced and metastatic disease. Inherited kidney cancers are often multifocal and bilateral, and present with multiple small adenomas. Among these multiple tumors, it is recommended that surgery be done for lesions 3 cm and greater and kidney parenchymal sparing technique should be used. Smaller tumors often behave as adenomas, and the cells do not have malignant features. Even with aggressive behavior, as in tumor extension into renal vein and vena cava, total tumor removal can yield some curative results. For metastatic disease, targeted therapy to known oncogenes, such as verolimus and soferanib, can result in some surprising responses.

Bladder cancers are nearly as common as kidney cancers, at 17 cases per 100,000 population. Males predominate 4:1, tobacco and other chemical concentrates in the bladder being the most common culprits. Transitional cell carcinoma is the most common histology, and interestingly squamous cell carcinoma can be found in bladders infected with schistosomiasis egyptii. Most bladder cancers are superficial, involving the mucosal lining and not muscle invasive. Hematuria, blood cells in urine, is the most common presenting findings and the diagnosis is confirmed with cystoscopy and biopsy. Microscopic hematuria is diagnosed only by urine analysis and not by visual inspection of the urine, a good argument for periodic urine analysis screening. The accumulation of mutations and oncogenes, such as RAS and P53 correspond to the step-wise progression into growth, invasion and metastases. Tumor grade is the histological correlate of accumulated oncogenes and higher grade and more bladder tumor oncogenes reflect poorer prognosis and aggressive behavior.

Superficial bladder cancers are treated with excision of tumor with negative lateral and deep margins and intravesical instillation of BCG or chemotherapy agents. Deeper muscle invasive cancers are treated with radical cystectomy. Chemotherapy agents are indicated for advanced disease as adjuvant or neo-adjuvant to surgery.

9.10 BONY AND SOFT TISSUE SARCOMA

The bony skeleton, muscles and associated soft tissues give us the important function of mobility. The evolution of the endo and exo-skeleton has been traced by paleontologists to earlier than 50 million years from fossil remains. Exoskeleton evolved from dermal elements and persists in the skull, sternum and ribs, while endoskeleton ramified into the spinal column, and long extremety bones. Osteo and soft tissue sarcomas as a group comprise the 10th most common malignancy and share some unique driver mutations. Second cancers in the skeleton are common in metastatic cancers and this predilection is found in prostate, breast, lung, uterus cancers and multiple myeloma. The incidence of sarcomas has a biphasic age distribution, first phase present in adolescence and the second in late adulthood. Half-century ago, the salvage treatment by amputation carried a frightening aspect for these tumors and fortunately, today, amputations are rarely necessary.

Both bony and soft tissue sarcomas have over 70 different distinct subtypes with unique histologies, clinical presentations and behavior. Bone, cartilage, muscles, nerves, blood vessels and tendons are thought to be inactive from growth activities, accounting for their uncommon presentation. The growth characteristics among the different mesodermal stem cells present some of these unique tumor features. Osteosarcomas occur in growth plates, commonly in the femur. Ewing's sarcoma, the second most common bony cancers, present usually in the pelvic bones, and is characterized by their small round cells. Chondrosarcoma are also found more commonly in bones around the pelvis and spine. Bony sarcomas can be found in soft tissues as in the periosteal and paraosteal sarcomas. Soft tissue sarcomas present with histology of fibrosarcoma, fibrous hystiocytoma, or PNET like tumors. Sarcomas rarely spread to lymph nodes, except for some subtypes (clear cell, rhabdo, epitheliod, synovial sarcomas in the 30% likelihood of lymph node metastases, versus liposarcoma and fibrosarcoma in the 2% range). Instead, sarcomas metastasize predominantly to the lungs.

EWS gene fusion with other RNA transcription factors is the most common molecular derangement in Ewing's sarcoma and among other sarcomas, osteo and PNET. EXT exostosis gene can be found in chondrosarcomas, PAX-FKHR gene fusions in rhabdomyosarcomas. Neurofibromatosis NF1 and schwannmatosis NF-2 have increased risks of malignant transformation into sarcoma. KIT mutations are common in GIST, gastrointestinal stromal tumors, also called intestinal leiomyosarcomas in the past.

Prevention efforts in sarcoma is focused on early diagnosis, as the disease can be cured in the early stages, even in the histological types carrying more aggressive behavior, such as the rhabdosarcoma, and small cell types. Pain is an early symptom, especially located in or around the bone. The pain can simulate an injury, and the bony or soft tissue changes from tumor can be mistaken for trauma. These early changes can resemble a swelling in the soft tissue or around bones often seen in contusions. Persitent pain that does not improve, as the usual case in injuries, should be studied with a simple plain X-ray. Sometimes the changes from osteosarcoma are subtle and missed on X-rays, thus persistent symptoms should not be ignored and should be followed by CT imaging. Subtle bony changes of early osteosarcoma can be missed on the radiographs, and recognized if the index of suspicion is present. Small soft tissue tumors cannot be seen on plain radiographs, however in locations such as the extremeties and some areas in the torso careful palpation can detect a mass effect. When in doubt after plain X-ray films and exam, a CT or MRI scans can be obtained. Dermal and subcutaneous masses are common and usually of the dermoid cyst and lipomatous type that can be differentiated from sarcoma by palpation and inspection. Retroperitoneal location of sarcomas makes diagnosis difficult, and usually found when grown to an advanced size. Neurofibromas can be differentiated from sarcomatous change by its consistency and softeness on palpation. Deeper neurofibromas that enlarges will need MRI or PET to study its nature. Li-Fraumeni syndrome with inherited P53 mutation should also undergo periodic screening for sarcomas.

Treatment starts with a biopsy to confirm cell type. Core needle biopsy is prefered and sometimes insufficient tissue is obtained for identification, due to sampling error. Sarcomas can have well differentiated areas among pockets of poorly differentiated components or normal tissues. If an open biopsy is needed for diagnosis, then the question is whether the entire mass can be removed safely prior to neo-adjuvant chemotherapy or radiation. This is the time when a multi-disciplinary approach can be of benefit for the decision-making process.

9.11 PANCREATIC CANCERS

Pancreatic cancers are found in 12.5 cases in 100,000 population, in the U.S., and they are responsible for 11.8 deaths per 100,000. Worldwide pancreas cancer account for the 13th most common cancer and 4th in cancer deaths. The more aggressive type, the adenocarcinoma is the most common and also accounts for only 5% cure rate. The neuro-endocrine cell type, or PNET, is less common, and although survival can be longer after treatment due to its slower growth rates, the cure rates are still poor. Risk factors are smoking, obesity, adult onset diabetes, chronic pancreatitis, mucinous cysts of the pancreas. There are links with inherited breast cancer, BRCA 1 and 2, Lynch syndrome and familial melanoma syndrome leading to increased rates of pancreas malignancies. The poor prognosis is partly due to late diagnosis and the presence of distant or regional disease at time of diagnosis. The pancreas is anatomically located deep in the retroperitoneal area of the abdomen, a difficult area to palpate. When small, most pancreatic tumors will not ellicit symptoms, which makes early diagnosis nearly impossible. Precursor lesions are the PaIN (pancreas intraepithelial neoplasia), PIMN (pancreatic duct intraepithelial mucinous neoplasia) and MCN (mucinous cystic neoplasm). Several oncogenes RAS, TP53, CDNK2A, SMAD4, BRCA1 and BRCA2 have been identified in pancreatic cancer.

Presenting symptoms include pain, bowel obstruction, and jaundice, usually indicating a locally advanced tumor. Mass in the pancreas can be identified on ultrasound, CT or MRI scans. Tumor markers CEA and CA 19-9 are usually elevated. Bilirubin and alkaline phosphatase are elevated due to obstruction of the common bile duct. Tumors in the distal pancreas can enlarge without biliary obstruction nor jaundice. Neoadjuvant chemotherapy can increase survival combined with surgical resection. Tumor resection with the Whipple procedure (pancreatico-duodenectomy) or distal pancreatectomy can be performed if tumor does not invade the portal vein or superior mesenteric artery, and in the absence of distant disease. Unfortunately, nearly 80% of pancreas cancers are not resectable. In addition, recurrences occur in the majority of resected tumors even in the absence of positive lymph nodes. Post operative radiation and chemotherapy treatments should be considered. Targeted therapies, like erlotinib and immunotherapy have not made significant strides in increasing survival rates. Neoadjuvant chemoradiation can lead to higher resection rates.

Neuroendocrine tumors of the pancreas (PNET) are relatively uncommon, 5-10% of pancreas cancers. They originate from the islet cells in the pancreas, and have variable and unique behavior, from benign (insulinoma) to metastatic behavior (carcinoid), usually depending on Ki67 marker or mitotic figures on histology. Multiple endocrine tumor MEA1, von Hippel Lindau and neurofibromatosis (NF1) syndromes have higher risks for pancreatic PNET tumors. Isolated PNET should be resected. Recurrent or metastatic PNET can respond to sunitinib or everolimus. Some metastatic foci can be resected with beneficial results due to their slow growth.

Prevention and early detection for pancreas cancer are challenging. There is no high-risk group for sporadic pancreas cancer that would benefit from screening. Tumor markers and imaging tests can be used for suspected pancreas neoplasm, however there are no reliable data suggesting benefits from screening. Cure rates are higher for early stage tumors, 30% 5-year survival rate after resection, reported from the John Hopkins' hospital surgeons. New molecular markers will hopefully provide new strategies for early detection in pancreas cancer.

9.12 THYROID CANCERS

Thyroid cancers are the most common endocrine malignancies, increasing in incidence partly due to the increase in neck imaging tests and diagnostic biopsies of thyroid nodules (Jegerlehner, 2017). The incidence worldwide is half a million cases yearly, and females predominate 3:1 over male, becoming the third most common malignancy in women, approximately 10 cases per 100,000 yearly in the USA. Thyroid cells develop early in the embryo from the primitive pharynx at the midline foramen cecum, later becoming the base of tongue, and decend into the anterior neck through the thyroglossal duct. Thyroid gland is functional at 12 weeks and thyroxine hormone is necessary for neural development. Fetal hypothyroidism can lead to multiple congenital defects including cretinism. Improper migration or development of the thyroid glandular tissue can lead to ectopic thyroid and thyroid hypoplasia such as thyroid rests and unilateral thyroids. Thyroid rests have higher rates of thyroid carcinoma, stimulated by TSH (thyroid stimulating hormone). Thyroid supplementation can reduce thyroid gland hyperplasia and subsequent malignant transformation. Risk factors for thyroid cancers include radiation, iodine deficient diet, carcinogens such PCB (polychlorinated byphenils) and interestingly living in areas near volcanic eruptions. For example, Icelandic and Hawaiian individuals carry higher risk for thyroid tumors. Radiation is known to increase the rate of RET/PTC fusion mutations. Oncogenes in thyroid tumors can yield information on the initiation and pathogenesis of the malignant thyroid cells. RET/MTC oncogene can be inherited in an autosomal dominant pattern and the identification of this oncogene can facilitate the management of familial MTC among MEA2. RAS, BRAF, hTERT, PTEN and PIK3CA are few of the oncogenes commonly found in thyroid carcinomas. Majority of these oncogenes, including RET, contribute to the MAPK signaling pathway where the proliferative activities are enhanced, favoring hyperplasia. The point mutations in these oncogenes can be associated with specific clinical behavior, like prognosis, recurrence rates and need for post-operative radio-ablation.

The majority of thyroid cancers are papillary or mixed papillary-follicular carcinomas. Follicular, medullary and hurthle cell histology comprise another 15%. Undifferentiated and anaplastic are subtypes with poor prognosis and fortunately less common, around fewer than 3% of thyroid cancers. The vast majority of thyroid cancers are indolent in their behavior, even when found in nearby neck lymph nodes. The five and ten-year survival is 98%, and the indicators for tumor recurrence is age, histology, stage and possibly newly identified oncogenes (Pstrag 2018, Abdullah 2019).

The diagnosis of thyroid cancers can be done by needle aspiration cytology of thyroid nodules. The cell appearance on microscopy, aided by gene micro-array, has a high degree of accuracy in differentiating benign versus malignant nodules (Shih 2019). Thyroid nodules are common, nearly half of individuals over the age of fifty will have thyroid nodules on ultrasound or by other imaging tests. Under 10% of nodules in the range of 1-2 cm are malignant and nodules over 2 cm have a 15% risk of malignancy. Since the overwhelming majority of thyroid cancers behave in an indolent manner, i.e., death rate of 2% at 10 years and low recurrence rates after surgery, it is recommended to observe nodules under 1.5 cm in size, in the background of multinodular goiter. Persistent growth in the nodule can prompt a needle aspiration biopsy. Blood tests can tip the balance for needle biopsy for nodules under 1.5 cm, i.e., elevated thyroglobulin and CEA levels. Although multiple nodules favor the diagnosis of benign goiter or thyroiditis, a dominant nodule among multiple nodules need to be followed or investigated, since these benign conditions carry some risk for malignant transformation (Fisher, 2018).

Total thyroidectomy is the surgical procedure of choice for thyroid cancer. Central neck compartment dissection is adequate for papillary or follicular carcinomas, while medullary carcinomas require a more complete neck dissection (Gambardella, 2019). Some investigators will limit the surgery to lobectomy rather than total thyroidectomy for cancers smaller than 1.5 cm. A large review of thyroid cancer cases showed increase in recurrences without postoperative radio-ablation with radioactive iodine uptake, even in small cancers (Mazzaferi 2008). Removal of all normal thyroid tissue, allows the radioactive iodine be taken up in residual malignant thyroid cells.

10

UNUSUAL CANCERS: LESSONS FOR CANCER BIOLOGY

"Observations of unusual occurrences can teach more than the usual ones", Darwin, 1859

Common cancers have the greatest impact on society and give us some general ideas of malignant diseases and shared common behavior and presentations. Prevention strategies are designed specifically around these common cancers, in the form of secondary prevention, early diagnosis and screening, most based on anatomic imaging tests and blood tests. In other words, despite advances in molecular medicine, much of the every-day clinical medicine revolves around the traditional organ-based disease. Additional clues and framework for cancer biology in the modern era, principally in the realm of the molecular medicine and genetic changes, could turn the tide of clinical medicine from anatomical to the molecular paradigm. The study of unusual and rare cancers can possibly give us a window to solving some of these molecular puzzles.

10.1 CANCER IN PATIENTS WITH ORGAN TRANSPLANTS AND IMMUNESUPPRESSION

The immune system has the important function of combating foreign invaders such as bacterial or viral infections and transformed cancer cells that can be detected as foreign. Many cancers do escape the immune surveillance. Not surprisingly, individuals with suppressed immune system by illness, drugs or auto-immune diseases may be suceptible to infections and cancer. Patients with allogeneic kidney or liver transplants often are immune suppressed to prevent organ rejection. This group of patients have been studied for secondary diseases such as cancers and how the malignant disease behaves under compromised immune function.

Interestingly, the most common cancer, in the immune suppressed individual, is skin cancer, and the second most common are the blood cell dyscrasias such lymphoma or leukemia. The skin cancers are of the squamous cell and basal cell carcinoma variety and some Kaposi's sarcoma, and very few melanomas and Merkel cell carcinoma. Several immune suppressive drugs used in transplant patients are also oncogene activators, such as azathioprine (Rangwalla 2011). Some studies showed that changing the immunosuppressive agents to mTOR agents which are also anti-neoplastic, cancer risks in transplant patients become lower. Often when the immunesuppression is stopped, the cancer is rejected and resolved, reaffirming the cause-effect relationship of immune effects on cancer growth and pathogenesis. Another observation is that cancer in a subclinical state can reappear after transplantation and during immunesuppression. For example, colon cancer metastatic to liver, are eligible for liver transplantation in hopes that the host liver is the only site of disease and with complete liver resection, patient will undergo a complete cure. Even when the transplant recipient does not receive immunosuppressive treatment, rapid recurrence of subclinical tumors appears not involving the allogeneic liver. These patients with liver metastases and substantial disease-free period (over 2 years), when resected with partial hepatectomy, have 40% of cure, conversely, 60% of these patients will harbor subclinical disease elsewhere in other organs that can eventually grow and recur. The time to recurrence in transplant patients is usually shorter.

Having one of the major defenses compromised, we have not seen complete chaos and overwhelming cancer growth. Although most common cancers have been found at higher rates in transplant patients, by low single digits, by far, the most common is skin cancer, which normally does not cause deaths nor major organ failures. In fact, the body does a remarkable job in containing most tumors, especially the aggressive types such as lung, pancreas, ovaryan, etc. Lung and heart transplant patients, compared to kidney and liver have a higher propensity to develop solid tumors, for some unexplained reason. Some studies have found that solid tumors have worse prognosis in transplant patients, however an U.S. transplant database, showed that when controlled for age and risk factors such as diabetes and cardiovascular disease, the prognosis is no different than in non-transplant patients.

The important lesson from these patients' experience is that the immune system is an important body defense mechanism, and even when this system is compromised, the body as a whole, has redundant defense systems at play that keep most tumors in check. What are these other defense mechanisms against tumors? In order for the tumor to grow, within the perview of the immune system, it has to find a protected or priviledged environment. This is illustrated in pregnancy where the fetal cocoon environment functions as an immune shield, as discussed in section 10.8, Trophoblastic Tumors in Pregnancy. Other possible scenarios include modulation of the check point inhibitors and other immune tolerance mechanisms. Some of these yet undiscovered mechanisms that prevent the immune suppressed individual from growing new tumors may be explored for new clues to cancer treatment and prevention.

Noone, 2019, compiled a large series of transplant patients that included larger numbers of lung and liver transplant patients. The rate of cancer deaths is higher than previously reported, 13% and the spectrum of cancers were lung, non-Hodgkins lymphoma, colorectal and kidney cancers. NHL was highest in pediatric patients and lung cancer in patients over 50 years of age. These new data do not change our overall concept of tumorigenesis in immune-compromised patients, however they bring up new questions of how the tumor growth process can be enhanced or accelerated.

10.2 CANCER IN CHRONIC WOUNDS

The classical example of a non-healing wound transforming into cancer is the Marjolin ulcer, a squamous cell carcinoma in the bed of an old burn wound with chronic ulceration and granulation tissue. Other examples of chronic wounds are osteomyelitis, diabetic venous stasis or decubitus ulcers, old chemical burns and anorectal wounds caused by viral warts. The duration of chronic inflammatory process is reported to be 30 years on the average, and shorter periods of 5 years have been reported prior to cancer development.

The relationship between wound healing, chronic inflammation and cancer has been reported by Virchow, 1863. Wound healing requires the participation of immune response with inflammatory cells, chemoatractants for angiogenesis, fibroblasts growth and epithelialization. Work with zebra fish embryos and RAS oncogenes has elucidated the early participation of neutrophils and macrophages in the transformation of cells into cancer (Antonio 2015). In this zebrafish model, melanoma would develop as early as 15 days after wounding in skin expressing the mutant RAS oncogenes. Inflammatory cells can modulate the growth rate of the experimental melanomas. Wounding and wound healing occur repeatedly in the course of a normal life and cancers in cutaneous wounds are rare and only occur in long standing open wounds. Controlled growth (fetal development, wound healing, hair and nail growth) undergoes many of the cellular and molecular signals that are upregulated by protooncogenes (growth pathways), the same genes behaving as oncogenes in cancer formation. Chronic wounds maintain an ongoing inflammatory process similar to conditions in chronic inflammation from infections such as viral hepatitis and H pylori gastritis resulting in hepatomas and gastric carcinoma, respectively. Both conditions generate cellular changes that favor gene mutations and continued signaling for cell division. Here is where some molecular changes are at the cusp of controlled growth versus uncontrolled neoplastic growth.

Experimental models show that the immune cells, in the context of wound healing, start on the pathway that can lead to cell transformation into cancer. Inflammatory cells are often found in abundance in tumors. Several clinical examples help illustrate their role. Ulcerated primary melanomas are associated with inflammatory cells and have a more aggressive biological behavior, noted in the micro-staging and the propensity for node involvement and recurrence. Medullary breast carcinomas are associated with lymphocytic infiltration and thought to be a sign of robust immune reaction, in this case, associated with better prognosis. Tumor infiltrating lymphocytes have been studied in other sub-types of breast cancers and point to the immune interaction and determines the ultimate cancer behavior (Cvetanovich 2016). Another clue comes from the plant domain where chronic inflammation and infections are found, with resulting tumor growth, however short of reaching cancer status, i.e., no spread to distant parts or local destruction compromising the survival of the plant. Stem and root galls from Agrobacterium tumefasciens are prime examples, see Chapter 16.

10.3 AGGRESSIVE AND INDOLENT CANCERS; THE BAD AND THE GOOD, SAME ACTOR?

As we have seen, common cancers such as breast or colorectal malignancies can have a subset of very aggressive and fast-growing tumors. Inflammatory breast cancers (IBC) present with breast skin swelling and redness associated with dermal lymphatic tumor invasion and rapid growth. The redness and swelling of IBC are not due to inflammatory response, but to the tumor emboli in skin dermal lymphatics, causing the dermal swelling and increase in blood flow. Only when the skin ulcerates from tumor involvement, then classical tissue inflammation develops with leukocytic infiltration. Some colon cancers spread to lymphatics and peritoneal surfaces, and are associated with high degree of regional recurences, but interestingly, a lesser frequency of liver or lung metastases. On the opposite end of this spectrum, there are very indolent cancers that have been referred to as an "over-diagnosis", by some physicians. Ductal carcinoma in situ (DCIS) of the breast, some occult prostate and thyroid cancers fall into this category. From a clinical approach, many tumors' aggressive or indolent behavior cannot be predicted to a high degree of certainty. Indeed, major operations are still performed for indolent tumors, justified by this uncertainty, while other doctors would refrain from aggressive treatments, and observe closely or treat with limited resection. Can we determine with greater precision, which tumors are bad actors and other tumors that will not spread or cause death? The keys to unlock the mystery and recognize their biological behavior beyond their appearance on conventional methodology (anatomy, histopathology, and past observations) is to explore the tumors' molecular footprint. DNA analysis and oncogene profiles will change entirely how we classify tumors, surplanting the anatomical origin, such as breast or skin cancers. Tissue of origin and histological appearance may be merely coincidental. Re-classifications have revolutionized the field of leukemia and lymphoma where the reconigtion of the transformed white blood cell progression from its normal progenitor cell to the differentiated lymphocyte or myeloid cell, has been expanded by the discovery of surface receptors and gene markers allowing refinements in the diagnosis and treatment of these neoplasms. Will the molecular footprint give a clearer prediction to the tumor biological behavior whether indolent, slow growth, or aggressive and capable of causing death? For each aggressive tumor we may need to address some basic issues; i) is the aggressive behavior inherent at the inception of the neoplastic change, ii) if not inherent, then the change from quiecense into phenotypic more aggressive behavior occurs later, with a predictable time table and measurable acquisition of new oncogenes? Clinical observations have documented slow growing cancers, present with minimal changes for long periods, then transform into a more aggressive behavior. Cases in point are, inflammatory breast cancer developing from an existing tumor mass and nodular melanoma growing in a bed of superficial spreading melanoma. Greater clonal and genetic instability in indolent tumors can provide means to acquire new oncogenes changing the phenotypic landscape into more aggressive tumors. If these changes are predictable, or measurable, then timely interventions can be devised to reach tumor eradication, prior to this critical change in tumor behavior and prognosis. If on the other hand, aggressive cancers are identified from the onset, the treatment approach should be more individualized and more urgent, i.e, a more intense treatment, with acceptance of greater morbidity. These lethal cancers need to be identified early from other more indolent cancers, possibly their close "siblings". In the past, traditional histopathology has identified some indolent cancers and failed in other cases. Molecular markers will likely reveal their true biological behavior and identity, and signal the change into faster growth patterns and metastatic behavior. This same question determines the need for systemic therapy, i.e., chemotherapy. When does the tumor change from localized to metastatic? Hopefully, genomics could be the key to unlock this good and bad behavior mystery. The third possibility is a combination of both indolent and aggressive tumor cells co-existing in the same cancer mass. This is called tumor heterogeneity, where the tumor cells are histologically similar, however different clones of tumor cells will emerge in the same tumor, as they acquire new oncogenes at a different rate. The clones with more aggressive behavior grow faster and become the predominant cells in the tumor with passing time. This understanding is actually consistent with the Darwinian view of living organisms and applicable to cells and even to molecules. Therapies, such as chemotherapy, can select resistant clones of tumor cells, which will continue to evolve new oncogenes enabling higher growth and metastatic behavior and thereby becoming the dominant and most prevalent cells in the tumor mass.

The dichotomy of the indolent and aggressive tumors can also be framed in the chicken and egg question, which came first? Life in general start with the single egg and matures into adulthood. The young embryonic cells are pluripotent as in stem cells, that can change into different adult tissues. Likewise, the transformed cancer cell, originated from stem cells, start from a single cell then changing into multiple clones, manifesting in heterogenous indolent or aggressive behavior. Returning to our question regarding "aggressive tumors" and whether it is inherent at inception or acquired at some point in the progression of the cancer, we can answer this paradox with the acquisition of new oncogenes. As the cancer start from the single cell, its biological phenotype is determined by the oncogenes transformed at the onset. Although not well established, the oncogene or combination of oncogenes in the early cancer cells determine the indolent or aggressive biology. Thus, in the subset of early aggressive tumors, prevention can achieve lesser impact on its eventual lethality. On the other hand, the majority of aggressive tumors acquire their aggressive behavior later in its "tumor life-span", allowing a window of time for prevention, diagnosis and screening. This indolent "life-span" can be in the order of 10-20 years. As mentioned, the innate aggressive tumors are most likely a very small minority of tumors, and not amenable to population wide screening programs. Another possibility, not often observed clinically, is that clonal aggressive behavior can revert back to indolent behavior. Most tumor cells show de-differentiation with progressive growth, anaplasia and aneuploidy, and is associated in continued acquisition of mutations and genetic instability. From a molecular standpoint, this would be akin to reversing entropy, which is potentially possible, as in conditions of superconductivity and life itself! In tumor biology, reversing the molecular mechanisms of oncogenesis, could arrest the uncontrolled growth, and acquire the characteristics of a normal differentiated cell. Several methods have been found successful in vitro with B cell lymphoma and pancreatic cancer cells using specific transcription factors, turning lymphoma cells into harmless macrophages and pancreatic cancer cells into normal pancreas cells. Transcription factors are proteins that attach to the back bone of the gene helix and can activate or silence the gene. Reprogramming of cancer stem cells has been achieved with several techniques used in stem cell technology. Incidentally, the reverse has also been achieved, turning differentiated cells back into pluripotent stem cells. These techniques have expanded significantly the applications in regenerative medicine (Dias Camara, 2016). Stem cells are pluripotent, philogenetically closest to the ovum and capable of renewing established tissues by supplying with young cells. Stem cells by nature are dormant until called upon to parcel out the "young cells". If a dormant stem cell is capable of harboring mutations, or for example a dormant malignant stem cell, then when awakened, rapid growth can ensue behaving as a manifest cancer. Thus, stem cells, or as cancer stem cells can accommodate the concept of indolent or dormant tumors and that of an aggressive tumor. From a cancer control point of view, the key signals for aggressive behavior need to recognized and their molecular features modified.

Tripple negative breast cancers (TNBC) are known for their propensity to metastasize and cause death compared to other categories of breast cancers. TNBC qualify as an aggressive type of tumor. The clinical management of this disease illustrates some of the aspects of indolent and aggressive tumors discussed earlier. TNBC are classified as the 10-20% of breast cancers that are estrogen, progesterone and Her-2-Neu receptor negative. Clinically presents as a bimodal age distribution; under age 50 and older than age 70. TNBC are associated with obesity, African-American ethnicity and some are BRCA1 gene positive. Molecular analysis show association with basal-like tumors, P53 mutations and loss of Rb1 (Neophytou 2018). TNBC are heterogenous group of tumors and further work need to characterize the more aggressive subsets, especially the non-responders to chemotherapy. Among TNBC, smaller and node negative tumors are associated with better prognosis, thus screening efforts should not be discouraged. Clinically pertinent molecular markers and targets need further elucidation as they can help in deciding which TNBC to be monitored more closely and which ones to be treated with "more aggressive modalities".

10.4 BRAIN CANCERS

Brain cancers are enigmatic and present some unique features which are still not completely understood. First, brain cells are long lived and have extremely low turn-over rate and consequently, brain cancer should be a rare occurrence. In fact, although not common, brain cancers are one of the worst malignancies in robbing the patient's quality of life. Secondly, the age distribution is unusual, higher in infants and disappearing by late teens and reappearing after age 40. It is the most common cancer in the pediatric age group, matched by lymphoproliferative disorders. Thirdly, males are more affected by brain tumors both in kids and in adults. And lastly, the presentation of different histological types varies by age, sex and have vastly different behaviors. The central and peripheral nervous systems are extremely specialized organs and may the foremost distinguishing feature of human-kind as a mammal. Our brains have developed a unique environment which is protected by the bony cranium, by the blood-brain barrier and by specialized lymphatics and by the cerebrospinal fluid. The neurons themselves are surrounded by special glial cells providing a privileged supporting micro-environment and stem cell niche. Not surprising central and peripheral nerve tumors, by and large, originate from the background cells; glial, astrocytes and oligodendrocytes. Pediatric brain tumors are much less common than brain tumors in the aged. More discussion in the next section 10.5, Pediatric cancers. Environmental factors have been implicated in the recent rise in incidence of glioblastoma multiforme in England, although no single factor was directly linked (Lamburn 2018). The use of cell phone has been implicated, however, multiple studies have not established a firm link. In-utero and maternal environmental exposures were not shown to be associated with pediatric cancer risks. The gender disparity is also unexplained. Overall male predominance in both early and late age brain tumors is 4:3 in favor of males. Mutations in P53 as in Li-Fraumeni syndrome, and in DNA repair enzyme as in Lynch syndrome increases the risk of brain tumors. NF 1 and 2 associated with neurofibromatosis and peripheral nerve tumors have weak links to brain tumors. Other common oncogenes found in gliomas are EGFR, IDH, PTEN, Notch1, TERT and ATRX (The Cancer Researh Atlas Network, 2015).

Glioblastoma multiforme (GBM), the undifferentiated form of astrocytoma, is the most common brain cancer in the adult, with incidence of 10,000 yearly in the U.S. The cure rate is extremely low, with average survival of one year, despite aggressive treatment with surgery, chemotherapy and radiation. Genomic analysis shows a ray of hope in managing this disease with some molecular signature changes. EGF receptor amplification was common (97% of GBM). PDGF receptor alpha over-expression, MGMT promoter methylation, and RTK (tyrosine kinase receptor) upregulation are features in GBM associated with prognostic significance and are potential targets for drug treatments (Brennan 2013). Research has been focused on finding key molecules that can be targeted for treatment. Better still, can we find molecular changes that present years ahead of the clinical manifestation of the tumor, i.e., neurological changes caused by the mass occupying part of the brain. On the other hand, one could argue that, we could not possibly screen for a tumor that is so uncommon. One would hope that these key molecular changes are shared by several mechanistic pathways for several diseases, as in growth signals, or important for nascent tumor formations, as in DNA repair.

GBM can arise from lower grade astrocytoma or de novo, which brings back our discussion of molecular nature of aggressive and indolent tumors as an evolutionary spectrum, section 10.3. Secondary GBM oncogene footprints seem to follow these very step-wise oncogene acquisition added to pre-existing mutational patterns found in astrocytomas. For example, the EGFR/PTEN/AKT/MTOR pathway seen in GBM could represent multiple gene combination of tumorigenesis (Mansouri, 2017).

10.5 PEDIATRIC CANCERS: A DIFFERENT PARADIGM FROM THE CANCER IN OLD AGE?

The vast majority of cancers worldwide occur in individuals over the age of 50 and the responsible mutational changes correspond to the accumulation of DNA damage over a life-time which also causes many other illnesses of old age. Inherited cancer genes lead to tumors at a younger age, by approximately a decade. Malignancies in the young are relatively rare and have unique organ distribution and behavior. Could there be different pathways leading to pediatric cancers compared to adult cancers? Mole pregnancy occur in the fetal tissues associated with the trophoblastic villi of the placenta. Neuroblastoma occur in the residual notochord neural tissues, and together with the nephroblastoma, they are the most common cancers in the newborn and early years of life. Childhood leukemias and brain cancers are the next wave of cancers in children that extend into early adulthood. Melanoma, ovaryan sarcomas and testicular cancers can also affect the young adult.

Malignant glial tumors of childhood and adults appear to be similar histologically, however clinically have different behaviors. The pediatric glial tumors are of lower grade and infratentorial, while the adult glial tumors usually progress to grade IV, called glioblastoma multiforme, and have grave prognosis. In the molecular analysis of childhood and adult glial tumors, the differences stand out clearly over several gene spectra. For example, adult glial tumors have low incidence of NF-1, a mutation that is the hallmark of neurofibromatosis. Pediatric brain tumors have a high incidence of NF-1. BRAF mutations, especially in pilocytic gliomas, differentiate pediatric from adult gliomas. Differences are also found in EGFR, P53, and other genes, (Gilheeny 2012). Many consider glialblastoma multiforme in adults as having transformation in glial cells exposed to a lifetime of carcinogen exposure. The same explanation would be difficult to ascribe to pediatric glial tumors. Toxin exposure in utero has been looked at, and no associations could be established. Based on tumor genes, four classes of medulloblastomas are recognized: WNT, SHH, G3, G4, reflecting clinical, therapeutic and prognostic differences.

A second malignancy that share many similarities and some noted differences in the childhood and adult stages is cutaneous malignant melanoma. Melanoma is discussed in Chapter 9.1. Clinically the manifestations and sites are similar including the propensity to metastasize to regional lymph nodes as studied by the sentinel lymph node dissection (SLND) mapping technique. In adult melanoma, the presence of lymph node disease is associated with more advanced stage and decreased survival, however, in childhood melanoma, occult lymph node disease is more common, and survival is not compromised. Recently, whole genome sequencing was done in a series of pediatric melanomas (Lu 2015), notable mutations were found in BRAF, PTEN genes, and no germ line gene mutations were found. Thus, gene analysis in pediatric and adult tumors, such as in astrocytoma and melanoma, significant gene mutational differences occur, pointing to potentially different treatment choices. Unfortunately, no silver bullet has been found yet, even after few new clues in molecular insights are discovered. Most adult cancers are associated with and caused by accumulated mutations, 6-8 driver mutations over 20-30 years (Vogelstein 2013). While in pediatric cancers, fewer mutations are found, one to two driver mutations. Alternate explanations for cancer development in childhood, include epigenetic changes in the genome, fragile chromosome sites, or synergism between oncogenes. This paradigm based on the double hit theory, explains the prevalence of cancer in late adulthood and in younger individuals with inherited oncogenes. Hereditary cancers present in young adulthood, however the scenario of germ line mutations driving tumors in infancy is not found. In hereditary breast cancer, the BRCA 1 or 2 genes, need to be paired with a second random hit on the opposite DNA strand, to fully express the oncogene. Genome wide studies have found 8% rate of germline mutations in pediatric cancers, and trio testing (parents and child) showed up to 20% rates of mutation and potentially other significant epigenetic changes (Kuhlen 2019), however these newly discovered mutations, most of unknown significance, cannot yet be linked to the pediatric cancers. GPR161 germline mutation has been found to be a predisposing factor in some medulloblastoma SHH (Begemann 2020). In time, we fully expect that genomics of pediatric cancers will explain the findings of fewer driver mutations, the apparent lack of pre-existing family history and yet the occurrence at an early age. These clues could also explain the basis for sporadic cancers.

10.6 LUNG CANCER IN NON-SMOKERS

Adenocarcinoma of the lung in non-smokers has shown a remarkable rise in numbers in the last decade, worldwide. Although a fraction of total lung cancers, 12%, there has been a 30% increase in the last few years. The basis for this change is not clear, noting that squamous cell type is still more common amongst male non-smokers, usually due to passive smoking (exposure to cigarette smoke). These new cancers are mostly of the adenocarcinoma type, (Sarnet 2009). The molecular signature of these cancers also sets them apart. These tumors have EGFR and HER2/ERB mutations, as opposed to RAS and TP53 mutations in squamous carcinoma type, mainly amongst smokers. These tumors can be treated with the EGFR antagonists erlotinib or gefitinib, however drug resistance develops eventually, despite the initial near complete eradication of tumor. Durable responses in chemotherapy and biological therapy were not observed except in pathological complete responses in the tumor. However, with the new checkpoint inhibitors, durable responses are seen even when the responses have been partial in the initial phases of treatment. The mechanisms of durable responses may give further clues into the therapy of cancer, (Bivona 2015).

Broncho-alveolar carcinoma has a typical cotton candy appearance on chest X-rays. In contrast, squamous cell carcinoma, found among smokers, present as a lung mass associated with bronchioles. In the original trials for EGFR inhibitors, this histological type responded to treatment, as opposed to lack of response in squamous cell type. Current work has been focused on identifying molecular markers that be set this disease apart. The carcinogens, tobacco and radon play a lesser role in broncho-aveolar type of lung cancer. The increase in broncho-aveolar carcinoma has been found worldwide, usually amongst residents of major cities. Urban air pollutants and second- hand smoke may play a role. The predominance in females remains a mystery.

These differences in lung cancers in never-smokers are also found in East-Asians, who have a higher fraction, up to 30%, compared to residents in Europe and U.S.A., where lung cancer in never-smokers account for less than 10% of all lung cancers, (Zhou 2018). Lung screening with CT scans developed for smokers, is now advocated in the Asian population of non-smokers.

10.7 KAPOSI'S SARCOMA (KS) AND CUTANEOUS T-CELL LYMPHOMAS

Angiosarcoma presenting in the skin of men, first described in 1872 by Moritz Kaposi, is an uncommon skin cancer. The epidemiology is unique by its prevalence in older men in Italy, Greece and other Mediterranean countries as well as in men of Jewish descent. It is much less common in older women, except in the African KS, where also affects children and young adults. In the U.S., KS incidence increased during the AIDS epidemic when young adults with HIV infections were commonly affected by a deadly form of KS. Co-infections and immune suppression, due to steroid treatment, for example, are conditions where KS can appear. KS is caused by latent KS herpes virus and the unique geographic distribution and presentation in men raise interesting questions regarding the pathogenesis. It is usually an indolent tumor, responding readily to treatment.

Mycosis fungoides and Sezary Syndrome are primary T-cell lymphomas of the skin presenting with reddish discolored plaques sometimes resembling psoriasis and eczema, created by the T-cell infiltration of the skin. These lesions can also be confused with KS. Skin is the second to GI tract as most common sites for extra-nodal lymphoma. The subsets of T and B lymphocytes in cutaneous lymphomas are unique and distinguished by their surface receptors. For example, Sezary Syndrome was thought to be the leukemic and aggressive progression of Mycosis fungoides, however they are now considered separate diseases, distinguished by their T cell origin (Fujii, 2018). Over a dozen of separate T cell lymphoma have been described with unique clinical features. CD4 small/medium T cell lymphoproliferative disorder is one such lymphoma with indolent behavior and usually localized, and is amenable to surgical treatment with potential cures. The skin microenvironment responds to the lymphoma by adopting unique chemokine ligands among the keratinocytes, fibroblasts and Langerhans cells. Cutaneous lymphoma populated by its transformed T cells of origin, and with unique cell surface ligands present platforms where cell surface molecules can be linked to specific clinical findings pertinent to tumor behavior as in skin tropism. These links will reveal greater insights into the molecular mechanisms of the unique cancer biology in cutaneous lymphomas.

10.8 TROPHOBLASTIC TUMORS OF PREGNANCY

Hydatiform mole and other tumors arising from the trophoblastic cells are fascinating neoplasms due to the fact that they originate from fetal tissue which is foreign to the mother. A successful pregnancy and birth of the healthy baby implies control of the normal immune rejection mounted by the mother in the placenta-uterine interface. The fetal trophoblast cells invade the uterine wall and the syncitiotrophoblasts establish a vascular rich membrane along with decidua basalis tissues of the mother's uterus to exchange blood oxygen/CO2 and nutrients between fetus and mother. The paradox is created in both directions of tissue growth control mechanisms. Preventing rejection of the baby by strong transplantation antigens, on the one hand, and preventing uncontrolled growth by the trophoblast cells, on the other. The failure of this entire process results in spontaneous abortions due to robust immune response from the mother, and much less common, the growth of trophoblastic tumors due to suppressed immune response, as in enhanced maternal immune tolerance.

Trophoblastic tumors, also known as gestational trophoblastic tumors, present in-utero mimicking a pregnancy that can be confirmed by elevation of beta-HCG secreted by one of the component cells, the syncytiotrophoblasts. The malignant potential is difficult to discern from the native placental cells, as residual placental tissue can grow independently, (Seckl 2013). The hydatiform mole occurs due to abnormal sperm fertilization and demonstrates an absence of the maternal ovum genetic contribution. Partial moles have the maternal genetic material as an embryo, and can develop along side the mole during the first trimester. These tumors can also develop after a pregnancy, long after the main placenta is shed from the uterus. Once malignancy is well established, these tumors can also be referred to as choriocarcinoma, and can occur outside the uterus and pelvis. Interestingly, placental and fetal cells can be found in the mother, during and after pregnancy, a finding called microchimerisms. These cells are found in multiple organs and perform beneficial functions, similar to those of stem cells, like anti-tumor and rejuvenation activities, (Sawiki 2008).

Fortunately, hydatid moles respond well to surgery and chemotherapy. The diagnosis is arrived at after ultrasound of the uterus reveals an abnormal mass and the absence of the fetus during routine follow-up. Since placental cells have the capability of invasion and rapid growth, much like a malignant neoplasm, the behavior of mole pregnancies suggest that the embryo and the mother have the capability of controlling the trophoblasts' growth, unlike other malignancies. The clinical presentation of these tumors and the fact that trophoblasts can without much alteration transgress the line between normalcy and malignancy, illustrate our lack of understanding of some crucial growth control mechanisms.

Some fetal cells are found in the maternal circulation well after pregnancy, fetal microchimerism, defying the maternal immune response (Sunami 2010), or perhaps an ingenious form of selective immune tolerance, also seen in other situations of chimerism in transplantation immunology. Some theorize that this phenomenon can explain lower breast cancer rates in multi-parous women, and lower rates of some cancers in women.

11

THE CANCER SURVIVOR: HOW TO PREVENT TUMOR RECURRENCE AND A SECOND PRIMARY CANCER?

There are over 15 million cancer survivors in the U.S.A., just under 5% of the population and these figures are expected to surpass 20 million by 2026. Some survivors have become disease free from early stage cancer or from an indolent form of disease while others had to struggle to overcome a more advanced stage cancer with more significant risks of cancer recurrence. The battle is long, and though the cancer was vanquished, fatigue and other consequences of surviving cancer, both mentally and physically can persist.

Cancer survivors are more aware of their own bodies and of the need to maintain themselves in good health and the importance of prevention practices. Each cancer will have its own characteristics of which organs are affected post-treatment and its particular risk of recurrence. In general, the recurrent cancers are local, regional, which include the nodal drainage areas, and distant sites of regrowth. Statistically, 75% of all tumor recurrences occur in the first two years after diagnosis. This pattern of temporal appearance speaks more to the escape of tumor cells from the initial treatment. The more delayed recurrence pattern reflects the dormancy of cancer cells reactivating into clinically relevant recurrences. The less common recurrences after 5 years of the initial diagnosis, implicate other means of tumor resurgence such as slow cell growth, or, field effect, also known as field cancerization, which is the concept that cells near the original treated tumor has greater chance to transform into a new malignancy (Lochhead, 2015). These late recurrences raise the issue of new or second primary cancers in the vicinity of the old tumor or at new locations. The risks of second primary tumors of entirely different cell types are also increased in cancer survivors. These second primary tumors can have predictable clinical patterns and anticipated patterns of molecular changes.

Local recurrence can result from microscopic residual disease after surgical resection, in the surgical site or in the regional lymph nodes. The art and science of surgical oncology have evolved from radical resections in order to remove strands of tumor extending beyond the central tumor mass and to encompass the malignancy extending into regional lymph nodes. Newer surgical approaches include neoadjuvant combinations of chemotherapy, biological therapy and radiation therapy. These modalities used prior to resection, can reduce the tumor size, shrinking tumor away from vital structures and eliminating strands of tumor cells extending radially from the main tumor bulk, or minor satellites of cells near the growing tumor edges. These methods called neoadjuvant treatment, consist of chemo, biological or radiation therapy prior to surgery, allowing more limited resections and reducing the local recurrence rates. Cure rates can be higher also due to reduction of subclinical metastatic disease. Radical resections are employed selectively for locally advanced disease or poor response from neo-adjuvant therapy. The necessity for node dissection has become more selective with the use of sentinel lymph node mapping. Some tumors, such as malignant melanoma, have a low but finite recurrence even at 10 years. Radical resection of tissues around a tumor was the standard of care prior to effective chemotherapy or radiation therapy. In addition, locally advanced cancers were more common. Even today, the choice between radical local removal of tumor and limited excision with clear surgical margins need careful consideration by the surgeon, balancing morbidity with risks of recurrence. Some recurrences can be indolent, isolated and amenable to re-excision, which are few of the factors considered in the surgical approach.

Another aspect of cancer recurrence is the lethality. Some tumors have high likelihood of recurrence and yet a low risk of causing death. Papillary and follicular thyroid cancers fall into this category of persistent indolent behavior after recurrence. The overall survival rate for these two types of thyroid cancer are better than 98% at ten years, even in the minority of patients that present with recurrences. The initial lymph node involvement in thyroid cancer does not infer a worse prognosis, unlike other cancers, such as breast cancer and malignant melanoma, in which lymph node spread implicates higher rates of local and distant recurrence. On the other end of the spectrum, there are cancers that become more virulent during and after recurrences, such as melanoma or phylloides tumors of the breast. Melanoma recurrences presenting in internal organs such as lung, liver or brain, as opposed to skin recurrences, carry more ominous prognosis. There are examples of patients with melanoma who were disease free for ten years, then present with recurrences which then behave aggressively.

Tumor dormancy can play a role in the delay in tumor growth after initial treatment. The low or absent growth rate is ascribed to the microenvironmental factors, i.e., the surrounding stromal tissues, capable of expressing a variety of lymphokines, immune cellular regulatory activities and tumor suppressive activity, (Linde 2016). The growth model fit the pattern of the cancer stem cell, covered in Chapter 21.2. The concept of field cancerization, can have similar overall effect affecting tumor recurrence, by modulating tumor dormancy or growth. Some of these recurrent tumors are actually second primary cancers and not a true recurrence of the first tumor. Anatomical location of recurrence, within 5 cm of the primary tumor, signals true local recurrence, while further away could be in-transit or a new primary tumor. The mutational changes as a response to genetic instability or exposure to carcinogens affecting the regional tissues, could have similar mutational hits or driver oncogenes as the initial cancer, hence the concept of field effect and propensity for second regional cancers.

As in primary cancers, the earlier and the smaller recurrent tumor is detected and treated, the more likely the chance of cure and favorable response to treatment. Prevention measures for tumor recurrence, called surveillance, are designed according to the stage of treated cancer and matching the temporal risks of recurrence, which will detect recurrent or second primary tumors at earlier stages or prevent the recurrence altogether.

First, a successful prevention strategy needs good compliance, and the understanding of how and why of tumors recur. The tumor stage at first treatment will affect the risks of the cancer to re-emerge after a certain number of months and years of growth. For example, stage I tumors, are smaller and have lower incidence of sub-clinical metastasis. At the initial treatment, surgery will have removed the tumor with clear margins, and being small, there are lower risks of undetected satellites or "roots". The risks for local or regional recurrences are low. Distant recurrences are unlikely and consequently there are no considerations for adjuvant or preventive chemotherapy. A more advanced tumor, with higher T stage, local failure rate increases and spread reaching lymphatics, regional lymph nodes or blood vessels are more common. In order to reduce local recurrence, radiation therapy is usually added to surgery, which is a form of regional treatment. Chemotherapy or biological therapy are considered systemic therapy, so that wherever the tumor cell lodges elsewhere in the body, the systemic therapy will reach the tumor cell.

These are the standard treatment modalities your doctors will offer. In addition, you can tip the balance for cure and lower risks for tumor recurrence, by harnessing your immune system to reject remaining cancer cells, by decreasing DNA damage and mutations, and by reducing damage from excessive reactive radicals which all adds up to optimizing the intracellular homeostasis. The discussions of diet, physical activity and avoidance of carcinogens covered in their respective chapters, would be most pertinent, as some of the important means to maintain cellular homeostasis and promote natural adaptive immunity or therapy (NAT) (Thomas 2018). The steps one can do in cancer prevention, repeated several times in our discussions, are as applicable to disease recurrence as well as to tumor initiation. Studies indicate survivors of cancer who enroll in regimens improving their daily diet and physical activity have significantly lower tumor recurrence rates.

There are also accepted surveillance protocols to detect early recurrences according to the tumor type and its corresponding stage at diagnosis. These surveillance methods include physical exam to detect any local or regional recurrence, i.e., surgical wounds and lymph node drainage areas, blood test for tumor markers, imaging tests of the affected area or potential organs likely harboring distant tumor spread. Each tumor type has targeted organs of potential spread, bones, lungs and liver for breast cancer, for example. PET (positron emission tomography) scan images the entire body and can reveal sites of tumor spread with the size of around 1 cm or less. This scan has been useful in determining sites of involvement of advanced primary cancers or in case of recurrences. Tumor driver genes can yield prognostic clues and help formulated the target sites for surveillance. Molecular clues to tumorigenesis can form the basis for prevention of recurrent cancer. The methodology will vary widely. One possibility is utilizing driver oncogene or unique molecular markers of the primary tumor and performing NGS genomics on liquid biopsies (Golemis 2018). Specific microRNAs have also been used for surveillance.

12

PSYCHOSOCIAL ASPECTS OF A DREADED DISEASE

The news of a cancer diagnosis could not be more unwelcome. Overwhelming thoughts of dying, pain and other dire outcomes of a malignant disease crowd your mind. Moreover, the impact on your loved ones is only one of many worries. The negative connotations of cancer, as an illness, transcend cultures. In some countries in Asia, the family does not want the patient to know the diagnosis of cancer, fearing that the psychological impatct will contribute to health decline. In addition, the fear surrounding this dreaded disease in one family member will burden the entire family in the eyes of the community. The immediate effects of the shocking news of having cancer is followed by the prolonged mental struggle with denial. Can the diagnosis be true? Could it be laboratory error or the tests inadvertently switched from another patient? The diagnosis is eventually confirmed, and irrefutable. One is overcome by constant and general anxiety, that spills over to self-doubt, leading to re-visiting past and future scenarios associated with illnesses. Feelings of guilt abound, along with many other remorseful thoughts. Eventually mental exhaustion sets in and unpleasant thoughts and images of dire consequences continue. Mental exhaustion is compounded by the real stress of undergoing the work of diagnostic tests and treatment.

Cancer patients need psychological support from family members and friends. Often professional psychotherapy can improve the outlook. The professional help start with your own doctor acknowledging your difficult journey, and that you should not feel alone since the disease does afflict a large portion of the population, at one time or another. Cancer is very democratic, afflicting everyone equally, by risk basis. Therefore, do not blame yourself. Your doctor should be the first to reassure you that there is hope in reaching a cure, albeit in some cases, the chances are slimmer. Your oncologists and nurses pursue the tasks of getting you on the road to recovery, and will provide the supportive psychological care that is an integral part of that journey. This is a time when one should slow down, accept your loved ones and friends help. Your daily tasks may appear more burdensome. It is a point to pause, take a deep breath and give time for your mind to clear and catch up. Convince yourself that the insurmountable is in fact a hill that can be climbed, new horizons are not far away, and better days are waiting ahead. Your mental health can be restored and recruited to fight the cancer. Some will encourage you to turn the negative into a positive. Your doctor's attention to your psyche is nearly as important as in finding ways of destroying your cancer cells while keeping your normal cells healthy. The patients' attempt to get the grasp of their illness will take time and will be an important factor in the healing process.

Chronic anxiety, mental depression and negative perception of stress are conditions that can lead to exhaustion or worsen the course of a chronic illness such as cancer. These negative health effects have been described since antiquity and treatment prescribed in the Chinese Traditional Medicine emphasizes return to harmony and equilibrium of the energy sources. It is interesting that with these philosophical approaches, many still prefer that their loved ones not be told of their cancer diagnosis. Most physicians will propose that being truthful about the prognosis is the best remedy, as the mental adjustments the patient need to navigate are better to faced sooner than later. The approach needs personalization as each individual deal with stresses differently, especially in young patients. Several interventional studies have been conducted with patients with breast and colorectal patients showing a measurable improvement in quality of life when the anxiety and stress are relieved through specific programs, such as group sessions, yoga, acupuncture, meditation and exercise. Few studies also demonstrated improved endpoints in cancer recurrences and survival.

Death, though not imminent, is a recurrent theme in the mind of the cancer patient, and will have to be faced and dealt with. This topic has been elegantly described by Kubler-Ross and points to the several phases everyone goes through to emotionally accept a life crisis or confronting death. The shock and denial phases are the initial reactions as one deals with the why now and why me; followed by anger, bargaining, acceptance and depression. The depression stage may be prolonged in the cancer patient, as most of the mentioned emotional stages and struggles have been experienced to some degree. Exhaustion is common, due to the prolonged and difficult treatment cycles. Fatigue can be caused by other physiological conditions as well: anemia, electrolyte imbalance, poor nutrition and drug side effects. A supportive family is essential for the patient and the caretaker, for their emotional as well as their health needs. It also helps to make sure all business matters and relationship discords are settled. Family dysfunctional interactions often resurface in these stressful times, accentuated by severity of the illness or by the cancer with poor prognosis. Just as the psychological needs of the cancer patient need attending to, this is the time to place differences aside and come together for the sake of the caretaker and patient. The family will be pleased to find that in time of one's poor health, there can be healing amongst family relationships. There are several published coping techniques for cancer patients and family. They share the common points of stepwise approach, pause and slow down and allow ample recovery period, find your "harmony" and look for hope and renewal. Sakura (cherry blossoms) in the Japanese tradition and lotus flower in Buddhism represent traditional concepts of survival and reverence for life despite earthly difficulties.

When do you cross the limit of prolonging life and start delaying death? We all have to come to terms with this question, with our loved ones or with ourselves. Despite, the wonders of medical advancement, the point in time when life cannot be sustained without cost to quality of life, dignity, and possible economic burden to the family, does arrive and need to be evaluated and discussed. Re-evaluation of life sustaining measures may be necessary. This question is faced, often, in the intensive care unit, when the patient is sustained on life support measures, like a ventilator. In other situations, when time is not pressing factor in the decision process, careful consideration and consultations with family and health advisors can be made to great advantage. These decisions do not have to be made alone or unilaterally, even if the family expects one particular member to take lead. For example, when the benefits of treatment may not be assured and the side effects can be greater than expected, then removal of cancer treatments can be withdrawn in consultation with the family. At times, there may be unexpected circumstances to delay the decision to scale down treatments. End of life care, spanning usually six months prior to death, is usually the costliest phase of care in the patient's life time. Yet, there can be a major disconnect between the patient, family and professional caregivers. The usual emphasis, in the acute care setting, is on prolonging life despite the fact that the end of life is imminent. Diagnostic tests and treatments are prescribed even though there are negligible benefits and cause a greater burden on the patient's well-being. When prolongation of life is not realistic then palliative care should be emphasized. Some argue that acute care and palliative care should always be considered together. Palliative care should be considered early in the course of illness and does not mean abandonment of care. The goal is to reduce suffering, and maintain or enhance the quality of life. When these goals are agreed upon by family, patient and the medical team, the fear of not providing for your loved one, is then, replaced by appreciation of life and preparation for a dignified end of life. These goals are simple, however in practice there are competing interests from within the family, caretakers, hospice and acute care institutions. There are instances when the family or caretaker feels responsible to make decisions for the patient. Guardianship should not change the dynamics of treatment or palliative decisions. Participatory decisions with the patient even in decline, in the end, get better results.

Occasionally, judicious use of palliation in the acute care treatment setting can benefit the patient by alleviating pain and enhance quality of life. The use of invasive surgical procedures, such as gastric feeding tube placement, drainage of abcess, relieving bowel or airway obstruction, takes careful evaluation in balancing risks and benefits.

12.1 ANXIETY AND FEARS FROM SCREENING EXAMINATIONS

The fear of cancer can be magnified during screening or diagnostic tests. This real problem leads to the low compliance rates for cancer screening. The anxiety becomes subliminal and manifests in minimizing the importance of screening tests. Some individuals are terrified that the findings on the examination will reveal the feared diagnosis of cancer. Doctors and public media should emphasize the opposite. The positives of early diagnosis should be highlighted, discovery of a small tumor is better, earlier than later. And more importantly, the screening for tumors will save lives. The denial may overlook symptoms of cancer leading to presentation of more advanced stages. Physicians should acknowledge the patient's feelings and anxieties surrounding medical tests. For example, examinations that involve discomfort such as compression of the breasts in mammograms, insertion of endoscopes in screening upper and lower gastrointestinal endoscopies, need to begin with full explanation of the indications and benefits, and assurances that patients' concerns are heeded. When indicated, sedation and drugs that relieve the discomfort of the procedure should be offered. Results of the examinations should be reported without undue delay and in clear unambiguous language. Many patients report anxiety in the way they receive their test reports, with wordings indicating possibility of bad outcomes, medical language unintelligible for the public, or disclosures of possible false negative results. Call back for additional tests is anxiety producing even for the normally even keel person. The recall letter or telephone notification should be coupled with assurance that majority of recalls are negative for cancer and done for reassurance. These letters for call back tests, without adequate explanation, are often thought of as positive results for the presence of cancer. Call back for additional views in mammography, are definitively feared by most women. Indeterminate results requiring further tests should be accompanied by explanations, such as additional views are required to clarify possible microcalcifications or lesions that will probably turn out not to be neoplastic. Medical terms such as malignancy cannot be ruled out and clinical correlation should be obtained, can be avoided in the patient communication, as to not create confusion and anxiety.

Compliance to screening tests recommendations is usually low. This can be the main reason for failing to achieve significant cancer prevention goals. Behavior scientists have developed several "nudge" techniques to improve rates of task performance and combat procrastination. Financial factor is one of the major barriers for cancer screening.

12.2 SYMPTOM RELIEF

Symptom relief is one of the oldest charges medical healers have accepted and able to ameliorate for their patients. The range of symptoms associated with cancer care varies widely, from pain, inability to swallow and nausea, abdominal bloating, shortness of breath, chronic aspiration with coughing, fatigue and nerve compression with weakness, pain and numbness.

The treatments and interventions can be simple, as an oral dose of pain medication, or more complex or invasive associated with greater risks and requiring greater thought in recommending the interventions. One of the most common symptoms in advanced cancer is pain, caused by tumor pressure on bone, soft tissue, nerves and other sensitive areas. Several formularies for pain relief have been developed with high degree of effectiveness and with ease of administration, either taken orally as a pill or elixir, trans-dermal or intravenous routes. Cutaneous electrical stimulatory devices can be helpful and more invasive methods are nerve blocks and insertion of probes or catheters for infusion of drugs or application of deep nerve stimulation. Most pain medicines will dull the mind, becoming an undesirable side effect. Alternatives to consider would be acupuncture, nerve blocks, epidural routes or trans-cutaneous stimulators. For difficult pain management cases, specialists in pain care should be consulted. Another common concern is subsequent addiction to opioids and other pain compounds. This can be a result after long term use and should be addressed by a professional instead of self-management.

Disturbance of the digestive process is common from cancer involvement of the alimentary tract, and from side effects of chemotherapy or radiation treatments. Nausea and vomiting can be alleviated with medications. Symptoms associated with blockage of the intestinal tract will require multidisciplinary management, and in some cases surgical intervention. The types of intervention can be personalized to the patient, from a major procedure such as removal or bypass of affected bowel, or use of minor surgery, such as insertion of a drainage tube in the stomach or dilated segment of the bowel. Weight loss and malnutrition is common. Food intake by oral route is always preferred and at times not possible. Use of alternate routes, such as tube feeding, or intravenous (parenteral nutrition) using peripheral or central veins are considered when the gastrointestinal tract does not function properly, usually as a temporary bridge for alimentary tract recovery. Cancer cachexia, a well-recognized phenomenon, is caused by the higher metabolic needs of the cancer and the release of several lymphokines, like TNF (tumor necrosis factor), which suppresses appetite and increases the metabolic rate. In the severe form of weight loss in the cancer patient, supplemental nutrition is provided, sometimes through a feeding tube. The decision to intervene with an externally placed route of feeding should be carefully evaluated with patient and family. Added nutrition in a patient with significant tumor burden may not improve quality of life nor prolong survival (Gullett 2011).

12.3 PALLIATIVE AND END OF LIFE CARE

Near the end of one's life, the reflection upon life's purpose and legacy becomes more philosophical and most will want to leave this world with notion that there was a small contribution made especially to your loved ones. For the cancer patient, as well, the end of life care should minimize the cancer burden and allow the proper reflection on one's life and attain quality and dignity in the remaining days. When life is limited by illness, quantity of life may not be as relevant as the quality of life. Usually, they are not mutually exclusive. When cancer is no longer curable, and prolonging life can be at expense of quality, the choices may resort to withholding treatments associated with severe side-effects, and emphasizing more on quality of life and symptom relief. Symptom relief requires more attention as the cancer side effects with compromising symptoms become more severe and chronic. In most instances, the most comfortable environment for palliative care is in the patient's home. This would require a hospice team and optimally would include the patient's family doctor. Occasional hospitalization in an acute care setting may be required to resolve a few health problems. The family doctor or nurse, who knows the patient and family, can best advise the best palliative choices and whether an acute or chronic in-patient care is required beyond the home environment. Consultation with a palliative care physician is advised.

13

GENETICS OF CANCER: How do molecular changes in genes, inherited and acquired, lead to cancer.

The double stranded set of paired 23 chromosomes packed into the nucleus inside each of our cells is the most amazing blue print, containing all the instructions for the cells to follow from inception to death and harbouring uniqueness that set us apart from our peers. The how and why of cancers encripted in our genes are ripe for discovery. The numbers of cancers associated with specific gene mutations are growing as new oncogenes, cancer genes are identified. Cancers associated with inherited genes account for only a fraction of all malignancies, fewer than 10%. The remainder large majority are called sporadic cancers. Some of these so-called sporadic cancers are found in clusters associated with ethnicity, geographic regions or common environmental exposures. These findings suggest that there are yet to be identified cancer genes (oncogenes) or interaction of multiple genes. These genes responsible for cancer transformation are found in somatic cells, cells that populate our organs, while germline cells are the reproductive cells in the sperm or ovary. Once transformation process produces established cancers, then dozens of mutated genes, oncogenes, are found. These dozens of oncogenes found at any particular time in the tumor cells, may not be the same oncogenes present in the early stages, as the "passenger and driver oncogenes" are constantly changing due to genetic instability, tumor cell heterogeneity and growth diversity (Romero-Arias 2018). Oncogenes and genetic polymorphisms, non-deleterious mutations, also called SNP or single nucleotide polymorphism, can interact in ways that increase the risks of cancer and other diseases. All oncogenes contribute to the cancer transformation by tilting the balance of growth signals towards uncontrolled cell growth. As the normal cell transforms into the cancer cell, multiple oncogenes are acquired. The key to reverse or stop this process is to turn on the cell death, apoptotic signals, or inhibit the driver oncogene, the very oncogene that is critical for the increased growth signals. The full significance of passenger oncogenes will be understood, as their roles would be unlikely to be solely passive. This will become clearer, as more genomic data are analysed in populations studies involving thousand of individuals. In addition, epigenetic changes, molecular moieties that can modify the function of the genes without changing its basic DNA backbone, can also modulate the risks of malignant transformation; like methylation, histone and microRNAs. Biochemical insults to our cellular organic structure, from reactive molecules, result in genetic mutations, damage, epigenetic molecular changes and the usual wear and tear of aging.

The molecular origins of cancer can be attributed to the multiple mutations in the genetic code. Each somatic cell, contains all the inherited mutations and new ones acquired during its lifetime. The renewal of somatic cells comes from dividing stem cells, which are subjected to the microenvironment of each tissue and undergo assault to their DNA with resulting damages and mutations unique to each clusters of somatic cells. In other words, though each somatic cell contains the same set of genes and inherited mutations, the epigenetic make-up and acquired mutations depend on the local micro and niche environments that differ from the organs, tissue and cells not far apart from each other. The corresponding stem cells could be dormant and only a fraction is actively reproducing new differentiated somatic cells and exposed to risks of mutations. In addition, the epigenetic environment for each stem cell and their respective generated somatic cells have different portions of methylated DNA, or microRNA content, which could be protective against DNA damage. The life time history of exposures that affects the particular genetic changes is your exposome (Section 15.2), which is a record of accumulated exposures, affecting the genome, just as accumulated SNPs provides a history of the particular cell or DNA. The risk and frequency of mutations can be modulated by the local environment around the cells, which in turn is affected by chronic infections, diet, local immune responses, reactive oxygen radicals and clearance of cellular wastes (Sections 15.3 and 20.3). This is also illustrated by twin studies, in whom the identical genes diverge immediately after birth. Clearly not all mutations can be prevented, and some established mutations cannot be eliminated by preventing further clonal expansion through apoptosis and immune cytotoxicity. DNA damage is a problem all living cells have dealt with since, literally, the beginning of life. Amazingly, 10,000 DNA damaging events, mostly single strand breaks, occur in a cell on a daily basis. Indeed, effective machinery in detecting and repairing DNA changes has been developed and evolved to the point where multi-organisms thrive quite successfully.

Testing your own set of genes for mutations, has become easier and more affordable. Several tests offer the convenience of in-home collection of a drop of blood absorbed onto a blot paper or mouth swab placed in a package for mailing. A small sample of DNA extracted from few cells recovered can be used to sequence and identify the genes and the presence of any mutations. Depending on the tests, accuracy, reproducibility and completeness may be an issue. The DNA can be purified and amplified through PCR (poly merase chain reaction), a technique developed by Kary Mullis in 1971, and awarded the Nobel prize 1993. Each cell contains 26,564 protein-coding genes and each gene contains an average of 750,000 nucleotides, and each nucleotice could be a target for mutations. These numbers can quickly become enormous and a non-targeted screening test could miss any number of nucleotide errors. In addition, the gene portions that do not code for proteins, referred as introns, compose most of the genetic material. Introns, interspersed between exons, were considered to be "non-coding" DNA. The non-coding label applies to protein-coding, and there are other overlooked functions of the genetic code, such as template for miRNA. There is a lot more to understand about the genetic code.

The information contained in the genetic code is, today, simply overwhelming for our comprehension or for computerized informatics. New algorithms and artificial intelligence are able to discern useful data obscured by irrelevant data, or background noise. For example, SNP are commonly present and scattered throughout our genome and commonly used to date or trace one's origin among our ancestors and different ethnic groups. These mutations are non-deleterious and do not change the basic cellular function in any significant way. However, some SNP may be associated with increase or decrease in cancer incidence or change cell function in a very small way. The significance of SNPs comes to light only after a large number of individuals are studied, matching the presence and absence of SNP to a variety of clinical data. Although these risk association studies can indicate interesting cancer risks, extrapolating these risks to the individual, is difficult. In other words, how do you translate the SNP based cancer risks to actionable steps, or how do you integrate into the overall risk assessment algorithm? Basically, as we gain sophisticated techniques to detect gene mutations, the clinical applications and valid interpretation of these data can still lag behind. Some diseases are associated with thousands of variant genes, each of which can have different interpretation (Rehm 2015). Several laboratories have pooled their results in ClinGen to clarify the clinical significance of the large number of gene mutations or variants.

13.1 ONCOGENES

The first RNA virus inducing sarcoma, a type of cancer involving soft tissues, was described in poultry by Peyton Rous, in 1911. He was able to take the sarcoma extracts, and induce the same tumors in other birds, by injecting the extracts into their muscles. Scientists debated for the next 55 years whether the Rous sarcoma virus, itself, was the agent inducing cancer and Rous was finally awarded the Nobel Prize in 1966. Human viral origin for cancer was not identified until years later in 1980, when the HTLV-1 (RNA virus) was found to cause leukemia first isolated in cutaneous T cell lymphoma, also known as mycosis fungoides or Sezary syndrome. About the same time, a cluster of leukemias in Japan was reported, and found to be associated with HTLV-1. Human DNA viruses have also been implicated in cancer, HPV as the inducing agent for cervical cancer, EBV (Epstein-Barr virus) for Burkitt's lymphoma and polyomavirus as the agent causing Merkel cell carcinoma. Approximately 20% of cancers worldwide are caused by viruses. Myc oncogene was discovered in the avian myelocytomatosis virus and later found in the human genome. It controls the transcription activities of the DNA and can either drive replication or apoptosis depending on the activity of multiple co-factors. It is a regulator gene and codes for a protein, a transcriptional factor, which facilitates nuclear phosphorylation with multi-functional activities. Its multiple normal functions in the cell are overshadowed by its oncogene activity when mutated and essentially becomes over active, in a constant "on" setting. Considering the normal functions and all what these genes do, the name oncogene, is actually a misnomer. The normal functioning counterpart of the oncogene is called proto-oncogene. The name proto-oncogene gives credit to the multitude of normal and life-sustaining functions it performs. The oncogene contribution to malignant transformation results from mutational changes in the proto-oncogene. Most of these genes have been conserved in the evolution of life-forms from viruses and bacteria to mammals, suggesting the importance of their functions in sustaining life. In fact, our cells incorporated some of these oncogenes from viruses, as their functions convey survival or performance advantage.

Bishop and Varmus were awarded in 1989 the Nobel Prize for their work on oncogenes. They were instrumental in determining the human DNA segment (cDNA) for the retroviral gene Src, a virus derived oncogene, found in animal tumors, could also cause human tumors. The term oncogene was coined by Hubner and Todaro, 1969, from studies of viral genes capable of causing tumors in animals. Tumor suppressor genes function to oppose the cellular activity that can lead to cancerous transformation, like promotion of cell division, inhibition of apoptosis (programmed cell death) and of autophagy (degradation of old and misshapened proteins). Mutations leading to lower activity of tumor suppressor genes, will also favor tumorigenesis. Table 13.1 below outlines a few well characterized oncogenes and tumor suppressor genes. The P53 gene, for example, controls the G0/S-phase transition of the cell cycle, and is known as the "guardian of the genome". P53 can delay mitosis to allow DNA repair, or direct the cell to undergo apoptosis, cell death, if the mutation irreversibly and deleteriously affects the genome. By signaling Bax/BCl-2 genes, the machinery for cell death is activated. Li and Fraumeni found several familial cancers caused by a variety of missence germline mutations in P53. Li Fraumeni syndrome is characterized by multiple cancers: sarcomas, brain and breast cancers, (Olivier 2003). Mutated P53 affects the function of TERT and c-myc, and other pathways contributing to tumorigenesis. Mutations on P53 are commonly found in sporadic cancers, in lung, pancreas and breast, to name a few. In breast cancers, several of these oncogenic activities are disrupted, by up or down-regulation, and are associated with a focal mutation in the P53 oncogene. A point mutation in the base pair number 270 of the P53 nucleotide sequence is found in breast cancers, while different codon mutations are found in colon tumors, for example 175, 245, a G to A and C to T transition leading to a single amino-acid substitution. Mutation affecting protein binding locus is also common. Rarely, germ line mutations in these oncogenes are detectable (Li Fraumeni tumors). A germline mutation will then be harbored in every single cell in the body. Search for oncogene mutations, as a blood test, has not turned out to be useful screening strategy in the population at large. Gene tests for germ line mutations are indicated for potentially affected family members and unsuspected carriers, i.e., cancer at young age or family members with cancer. For certain situations, pre-malignant cells could be tested for oncogene mutations as markers and gauge risk for future cancer transformation. Oncogene testing in tumor tissues usually yields multiple gene mutations and the pattern of mutations can potentially lead to treatment modifications (Vogelstein, 2015). Despite the multiplicity of mutations, characterized by the genomic instability in cancers, a dominant oncogene can be targeted and result in surprising therapeutic outcomes in tumor shrinkage as in GIST (gastrointestinal stromal tumor), a subtype of sarcoma, with the use of imatinib, a tyrosine kinase inhibitor. This main oncogene, determining growth characteristics of the tumor, KIT (tyrosine kinase inhibitor)/PDGFRA (platelet derived growth factor receptor A) driver oncogene, producing a state known as oncogene addiction.

In the current era of "gene sequencers" (NGS) and genomics, the entire human DNA can be deciphered for each individual. For the scientist studying cancers, the person's entire genome is essentially all the information one needs to know about the risk for developing cancer, by identifying all the oncogenes in the genetic code. Well folks, we are not quite there yet. The reality is more complex. The individual's genome can be known and yet many of the genetic code and hidden oncogenes are not well understood. Much of the gene sequences is in the non-coding regions and more oncogenes have yet to be discovered. On the average only 5% of individuals in the population tested, have know germ line oncogenes. This figure will increase as more oncogenes are discovered. In addition, most cells at risk of mutations cannot be tested easily since only leukocyte DNA is tested on a liquid biopsy. cDNA oncogene fragments are detectable in liquid biopsies. Tumor cell genome, on the other hand, has acquired dozens of oncogenes, and can be tested on a sample of cancer obtained by biopsy. Thousands of oncogenes have been catalogued and their molecular signature and clinical significance studied through several cooperative tumor tissue banks. The oncogene profile of tumors can yield information leading to novel treatments beyond what clinical and routine pathological information can provide (Malone 2020). Early acquisition of oncogenes in somatic cells is most pertinent for the science of cancer prevention, especially for the majority of tumors, the sporadic cancers. The model of tumorigenesis proposed by Fearon and Vogelstein for colorectal cancer, the adenoma-carcinoma sequence, mirrored the step-wise accumulation of Wnt/beta Catenin, Ras, P53 and Smad4 pathways mutations. This model was revised with addition of the serrated polyp progression to cancer, following other pathways including epigenetic hypermethylation MGMT and MLH1 genes, associated with microsatellite instability (MSI), (Testa 2018). This cancer development model (tumorigenesis), as a clinical template bridge to the molecular approach, the world of oncogenes, can be replicated for other organ- based tumors, i.e., breast, lung, prostate, or thyroid. The molecular map for these different cancers can have different oncogene patterns and not surprisingly many of the same, supporting common pathways to tumor formation, which can then be dealt with some common basic cancer prevention strategies.

Searching for early oncogenes in some deep seeded cells in our body would be a difficult if not inconvenient task. However, the DNA information needed can be provided by circulating tumor DNA, obtained by routine blood tests. These snipets of tumor DNA can reveal the hallmark signature of these oncogenes. Circulating tumor cells were studied by investigators looking at the biology of metastatic cells since the 1950's. Currently, these tests can detect tumor oncogenes from circulating tumor cells or free fragments of tumor DNA (Merker 2018).

Although we do not have clear recommendations for genomic testing for screening sporadic cancers, we are entering exciting times for a new molecular paradigm, risk assessment and diagnostics for cancer and cancer prevention. Developments in new generation gene sequencers, genomics, proteonomics, epigenomics, microRNAs may soon give us new insights into molecular and precise diagnosis of cancer and pre-malignant conditions.

TABLE 13.1: ONCOGENES and TUMOR SUPPRESSOR GENES (incomplete list)+

Cancer Type	Oncogene (s)	Suppressor Gene	Function^	Comments
Breast *		BRCA 1&2	DNA repair	
Colorectal *		APC	WNT signaling	
Lynch syndrome	MLH1,MSH2, MSH6,PMS		DNA repair	
Pancreas*, Melanoma*		P16 (CDKN2a)	Cell cycle regulation	SNP link to heart dis
Li-Fraumeni		P53	Cell cycle arrest apoptosis	Sarcoma*, brain tumors*
MEN 2	RET		Neutrophic signaling	Thyroid* Hirschsprung's
Cowden		PTEN	phosphorylation	Harmatomas, prostate Ca
Gastric*		CDH1	Membrane protein, adhesion	EMT
Neurofibromatosis		NF 1&2	GTPase	Von Recklinghausen
Retinoblastoma*		RB	Cell cycle arrest	
PJS		STK11	P53 binding	
VHL	VEGF		angiogenesis	Kidney*
Pancreas#, Lung# Colorectal#, Endometrial#	K-RAS		GTPases	
Melanoma #	B-RAF		ST kinase	Birth defects
Breast #, Gastric #	ERB2 (HER2)		Growth factor receptor	Epithelial cancers
Lymphoma #, colon#, breast#, prostate#	MYC		Transcriptional factor	
Glioblastoma #	IDH 1&2		Electron transp	Chondromatosis
Xeroderma pigmentosa	XPA, ERCC3, XPC		DNA binding	Skin*

Abreviations: MEN multiple endocrine neoplasia, PJS Peutz-Jeghers syndrome, VHL von Hippel Lindau syndrome

** Inherited cancer, # sporadic cancers (oncogene probably appeared later in the oncogenic process, in contrast in inherited cancers in which responsible oncogene is the instigator of oncogenesis)*

+ There are hundreds of newly found oncogenes, clinical significance yet to be identified.

^ one of multiple functions.

13.2 HEREDITARY AND "SPORADIC" CANCERS

Nearly 40% of Americans have a family member who has been striken with cancer. Their fears are heightened when news and print media carry unfortunate stories of young patients dying of cancer. The fact that the risks of cancer are carried in ones' genes is not new, but the fact that known risks are manageable is not well appreciated. We want to be in a comfort zone and the risk that we may be carriers of a defective gene with potential implications of causing cancer is, to say the least, frightening. Most of us would not want to think about the diagnosis of cancer, and simply push it into the bin of denial. Knowledge about genetics of cancer can reduce the fear factor by showing what the risks are and that they can be reduced and managed. Getting genetic testing done can take some extra fortitude, however, not all family history of cancer will require gene testing.

To date only approximately 10 % of cancers have been found with a known germ line mutation and are classified as hereditary, i.e., a cancer gene passed from one generation to another through their germ line. The cancers with strong family association, and without specific cancer gene identified, are classified as familial, and the remaining majority of cancers are "sporadic". As the the molecular basis of cancer is better understood, other cancer genes will be discovered, and the genetic patterns of familial cancers will be more predictable. The sporadic cancers will likely be caused by a more complex interaction between multiple genes. Indications for gene testing has expanded to include more individuals with risks of familial cancers. For example, individuals diagnosed with cancer at younger age of 50, or with two family members diagnosed with cancers. In addition, the multi-gene panel testing and the new generation gene sequencer have made gene testing more practical and more efficient in finding other less frequent oncogenes. In individuals at risk for breast cancer, BRCA is most commonly found, however studies with multi-gene panels are finding another 10% of individuals with other oncogenes such as CHEK2, PALB2, CDH1, TP53, (LaDuca 2019). Amongst pancreatic cancer patients for example, nearly 50% of these patients were found with a pre-existing somatic mutation (Price 2018). To be clear, oncogenes found in circulating white blood cells by routine blood gene test have a low positive rate, about 5% in the general population. However, newer techniques are finding new genes in higher proportions of the population at risk for cancer. Some of these oncogenes found in one individual, can be tested in other non-affected family members, with potential preventive implications. Let us illustrate some of these points by first discussing the hereditary cancer genes.

13.2.1 BREAST CANCER GENE, BRCA1 AND BRCA2

BRCA1 was identified by Mary Claire King, then at UC Berkeley, and Mark Skolnick at Myriad Genetics, in 1994. A year later BRCA2 was identified by Michael Stratton at the Institute Cancer Research, UK and scientists at the WellcomeTrust Sanger Institute, (Woosley 1995). Both genes play roles in the DNA repair process, cell cycle control and degradation of proteins through ubiquination. BRCA1 is located on 17q and BRCA2 located on 13q, long arm of chromosome 17 and 13 respectively. Women with BRCA mutations are at risk of developing ovarian cancers (70% life-time risk) and breast cancers (80% life-time risk). These breast cancers develop at younger age, by a decade on the average. Second cancers, such as melanoma and pancreas carcinoma, can also occur. Ashkenazi Jewish individuals have a 18% incidence of BRCA mutations, while other ethnic groups such as Hispanics and Asians have an incidence similar to other Caucasians, around 5%. Distinct founder mutations have been identified in particular ethnic groups, as in the Ashkenazi ancestry and in the Spanish and Icelandic ancestries, (Janavicius, 2010). BRCA 1/2 account for just over 8% of all breast cancers, and another 15% have familial links, strong family history. Other genes with mutations carried in the germ line associated with significant increase in breast cancer, have been identified, i.e., P53 as in Li-Fraumeni syndrome, CHECK2, PALB2 associated with Fanconi anemia, CDH1 associated with lobular breast carcinoma and hereditary diffuse gastric carcinoma. These genes, other than BRCA, account for less than 2% of the familial breast cancers. Mutations, not clearly deleterious, i.e., found with lower penetrance by population-based studies, are the SNP (single nucleotide polymorphism). SNPs play a role in sporadic breast cancers, and their significance are more difficult to interpret, since multiple SNPs and genes are involved (Skol, 2016). The biological behavior of BRCA positive breast cancers is similar to sporadic breast cancers with a few exceptions. Histological type is characterized by invasive ductal origin, with a preponderance of poorly differentiated microscopic appearance, with medullary pattern and lymphocytic infiltration. Metastasis to lymph nodes is less predictable by tumor size. BRCA1 breast cancers have disrupted estrogen receptors and most often do not express the epidermal growth factor receptors, consequently significant higher number of these tumors are classified as triple negative of the basal type. These tumors tend to be more aggressive and do not respond to hormone nor to HER2neu targetted treatments.

Indications for testing for BRCA genes, among women at risk, are: young age at diagnosis (less than 50 years), two first degree relatives with breast or ovaryan cancers, Ashkenazi descent, and a relative with BRCA. A patient with newly diagnosed breast cancer, fitting these criteria, can benefit from BRCA testing in several ways. First, the decision for contralateral prophylactic mastectomy and oophorectomy can be swayed based on the results, and secondly, other family members can also be affected by the autosomal dominant inheritance. Although BRCA1 and BRCA2 breast cancers have higher rates of multifocality in the ipsilateral or contralateral breast, breast conservation surgery can still be considered. In the conserved ipsilateral breast, the recurrence rate can be higher, however, the survival rate is not affected compared to mastectomy. Dr King, in 2014, advocated for testing every young woman for BRCA 1 and BRCA 2, a position that was based on study done in Israel. The unexpected finding was that 50% of women tested positive did not have a family history of breast cancer. Thus, the current criteria based on family history, would miss the opportunity of preventing many breast cancers in the young female population. The scientific community in the U.S.A. was generally against wider population-based testing. The yield for wider testing is estimated to be lower than the 1 in 300-500 women tested in Israel. The benefits of breast cancer prevention in this cohort of young women is complicated by the risks of misinterpretation of the genetic test and of mammographic test results. The polymorphism in the BRCA1 and BRCA2 genes are recognized with wider population gene testing, and do not behave as oncogenes, thus associated with unknown significance. Wide population studies with well documented clinical consequences, rigorous longitudinal follow-up and collaboration with research and commercial data libraries can eventually lead to greater accuracy in reading the test results. In addition, among women with BRCA mutations, at least 20%, do not develop breast or ovary cancers and interesting lessons can be learned from this apparent escape from breast cancer predisposition and tumorigenesis.

What are the clinical applications of BRCA testing? The most common scenario is the young woman with newly diagnosed unilateral breast cancer, often with a family member afflicted by the disease already. The positive BRCA mutation may affect the decision of treatment options toward bilateral mastectomy and breast reconstruction. In the last ten years, even prior the news coverage of actor Angelina Jolie own family history of breast and ovaryan cancers, the rate of bilateral mastectomies had been increasing. Other reasons for this increase, is the use of breast MRI, where contralateral suspicious breast nodules are found, and the increase findings of DCIS in younger women.

If one of your relatives has a known BRCA mutation, then the same mutation can be tested in your blood sample, which is a simpler test, rather than surveing the entire gene (125,951 DNA bases). And if positive, your life-long risk of breast and ovaryan cancer is in the neighborhood of 75%. This information although of serious concern, does not call for urgent treatment such as prophylactic mastectomy nor oophorectomy. First, a confirmatory test is indicated, such as repeating the test, especially if other near-relatives have tested negative. Secondly, mammograms, breast MRI and trans-vaginal ultrasound of the ovaries should be done in newly diagnosed BRCA gene mutation carriers over the age of 40 years. If negative for occult breast or ovary cancer then, there is a period of time to allow personal preferences such as moving up the schedule for a desired pregnancy. If one has reached menopause, then is reasonable to undergo prophylactic salpingo-oophorectomies. Few studies have shown that decreased estrogen levels post oophorectomy can be protective against breast cancer. Prophylactic mastectomy for positive BRCA gene test and negative findings of breast cancer on MRI and/or mammograms is an elective procedure and should be given plenty of time and thought for the decision. New data suggest that salpingectomy may lower the risk of ovaryan cancers without prophylactic oophorectomy, hence preserving ovaryan function. This concept has not been validated in large group of patients.

Male carriers of BRCA genes have higher risks of prostate and breast cancers. Majority of breast cancers in males are associated with BRCA2 oncogene, and present at younger age and associated with higher rates of nodal metastases. Prostate cancers are more common in BRCA2, nearly 50% higher incidence and usually have higher Gleason's score on biopsy.

13.2.2 FAMILIAL ADENOMATOUS POLYPOSIS

Polypoid growths in the large colon and rectum were recognized, since mid XX century, by pathologist Cuthbert Dukes and surgeon Lockart-Mummery at St Marks Hospital, London, as precursors and indicators of risks for colorectal cancers (CRC). Autosomal dominant inheritance of CRC in individuals with numerous polyps was recognized, prior to the discovery of the APC gene. Most afflicted family members had too numerous small polyps to count and by the 4th decade of life nearly all affected individuals will have developed CRC. The APC gene was sequenced in 1991 and found to be located on chromosome 5. The race to identify the APC gene sparked a friendly competitive collaboration between three labs, one in England, and two in US, in Baltimore and Salt Lake City (Rustgi, 2007). The APC wild type protein is considered to have cancer suppressor function by phosphorylation of beta-catenin. Mutated APC allows unchecked growth signal by nearly 10-fold. Although risks of several tumors are increased including brain, endocrine and pancreas, by far, CRC is the predominant cancer found with this mutation. This aspect of the differential phenotypic expression of the mutant APC gene is still unexplained. Possible explanations include tumor niche effect and gut carcinogens being more mutagenic to cells with APC gene. Association with soft tissue benign growths (Gardners' syndrome), brain meningiomas (Turcot's syndrome), desmoid tumors and ampullary carcinomas are more common secondary tumors. The treatment of choice is prophylactic total proctocolectomy in the 2nd decade of life. The timing of prophylactic colon surgery is framed by the time when these hundreds of adenomas are likely to develop into malignancies, increasing dramatically in the fourth decade. The second consideration is to minimize the psychological consequences if surgery is performed in early adulthood, prior to 4th decade. These concerns result from the multiple bowel movements after total procto-colectomy that impact social interactions. Preservation of the rectum is controversial and usually improves the quality of life by avoiding the consequences of ileal pouches, including multiple bowel movements and pouchitis. Development of rectal cancer in the remaining rectal stump is determined by the adenoma burden and can be as high as 50% in patients followed long term. The higher risks have also, more recently, determined to be associated with several specific APC mutations, (Bertario 2000).

13.2.3 HEREDITARY NON-POLYPOSIS COLON CANCER OR THE LYNCH SYNDROME

Lynch syndrome, described by Henry Lynch, after reviewing records of hundreds of family members with CRC over several generations, is characterized by presence of few colorectal polyps, far fewer than found in familial polyposis, thus the name HNPCC (Hereditary Non-Polyposis Colon Cancer Syndrome). This registry of familial cancers spans nearly a century and interestingly, in the 1930's, Lynch syndrome families manifested with more gatric cancers than CRC. The genes associated with HNPCC or Lynch Syndrome are actually several related genes, grouped as the genes for DNA repair enzymes (Vassen, 2007). The phenotypic expression is variable and the risk of CRC is in the range of 60% life-time risk. Other associated cancers are gastric, kidney, ureteral, uterine cancers and cutaneous sebaceous gland tumors (Muir Torre Syndrome). CRC in HNPCC are usually in the proximal colon, histologically with cells containing more mucin and showing diffuse lymphocyte infiltration and are microsatellite unstable. Mutations are usually found in MLH1, MSH2, MSH6 and PMS2 DNA repair genes. Microsatellite instability (MSI) is a general description of tumor DNA showing grouping characteristic of DNA short tandem repeats of GC/AT bases due to skips on DNA replication and faltered repair. Approximately 15% of sporadic CRC are MSI high, compared to others that are low or stable, and have all the characteristics of Lynch syndrome CRC. In addition to Lynch syndrome, other MSI CRC may be caused by hypermethylation of the promoter gene for MLH1, resulting in poorly functional mismatch repair proteins. MSI high tumors have more favorable clinical behavior, manifested with higher rates of synchronous and metachronous polyps, with overall higher patient 5-year survival, lower rates of lymph node and distant metastases, and interestingly, lower response rates to chemotherapy treatment, like 5-fluoro-uracil (5-FU). MSI high colon cancers respond to checkpoint inhibitor immunotherapy, while MSI stable colon cancers do not.

The index case, the first in the family suspected of inherited trait, should be tested first, especially if the tumor tissue is available for testing (MSI or mismatch repair enzyme). In other instances, the guidelines to test for HNPCC genes depend on the Amsterdam criteria. These guidelines have been revised to include non-CRC tumors including uterine and other gastrointestinal malignancies, referred to as the Bethesda criteria.

All CRC should be tested for MSI; if high, then the tumor should be tested for Lynch syndrome. IHC staining for MMR proteins can be used first as a screen for further gene testing of MLH and MSH mutations. These criteria for testing have been changing as the multiple gene panels are becoming more routine. All patients with CRC can be tested with a wide array of genes and the results may benefit the family members.

Lynch syndrome carriers can be screened for CRC at more frequent intervals. Prophylactic colectomy can be performed for high burden polyp phenotype, although endoscopic polypectomy can be an option. Lynch syndrome carries risk for endometrial cancer in the female, renal, gastric and small bowel cancers. Because of cancer risks beyond the colon and rectum, prophylactic colectomies may not be the best option for prevention.

13.2.4 JUVENILE POLYPOSIS, AND THE HAMARTOMA POLYPOSIS SYNDROMES

In contrast to the familial polyposis and Lynch syndrome in which the molecular changes lead to the clinical progression of adenoma to carcinoma sequence, the more uncommon juvenile polyposis and hamartoma syndromes, follow a less understood path to colon cancers and other extra-colonic tumors. Juvenile Polyposis, Peutz-Jeghers syndrome (PJS), and the less common Cowden syndrome, hereditary mixed polyposis syndrome, make up interesting presentations of hereditary polyps and cancers in the gastro-intestinal tract. The harmatoma polyps consist a mixture of mucosal, fibrous and muscular elements, and the hyperplastic adenomatous component can degenerate into cancerous cells, mostly located in the large bowel. The polyps present predominantly in the young adulthood prior to 20 years of age. Peutz Jeghers syndrome (PJS) patients have the characteristic of lip melanotic spots and Cowden syndrome patients have tongue polyps. The gene mutations, in Juvenile Polyposis, are in the BMPR1A and SMAD4 genes, that lead to TGF-beta binding domain malfunction which in turn misregulates protein transcription. PJS present with defects in the STK11 and LKB1 genes, which are linked to P53 and WNT signaling, and up-regulates cell multiple cycle functions. The harmartomas in the small intestine can persist throughout lifetime, but most regress during adulthood. Bowel obstruction secondary to small bowel intussusception and intestinal bleeding may require surgical intervention. PTEN gene mutations can result in intestinal hamartomas in the Cowden's and Ruvacalba syndromes. There are several poorly understood developments in the intestinal harmatomatous syndromes. How do the diverse gene abnormalities lead to intestinal hamartomas and then what is the association of hamartomas and cancer? Hamartomas could represent a disruptive growth of the niche cells around the epithelial cancers of the bowel, composed of mesenchymal cells. Hamartomas show growth of cells of diverse cell lineages, from ectoderm, mesoderm and endoderm. Intestinal hamartomas have smooth muscle, nerve and endocrine cells. Could the pathways to cancer, illustrated by the molecular basis of tumor development in Juvenile Polyposis and PJS, represent growth defects around the niche cells and their interactions with the epithelial component? Most neoplastic growths are driven by clonal growths of one type of cells, with clonal heterogeneity limited to the original cell lineage. Harmatomas, on the other hand, are disruptive growths of more than one cell lineage. The association of hamartomas in juvenile polyposis and adjacent epithelial adenomatous neoplasms brings up the question whether niche cells for stem or cancer cells can grow in unison to form hamartomas. This hypothesis is yet to be verified. Though, the intestinal epithelium carries nearly hundred-fold greater numbers of cells than the large colon, carcinomas of the small bowel are rare in comparison, approximately a hundred-fold fewer, mostly in the form of lymphoma or neuro-endocrine tumors which do not arise in epithelial cells. In the hamaromatous polyposis syndrome, the incidence of small bowel carcinomas is increased by 10-15 times, and interestingly usually does not arise in the hamartomatous polyps, but rather the dysplastic mucosa develops in the vicinity of the hamartomas. The complexities of the Juvenile Polyposis and other harmatomatous polyp syndromes extend to several congenital defects as well as propensities of tumors in the breast, thyroid, ovaries and other glandular tissues.

13.2.5 TP53 MUTATIONS AND THE LI-FRAUMENI SYNDROME

TP53 is called the "guardian of the genome" for many of the important central functions it plays and for the linkage with other important gene pathways, governing growth, apoptosis, cell cycle checkpoint, and protein degradation. In 1969, Frederick Li and Joseph Fraumeni described several patients with cancers that shared the germline mutation in TP53. Li-Fraumeni syndrome manifests in several cancers, breast, sarcoma, brain and adrenocortical carcinomas, being the most common. Other lesser known aspects include blood dyscrasias, melanoma, GI cancers and others. The specific mutation on the gene determines the predilection of tumor types. TP53 harbors large numbers of polymorphisms and most mutations are deletions and point mutations. P53 oncogene derived protein in turn modulates hundreds of other downstream genes and proteins. The mosaicism of tumor types gives clues as to which tumors to screen for. The Brazilian founder mutation TP53 R377H predominantly leads to adrenocortical carcinomas. The screening strategies include searching for early breast cancers, sarcomas and brain astrocytomas, glial and choroid plexus tumors which account for over half of the tumors found. Other prevention methods include modulation of p53 function, with small molecules, for example, PRIMA-1 and RETRA.

13.2.6 MULTIPLE ENDOCRINE NEOPLASIA

Multiple endocrine neoplasia is characterized by more than one endocrine tumor in the same patient, first described in 1903 by Erdheim, a patient with acromegaly, pituitary and parathyroid adenomas. The inherited patterns were recognized in 1954 by Wermer in a patient with MEN1. Today, several gene mutations have been identified, allowing for the diagnosis of these tumors at earlier stages. MEN1, Wermer syndrome, comprises of primary hyperparathyroidism, pancreatic endocrine tumors and pituitary adenomas. MEN1 mutation shows up as menin protein deficiency or defects. MEN2, Sipple syndrome, previously MEN2A, presents with medullary carcinoma of thyroid (MTC), pheochromocytoma and parathyroid tumors. RET proto-oncogene was identified in 1993, that encode a large protein transmembrane ligand with receptor for multiple other phosphorylation ligands. MEN2 syndrome accounts for 25% of all MTC (medullary thyroid carcinoma). MEN3, previously MEN2B is characterized by MTC, pheochromocytoma, marfanoid habitus, intestinal ganglion malfunction with possible megacolon and mucosal neuromas. MEN3 are much less common than MEN2, and their RET mutations are specific to the loci M918T, exon 16, and A883F, exon 15. MEN4 was discovered as MEN1 mutation negative patients, instead, carrying CDNK1B mutation encoding the cyclin-dependent kinase inhibitor CK1 p27kip1, a recessive gene inherited pattern. MEN4 syndrome is rare and presents with parathyroid, anterior pituitary, adrenal and renal tumors.

There are several biochemical markers or hormones produced by these endocrine tumors that can be used for screening and diagnosis. Calcitonin and CEA for MTC, parathyroid hormone for parathyroid adenomas, urinary or serum catecholamines for pheochromocytomas, prolactin for pituitary tumors and others that can be measured with a blood or urine sample. Familial cases can be screened with the appropriate mutations on the respective protooncogenes. In MTC tumors for example, advanced cases have high propensity for lymph node metastases, with corresponding lower rates of cure. Prophylactic thyroidectomy in RET oncogene carriers detected by early increase in calcitonin levels have dramatically increase the cure rates. Surgical approaches for adrenal and pituitary tumors can achieve good long-term results.

13.3 FAMILIAL AND SPORADIC CANCERS: RATIONAL DECISIONS FOR MANAGING YOUR RISKS

Family history of cancer is common, and sometimes kept a secret, with the rest of the family uninformed, trying to protect them from undue anxiety. It is common belief that changes to your genes and their behavior are random processes, a draw of the luck, not much that could be done about it. On the other hand, the apparent randomness of molecular changes has deeper mechanistic patterns. The high number of molecular hits, causing tissue degradation in its very microscopy dimensions, can be reduced by other molecular pathways, in the constant process of preserving cellular homeostasis. The frequency of DNA damaging events is in the order of 10,000 per day, in a single cell, and through hundreds of million years, cells have evolved solutions to maintain the integrity and function of their genes (Tubbs 2017). The molecular events leading to DNA damage and the cellular ability to maintain DNA integrity are better understood, today, and the science behind these wonders of biology will be elucidated. This apparent randomness of genetic hits can be modified to our advantage, by the very choices in our daily lives. Some of the daily choices in our diet, activities and environmental exposures will impact on our cellular capability to achieve homeostasis. Research in biological science and molecular medicine has given greater clarity into these matters. In brief, the cellular environment favoring DNA damage and mutations can be minimized while the environment for homeostasis and DNA repair be maximized. The underlying genetic basis, for tumors in the category of inherited oncogenes, was discussed in previous Section 13.2. Beyond the 5% of tumors with known inherited oncogenes, there are another 15-20% of familial tumors, leaving the majority of cancers in the category of sporadic cancers whose genetic basis are yet to be identified. It is thought that some familial cancers and most of the sporadic tumors are caused by multiple oncogenes. Are there any gene-based clues for early diagnosis and prevention of sporadic cancers? Each type of cancer is associated with a spectrum of oncogenes, some common to many cancers and others more unique. Fragments of these oncogenes can be detected in peripheral blood specimes, and become potential early markers for these cancers (Cohen 2018).

Although the genomics of cancer is a work in progress, the risk of developing cancer and how to reduce these risks can be measured, monitored and manageable today. How can we estimate our own risks based on the information of family and clinical history and on established biological markers? How do we proceed with testing and screening for known genes and biomarkers? These are questions that can be answered today and will guide our management of cancer prevention in the era of "more" precise medicine.

13.3.1 CANCER RISK ASSESSMENT

Tumor registries and population mortality data accumulated by SEER (Surveillance, Epidemiology and End Results, National Cancer Institute), IARC (International Agency for Research on Cancer), and others, have kept fairly accurate figures on cancer incidence and death rates. These figures can yield average personal risk for each cancer, i.e., 40 new cases of colon and rectal cancer diagnosed per year per 100,000 persons, can be translated into a more understandable personal average life-time risk of colorectal cancer: one in twenty-two, or 4%, in the U.S. These rates can be modified and personalized to the individual by incorporating family history, personal history of colorectal adenomas, gene mutations, tobacco use, diet, among other factors. The risk of 4% life time risk seems small and compared to other life events one is tempted to disregard these matters. However, a more realistic picture is that the 4% risk can increase according to our daily habits, such as eating a high caloric and red meat-based diet. The risk can reach over 10%. In reviewing available published information, cancer risk assessment could be a formidable task (Weitzel 2011), especially when the new advances in molecular medicine are incorporated in the calculations. A simpler and user-friendly nomogram has been developed in the field of heart health, such as in BMI, blood pressure, heart rate and cholesterol levels. A similar nomogram would be the ideal tool for cancer risk management, however, this has not been verified, though many strategies in cardiovascular health and prevention reflect those for cancer prevention. Currently, the risk assessment score differs for each type of cancer, however from the molecular view point and the molecular pathways leading to cancer, the cancer risk scores could track closely together for many types of cancers. Thus, the genomic and proteomic markers for cancer risk assessment, should be applicable across most malignancies and for the individual, these markers could initiate and point to diagnostic tests for pre-cancerous conditions and early stage cancers (Rodriguez 2018). The simpler cardiovascular health nomograms should also serve as a guide to cancer prevention.

13.3.2 WHO SHOULD BE TESTED FOR CANCER GENES?

You have just visited your close family member who have recently been diagnosed with cancer. In the family reunion, the conversation turns to other relatives, and you learn the past history of cancer amongst other members in the family. The anxiety amongst your family members is clearly seen on their faces and one of you asks about hereditary or familial cancer risks. Who are candidates for gene testing?

The medical community refers to the appropriateness of gene testing as the eligibility criteria for testing. These eligibility criteria have been worked out for each of the tests and they all fall into the 10% threshold range. For example, if you have a 10% chance of being a carrier for a cancer gene, then you meet the criteria for testing. The criteria for BRCA 1 or 2 breast cancer gene testing include: i) 2 or more first degree relative with breast cancer, ii) personal history or one first degree relative with breast cancer younger than 50 years of age, iii) any relative with BRCA mutation. In HNPCC, where family history of colorectal cancer and other gastrointestinal cancers can present in different generations, the criteria for microsatellite instability (MSI) and DNA repair enzyme measurement are spelled out by the Bethesda criteria: i) 3 relatives with CRC or GI cancers and others (uterine, renal, gastric) in 2 separate generations, ii) CRC younger than age 50, iii) MSI-H (microsatellite instability high) tumor in patient under age 60 or in any relative under age 60.

New genomic technology is changing some of these criteria and expanding the relevance of these tests for sporadic cancers. In addition, tumor markers, proteinomics will expand the techniques in detecting early cancers or cellular and even molecular changes associated with the pre-cancer stages. These eligibility criteria for testing will change with medical and scientific advances, and the established historical criteria and past benchmarks gene testing are constantly revised.

13.3.3 TESTING FOR CANCER BIOMARKERS

Biomarkers are biological molecules such as protein, glycoproteins, gene cDNA, RNA or DNA segments, SNP (single nucleotide polymorphism), or clinico-pathological entities, colon adenomas or dysplastic nevi, for example. Some of these biomarkers can be considered intermediate markers, as they indicate a degree of risk for developing a malignancy. These markers can also be useful in treatment and surveillance planing. A panel of DNA gene arrays, which signal gene transcription activity into mRNA, has been used for tumor prognosticator, or indicator of potential benefit from chemotherapy treatment in breast and colorectal cancers. Other biomarker tests can have indicators of other cellular characteristics, such as sedimentation rate, or cellular proteins reflected in the staining pattern by immunohistochemistry (IHC) of tissue sections. Caution is in order when interpreting these tests since normal or elevated results are relative to its value in sensitivity and specificity for a particular disease state.

Although the specific nature of the tests is diverse and evolving, the concept and the use of markers to characterize risks of developing a disease, and to characterize the prognosis of the disease, has been well established. For example, carcinoembryonic antigen (CEA) is a cell surface and intracellular glycoprotein shed into the blood pool. CEA was isolated by Gold in 1965. Embryonic gut cells express this protein as well as neoplastic and hyperplastic gut mucosal cells. This protein is also expressed by variety of tumors including lung, breast, gastric, and pancreas cancers and especially medullary thyroid cancers. Adult normal cells have extremely low expression of CEA. The FDA has only approved the marker as an ancillary marker, i.e., to follow progression or recurrence of tumor and not as a diagnostic aid. In clinical practice, the applications of CEA are helpful in several ways. In primary tumors, it can guide the work-up towards metastatic or metachronous sites; in metastatic sites of presentation, it can guide in finding the primary site. High CEA values would signal higher risk of metastatic disease, while CEA producing tumors in a metastatic setting, would favor GI primaries. During surgical exploration, a CEA-tagged nuclear scan, can aid in localization all involved sites of disease. And in the immediate follow-up after surgical resection, CEA levels can give additional information regarding the presence or absence of residual disease. In the diagnosis of tumor recurrence, CEA levels, especially a series of values showing slow elevation, are strong indicators of tumor recurrence. Indeed, there are plenty of pitfalls, that need to be excluded. When the follow-up test involves an invasive procedure or tests associated with serious risks, further care needs to be followed to exclude false positives. For example, rising CEA can be false positive due to renal insufficiency, liver dysfunction, tobacco use, and inflammatory conditions. Thus, to avoid chasing an elevated value with multiple diagnostic tests, first a true elevation of CEA due to potential tumor growth needs to be verified.

11.3.4 TUMOR MARKERS AS A GUIDE TO ADJUVANT THERAPY

Adjuvant treatments with chemotherapy have been accepted into cancer care after well-designed phase III studies demonstrated clinical efficaccy. The tumor stage and other clinical criteria predict risks for tumor recurrence. The benefits of additional treatments with chemotherapy become smaller for early stage cancers. Stage IA breast cancer falls into this category, node negative and primary tumors less than 1 cm in size. Oncologists have adopted the use of some tumor markers to identify an intermediate risk group, within Stage IA breast cancers, that can be considered for adjuvant treatment. This intermediate risk group could further be stratified into a higher risk sub-group that would benefit from the treatment versus a lower risk sub-group that can be followed without adjuvant treatment. Tumor gene-expression tests, using the panel of multiple gene mRNA assays, profiling a set of up-regulated and down-regulated genes, can discriminate between subsets of tumors more or less likely for recurrences. In colon carcinoma, stage II, T3 node negative has a 20% risk of recurrence and in several studies, these patients did not benefit from adjuvant chemotherapy. Stage II colon cancers with elevated CEA, pre-operatively, and especially post-operatively, have an additional 5-10% risk of recurrence. In addition, a gene panel can select a subset of stage II colon tumors with greater risk for local and distant recurrence.

13.4 GENE MUTATIONS IN CANCER PROGRESSION AND METASTASIS

With unchecked tumor growth, some tumor clones acquire further genetic instability and oncogenes capable of expressing metastatic properties. Tumor spread to vital organs such as the liver, lung or brain often leads to death. Histological appearance of the metastatic cell can bear resemblance to the original primary tumor with some signs of de-differentiation, meaning further degeneration of normal cell structural anatomy, with nuclear aneuploidy and cytoplasmic atypia. These cytological characteristics correlates with more aggressive growth and metastatic behavior. Experimentaly, the steps in metastasis require properties of cell invasiveness, motility and dissociation. These properties allow cancer cells to sqeeze between normal cell boundaries and penetrate blood vessels and lymphatic channels, finding the conduit to travel to distant organs. In order to survive in the extra-cellular environment, in the lymphatics or blood vessels, rather inhospitable cytotoxic environment, where the tumor cell is exposed to complement/antibody system and to the immune surveillance apparatus. The metastatic cells are well equipped and adapted for survival by arming their surface membrane with proteo-glycans capable shielding and escaping direct cytotoxic attack. On arrival to the host organ, the metastatic cell interacts with the new local stromal environment, establishing the ground work for survival and growth. The new host tissue stroma is adapted to protect the metastatic cell survival. Anti-tumor immunity is counter-balanced by immune suppression or tolerance mechanisms exploited by the metastatic tumor through inflammation promoting factors and angiogenesis (Blomberg 2018). In mouse experimental model, one could isolate different clones of metastatic cells that would only populate a specific organ, such as lung or liver, after tail vein injection of these cells. These events illustrate the seed/soil hypothesis, described by Paget (1889) and popularized by Fidler (1977), which simply captures the concept of the biological capability of the metastatic cell to end up in a distant organ and grow with a certain degree of determinism (ability to modify recipient soil, niche and tumor associated macrophages, TAM) as opposed to a random process of embolic tumor cells flowing into recipient vasculatures. The seed/soil concept stimulated numerous research projects in the field of cancer metastasis. VEGF (vascular endothelial growth factor) is one of several proteins released by tumor and endothelial cells that increase vascularization of the tumor mass and contributes to the loss of cell adhesiveness by action of stromal fibroblasts, through MMP (metalo proteinases) and other enzymes like LOX. Cytokines are released that recruit bone marrow cells that reject or protect the metastatic cell in route through the lymphatics or venules, through immunesuppression. In addition, the tumor evolves into multiple clones with varied metastatic potential by acquiring multiple oncogenes enabled by genetic instability. This same process explains the propensity of metastatic cells to grow at the surgical wounds, due to the local growth factors. Thus, tumor recurrences at surgical wounds can be due to circulating tumor cells rather than spilled tumor cells during the surgical procedure (often avoided by astute surgeons). Advanced or aggressive tumors with metastatic potential are more likely to have circulating cells from primary and distant sites that can then arrive to the surgical wound and grow to what appears to be a local recurrence. Resection of small and "early (non-metastatic) tumors" have higher rates of success with much lower risk of local and regional recurrences.

The molecular basis for the phenomenon of metastasis is complex. We can agree that the first step is the accumulation of multiple mutations, and several of which, drive the metastatic process. The driver mutation concept states that a dominant mutation is responsible for ultimate tumor behavior, as the dominant growth driver, and in blocking the driver gene mutation, will ultimately lead to prevention of metastasis and/or tumor cell death. Consequently, once the metastatic stage is reached, other mutant genes may overcome the driver mutation effects. These findings are a set-back to the researchers in the field of metastasis, as they were hoping for a simple and hopefully single molecular switch responsible for this event. For example, TP53 mutation can be the initial driver mutation for sarcomas in Li-Fraumeni syndrome. When TP53 is acquired as a passenger mutation in lung cancer, it can indicate poorer prognosis and higher likelihood of metastasis. Mdm2, a gene that induces EMT, epithelial mesenchymal transition, was thought to be the gene responsible for metastatic disease. Today, multiple genes were found responsible for the metastatic behavior for advanced and aggressive tumors. Accumulation of multiple oncogenes are found in metastatic tumors, in greater numbers than non-metastatic tumors. This is consistent with the stepwise transition of tumor cells with growth potential only, to metastatic cells with additional invasive and tissue disruptive behavior. EMT was first described in embryonic development, with epithelial cells losing polarity and adhesiveness, as in mesenchymal cells. Each step of EMT is associated with specific gene activation and protein function, as in E-cadherin calcium depent membrane adhesion molecule. In cancer, the metastatic property for the particular cancer is acquired after undergoing EMT related oncogene transformation. If a few oncogenes were drivers of metastases, then modification of these genes could then potentially lead to inhibition of metastasis. EMT was first described in the embryo in which several cell groups migrate during fetal development, as in neural crest and gonadal germ cells. It is interesting to contrast the different molecular pathways guiding this orderly migration in embryogenesis to that of the destructive EMT process of tumor metastases.

Metastatic disease leads to eventual demise and blocking or preventing metastases will prolong life and improve quality of life. Will oncogenic drivers and other molecular signals provide targets to control the metastatic process? Can these molecular pathway switches be identified? There may be clues in the clinical features of metastatic diseases:

1. Lymphatic dissemination versus hematogenous. Tumor cells disseminated in lymph nodes can be eliminated with curative outcomes in 30% of patients, after a procedure known as node dissection. These clinical findings point to one scenario of tumor progression, step-wise from localized mass to regional lymph nodes then to distant sites.
2. Hematogenous dissemination into solid organs can be solitary or multiple. Metastasectomy can yield long term survival in selected cases of isolated metastases, depending on number and organ involved in the dissemination. Interestingly from a "soil" standpoint, skin involvement carries a better prognosis than solid organ involvement as in liver, lung, adrenal, ovary or brain. This is true for different tumor types, melanoma and breast cancer, for example, even when lymphangitic skin spread is excluded. Estrogen-receptor positive breast cancer metastasis is associated with skin and bone spread compared to lung or liver sites. Can these clinical scenarios provide clues to the molecular signals for cancer cells to become metastatic? The cellular properties of invasion, also characterized as EMT, and other cellular changes as in angiogenesis associated with hypoxia, dissemination and finally growth in new tissue niche, are all steps needed for the success of the metastatic cell, (Pachmayr 2018). The molecular pathways are numerous, and key switches may be difficult to identify. Pachmayr et al suggest some signal molecules that can be targeted. HGF/Met and S100A4 are examples of key molecules that can be blocked. The molecular mechanisms to metastatic tumors were narrowed down to five key pathways. Blocking the tumor initiated immune tolerance is one

pathway successfully explored through the checkpoint inhibitors (Blomberg 2018, and Chapter 8). Slow metastatic progression is another biological behavior that is used for treatment management. Molecular marker for slow growers would be indeed helpful. For example, slow growing metastases may be amenable to resection followed by chemotherapy.

14

MOLECULAR MEDICINE, and cancer prevention.

The paradigm of cellular function and understanding of diseases is shifting from the anatomical to the microscopic dimensions of the subcellular organelles and beyond, to the molecular interactions. The study of cancer shows this shift through the terminology used and new findings in genomics and proteinomics. Molecular, precise or personalized medicine are commonly used terms to designate this change. This paradigm shift in the science encounters some inertia in the practice of medicine, i.e., in the clinics and in the doctor's offices. In the futuristic science fiction depictions, the doctor would place the patient on a special table connected to electronic devices and a large computer-like screen. After waving a probe over the well sculpted supine torso, data on organ function and tissue composition would appear on the screen showing simultaneously some internal organ scans, and quickly followed by bold print of the diagnosis. Treatment is quickly rendered through changing the electromagnetic fields around the patient or with a quick painless injection. No, we are not there yet, and many of the doctor's office have the same wooden examining table, the stethoscope, blood pressure cuff and ear speculum. This is in no way a denigration of the family doctor, but quite the contrary. The art of medicine practiced effectively by many aging family doctors, is still very much alive and absolutely effective. The art of observation, gathering patient's history, synthesis of physical findings and test results are essential in reaching the proper diagnosis and designing disease management with the patient and family input. The art of medicine is confidently displayed. This is the real personalized medicine. This endearing reference was taken recently to designate modern molecular paradigm that is capable of precision to the point of narrowing the treatment choices to the individual findings. If I were in the position to seek the best medical advice, I would want both, the family doctor and the availability of the latest molecular and genomic testing. In the last few decades, scientific and technology advances in medicine have generated significant new treatments, drugs and diagnostic methodology. However, the proper application of new technology requires a dedicated physician with a wealth of experience. The translation of basic molecular discoveries to bedside treatments needs well planned clinical trials. New drugs are approved by the Federal Drug Administration (FDA) after trials in volunteers to verify safety, toxicities and effectiveness. For example, the majority of new anti-cancer drugs, approved by the FDA, have demonstrated efficacy in the ranges of 15% and a few reach the 40% mark, in shrinking tumor size or keeping tumors in check without progression for average of 6 months. Some of these drugs are very promising, since their mode of action are novel and targets new molecular sites in the cancer cell. There are a few treated individuals that had remarkable results, and even complete cures. Yet, the overall improvement amongst all patients, and prolongation of survival are less than hoped for. This is not because of failures of precise medicine or new pharmaceuticals. This is a statement on the complexities of cancer and molecular medicine. Technological advances in medicine take us several steps forward and sometimes suffer a few failures taking the progress a few steps back. Minimally invasive laparoscopic or robotic techniques illustrate these realities. It is now the standard in gallbladder surgery, however in the beginning, injury to the main bile duct was problematic during laparoscopic dissection, until a few new methods were adopted. Surgery for intestinal cancers, in its early days, had instances of tumor contamination of the port site wounds resulting in local tumor recurrence. The problem was solved when techniques improved, and the choice of surgical cases were limited to less advanced tumors. In the area of genomics, the use of gene testing in the clinics is accompanied by a whole hosts of implementation issues, such as tests results interpreted without the expertise of genetic counseling. The costs, reliability, options in therapy, criteria of who should be tested, standardization of test methodology are current implementation issues. These are issues that are still pertinent to gene tests today despite over 15 years of clinical use. The breast cancer gene (BRCA) is a case in point. BRCA test can result in finding new mutations whose function are unknown, possibly non-deleterious or ambigous. The implementation of newer tests, and potentially ground-breaking ones, like whole genome testing, would raise many more scientific issues regarding the very meaning of new mutations (oncogenes) found, in the context of thousands of other genetic changes discovered.

Tumor DNA genomics is a good example to point out the applicability of the new molecular advances. Since the development of newer DNA sequencer machines and the publication of the entire human genome in 2001, the availability and the cost of DNA tests have significantly decreased. The analysis of entire genome for mutations in somatic and tumor cells has allowed a tremendous new insight into the genetic basis of cancers. The significance of large amount of data relies on computerized statistical methodologies and large data banks gathering genetic data and and correlating to clinical information, in order to understand the phenotypical expression of these genes. Large genomic data sets are being built, as the GenBank by NIH which is member of the International Nucleotide Database Collaboration, which includes DDBJ, the DNA Database of Japan and the ENA, European Nucleotide Archive. The accurate clinical interpretation of these new molecular changes requires the collaboration of clinicians with interest in genetics, molecular biologists with interest in clinical medicine, and computation analysts. One method of exploring the genomic database is by taking established clinical landmarks (disease characteristics, personal traits, biomarkers) and linking these known and proven clinical characteristics to a particular set of gene data. This has already evolved in the early days of genetic and inheritable syndrome studies, where a named inheritable syndrome has well characterized clinical landmarks associated with known gene mutations.

The number of DNA mutations in a particular cancer cell can reach into the hundreds and follow the concept of the mutator phenotype, i.e., in the process of a normal cell turning in to a cancer cell by accumulation of DNA mutations. This change creates evolving genetic instability, since the mutations weaken or suppress the DNA repair process, and up-regulates the oncogenes favoring increased growth and accumulation of more hits to the genome. With malignant transformation, the appearance of the cells and the nucleii will change to a more irregular shape with larger and darker staining nucleus. These changes in the genes correspond cytogenetically to chromosomal features of aneuploidy, an abnormal number of chromosomes. The link between aneuploidy and cancer has been noted over 100 years ago by Theodor Boveri. There are some noted exceptions as in yeast and plants, in which, aneuploidy and tetraploidy are consistent with normal cell function. Another exception is in Down's syndrome, trisomy 21, though associated with increased incidence of leukemia, these individuals have lower incidence of other cancers due to increased levels of anti-VEGF angiogenic protein which is coded by DSCR1 located on chromosome 21. Aneuploidy, the increased number chromosomes, results from centromere and tubules defects, that interferere the orderly separation of duplicated chromosomes during mitosis stage of cell division. Cells with aneuploidy and poorly differentiated nuclei are associated with more aggressive and faster growing tumors that eventually acquire membrane properties that will allow invasion into surrounding tissues and spread as metastatic cells, the ability to travel to other organs in the body through the blood vessels and lymphatics, and moreover survive the implantation in new organs. On a molecular level, the mutations affect growth regulating genes, TP53, RB, and DNA repair genes. Signature mutations have been identified in several types of cancers. Some of these oncogenes are associated with specific carcinogenic agents, such as aristolochic acid inducing kidney cancers with specific TP53 and RAS gene mutations. More common carcinogens, like tobacco by-products, are associated with CHEK2 and P16INK4a gene mutations in lung cancer, and exposures to UV light or benzo(a)pyrene chemicals have their own associated mutational changes (Brennan 2015).

Mutations in the genes encoding the tyrosine kinase receptor family, which include the epidermal growth factor receptor (EGFR), can be identified in several common tumors, and serve as clues to clinical behavior. These very targets can be modified by monoclonal antibody inhibiting tumor growth and used successfully in the clinics. A mutation in TP53, codon 249, indicates in patients with hepatitis, a higher risk of developing hepatocellular carcinoma, with 5 years lead time prior to clinical disease, on average. Moreover, this mutation can be detected in peripheral blood samples. Although DNA and RNA are quickly degraded outside the nucleus, small amounts of cDNA are detectable, including DNA products of tumor cells that could be used as diagnostic or monitoring tools. Clearly, access to tissue samples may require invasive means, while samples of peripheral blood are more readily obtainable.

The personal genome information can now be evaluated for every single individual. DNA obtained from white cells in a few drops of blood can be run through the NGS DNA sequencer and data on all the mutations in the somatic cell, the white cell in this case, can be read. The germ line genetic information is passed down from your parents, present in every single cell. Even though our DNA is 99% equivalent to other humans and 96% to primates for that matter, the 1% is what makes us unique. Some of the inherited mutations are deleterious, however the effects are only triggered by a "second hit" mutation, on the paired DNA strand. In the cases of breast cancers secondary to BRCA 1 and 2 mutations, the life time risks are in the order of 75%. The mutations that we acquire during our lifetime, combined with others we are born with, are the underlying origins of cancer and other diseases. How can we screen for these potentially harmful mutations and possibly reverse their effects? The inherited mutations can be tested in individuals with known family traits of cancer, covered in section 13. The sporadic cancers are not necessarily as results of bad luck, since there are known risks factors that can be altered. If significant exposure to these risks (exposome, section 15.1) has taken place, then certain targeted screen for specific mutations can be done. For example, current tobacco users with 10 years of smoking, can have their bronchial cells screened for 12 genes and checked for mutations. A high risk of lung cancer category determined by this genomic screen will then lead to further testing, bronchoscopy and lung CT exams (Yeo, 2017). The US Prevention Task Force recommends low-dose Chest CT scans for smokers 55 years and older with 10 years of active tobacco use.

Calculations from epidemiological data in cancers using age and incidence, an average of six driver mutations in the cell were necessary for malignant transformation. This view was challenged by Tomasetti (2015), who revised the calculations that three consecutive driver mutations were sufficient to complete the malignant transformation in lung and colorectal cancers. These authors used the new genome wide sequencing data on these two solid tumors comparing the presence of known factors of tobacco use and MMR (mismatch repair) deficiency in lung and colorectal cancer, respectively. This revision can be meaningful as treatments aimed at these driver mutations can be yield cures and provide insights into prevention of these tumors.

Complete genome analysis is a powerful tool to understand and accuratively characterize the cancer. Patients with metastatic or recurrent cancers have benefitted from genomic analysis, and using TCGA data to compare and identify driver mutations. Their tumors contained a mutation that yielded treatment response to specific targeted drugs (Gagan,2015). The future of cancer biology can be completely altered as genomics have identified approximately 12 major oncogene pathways leading to cancer transformation. The scaffold tissues around the tumor play an important role, as in the health of the stem cells. More on stem cells in Chapter 21.2. Genomics can also tease out the genes that synergize with tumor growth. The heterogeneity of tumors lay at the difficulty in devising a single treatment strategy, with drug resistance, tumor dormancy, recurrence and metastases, all moving in different directions genomically. This very issue can also present challenges to the molecular genomics approach (Li, 2014).

Prevention of cancer will be transformed by genomics research. As the normal cells acquire genetic mutations, they will transform into a pre-cancerous stage prior to becoming a true cancer. By eliminating these pre-cancer cells, one is achieving cancer prevention. Kensler, (2017), proposed a PCGA, pre-cancer genomic atlas, which can yield a diagnosis in the pre-cancer stage, and when recognized clinically, it can be appropriately excised, or eliminated by medical or targetted treatment. The micro-environment facilitating DNA injury and mutations varies between tissues, large bowel or the bronchial mucosa, for example, are subjected to ingested sources of carcinogens or resident microflora versus inhaled air pollutants, tobacco smoke or air-borne microbes.

MicroRNA closely modulates messenger RNA (mRNA) function in the normal as well as the cancer cell. MiRNA dysfunction as result of mutations, changes in target mRNAs, and availability of appropriate miRNA are essential factors in the progression of tumor from transformed cell to invasive cancers. Genomic studies of somatic cell mutations can reveal some key miRNA changes in cancer, (Bhattacharya 2013). Blood miR levels may reflect cancer risks and represent means of selecting individuals for genomic profiling or interventions with chemopreventive agents or phyto-compounds. MiRNA could be the second molecular rail to tract and modify tumorigenesis, the first being oncogenes. The third rail is proteinomics, which holds more promise in the therapy and intervention of the malignant cells. All three disciplines, genomics, epigenetics (micrornas) and proteinomics, in coordination will be needed to understand the molecular pathways to oncogenesis and cancer.

15

ENVIRONMENTAL RISKS: BEYOND TOXINS AND CARCINOGENS

Pioneers in the field of radiology, often did not wear protective gloves, and many developed skin cancers on their hands and fingers. Chimney sweepers exposed repeatedly to coal tar, developed scrotal skin cancers. Radium dial workers, who painted watches and clocks dials and exposed themselves to radium by licking their brushes, were at risk for bone sarcomas and mastoid and sinus carcinomas over the next 7 to 60 years. These are three examples of carcinogenic exposures among countless others that alters the cellular homeostasis in some specific and yet not entirely understood pathways resulting in malignant transformation of normal tissues. The field of carcinogenesis originated from these early observations of cancer development with strong association to suspected carcinogens. The path from carcinogenesis to cancer is classically divided into three stages; exposure to carcinogens (initiation), promotion (exposure to co-factors) and a latency period. These stages are comparable to pathological changes following exposure to a dose of infectious organisms leading to the development of the clinical infection and to molecular alterations leading to the classical two-hit theory of gene mutations. Histological corrolates of carcinogenesis stepwise progression correspond to hyperplasia, dysplasia and carcinoma. The latency period allows time for prevention interventions, especially when intermediate markers, both molecular and clinical, can be identified to aid in the understanding and management of the tumorigenesis process.

15.1 COMMON ENVIRONMENTAL CARCINOGENS

It is accepted that chemical and environmental pollution in our urban and industrialized society is reaching higher levels and the frequency of exposures is becoming commonplace. Air pollutants, water contaminants, reliance on processed foods, increased household use of cleansers, fire retardants on clothes and furniture are becoming difficult to avoid. Yet, some of these sources of carcinogens can be reduced and exposure to these agents minimized. First, we have to be aware of our environmental changes and what are the sensible steps to lessen exposure to deleterious agents. Electromagnetic wave emittors surround us, however their energy dispersion drops off by logarithmic rate of the distance from the source. This translates to lessening exposure just by staying at some distance from the source of radiation or electronic equipments. Air pollutants are more concentrated near major highways and manufacturing plants. Human activities are not the only producer of environmental carcinogens. Compounds that contribute to cancer and other ill health effects can originate from plants, naturally occurring radiation and pathogens. For example, chewing tobacco and beetle nut can cause oral cancers. Virus infections can lead to liver cancers, as in hepatitis B and C; and HPV is the main cause for cervical cancer. Many of our edible plants and fruits contain phytochemicals that have anti-cancer properties, however, there are some notable plant products that are carcinogenic. Aspergillus flavus can grow on stored rice grains and produce aflatoxin B1, that is linked to gastric and liver cancers. There are other mycotoxins that can contaminate foods, becoming of higher concern with climate warming. Cycad nuts that are consumed in Okinawa contains cycasin that is a known carcinogen. Animals grazing on Braken ferns have developed intestinal inflammatory disease and cancer and is consumed by the Japanese for presumed health benefits, (Sugimura, 2000). Obesity now affect 50% of adult population in Europe and North America, and is considered to be an imbalance of food intake, invariably associated with increase intake of modern processed foods, (Eskola

2019). Obesity increases the risk of cancers and other chronic diseases also through increased systemic inflammation.

Air pollutants from auto, coal plants and factory emissions can compromise the air quality. Air quality index (AQI) measures the level of air content of five major air pollutants: ground level ozone, particulate matter, carbon monoxide, carbon dioxide and sulfur dioxide. Levels below 100 are considered good air quality, and between 100 and 300 can cause problems to sensitive individuals, such as asthmatics, and over 300 are considered hazardous. Chronic exposure to increased air pollutants increases deaths from chronic lung and cardiovascular diseases, and from cancers of the lung, esophagus, nasopharynx, and gastrointestinal tract (Bofetta 2003). The acute effects of air pollution in terms of upper respiratory irritation increases at a level of 150 AQI, and these levels have been reached in many cities around the world, as in the USA, China, India and Europe. In Los Angeles, USA, for example, air pollutants are contributed mostly by automobiles and trucks and measures to curb these emissions directed at elimination of lead content, and improved fuel-efficient automobiles, have been very effective. Recent air quality alerts were issued due to regional wild fires, rather than from car emissions. Local air quality can be changed by presence of passive tobacco smoke. Indoor and home ambient conditions can change drastically by adequate ventilation and use of air filters. Another surprising source of air pollutant are the blowers used in gardening where ground particles and microbes can be pushed into the air. Increased deaths from other chronic diseases (cardiovascular and pulmonary) due to increased air pollution can be several times greater than deaths from cancer.

Notable environmental risks include some uncommon compound, like asbestos exposure and subsequent development of mesothelioma, a cancer of the lung and chest cavity covering, called the pleura. Today, asbestos is no longer used in insulation products, however, one needs to be attentive to other industrial chemical exposures, at work or at home. Drinking water contaminants such as lead, and other known carcinogens, can be of concern. Chlorination to eliminate microbial contaminant and its byproducts, TMH (trihalomethanes), HAAS (haloacetic acids), and agricultural pesticides can be found in residual amounts in potable water systems (Sciacca, 2009). Obtaining a filter for in-home use can decrease some of the drinking water contaminants. Dietary exposure to carcinogens will be discussed in Chapter 19.

15.1.1 ETHANOL, AND OTHER EXAMPLES OF COMMONLY CONSUMED CARCINOGENS

A common misconception of environmental toxins is that we are passive recipients of environmental toxin exposure, and ethanol in forms of wine, beer and spirits, is a good example illustrating that we can be willing consumers of mild carcinogens, which can be modified by our awareness of daily life activities. Other examples are part of our food supply as emulsifier, or preservatives consumed in small quantities, for the most part harmless, however over years, these organic compounds contribute to chronic diseases.

Ethanol consumption, even at low doses (one drink per day) has been found to increase cancer risks in breast, oral and upper digestive tract, liver cancers and to a lesser extent colorectal, (Bagnardi 2013). No association were found in lung and prostate cancers. The chemical effect of the two-carbon ethanol molecule should be straightforward, from a carcinogenesis standpoint. Ethanol is oxidized to acetaldehyde which is harmful as a reactive radical. Acetaldehyde is then converted to acetate, which is harmless. Several enzymes catalyze these two steps, ethanol to acetaldehyde to acetate, and their respective genes have polymorphism that renders different activity levels to their enzymic activity. For example, East-asians have up to 48% rate of polymorphism to gene ALDH2 (aldehyde dehydrogenase 2), and their rates of esophageal cancer amongst alcohol consumers are the highest. Acetaldehyde can react with DNA resulting with the damaging adduct 8-oxo-dG. The carcinogenesis full story is played by ethanol effects on other tissues with more indirect and chronic consequences. Alcohol affects liver function and hormone metabolism resulting increases in estrogen, estrone and DHEAS (dehydroepiandrosterone sulfate). Alcohol inhibits retinoids that participate in the regulation of cell growth. These secondary effects in the liver cells and mammary epithelium, in particular, increase the risks of cancerous transformation. Alcohol exposure in adolescents and young adults causes mammary epithelium proliferation, ducts branching and hyperplasia. Alcohol consumption has been correlated with increased breast density on mammography.

Other common carcinogens consumed in foods have significant impact in our bodies, nitrates, trans-fats, bisphenol A, titanium dioxide as a few examples. A 10% of our total food consumption in the form of processed food can increase our risk of cancers (Fiolet 2018). Further discussion of processed food and chemical additives in Chapter 19, Nutrition.

15.2 EXPOSOMES

The current concept of an individual personal environmental exposure in totality can be measured as the exposome, first proposed in 2005 (Wild). Environmental factors that stress our internal homeostasis, such as exposures to toxins and to carcinogens, alter the genetic molecular make up at the nuclear and cellular levels. Hence, your interaction with the environment leaves a mark on your molecular structural make-up. There are some unusual examples of exposomes determining some key physiological changes. For example, nutrients and feromones can determine the social role of bees, such as the relationship between worker bees and the queen bee, and ethanol consumption in mice can determine the fur color of the offsprings. In humans, the exposome has a role in many diseases such as obesity, diabetes, allergies and cancer. The exposome also reflects the exposure history from in-utero to end of life, much like the rings in the tree trunk or climate history absorbed into the ice in the artic and antartica. The genome in identical twins can be modified beginning in utero and this explains the phenotypic differences seen beginning in infancy. Cancer and chronic diseases have been studied in twins, in order to elucidate the debate of nature or nurture. The contribution of exposome and inherited genes to cancer risks, as studied in twins, is approximately equal. By characterizing their respective exposomes, the epigenetic changes to diseases can be better understood. The exposome can be interpreted through the accumulated changes in the methylation patterns in the cPG islands, microRNA transcriptional patterns, and other epigenetic changes. The changes to the genome itself include DNA adducts and mutations. The exposome can reveal insights into many forms of cancers. Squamous skin cancers, for example, occur in sun damaged skin, usually after many years of accumulated exposure.

There are a host of natural occurring compounds produced by our surrounding plants and animals that contributes to the DNA mutational pressures or may be functioning as promotors to other known carcinogens. Indeed, our own body excess oxygen radical production, reactive oxygen species (ROS), are both actors and promotors for mutations. Thus, the contact of our cells to the environment is recorded as epigenetic and genetic changes in our genes as the exposome. By looking at the genome in its totality we will have a record of exposome that help us predict and manage our disease states.

How do we take the exposome and give us measurable clues for our risk for cancer and chronic diseases? Much like the entire genome, all the clues may not be known, however we know where to find them and construct a practical gauge for risks and prevention strategies. The exposome provides a convenient map and guide to a trove of new information in tumorigenesis and the prevention of cancer. One possible marker that reflects the exposome are the ubiquitous microRNAs (Vrijens 2015).

15.3 ENDOGENOUS REACTIVE OXYGEN SPECIES (ROS)

Oxygen is a reactive gaseous molecule released in the atmosphere by the action of photosynthesis, and is a necessary element of aerobic life. The rapid proliferation of early life forms around the Cambrian period, 500 million years ago, is partially attributed to the increase in atmospheric oxygen. As a necessary element for electron transport and energy transfer on the cellular level, oxygen and nitrogen reactive compounds sustain life, and other hand can also destroy life. Early life forms have evolved complex mechanisms to generate ROS and use their ability to donate electrons and transfer energy in molecular signaling. At the same time, cells have developed an elaborate schema to control and neutralize ROS beyond its immediate sites of molecular signaling and protein synthesis, as in the mitochondria, around the membranes, endoplasmic reticulum, ribosomes, and lysosomal vacuoles. The importance of these mechanisms and their biochemical simplicity have been passed on and conserved from unicellular organisms to eukaryotic cells, plants and in animals. These are some of the properties that define and maintain homeostasis in cells necessary for life. Each molecule has its ideal range of numbers (concentration) and performance within the cell. Low oxygen levels fall short of energy transport to sustain life, and abundance of oxygen leads to excess oxygen radicals that degrade cell molecular structures. Despite these checks and balances, a small amount of ROS does escape into the nuclei and cytoplasm, where ROS can react with DNA, lipid and proteins. These altered molecules can lead to apoptosis, mutations, membrane lipids and cell adhesion defects, denaturation and aging of proteins. Innate mechanisms to control ROS consist of a variety of enzyme systems, such as catalase, glutathione peroxidases, superoxide dismutase, and the NADPH system. As mentioned, ROS facilitates the very cell functions of signal transduction, protein synthesis, and several ligand-receptor functions. The ROS supplies the electrons that are transferred in the phosphorylation of the ADP-ATP system, the energy source to run the entire cellular molecular machinery. Oxidative stress is the overall imbalance of free radicals, the abundance of ROS and nitrogenous radicals in excess up-regulates the production and function of anti-oxidative elements. Persistent oxidative stress will lead to DNA, lipid and protein deleterious changes (Gorlach, 2015). In turn, the deleterious changes to our building blocks (DNA, RNA, lipids and proteins) can lead to chronic diseases and aging, such as atherosclerosis, diabetes, build up of intra-cellular wastes, dementia and cancer.

When ROS reacts with pyrimidines and purine moieties or with the ribose backbone in the double helix, DNA adducts form, and alter the DNA configuration and intermolecular bond potentials. As a result, conformational deformities with base mismatches and breaks in the DNA helix occur. If not repaired, these events will lead to deletion mutations and transcriptional changes during mitosis (Maynard, 2009). DNA repair enzymes for the most part, excise these adducts and associated DNA changes and replace them to preserve the functioning structure of the DNA sequences. Excess oxygen radicals react with lipids resulting in peroxidation of the carbon double bonds, which are plentiful in PUFA (polyunsaturated fatty acids), present more often in animal than plant lipids. ROS excess can react with proteins in several ways, some as in the normal sulfur-protein bond reactions for signaling and others more permanent as in a carbonyl-protein bonds that can also involve lipid aldehydes, which in themselves are also reactive byproducts of excess ROS. These protein changes can lead to dysfunction, or worse, misfolding and aggregation into clusters with intracellular accumulation such as amyloid plaques. These reactions can be reversed by anti-oxidants combining and releasing the ROS from reversible oxidative coupling with tissue molecules, like in the cysteine-thiol moieties. This constant balancing act between ROS and anti-oxidant reaction is in active equilibrium. The imbalance in favor of reactive radicals occur during infections, inflammatory responses, acute phase of exercise, with malfunctioning mitochondria, and with overproduction of ROS. This fluid balance is referred as the redox (reduction/oxidation) homeostasis. The cells are actively sensing the redox homeostasis and compensating any ROS excess by activating the ARE (anti-oxidant response element) genes and proteins to provide the optimum level of ROS. Exercise, for example, generates ROS and at the same time responds in activating ARE and autophagy, the importat health benefits from muscular activity. A secondary line of mechanisms providing checks and balance of

ROS cellular functions and its potential damaging effects are the innate apoptotic system, located around mitochondria and cell membranes. It initiates cell death when excess damage from ROS occurs.

Chronic excess ROS constitute one of the causes of cancer and aging of tissues, dementia, diabetes, obesity and others. As ROS can damage cellular building blocks, if unchecked, mutations and build-up of intra-cellular wastes become the basis of continued DNA damage and cellular dysfunction. Conditions of chronic excess ROS are found in inflammatory conditions, such as high caloric and fat diet, hypoxic tissues, nutrient deficiency as in the lack of methionine in alcoholic hepatitis.

Reversing the effects of ROS with exogenous anti-oxidants can be demonstrated in controlled animal models. In human studies, health benefits of anti-oxidants could not be confirmed by controlled experimental measures. The end effects of ROS and associated products, such as DNA adducts in humans are difficult to evaluate, and there is no consensus on measurement criteria. Studies have used several methodologies in measuring ROS products and ROS molecular damage. There are no agreements on which endpoints to measure and reproducible results are lacking. Nevertheless, most experts agree with the hypothesis of health benefits in consuming anti-oxidants, especially from dietary fresh fruits, vegetables and nuts. Controlled animal experiments have verified the biochemical effects of ROS in diseases, cancer and aging and serves as a theoretical proof of principles. In these experiments, intervention with anti-oxidants have also shown protection from ROS damages in tissues (Samoylenko 2013). In human cancer studies, treatments with anti-oxidants have not shown clear benefits. For example, the CARET trial, a large controlled human study using tocopherol and carotenoids in lung cancer. The CARET study showed harm, in terms of higher cancer rates in the group of smokers. The selenium and vitamin E trial in prostate cancer resulted in no measurable benefits.

DNA damage caused by ionizing radiation has been a good experimental model. When a small dose of radiation is given, producing minimal DNA double strand breaks, a small burst of ROS is also produced that can be studied. In this experimental model, ROS was produced by hydrolysis on intracellular water, disruption of mitochondria and generation of organic radicals, including RNS (reactive nitrogen species). The effects of ROS can also be measured in a controlled manner. For example, DNA strand breaks, mitochondrial function, autophagy, apoptotic responses, and generation of anti-oxidants can all be observed in a controlled environment. The reason for the disparities between animal and human experimental findings lies in the complexities in the cellular control of ROS.

The dual role of ROS is paradoxical, essential for energy production for life sustaining molecular activities, and on the other hand, harmful to the very molecules sustaining the homeostasis of life. In order to accommodate these contrasting function of ROS, multiple diverse coping mechanisms are incorporated into the metabolic pathways of stress response, ARE (anti-oxidant response elements), autophagy and apoptosis, (Jia, 2011). Like the pathways to mitigate DNA mutations, anti-oxidant pathways are also multiple, redundant and overlapping. Similarly, a single cellular process of autophagy, which participates in ROS control, digestion and disposal of waste product, recycling cellular ingredients, anti-microbial and anti-cancer activities, may by default represent a good surrogate for ROS balance measures. In ROS homeostasis, autophagy eliminates the damaged mitochondria responsible for ROS leakage into the cell, also referred as mitophagy.

16

WHY PLANTS DO NOT DEVELOP CANCERS? Can plants teach us how to prevent cancers?

Multi-cellular organisms develop cancers through the same molecular mechanisms of genetic mutations and transformed cell growth as in humans. Mutations are derived from a single or multiple DNA nucleotide replacement, chromosome transposition or deletion, which can be inconsequential or be deleterious, resulting in modified protein translation, be it quantitative or qualitative, and a change in the function or structure of the protein. DNA repair, cell arrest and apoptosis or programmed cell death are very elegant and efficient solutions to mutations or DNA damage. These mechanisms counter the deleterious effects of mutations, and are necessary for life as they are conserved over millions of years.

Plant genes are subject to mutations and have similar apoptotic mechanisms to handle deleterious genetic changes. Interestingly, plants defy findings in most organisms, and not develop unchecked growth, such as cancer. Plants do develop benign tumors such as galls, burls and tuberous formations. Progression from benign to malignant tumors occur with uncontrolled growth and the acquisition of multiple mutations. In plants, the benign tumors can attain large proportions without evolving into cancers. The important point is that these tumors do not grow to the point of causing the death of the plant or losing a significant portion of its foliage or tree branches. Here caution calls for some clarification, since plants have an ability to limit its growth to an established portion of its system through apoptosis or programmed cell death. For example, a limb of the plant can wither or not grow at all, in favor of another branch that receives more nutrients, water or sun rays. Human cells use apoptosis, as a basic mechanism to combat cancerous cells. Cancers do eventually develop as a result of failure of anti-tumor mechanisms, not just apoptosis, but also mitotic arrest, immune cytotoxicity, activators of tumor oncogenes and inhibitors of suppressor genes. In plants, genetic control for growth employs similar molecular pathways as in mammalian cells. Apoptotic signals are probably more robust in plants, however, may not be the only anti-tumor mechanism that render such remarkable solution to the cancer question. More about apoptosis will be addressed further in in this chapter.

Cancer is a disease of older age due to accumulation of chromosomal insults with greater risks of acquiring oncogenes. Plant cells are subject to mutations, however the accumulation of oncogenes and genetic instability leading to cancer have not been observed. Some trees and fungal webs can survive thousands of years without evidence of cancer. Old tree trunks can sprout new shoots, deciduous plants renew itself seasonally with new growth, and seeds can stay dormant for dozens of years. These plant growth characteristics argue against the rigid plant cell walls hypothesis as barrier to cancer invasion and spread. In fact, there are many stem cell and cell growth properties that are common in both plant and mammalian cells as the epithelial mesenchymal transformation in early meristem formation, which can occur in mature trunk sites in trees. Old tree trunks, although the bulk is composed of acellular wood, have growing cells in the cambium layers, contributing growth to the bark and new layers of wood.

Telomeres represent a key growth molecular pathway that have been preserved nearly identicaly in both plants and animals. Telomeres have the identical tandem repeats in plants as in humans. Telomeres are located at the end of each nucleic acid strands of the chromosome, protecting the ends from reacting with other segments of DNA and also allowing replication of the gene, during mitosis, all the way to the its last nucleotide, as the telomere provides the extra length for the docking of the DNA polymerase, and other replication machinery, solving the terminal replication problem. The telomere shortens with each mitosis and at some point, the telomere length limits the mitotic process. The telomere-telomerase system has evolved roles in different growth needs and patterns, from the embryo and seeds, to well differentiated tissues, annual seasonal growth, and cancer. The telomere system illustrates growth controls or checkpoints that are quite similar in plants and in the animal kingdom.

Plants do undergo changes in their DNA due to mutations. Mutations, affecting plant leaves and flower structures, color and fruiting, were noted by Darwin, and influenced his formulation of the evolutionary theory. Darwin was not aware of molecular biology and the gene, however, his concepts of selective natural pressures that shape the genetic and epigenetic changes, hold true today. These phenotypic changes have been cultivated for centuries by humans in selecting new qualities in the flowers, fruits and grains. Tumor growth in plants demonstrates the potential for hyperplasia. The molecular pathways of increased growth are analogous to the mammalian cells as illustrated in the plasmid of Agrobacterium tumefasciens incorporation into the plant DNA. This bacterium found in the earth can interact with plants inducing gall formation. There are other organisms that can induce gall formation, including mites, fungi, and viruses. All living cells have the same challenges of keeping their inner homeostatic environment protected from the harsh outside environment with potential predators and invasive organisms. Multicellular organisms have developed varied ways of coping with the outside world from mobility to protective shell, skin, and hair. Plants, similarly, have developed thick cell walls, bark and especiallized root system to ward off invasive organisms. On a cellular level, some of these strategies are similar, and some are actually incorporated from bacterial and viral genome. We know it as our natural defense, the immune system, with humoral and cellular components, consisting of antibodies, cytokines, and white cells and other phagocytes. Once we encounter a localized or a wider infection, the foreign invaders are recognized by their surface antigens, and a brisk response is mounted resulting in the inflammatory response. Local infections, starting in the skin for example, will lead to skin redness, swelling, pain and eventually a pustule. The pustule contains white cells, invading foreign organisms and dead cell debris, all in the effort of containing the infection. The same mechanism is also involved in tissue repair and healing which requires cell growth and differentiation.

In plants, the reaction against invaders is limited to the humoral response, since the flow of phloem does not contain immune cells. Humoral components include axins, phytolexins, antimicrobial peptides, polyphenols. Plants have developed several chemicals, like cysteine rich anti-microbials, that are toxic to invading organisms. Penicillins are fungal products to limit bacterial growth. Another basic mechanism employed by all living cells are short strands of nuclear material known as microRNA. We will devote a full chapter to microRNA (mirR) since it plays many roles in the multiple cellular activities including in cancer and disease development. In the process of converting the genetic information into working proteins, the messenger RNA (mRNA) is generated from the DNA and travel to the ribosomes and lines up the amino-acids into production of proteins. Some of the by-products of mRNA are short inhibitory RNAs (siRNA) and can pair with the mRNA resulting in inhibition of protein production. In biology, several molecular pathways generate their desired response and incorporate an inhibitory reaction to attenuate the initial response, usually derived from down stream products of the same molecules. This regulatory mechanism paralells the first Newton's Law of physics, where for every action there is a reaction. This strategy is so useful that it is incorporated into the genetic information of all living organisms for miRNA. The difference between microRNA and small inhibitory RNA (siRNA), is that siRNA is derived from larger messenger RNA, while miR are coded by segments of DNA intron.

Despite our accumulated knowledge in human and plant biology, the abscense of cancer in plants is unexplained. Doonan, 2010, postulated that the rigid plant cell wall was a deterrence to cancer growth. However, this concept may not be the explanation since young shoots can grow out of mature trunks with thick bark and out of tumorous growth, like burls. Cell walls in dividing plant cells are not rigid. In addition, some botanists claim that rigid cell walls, impede cell migration and metastases.

As more scientists are now convinced that plants do not develop cancers, there has been growing enthusiasm in investigating plant unique ways capable in rejecting malignant transformation. If these plant mechanisms that reject malignant tumors could be applied to humans, this would be a major breakthrough for curing cancer. For example, plants may have a novel molecular pathway in apoptosis, that when induced in the human cells, could inhibit tumor growth. Plant cell walls may trigger signals to prevent EMT (epithelieum to mesenchymal transition). EMT in mammalian cells provides the plasticity of the embryonic stem cells in fetal development and also the transition of epithelial cells into malignant cells. EMT determines the capability of regeneration of tissues. In salamanders, for example, the regenerative tissues can grow into entire functioning organs. In plants, the meristem cells undergo similar transition providing the growth in seedlings, apical and root growth. Meristem cells when cultured can be grown into separate clones of plants. Plants do provide large part of our nutritional diet and provide medicinal compounds with anti-oxydative radicals, anti-inflammatory and anti-cancerous effects. MicroRNA in plants and humans, sharing much in common, may provide further clues into this phenomenon of being cancer free. MicroRNA in plants when ingested, crosses the gut into our blood stream and can interact within our cellular molecular machinery and thus, considered as a micronutrient and behaves as a biomarker of phytochemicals medicinal actions within us.

Botanists have long thought that plant tumors, such as crown galls, were equivalent to cancers in humans (Aktipis 2015). This biological comparison is incorrect, since plant tumors are more like benign tumors and rarely destroys the plants, and in fact, new branches can arise in trunk galls and burls. The thick plant cell wall and the acellullar wood were thought to inhibit cancer transformation. In fact, from a cellular view-point, the budding and growing portions of the plant, the meristem, would be most susceptible to mutations leading to a malignant plant tumor, however such occurrence has not been observed, though mutations leading to changes in leaf shape, pigmentation and flower formation, are commonly observed and taken advantage of by horticulturists. Comprehensive review of tumors in all multicellular organisms point to the common thread of disruptive behavior of the tumor cells growing among normal cells that disrupts the normal cellular architecture resulting from cooperative growth (Albuquerque, 2018). Oncogenes in human cancers are one of the driver mechanisms behind the transformed cell evolution into cancer. Only a few plant oncogenes have been identified, mostly associated with Agrobacterium tumefasciens, responsible for galls, elaborated in Section 16.2.1. Genetic instability, a hallmark of oncogene accumulation in human tumors, is lacking in plants.

As we lack a clear explanation of why cancers do not develop in plants, few molecular pathways, apoptosis, telomeres and EMT (epithelial mesenchymal transition), were reviewed to point out potential mechanisms that may explain plant unique ability for cancer resistance. Moreover, few plant products have proven anti-tumor properties in human cancers. Plant mirnas are among the candidates to be promising cancer therapeutics and explain the unique plant resistance to cancer.

16.1 MOLECULAR CHANGES IN CROWN GALLS

Crown galls and burls develop in response to invading microorganisms. In many cases of infestations, hypersensitivity develops as results of plant defenses and can lead to death or parts thereof. In other cases, the hypersentivity reaction in plants, akin to the inflammatory reaction in humans, activates several growth signals, initiating the findings of galls and burls. The dimensions of the tumor growth are proportional to the activities of the invading organisms, and even in the large tumors, such as burls, there are no reported cases of uncontrolled growth, leading to destruction of plant structures. This is in direct contrast to human cases, where chronic infections will lead to some uncontrolled growth and cancers.

Agrobacterium tumefaciens is a common bacterium found in soil and is responsible for generating galls in several plant species. Agrobacterium nucleus contains a gene sequence, referred to as plasmid T-DNA, as it is incorporated into the plant DNA, inducing the gall transformation. Agrobacterium plasmids have been used as vectors to introduce several desired properties in rice and other crops by using transgenic engineering (Gelvin 2003). Today, several other vectors are available for gene insertion into the desired plant cell. Several oncogenes in human oncology have similar counterparts in plants. The bacterium T-DNA transforms and activate some of these oncogenes, including roL1,2. Gomez, 2011, elegantly showed that many cell-cycle genes, closely modulate the cell reproduction mechanisms, and that these genes, common in plants and humans, are conserved with minor differences, despite having diverged genetically 1.6 billion years ago. In addition, activation of these growth genes in the meristem stem cells are responsible for increased proliferation rates. Apoptotic mechanisms were demonstrated to prevent progression in mutated seed formation. Transforming T-DNA incorporated into plant DNA, like Nicotiana, lead to spontaneous tumors, however experimental progression to cancers has not been accomplished. The retention of T-DNA renders some survival advantage, such as bulkier roots with better water retention during droughts.

The mutagenic and molecular entropy pressures on plant cellular genome is similar to that on human genes. Henceforth, the accumulation of oncogenes is a pre-requisite for malignant transformation. In contrast, plant oncogenes are few and associated with T-DNA of A tumefaciens (Lacroix, 2013), known to cause crown galls and “hairy root” in plants. Genetic instability in galls is not a hallmark. Multiple copies of DNA are common in plant cells, while aneuploidy and polyploidy are common in human cancer, aneuploidy in presence of polyploidy in plants is not associated with tumorigenesis. Unique tumor suppressor check points in plants may account for the absence of cancer, and these molecular mechanisms could be exploited for the human cancers.

16.2 DO PLANTS HAVE UNIQUE APOPTOTIC MECHANISMS TO WARD OFF CANCER?

Mechanisms that promote cell death are at the front and center in the fight against cancer. Apoptosis, self-programmed cell death, is the aggregate of all the pathways that lead to cellular self-sacrifice. This is a normal process in life, a process of "group cellular homeostasis", as a need to eliminate deleterious mutations, and as normal part of wound healing and fetal growth. These are coping mechanism for irreversible cell injury, wound healing and remodeling, deleterious mutations, starvation, or developmental attrition and normal immune-suppression. In plants, during the seasonal deciduous cycles, apoptosis slows and then stops the growth of new leaves and promotes the shedding of old leaves after much of the nutrients have been diverted away, (Keskitalo 2005). Apoptosis also slow the growth of the new shoots and growths in parts of the plant with less sun exposure and nutrient supply. In humans, for example, apoptosis regulates the embryo development in parts such as tissue between digits, avoiding a webbed hand, and in the terminal coccyx segments, eliminating the remnants of the tail. The transformed normal cell, in stepwise tumorigenesis, has to overcome many of its internal checkpoints to continue surviving. These molecular screens are like the quality control manager that screens out defective cells. These quality control gates are at every step of the internal cellular machinery, such as, DNA repair, cell cycle and mitosis, protein translation, and immune surveillance. Key genes and proteins are at the center of these checkpoints, such as the BCL and Bax (intrinsic process of apoptosis), P53, NFK-beta. Caspase degradation proteins are induced early. There are other (extrinsic) pathways including actions of cytotoxic lymphocytes (CTL) and natural killer (NK) cells activating TNF (tumor necrosis factor) and death domain receptors Fas, TRAIL, which all contribute to the apoptotic function, (Hassam 2014). Consequently, apoptosis is a key mechanism in eliminating the early cancer cell.

Plants have a more robust apoptotic mechanism. For example, entire limbs can be sacrificed to sustain the vitality of the whole plant, by maximizing sunlight exposure, through the apoptotic mechanism. In the development of multicellular organisms, mobility provided special survival advantage, in order to gain new feeding grounds and to escape predators. The locomotive properties of the organism are provided by the coordinated action of muscles, skeleton, and nervous system, that are all important for self-preservation, which in turn translates into inhibition of apoptosis in certain situations. Infections on the periphery of the plant branches, can be solved by allowing the branch to die off, not an option for mammals. Some of these mechanisms are hijacked by the cancer cell in maintaining its independence from apoptotic pressures. P53 is considered to be a tumor suppressor gene by promoting apoptosis. P53 mutations are the most common oncogenes encountered in human cancers.

Plants have to adapt to more extreme ambient conditions, in temperature fluctuations, in dry or wet seasons, and during scarcity of nutrients. Developing robust mechanisms in conserving resources, plants can survive in conditions inhospitable to animals and humans. Lacking the cellular component of the immune system, plants rely on apoptotic systems to shed infections. Apoptosis is the mechanism of choice to reduce or sacrifice cells for adaptation to infections and environmental stresses. Tuberous growth in the attempt at isolating or walling-off the invaders, is another method used. Agrobacterium tumefaciens, bacterium commonly found around plant roots, can induce galls in the root, trunk, stem and leaf system. A tumefaciens inserts its plasmid into the plant cell DNA and activates a host of genes, some of which are growth inducers, resulting in gall formation. This process also activates a complex cascade of apoptotic mechanisms (Hansen, 2000) and most likely limits the hyperplastic gall formation to a “benign tumor”. To date, there have not been any descriptions of these benign growths, hyperplastic growths, undergoing malignant transformation, into dysplastic tissues nor carcinoma.

Apoptosis studied in plants and humans, share many common genes, supporting the fact that apoptosis is essential to organisms, dating to period of the first multicellular organisms (Reape 2008). We postulate that some apoptosis genes or pathways are absent or repressed in humans, allowing tumorigenesis to proceed, and that, they are active in plants. Unfortunately, genes having tumor suppressor properties have not been the focus of research in plants, unlike in human cancer research. Hopefully, this will change, as the molecular biology of plant apoptosis may yield novel genes or compounds applicable in human tumor biology. This hypothesis is not far-fetched. Several phytochemicals have anti-tumor activities in human cancers, principally through increasing apoptosis in human tumors (Firoozinia 2015). Several of these plant compounds are produced as mediator to ward off invaders and pathogens. Some mediators of apoptosis in plants, ceramides, peroxides, nitric oxides, induce programmed cell death pathways in humans. Paclitaxel (taxol) isolated from Yew tree bark and needles has been found effective in treating ovary, breast and other cancers, by increasing apoptosis in these tumor cells. It is produced in the Yew trees to protect themselves against fungal invaders.

Apoptosis can be modulated by ROS, reactive oxygen species. ROS is generated mainly in the mitochondria, some at the ribosome, lysosomes and cellular membranes and is used for signal transduction and activation of molecular pathways, such as apoptosis, autophagy and immune reactions. In plants, photosynthesis in the chloroplasts is also a common source of ROS generation as oxygen is released, when CO2 is fixed into organic compounds. Plants and human cells are exposed to greater ROS under stress of extreme temperature, of radiation, of concentrations of metals, salts, oxygen greater or lower than homeostatic conditions. In the early phases of cancer development, ROS excess is common and, coincidentally, is an important signal for apoptosis and autophagy. This balance spells the importance of maintaining homeostasis and prevention of the tumorigenesis proceeding into clinical cancers (Petrov 2015).

16.3 HOW DO PLANTS DEAL WITH CHRONIC INFECTIONS?

Humans can harbor infections for years, called chronic infections, in a way where a stalemate between invading organisms and the host exists. Several examples come to mind: Hepatitis causing liver cirrhosis, Helicobacter pylori living in the wall of stomach leading to ulcers and Human papilloma virus (HPV) can infect the oral and vaginal cavities resulting in verrucous lesions. Long standing infections can lead to cancer, as in liver carcinoma in chronic hepatitis, gastric cancer in long standing H pylori infection, cervical and oral cancers associated with HPV infections.

Plants have the same issue of managing infections by viruses, bacteria, fungi and mites. By contrast, the ability of literally walling off the invaders in galls, and in thick woody shells is unique and not found in the animal world. The humoral mechanism in plants responding to infections appears to be paltry, while in animals and humans, the cellular response with inflammatory leukocytes along with the humoral response with antibodies, complement, lymphokines and numerous other plasma components, play crucial roles in microbial defense and wound healing. Chronic infections in humans that can facilitate changes leading to cancer, is essentially absent in plants. Infected areas in plants can be shed, be it leaves or a major branch, which circumvents the problem of chronic infections. Even in the uncommon cases of galls and tumorous growth secondary to infections, progression to cancer has not been observed. The underground root system, where there is direct contact with multiple soil organisms presents unique challenges. The close and constant contact with these soil organisms could be a source of chronic infections. In humans, the analogy is the gut interface with the gut microbiome. Colorectal cancer is the second most common cancer in humans and the etiology partly rests on the interaction between the microbiome and colon mucosa. The root microbiome, or rhizosphere microbiome, demonstrates remarkable degree of cooperation between plant roots and soil flora (Mauchiline, 2017). In humans, microbes can be found in association with different organs, as in the skin, nasopharynx and lungs, deemed in the past as free of micro-organisms. The presence of these apparent foreign microorganisms can generate host immune reactions, as in fighting an infection, or to a lesser degree as in chronic infections, and a third option in the microbial-human interaction is an interface with no immune activation, as in commensal organisms, the normal microbiome on the skin, in the oral cavity, and gut. In plants, similar association with microbes are found. Chronic infections in plants can be manifested as bulbous growths, also found in the root system, root galls, (Gravot 2016). Chronic infections in humans lead to a state of constant growth, as in tissue hyperplasia, that can progress to cancer. In plants, hyperplastic growth is controlled and limited, probably by more robust programmed cell death, apoptosis, and does not progress to cancerous growths. In comparing the immunity to foreign invaders in humans and plants, a potential fallacy like apples and oranges, the analogy of a battle is used and often a stalemate, truce and even cooperation is found. The absence of cellular immunity in plants is understood, and it does not place them at a disadvantage towards infectious diseases and possibly factor in their answer to oncogenesis.

17

MicroRNA and Human Cancers

MicroRNAs (mirna) were discovered in 1993 by Lee and colleagues in the worm C elegans, where the short 17-23 nucleotide segment of RNA were found to suppress the production of protein by inactivating messenger RNA. Anti-sense small segments of RNA binding to mRNA, and inhibitory RNA, siRNA, were known to silence transcriptional activity by inhibition and degradation of mRNA. This was demonstrated elegantly by Napoli and Jorgensen, in 1990, who attempted to enhance the violet color in petunias, by introducing additional copies of T-DNA of chalcone synthase. This maneuver resulted unexpectedly in a range of pigmentations including all white petunias. Later, the authors realized that the observed unexpected results were not due to "co-suppression", but rather, due to silencing by siRNA. In contrast to small inhibiting RNA, siRNA, which originates from break-down products of messenger RNA, miRNA generation starts in the genetic code. The precursor miRNA is transcribed from the intron segments of DNA and cleaved by enzyme complex Drosha. A second RNA enzyme Dicer cuts the remaining pre-miRNA into duplex miRNA that are passed onto carrier protein AGO and RISC (RNA inducing silencing complex), leading to the coupling with one or more messenger RNA, achieving the protein translation inhibition. The protein carrier complex is transported into cytoplasm where portion of mirna complementarity binds to the associated mRNA causing inhibition and depending on the binding characteristics, degradation of mRNA and miRNA ensue. Due to the incomplete complementarity, miRNA in humans, can bind to several related mRNA and lead to mRNA inhibition without degradation of the mRNA itself. By contrast, siRNA has complete base (binding) and is specific to its corresponding mRNA and leads to degradation. Mirna in plants carry exact complementarity to their respective messenger RNA, which is one of the notable differences compared to human mirna.

Mirna and the class of siRNAs, are probably one of the most significant discoveries since the DNA double helix, by Watson and Crick, in 1953. The significance of mirna will play out in the near future, especially for the field of oncology. It closely modulates DNA function. Mirna is more stable than other configurations of DNA or RNA. DNA and RNA segments found outside the nucleus, mitochondria and outside the cell, are immediately degraded by enzymes. Mirna, on the other hand, is more stable and can be measured in the serum and in other bodily fluids. In addition, mirna is exchanged between species and used for trans-zootic communication, interface between species, so called trans-kingdom cross-talk. For example, interactions between the microbial species and humans or between microbes and plants, have been characterized as adversarial. The exchange of mirna between species is fascinating and mediates cooperation and is one of the mechanisms negotiating unique co-existence between different organisms, as in our own microbiome, (Viennois 2019). Gut micro-organisms can become invasive, however can co-exist in a symbiotic fashion, and this unique behavior can be mediated through mirnas (Liu,2016). Similarly, in the Plant kingdom, the root system, embedded in the complex soil ecosystem, the rhizosphere, has several ways of interacting with the soil microbiome deriving mutual benefits and avoiding diseases. Mirnas are employed by plants to reduce microbial invasion and employed in agriculture crops. Transgenic RNA silencing of potato leafroll virus is used to protect potato farming from this leaf virus, (Eamens, 2008).

Mirna modulates the translation of gene information into proteins. This function means that specific mirnas chaperone each one of the myriad cellular activities initiated by messenger RNA translation. Mirnas modulate gene function without changing its structure, classified as the epigenetic role of the gene, changing cell functions, as in growth, basic housekeeping functions, and transformation into cancer. Other examples of epigenetic modulating molecules are histones, transcription factors and methylation of DNA bases which affect the helical structure and phenotypic gene expression into messenger RNA.

Mirna is conserved throughout the evolution of living organisms. Plants adopt a portion of the viral, fungal or bacterial mirna to use against the replication of the invaders themselves. Human infections are modulated by a myriad of mirnas, some specific modulators of effector lymphocytes and NK cells. Specific mirna affects the virulence of an infection, modifying the replication of invading organisms, their toxicity and the host response.

Over 18,000 human mirnas have been identified and cataloged in miRbase, and other sites, miRCarta, (Backes 2018). Mirna are more stable than other gene products that are quickly degraded in human blood and other bodily fluids. Mirna can be isolated and measured in tissues, serum, milk and urine. Consequently, mirnas are not only important in cancer biology, but more accessible for study and tracking through time. Nearly 10 years after discovery of mirna, Calin and Croce found mirnas 15a and 16-1 in the region of chromosome 13q14. Instead of tumor suppressor genes they were looking for, they isolated oncomirs, tumor promoting mirnas. This region is known for frequent chromosomal deletions, commonly found in B cell chronic lymphocytic leukemia (CLL). Since this first discovery of mirna link to cancer, hundreds of mirna have been implicated in oncogenesis, as oncomirs or tumor suppressors.

Oncomirs and tumor suppressor mirnas roles in the signaling and growth pathways that can lead to oncogenesis have yet to be fully understood. For example, mirna 34 transcription is regulated by P53 and in turn mirna 34 family down regulates P53. Apoptosis is modulated by let-7 mirna by targeting RAS gene, which in turn affects cancer growth. Mirnas are intrically associated with all gene functions, and more examples will be mentioned when specific tumors and their associated mirnas are discussed. Mirna 10-b regulates cell invasion and migration in breast cancer cell line and activates

RHOC gene, known to promote metastasis. Other mirnas can inhibit metastasis, as in the case of miR 126. Since the experiments on mirna are more feasible in the animal and in tissue culture environment, the significance and applications of these pre-clinical findings, need to be validated in patients.

All cancers studied, thus far, have aberrant mirnas, measurable in cancer cells or detectable in the blood of cancer patients, either in lower or higher concentration levels than normal. The group of aberrant mirnas are unique to each type of cancers. The differences in different mirna levels present an opportunity to diagnose cancers, perhaps at a very early stage, such as in polyps in the large bowel (Ahmed 2012). Table 17.1 shows a list of mirnas that are either down or upregulated in cancer, along the potential genes and pathways that the mirnas regulate. Mirnas have been associated with response to treatment and predictive of biological behavior, namely, propensity for metastasis and indicators of mortality risks. For example, the mirna let-7, one of the first identified mirna in nematode C elegans, plays a role in human lymphoma, and is a member of a nine mirna family, acting as cancer suppressors. They are downregulated in several cancers including lymphoma, lung, breast and colon cancers. Several mirnas play integral roles in the molecular changes leading to cancers of several different cell-types, and they are refered to as oncomirs. Oncomir 21, for example, targets PTEN driving proliferation and impairing apoptosis and also promotes genes facilitating invasion. A panel of serum mirnas can provide a pattern diagnostic of specific cancers such as breast, colorectal, lung and others. Most studies are from single institution and are limited to under a few hundred individuals and some far fewer. The studies are retrospective in nature and controls subjects are matched and not randomized. The panel of mirna range from few 3-5 to over 10, and the positive criteria established by statistical analysis, $p<0.05$. No sensitivity nor specificity are established due to the small numbers and that true negative has not been rigorously established. The real value of mirna in the diagnostic arena, will only be established, when asymptomatic volunteers are tested with the pre-determined panel of mirna, and the sensitivity and specificity of the test measured. In other words, the studies need to be done in a prospective manner. The sensitivity and specificity of a new test system does not need to approach 100%, since it can be used to select a higher risk group for a screening or diagnostic test, such as a mammogram in breast cancer or chest CT for lung cancer.

In the clinical setting, mirna can also be used to provide prognostic information, more specifically, what are the risks for the treated cancer to return as a significant growth, spread to other organs and cause death? In several cancer types studied, breast, colorectal, renal, that have been studied, an array of mirna closely resembling the panel for diagnostic capability, will also yield prognostic information, that can be used to employ additional treatment modalities, namely, adjuvant chemotherapy. This information can also be used for surveillance strategies, for example, how soon and how often, to obtain imaging tests or other monitoring exams such as endoscopy. Ovarian cancer is a case in point. Zheng et al have studied 360 patients with ovarian adenocarcinoma and 200 controls, and found 2 mirna, in particular, let 7f and 205 can discriminate between cancer and non-cancer groups, and continue surveillance with tumor marker CA-125. In addition, let-7f levels was associated with improved survival among stage III and IV patients. Malignant melanoma is one of the cutaneous cancers that when discovered at late stage, with deep penetration of the skin, can metastasize and regrow locally despite initial successful treatment. The melanoma characteristics by depth of invasion and lymph node spread, as seen on microscopic examination, can predict future behavior and risks of recurrence. Several mirnas (mir-214, mir-9) in malignant melanoma can signal its presence, especially in hard to diagnose cases, as in mucosal melanoma, which can be hidden in unexposed internal lining of sinuses, for example. Moreover, hidden melanoma cells that have already travelled to other organs through the venous route, would be difficult to detect. In these cases, mirna profile in malignant melanoma, would be very usefull indeed, such as mir-221 and mir-191, (Segura 2012).

Mir 122 and 221 play important roles in the tumorigenesis process and modulate the nuclear receptor HNF-4alpha target which also in turn induces proliferation, metastasis and apoptosis. The normal functions of HNF-4alpha include binding to promoter regions of several hepatocyte associated genes responsible for growth and differentiation of hepatoblasts during the embryonic stages. Mir 122 and 221 are among a group of mirna that are dysregulated during the progression of hepatocellular carcinoma and can be followed for diagnostic and prognostic clinical use. Mir 122 loss and mir 221 increase, along with mir 124 and mir 24, have closely mirrowed the growth or regression of liver cancers. Encapsulated liposome delivery of mir 124 and 122 have been used for treatment of liver cancer and Hepatitis C viral replication in liver cells (Cougelet 2013). The promise of miRNA as biomarkers of early cancers, or as indicators of molecular micro-environment conducive for oncogenesis could propel miRNA as the key diagnostic tools for cancer prevention (Dufresne 2018). A study among fire fighters miRNA profiles yielded interesting differences in subjects at risk of cancer, with clear implications for possible early opportunities for cancer prevention strategies (Jeong 2018).

Table 17.1. EXTRACELLULAR MIRNAS in Diagnostics of CANCER

Cancer Types	MIRNA	Functional Pathways
	Mir 21	(+) anti-apoptosis
Colorectal	Mir 29	(-) pro-apoptosis, dyslipidemia
(Chen 2019, Guo 2018)	Mir 141	(+) Mir 8, 200 homology
	Mir 125	(-) down-regulates IFN gamma
	Mir 21, 24	Regulation of p16
Breast	Mir 133	(-) Regulation of p53 and p21
(Bhat 2019, Hamam 2017)	Mir 92	(-) activation p13
	Mir 10b	
	Mir 145	Target angiopoietin-2
Lung	Mir 21	

(Yang 2019, Filipow 2019)	Mir 15	Target Bcl-2
	Mir 205	Regulates E-cadherin
	Mir 17	Target Myc
Prostate	Mir 185	Regulation of DNA methylatio
(Urabe 2019)	Mir 152	Target FGF, SOS, HSP90
	Mir 210	Regulate HIF2A
Kidney (Braga 2019)	Mir 378	Hypoxia, angiogenesis signaling
	Mir 7	NF-KB
Gastric (Link 2018)	Mir 148	Target SMAD2, CCKBR

(+) concentrations higher than normal. (-) concentrations lower than normal.

17.1 PLANT MICRORNAS (MIRNA): POTENTIAL ROLE IN HUMAN CANCERS.

MicroRNAs are found in mammals, plants, unicellular organisms including bacteria. Plant miRNA has exact complementarity to segment of mRNA and leads to complete inhibition and eventual degradation. Human miRNA, on the other hand has partial complementarity to their respective mRNA, thus enabling partial inhibition of multiple mRNAs at multiple encounters without degradation. Bacteria employ miRNA to blunt the host response and allow establishment of atenuated co-existence within the host. These interactions between organism has been characterized as "cross-talk" between molecular networks and between organisms. Bacteria, fungi and viruses populate our skin, gut and other organs and interface with our cells and anti-microbial defenses via miRNAs (Yuan 2019). The importance of miRNA in plants and humans is evident in the role mirnas play in normal physiological functions and in disease states as in cancer. In the gut, for example, miRNA from microbiota, ingested plant products, and from our colonocytes interact to determine composition of bacteria and fecal micronutrients that affect our general health and risks for neoplasia, colorectal cancer. MiRNA is surprisingly stable in different body fluids, in the blood stream, urine, saliva and milk. Strands of DNA and RNA outside the nucleus are degraded rapidly by enzymic activity. Stability of miRNA is also enhanced by carrier proteins and conveniently allow scientists to collect, measure and study its significance.

Plants in turn has used mirna to ward off some common invaders by modulating their ability to reproduce within the host, (Palaez 2013). Several animal and human cancers are caused by oncogenic viruses. In avian leukomogenic virus, for example, the retrovirus capsular protein fuses with the target cell and the RNA is copied into DNA and inserted into the host DNA in the promoter region, where multiple copies of viral DNA are made. In the latent phase, the viral proteins alter the normal cell mechanisms of cell growth, apoptosis and DNA repair, inducing growth and transformation of lymphocytes into leukemic cells. Likely, plants have evolved a system of mirnas capable of turning off the viral induced oncogenes and able to ward off cancers originating from other molecular alterations such as mutations.

How do miRNAs exert anti-tumor activity in the plant kingdom? Plant small regulatory RNAs and mirnas have similarities as in humans, and when ingested the plant mirna are active in the human cells and plasma. Plant mirna have numerous roles in plant physiology. We have grappled with the hypothesis that programmed cell death pathways in plants responsible for the absence of cancer in plants, could potentially be applicable in human cancer treatment. In fact, several phytochemicals have been found to have anti-tumor activity in humans, through apoptotic enhancement in cancer cells. In Arabidopsis root galls during nematode infestation, several mirna are increased or suppressed during the tumorigenesis, with close coordination gene activation and deregulation (Cabrera 2016). In humans, several classes of microRNA have been identified in close association with apoptotic pathways involved in various dieseases and cancer (Yang 2009). Structure similarities in human and plant microRNA, including functions, have been found implicating the evolutional conservation of these important molecular pathways in life (Arteaga-Vasquez 2006). Plant products is the majority of our food consumption and health promoting benefits of certain fruits and vegetables are well established including their direct molecular effects on human microRNAs. Nutritional plant science has narrowed these ingredients to phytochemicals and their modulation of our microRNAs (Lin 2017). A further progress is to trace these effects from plant microRNA to human microRNA (Bellato 2019). Plant mirna may well be the ideal biomarker for phytochemicals with potential anti-tumor activities and become the holy grail for cancer preventive diet.

Returning to the concept of tumor development, common to both plants and vertebrates, the struggle for survival of all living organisms is centered around keeping different invading organisms at bay, be it viruses, bacteria, insects or other parasites. The evolution of armaments in this struggle are common to most species, such as the immune system, activation of products capable of eliminating the invaders such as antibodies, and a host of noxious products, in plants. One notable difference in the immune system of plants is the lack of the cellular immune component, namely the neutrophils, NK cells, macrophages and lymphocytes. The limitation in the inflammatory response and allowing the invaders succeed in a limited capacity is a useful strategy considering that in plants one can literally sacrifice their limbs. This strategy has been abandoned by the vertebrates for the obvious advantage of self-mobility. With this evolutionary requirement, the humans also inherited the consequences of chronic inflammation, collagen vascular diseases, and an important venue for cancer development.

Another common evolutionary problem, second to the above discussion of invasive organisms, are the internal insults on the molecular homeostasis, including the genetic backbone, the DNA, by reactive radicals, mainly ROS, and other mutagenic assaults. The changes leading to poor cellular function would be self-limited, leading to aging and cell loss. However, the changes that lead to increased growth as in tumors and eventually cancers, can also lead to eventual death of the organisms or the patient. We have made a case for special mechanisms in plants to explain the absence of cancers, pointing to the robustness of apoptosis and miRNA in plants. MiRNA as a messenger in cross-talk between molecular anti-tumor mechanisms, can be an intriguing mediator from plant to humans modulating cellular physiology including interacting with protooncogenes, oncogenes and tumor suppressor genes (Li, 2018).

18

Nature's solution to cancer. Individuals and animals with lower rates of cancer.

Cancer has been diagnosed in all species of mammals, in birds, fish, reptiles and amphibians. Molecules supporting life are under pressure of oxidative stress, structural damage and in the case of DNA backbone, mutations. These molecular changes result in cell aging, death (apoptotic or necrotic), dysfunction (illnesses) or cancer. All cells evolved mechanisms to minimize damage to their internal collection of biomolecules, functioning in homeostatic balance. In this context, chronic illnesses, cancer and aging are not random occurrences, but a result of successful or failed cellular functions. Cancer has been characterized as a "roll of the dice" as the gene mutations resulting in malignant transformation occur in a random fashion. From molecular viewpoint, the laws of entropy are a fact of life, and overcome by molecular pathways that defines living organisms. Multicellular organisms have evolved elegant mechanisms to compensate the constant mutagenic pressures on their genome. The human body constitutes an ecosystem of its own and certain conditions can lessen the frequency of gene damage and mutations. Epidemiological studies point to individuals with lower cancer rates, as in some individuals with special diets, vegetarian, meditarranean or the hunter- gatherer diets (Key 2004). More discussion in the role of diet and genetic health, later as a segue to the next chapter 19, on nutrition. A gene mutation, refered also as a genetic hit, can be random and unpredictable, however, this is only one aspect of the cancer story. The molecular basis of biological events or the inner cellular machinery of molecular pathways can be channeled or altered by gene repair mechanisms, cell growth signals, cell death or arrest pathways and so on. In addition, a single hit eventual target site is unpredictable, however the innumerable intracellular molecules and their interactions as an ecosystem are very predictable and follow observed events of biological sciences. Let us look into nature's solution to the cancer questions, not just in plants, but also in the example of the naked rat mole, Peto's paradox and humans with exceptional lower rates of cancer.

18.1 CANCER RESISTANCE: THE NAKED MOLE RAT

The naked rat mole is a rodent living underground in large colonies with remarkable qualities, such as surviving much longer than comparable member of the specie, by a factor of 10, and being free of cancer except for some rare reports (Gorbunova 2014). Surprisingly, these animals can survive much longer under oxygen deprivation, and able to switch to glycolytic metabolism. The laboratory mouse and rat have been the work-horse experimental animals for cancer research and not surprisingly when a cousin rodent, as the naked mole rat is able to defy the well studied oncogenic mechanisms, scientists take notice. The entire genome for the naked mole rat has been deciphered and compared to that of the rat, and the oncogenic pathways were investigated and contrasted. The ideal finding is to pinpoint a single "master" gene that would explain the cancer resistance in the mole that could potentially be applied to the human cancer problem. In fact, what was found were family of genes in several pathways forming a network of genes (Lewis, 2016). In many ways, this finding is conforting, since cellular mechanisms are richly redundant, intertwined and inter-dependent; a true characteristic of an ecosystem in molecular pathways evolved over million of years. For example, the naked rat mole was found to manufacture a different large mucinous material called hyaluronic acid (HA). HA is produced in abundance, to allow a pliable wrinkled skin, which is best adaptable for underground tunnel activities. HA occupies the cellular interstitial spaces and can affect inter-cellular signaling and the stromal tissue feedback in the cell growth. HA in the naked mole rat could be the key compound accounting for the cancer resistance. In addition, the diet of the naked mole rat consists predominantly of plant roots that contributes to the anti-cancer story. Plant products contain a variety of phytochemicals known for their anti-cancer properties. Plant based diets are associated with lower cancer rates (Lanou 2011). Elephants who are primarily vegetarians, are studied for their low cancer rates in the context of Peto's Paradox.

18.2 PETO'S PARADOX

Richard Peto is a statistical epidemiologist from University of Oxford, who in 1977, proposed the hypothesis that cancer rates among different species should vary according to mass size and life expectancy, i.e., number of cells at risk for mutational changes. Herein, lies the paradox that observation in nature shows the contrary. Humans have a lower rate of cancer than rodents, despite a 1,000-fold greater number of cells. Similarly, elephants and whales' risks for cancer are lower than humans (Nunney 2016). The explanation for this paradox is that evolution is able to provide the solution, otherwise, these large mammals could not exist. The genetic basis of these molecular pathways has developed "cancer resistance" solutions that can overcome the random and relentless battering of the DNA structures. For example, elephant cells have been found with multiple copies of P53 genes which are tumor suppressor genes (Caulin 2011). In general, smaller mammals' life span is shorter, reproduce at greater numbers and have developed fewer protection against DNA damage and mutations. According to Peto's hypothesis of cancer rates, animals with greater numbers of cells will succumb to cancer at greater rates, hence the evolutionary pressure to select effective tumor suppressor genes.

18.3 CANCER RESISTANCE IN DOWN SYNDROME AND LARON DWARFISM.

Down's syndrome (DS) occurs in one of 800 births in the U.S. and is associated with several birth defects; variable mental retardation, heart defects, and extra 21 chromosome, trisomy 21. DS individuals are surviving into their sixth decade and is becoming clear that risk for solid tumors are significantly lower (Xavier 2009). DS has higher rates of childhood leukemia and testicular cancers. Genes on chromosome 21, are up-regulated, and genes DSCR-1 and DYRK1A can explain the cancer resistance from anti-angiogenesis to interferon response (Elshimali 2012). The cancer story from angiogenesis point of view was explored by the pediatric surgeon Judah Folkman (1933-2008), when working with tumor growth in organ explants in culture, and noted the appearance of new vessels as a requirement for tumor growth. He pursued the molecular signals for this angiogenic phenomenon and identified several angiogenic and anti-angiogenic factors. These molecules and their receptors are natural targets for pharmacologic blocking agents that are used today in the clinics, in order to modify tumor growth and to treat diabetic retinopathy.

Laron syndrome is characterized by mutations in the growth hormone (GH) receptor, resulting in smaller stature, high levels of GH and low levels of insulin and of insulin growth factor (IGF). Absence of diabetes and cancer (1% rate versus 20% rate in non-affected relatives) are features of interest in these individuals. Truncal obesity without diabetes in these individuals is paradoxical and not understood. The molecular defect in Laron syndrome may point to potential pathways that could prevent cancer. Caloric restriction results in longevity and lower cancer rates in humans and experimental animals. Metabollic studies revealed some interesting links with diabetes, sugar metabolism, insulin and insulin growth factor (IGF), and growth hormone (GH). Lower levels of IGF is associated with low BMI, relatively active muscle mass, alertness, and lower cholesterol levels. The molecular pathways impacted by these metabolic changes involve maintenance of interleukins and immune response, usually at normal levels compared to responses associated with older age, diabetes and obesity. Other affected pathways are maintenance of the oxidative balance, shock response proteins, and growth responses. Laron syndrome resistance to cancer and increased longevity paralell the findings in caloric restriction studies that are also associated with low levels of IGF. As the metabolic contributions to health and specifically to cancer and aging are analysed, GF, IGF, obesity, diabetes, and glycolysis are all potential players, as discussed in the next chapter 19, Nutrition. Indeed, the additional factor is autophagy which is also linked to glucose and amino acid balance, through fasting and exercise, discussed in chapter 20. The interdependent roles of IGF, GH, nutritional metabolism, physical activity that impact mutagenesis and oncogenesis, could be exploited for cancer treatment. For example, in blocking GF receptors, with pegvisomant (used in the treatment of acromegaly), it was found to have anti-tumor activity against breast cancer (Janecka 2016).

18.4 ANTI-TUMOR SECRETS IN CENTENARIANS?

Numerous investigations have been launched to study the secrets responsible for longevity in centenarians. This search for answers or secrets to longevity could lead to the real "fountain of youth" or to a simple answer, such as a diet rich in beans. Others are content to join the scientific nihilistic camp and ascribe the individuals living past 100 years as being lucky. Studies do show that longevity is associated with fewer chronic illnesses and lower incidence of cancer (a no brainer). Genome wide studies have identified several genes exerting special activities in centenarians, including APOE, IGF-1, DNA repair and hTERT (Serbezov 2018). It is not surprising that these proteins play important roles in longevity, APOE being a transport moiety for lipids, IGF-1 sits at the center of sugar and fat metabolism, hTERT a constitutive component of telomere modulation of mitotic activity and DNA repair a necessary maintenance tool of genetic information. All genes and metabolic pathways, in one way or another, allow the cell to maintain molecular homeostasis and allow a quick return cellular integrity after different forms of stresses and disruptions. The wear and tear of normal living and the heretofore mentioned stresses lead to aging, chronic diseases and acquisition of oncogenes, through mutations, and eventual cancers. The individuals reaching a rather extreme older age, the centenarians, by definition, have solved many of the molecular endpoints of chronic diseases, aging and cancer, which we have weaved together as a group of molecular diseases as result of molecular degradation and genetic mutations. Thus far, scientistists have not unraveled the nature's molecular formula to achieve longevity, to the point where science could recommend a treatment with reproducible results of good health in older age. Some of these pathways may be a seamless sequence of DNA repair, autophagy or apoptosis among the many molecular functions the cell has at its disposal. Some of these pathways may require minor "tweeking" in order to treat or prevent cancer in the vast majority of us. There is one centenarian for over 4,000 seniors over 60 years of age. This fact could give confort for most of us who are expected to be diagnosed with cancer. One is reminded that studies on certain diets and programs including physical activities have shown health benefits for older age and in decreasing cancer risks, more discussions in the next chapters on nutrition and exercise.

19

NUTRITION

"Don't eat less, just eat right,
and eat healthy". (author unknown)

Balanced diet is the basic mantra of nutrition experts. Essentials of a balanced diet include grains, meat, fish, vegetables, fruits, nuts and dairy products. Though nutrients consisting of only rice and beans can sustain the human body, a variety of foods can provide the best guarantee of sufficient essential amino acids, starches, fats, vitamins and multitude of other elements deemed best for a healthy existence. The science of nutrition is based on the biochemical classification of essential foods, which are, in general terms: starches or sugars, protein or amino acids, fats or lipids, nucleic acids, vitamins, rare elements, and other micronutrients.

Several measures of population health including longevity and low incidence of common illnesses have been attributed to improved medical delivery systems. However, the major contributors to improved health in most populations around the world, are indeed due to improved nutrition and hygiene, namely the access to clean water, adequate waste disposal and sufficient foods. Good nutrition takes on many meanings depending on which aspect is emphasized. As an example, the lack of food insecurity, balanced diet, pleasure of sharing and consuming food in a social setting are different aspects of good nutrition. The personal connection between food consumption and production, has been generally lost in the modern era. Not more than a generation ago, we had amongst our peers, a farmer or a grocer close to the source of food production. Since, we have favored convenience over traditional whole foods and preparation methods. In addition, food advocates in the immediate post-war era convinced households that new techniques in food processing to purify the food elements were superior to whole and fresh foods. The attraction to this new process came along with the allure of modernization, with new kitchens, stoves, refrigerators and cleaning accessories. Nutrition sciences, in the post-war era of modernization, largely ignored the importance of micronutrients in the whole fresh vegetables, for example. Extracts of fruits and vegetables provided in cans and plastic containers were advertised as "improved" while much of numerous micronutrients were lost. The obesity epidemic, followed by the increase in diabetes and cardiovascular diseases, can be traced to this time, and began with increase consumption of processed foods, rather than the widely believed increase in caloric consumption.

19.1 ELEMENTS OF NUTRITION: WHAT IS THE BEST FORMULATION FOR GOOD NUTRITION?

We will make our starting point of discussion the recommendation by the US Department of Agriculture on the food pyramid, issued in 1952. The emphasis on balanced diet was simply the consumption of all components on the chart (grains, beans and starches; dairy products; vegetable and fruits; meats, and proteins), more of the components on the bottom of the pyramid such as starches and grains, as compared to the top of the pyramid such as animal protein, or meat. Healthy eating index has been proposed few decades later, to encourage improved eating habits, however, its complexity prevented its wide use. As the obesity epidemic took hold in this country and in the rest of the world, the diagram was revamped with a circular plate of macronutrients without emphasizing quantities or quality. As we will see from our analysis of recent studies, the culprit for some of the modern-day diseases, obesity, diabetes and heart disease, may not be the quantity but rather the types of food, especially processed foods. Macronutrients are the elements of nutrition that are used as fuel to run the body machinery, on a daily basis, such as starches, proteins, fats, and water, while, micro-nutrients are elements that are required for "fine tuning" of the system, such as iron. Iron is incorporated in hemoglobin for oxygen transport and in several enzymes. Other micronutrients include vitamins, minerals (calcium, zinc, copper, magnesium, etc), some of which can be considered essential, as relative deficiencies can result in disease states. Some elements of macronutrients, such as essential amino-acids, which include histidine, leucine, isoleucine, lysine, methionine, phenylalanine, valine, tryptophan and threonine, are rarely a source of deficiencies, since most protein sources include these essential amino acids, including vegan diets.

Recommendations for a balanced diet or good nutrition do not specify exact amounts of macro and micronutrients. The range of quantities of macro and micronutrients intake is usually wide enough to encompass the diversity of body habitus, and physical activity. The minimum requirements of food components and higher toxic limits are usually not an issue. The plain truth is that there is no general agreement as to specific standards in diets, amounts, and which combinations of foods are better than others. Most cultures have specific ways of food preparations, different amounts of macronutrients such as starches, whether based on rice, potatoes, wheat, or corn. Fat consumption differ by use of plant or animal based, or whether is combined with different uses of spices, or vegetables. The common elements of good diet from different parts of the world, is the use of wide variety of foods and sources of nutrients that fulfill the criteria of a balanced diet. There are essentially no standards in ways of measuring the endpoints of nutrition. For example, for an athlete, the measure of good nutrition would be different than the needs for intense mental exercises, such as for students prior to a major school exam. In the case of athletic endeavor, one could use weight lifting or speed in a race as the measurement criterium; and for a college exam, brain MRI can be used for a few mental calculations. These measurements or studies are designed narrowly to illustrate a metabolic or a digestive process and usually difficult to generalize to our daily nutritional needs. The nutritional intake is usually measured as grams of certain ingredient, whether being macro or micronutrients. These measures, though precise, may not be sufficient to compare across different nutrients. For example, different nutrition sources have different nutritional values, i.e., starches from taro roots are digested differently than starches from wheat flour. Through our discourse on nutrition, we will demonstrate that the notion of refined foods is antithetic to good nutrition. Whole foods in the form of fresh potatoes, corn on the cob or ripe fruits, have higher nutritional value and contain elements that are lost in the process of refinement or packaging for convenient consumption and storage.

The end point measurement of a good nutritious diet has escaped most investigators. Practically, body weight, energy level, sense of well being could be measurable end points to judge the quality of nutrition. Biochemical measurement of blood electrolytes and metals, such as sodium, chloride, potassium, iron, zinc and vitamin levels would give hints of disease states, but not useful measurements of nutritional quality. In order to measure or achieve a menu of good nutrition, we need to agree on the definition of good nutrition. The definition would encompass several concepts of good foods, health and well being. If we narrow the scope of analysis, i.e., looking at what kind of diets are best for specific health conditions, for example, minimizing heart disease, obesity, diabetes, or cancer, we find greater numbers of studies and get closer to a scientific consensus.

Nutritional sciences have emerged in the early twentieth century with boost in the medical, biological and plant sciences. Understanding the nutritional deficiencies occupied most investigations as famines, and pediatric developmental deficiencies from poor nutrition were common, such as rickets, pellagra and goiter, (section 19.5). By the the 1980's, the focus shifted to diseases of nutritional excess, such as obesity, diabetes of adult-onset and heart disease. The types of food intake were implicated as the findings of glycemic index, a rise in blood sugar after nutrient intake, was higher with more refined starches and sugars. The association of cholesterol blood levels, high blood pressure and of fat consumption to arterial plaques, have emerged. Arterial plaques are the hallmarks and end results of these multiple factors (diet, sedentary life style, hypertension, etc) in elevating cardiovascular risks for adverse events. The current dietary concerns, not only address avoidance of disease conditions but also what is best to maintain good health and body function. Popular literature and the internet are profuse with advice on dietary do's and don'ts. Nevertheless, not many nutritional advices are based on rigorous science, especially when a particular product is reccomended. With the caveat that good nutrition covers a lot of ground, and that there are individual variabilities, with different levels of physical and work activities, we can discuss some guidelines based on sound investigations. Pertinent to our subject of cancer prevention, it is fortunate that the same guidelines for dietary consumption to optimize cardiovascular health and longevity, will also lower the risks for cancer. The coincidence or serendipity that good diet results in better health, lower rates of chronic diseases in old age and of cancer risks, rest on the some of the basic underlying causes of these diseases, namely, genetic code damage and mutations. Thus, the simple rationale in healthy eating is to maintain our internal homeostasis, minimize the risks of gene damaging effects. Some foods or their by-products will increase levels of ROS, reactive oxygen species, generating stresses on genes, proteins and other intracellular structures. While others, plant products, fresh and whole foods, often refered as anti-oxidants, will decrease ROS and optimize maintenance of homeostasis.

Skerrett (2010) summarized findings in the Nurses' Health Study, the Western and the Mediterranean diets, and the DASH diet (Dietary Approaches to Stop Hypertension). Notable findings that cannot be ignored are the 80% lowering of cardiovascular risks among some individuals adhering to a few dietary guidelines. Cancer, cardiovascular, Parkinson's and Alzheimer's risks all decreased in groups consuming foods similar to the Mediterranean diet. Schulze (2018) pursued a similar review and tried to find a common thread between established dietary patterns and nutritional elements in affecting the common diseases of cardiovascular, diabetes and cancer. For example, the Mediterranean and Paleolithic and vegetarian diets had many elements in common. The more extreme Atkins diet of carbohydrate restriction will reduce the fat stores by converting to needed glycogen by autophagy in adipose tissues and through glugoneogenesis using lipids resulting in relative ketogenesis. There are no long-term health assessments of the "keto-diet", however intake of animal origin saturated fats could increase incidence of atherosclerosis. The common thread in these dietary regimens includes lowering overall caloric intake (for BMI over 25), eating fewer components of red and processed meats, increasing consumption of fresh fruits, vegetables and nuts, and restricting consumption of processed drinks, foods, refined sugars and salts. Physical activity and exercise have to be included in this discussion, as the metabolic machinery that incorporates the nutritional elements into the cells, has cogs and wheels connected with one and another to physical activities, the muscles that literally move our engine, (chapter 20, Exercise and Physical Activity).

19.2 MORE ON NUTRITIONAL SCIENCES

The major components of everyday foods are starch, protein and fats. Starch is the prefered form of energy storage in grains which is composed of chain of repeated units of sugar and glycogen. Breakdown of starches into glycogen and sugar units begins in the mouth with salivary enzymes and continue in the stomach and small bowel with mechanical mixing with acids and pancreatic juices. The sugar units are transported past the gut mucosal cells into the blood stream transporting these glucose units to the liver by the portal vein. The liver stores the sugar units as glycogen, maintains blood glucose levels through gluconeogenesis and distributes glucose to all organs for fuel. Excess sugars are also stored in muscles as glycogen and coverted into fat in adipocytes. Proteins are in meats, poultry, fish, milk products, plant seeds, fruits and vegetables. The digestive process breakdowns the proteins into their component 20 amino acids, five of which are essential, not produced in our cells. Absorbed into the portal vein, amino acids are processed in the liver to maintain a narrow concentration range in the blood compartment. Liver can break down excess amino acids by deamination. Muscles are the largest organs converting amino acids into protein, and conversely, releasing amino acids into the blood stream in fasting conditions, in protein deprivation, or when protein is broken down by proteolysis and autophagy. Fats are found in both animal and plant sources. There is a major distinction in the fats, by the hydroxyl side chains which in practice renders the animal fats in the solid form at room temperature, while in the liquid state for plant derived oils. There is evidence that arterial sclerosis and heart disease are decreased with predominant plant oil use, i.e., avoiding animal fats. In addition, omega-3-fatty acids present in both fish and plant oil can reduce cancer risks (Tuso, 2013). A comprehensive review of food components and their biochemical make-up examined health consequences in terms of cardiovascular diseases, strokes and diabetes, (Mozaffarian, 2016). The general findings were not surprising, as most studies agree on the importance of diet in affecting risks for several common diseases. Caloric excess, diets high in meats and fats, foods with chemical additiives are linked to microbiome changes, obesity and reactive oxygen radicals (ROS) excess resulting in greater molecular degradation and DNA mutations.

19.3 NUTRITIONAL IMBALANCE AND DISEASES

19.3.1 OBESITY: TOO MUCH OF A GOOD THING?

Obesity is usually thought to be a result of abundant food consumption and is becoming more common worldwide. The beginning of the obesity epidemic was observed first in the Western countries, starting in the 1950's then becoming more prevalent in the major cities of developing countries. This period also coincides with the beginning of the era of food industries and mass consumption of processed foods. Looking further beyond just number of calories consumed, there are some interesting revelations regarding the dietary habits of the overweight individuals. Obesity increases the risks for other illnesses, like diabetes, heart disease and cancer. First, most components of our diet have an optimal range, such as sugars, protein, total calories, fats, salts and vitamins. A deficiency or an abundance of each category can be problematic. Indeed, obesity, a reflection of abundant nutrition in one or another category, is not synonomous with good nutrition. That means well fed is not the same as well being. Obesity can still mask significant malnutrition such as a lack of some important nutrients, like protein and vitamins. Secondly, the type of fats or sugars can make a difference. For example, animal fat, such as lard or what is used to fry potato chips or fries as opposed to vegetable oils such as from corn or olives can lead to obesity. In case of consumption of sugars, processed sugar cane (sucrose) or corn molasses as opposed to fruit sugars, can have significant health implications. The types of fat consumed can potentially change the *metabolism of cholesterol to gut resorption of nutrients due to changes in gut flora*. As a result, the trafficking of these compounds through the body, referred to as metabolism and storage of fats, glucose and protein, can be altered and contribute to the obesity problem. Obesity is the canary in the coal mine, indicating an imbalance in our diet.

Let us start addressing the bigger problem in nutrition. The modern life-style has taken us well away from the hunter-gatherer food consumption patterns. Hominids appeared a little over a million years ago and the hunter-gatherers had to adapt to their environment to survive. The paleo diet (paleolithic era, 50,000 – 10,000 years BC) consisted mostly of plant based: leaves, fruits, roots and nuts. Meat and fish were available only after a hunting endeavor that consumed considerable degree of physical activity, estimated to cover an average of 10 kilometers. It is safe to assume that our genes have evolved with and adapted to the palelithic life-style. Several hunter-gatherer tribes survived to the modern era and their health status has been studied. What stood out was the absence of cardiovascular diseases. Agriculture and animal husbandry and later the industrial revolution ushered a greater change in our diet, characterized by greater amounts of grains and starches, sugars, animal protein and fats. The Western diet, that most Americans are now consuming, is the present-day result of the dietary changes of the modern western industrial revolution. The common diseases in the latter 20th century, diabetes, cardiovascular, Alzheimer's, cancer and obesity, can be partly blamed on this modern diet.

The gene divergence between humans and chimpanzees are centered around metabolic functions and nutrition acquisition (Hunter, 2008). The paleolithic hominids shaped our genes and their response to the paleo type of nutrition. This is simply the most convincing reason to examine the benefits of the paleo diet. Insulin resistance genes have been closely linked to the metabolic syndrome, and a starting point to evaluate links of diet and molecular basis of chronic diseases associated with obesity, vascular diseases and cancer (Brown 2016).

Processed foods have become a significant portion of our diet. Fresh and whole foods are transformed into bite size portions, garnished with preservatives, to prolong shelf life, enhanced with artificial colors, and emulsifiers for improved appearance, prior to reaching our tables and our palates. We should not disparage all stored foods, since this practice goes back in our heritage, such as pickled and fermented foods, and storage of nuts, grains, pumpkins and dried vegetables and fruits. Prolonged food storage and fermented foods when consumed in limited quantities may be a source of new microbes in our gut, a newly understood modulator of dietary absorption and health. The rise of processed foods and their increased consumption parallel the rise of obesity. The picture of gluttony features obesity in close association, which appears to be the inescapable explanation. The entire story of proper nutrition is not as simple. Gluttony interspersed with periods of scarcity is part of the natural cycle of life in our hunter-gatherer ancestry; just as seasonal rains, drought conditions, or freezing winters determine food supply in nature, and whether the harvest or hunt will be bountiful or bare.

Research in the human body microbiome revealed the importance of commensal microbial contribution to our health, especially the gut flora (Devaraj 2013). The total weight of the gut microbes approaches half a kilogram, which is half of the volume of daily food in the gut. Among the many species of bacteria, viruses and fungi, the Bacteroides and the Firmicutes bacteria are the most numerous and their numbers and function with regards to short chain fatty acids production can change with diet and the microbiome itself modulates our immunity, neurohormones. Changes in the microbiome composition can lead to obesity and to other illnesses, as well as colorectal cancer. Greater consumption of processed (and ultra-processed) foods has direct impact in the gut microbiome. Emulsifiers in processed foods, detergent-like compounds that extend shelf-life of packaged foods, have been found to be one of the culprits in promoting gut wall inflammation, the metabolic syndrome and changes in the gut microbiome (Chassaing, 2015). This concept of the gut microbiome as being important to general health is being embraced by some segments of the food industry by decreasing artificial food coloring and other chemical additives and promoting commercially available pre and pro-biotics. Greater public understanding of the gut microbiome is changing the conversation about healthy foods, but may not be enough to change the tide of processed food consumption, as the economics of food supply, convenience and ready availability dominate the future of food consumption habits.

The discussion of obesity and nutrition needs to include the ultimate measure of good health, and that is longevity. In fact, in nutritional studies, the end point of longevity also correlates with lower risks of cancer and chronic diseases. Life span has been increasing in the last three centuries from 30-40 years to a median of 65 years, measured in 1950, and today the median survival is nearly 80 years. The height of the average male and female has also increased from 45-55 inches to today 65-75 inches. In addition, laboratory animal studies and some human trials, show that a 15% reduction in normal caloric intake results in approximately 5-10% weight loss, leads to longer survival, and to fewer illnesses such as cancer and heart disease. This concept of caloric restriction being health-wise beneficial, came to light after large numbers of individuals that have lived through significant periods of food deprivation, such as during economic depressions and survivors of concentration camps were studied. The surprising finding was that the general health was not negatively impacted, and on the contrary, their overall survival improved. These findings have stimulated further research in nutrition, finding correlative changes in hormones, such as insulin growth factor, immune system and brain function improvements. There is correlation between dietary restriction, fasting, physical activity and metabolic activity in cells, lower IGF (insulin growth factor) and increased autophagy.

The association of nutrition and stature, as seen through the last couple of centuries, appear to be an exception, perhaps a paradoxical finding. The overall increase in stature of humans through the last centuries apparently due to improved nutrition seems to contradict the potential harm of prolonged, above average food consumption. This apparent contradiction can be explained by the nutritional impact in the young compared to increased consumption in the aged. Abundant nutrient intake in the formative years prior to puberty contributes to increased stature and possible improved health, while in the late adult-life, abundant nutrient intake may actually be detrimental to overall health. Height is associated with higher cancer rates, which is concordant with the expectations of Peto's law regarding cancer rates and body mass, being proportional to the number of cells at risk. Short stature associated with low IGF1 (insulin growth factor), Laron syndrome, is associated with longevity and lower cancer rates.

Not surprisingly, obesity is associated with lower longevity rates and with higher rates of chronic diseases and cancer. Obesity increases the incidence of adult onset diabetes, arthritis, cardiovascular diseases and cancer and these problems regress with weight reduction, by a combination of sensible diet and physical activity. The link between obesity and dietary consumption of processed food is fairly clear and, in turn, the link between chronic diseases, cancer and the "modern diet" is strong. The understanding of the common etiology of these chronic diseases based on the microbiome, genetic damage and mutations, provide a perspective on how the known factors in genetic hits interact with nutritional elements to reshape their risks. Intake of processed foods, compounds with potential carcinogenic effects and fewer phytochemicals lead to changes in the microbiome, disruption in the oxidative balance and chronic homeostatic imbalance, which in turn, increase the risk of genetic damage. These interdependent factors of nutrition, physical activity and microbiome on obesity and chronic diseases are well integrated in the context of molecular medicine. Molecular pathways designed to perform tasks of housekeeping, cell growth, immune functions and maintenance of homeostasis are modulated by dietary elements and exposure to carcinogens. Molecular homeostasis allows conditions of lower ROS stress, proper tissue and DNA repair and robust autophagy. These conditions favoring homeostasis will guarantee lower risks DNA damage and mutations.

19.4 THE GUT MICROBIOME

The large intestines carry trillions of microbes, from bacteria, viruses to fungi, amassing nearly a kilogram. Resident microbes on our skin, gastrointestinal tract and other areas of contact with our environment, have a collegial role in our health maintenance, also refered as the hologenome (Rosenberg 2016). In the gut, the microbes are established early after birth and share the mother's microbial make-up. The relative numbers of microbial species, Firmicutes, Bacteroides, Lactobacillus, and more, can be determined by DNA assay and are fairly stable throughout life and can be altered by diet, antibiotics, and gut infections. The beneficial and symbiotic functions include production of vitamins, short chain fatty acids, and essential amino acids that are important for the local intestinal cells, mucous barrier and immunity, as well as important modulations in other unexpected organs such as in the brain, liver and in adipose tissues (Singh 2017).

The modern diet with higher caloric and protein consumption as well as higher concentration of food additives alters the microbiome with consequences on several chronic diseases in the aged. The microbiome of the paleo-diet consuming individuals has been characterized, and mimics that of individuals on diet high in fruits, vegetables, nuts and low in processed foods (Schnorr, 2016). The entire significance of the microbiome is still being discovered, especially the role in colorectal cancer and opportunities for prevention of other cancers. Microbial DNA signatures developed in the study of the microbiome has been used to study cancer tissues themselves, and interestingly, predictable patterns are found in different cancer types. These microbial signatures can also be detected in cancer patients' blood. The opportunity then arises for the study of cancer diagnostics and of novel tumor interactions with the microbiome, (Poore 2020). Severe life-threatening colitis, refractory to antibiotic treatment, has been successfully treated with re-introduction of normal microbiome organisms.

19.5 NUTRITIONAL DEFICIENCY AND DISEASE STATES

Scurvy was described as a condition common among sailors during long ocean crossings without fresh fruits and vegetables. Swollen and bleeding gums, painful joints can appear in in one month after vitamin C deficiency. In 1747, Navy doctor Lind found that citrus fruits were able to prevent scurvy in one of the first clinical trials conducted. Not until 1932, vitamin C was isolated and discovered to be the active compound against scurvy. This event marks the first micronutrient to be characterized. For the next two decades, many other micronutrients were linked to single nutrient deficiency associated diseases; thiamine to beriberi, niacin to pellagra, iron to anemia, calcium to rickets, etc. In 1941, President Roosevelt convened the first National conference on nutrition and deficiencies. This meeting stimulated the drafting of the Dietary Minimum Allowances of several nutrients.

Nutritional deficiency studies have been instrumental in discovering specific nutritional problems among children suffering from famines, food deprivation in wars, and from other natural catastrophes. Subclinical micronutrient deficiencies can also be found closer to home in many urban areas. Molecular pathways of micronutrients, vitamins, minerals have been elegantly worked out in their biochemical interactions, however, the clinical manifestations can take several disparate forms and not necessarily expected from their molecular functional profile. This is the beauty and wonders of the complex constellations of molecules, absorbed from the gut, transgressing tissue cells and playing important physiological roles, much as we see in the progression of cancers.

In severe protein deficiency, the symptoms and signs of marasmus can be clearly apparent, characterized by apathy, irritability, low weight and tissue edema. The term Kwachiorkor is reserved for the presence of severe edema, ascites, and often hepatomegaly. In the U.S., skin rash, a diffuse dermatitis is seen, and infants are usually thought to have milk allergy or given fad diets (Liu 2001). Zinc deficiency and HIV infection need to be ruled out. Thiamine, vitamin B1, deficiency is a major cause for infant mortality in some regions of the world, where the staple of polished rice is devoid of the rich vitamin content in the bran husk of the rice grain. In addition, few foods can bind thiamine, like fish sauce and soda drinks (Barennes, 2015), and result in thiamine deficiency with clinical signs developing in children that are apparently well fed. Heart failure can be the first sign of thiamine deficiency and is sometimes confused with other conditions of cardiopulmonary infections. Administration of thiamine results in rapid recovery and prevention of Beriberi can be achieved with vitamin supplementation to the expectant mother and during breast feeding.

Key deficiencies during pregnancy are associated with specific fetal developmental syndromes. For example, neurotube defects, anencephaly and spina-bifida, occur at a rate of 3-10 births per 1000. Multiple factors are associated with these defects, including maternal smoking, malnutrition and alcohol consumption. Niacin supplementation can decrease the incidence by about 70% (Beardin 2009). Folate is key in the one carbon transport and synthesis though the methionine pathway and important in the thymidylate biosynthesis, all required in rapidly growing tissues, especially in the early neural structures. Maternal and infant iodine deficiency can lead to hypothyroidism which will affect neural tissue development and increase incidence of mental retardation.

19.6 INSULIN GROWTH FACTORS (IGF) AND NUTRITION

IGF 1 and IGF2 are small protein hormones made in the liver, and to a lesser extent in other tissues, in response to growth hormone (GH) and other signals in the complex metabolic world of nutrition and cell function. IGF interacts with multitude of other hormones (thyroid, insulin, leptin) in close response to overall nutrient metabolism. IGF-1 stimulates cell growth, differentiation and maintenance of stem cell niche. It is bound to a carrier protein, and has relationships to all metabolic related pathways, so that it can be considered as a master hormone (Youssef 2017). Its concentration in the plasma and interstitial cell spaces correspond to body mass in children and reflects malnutrition with protein and caloric deficiencies. IGF-1 has been proposed as a marker for nutrition and possibly key player in carcinogenesis and chronic diseases associated with obesity and diabetes. Experiments with mice and worms with down-regulated insulin/IgF/receptor axis could increase longevity. Studies in centenarians likewise showed lower IgF and glucose levels, as opposed to usual findings of insulin resistance in older age groups associated with higher glucose levels, as in pre-diabetes. Laron syndrome characterized by GH receptor mutations, results in GH insensitivity, in small stature, low IGF-1 levels, and live longer with significantly lower risks of cancer compared to siblings and relatives with normal GH receptor gene. These findings also corroborate the health findings in diet restriction studies. IGF-1 is lower in late adulthood and lower with lean body mass, however with BMI in the range of obesity (higher than 30), the IGF-1 levels are more variable. It is possible that the protein bound IGF is higher in obesity. Higher nutrient intake in young adulthood is associated with higher IGF-1 level. IGF coordinates glycogen, lipid and protein balance. IGF plays a central role in hormone homeostasis in regulating cell growth, metabolism and energy expenditure. Whether, the level of IGF1 can be used as a marker of nutritional status, longevity, physical activity and risk for cancer remains to be seen. The interaction of IGF in cancer metabolism has been a hot topic of research, devising techniques in lowering IGF by drugs, like PARS inhibitors, or lowering sugar availability to the malignant cell.

19.7 MICRONUTRIENTS

Vitamins, minerals, and trace elements are the major categories of compounds grouped as micronutrients. These compounds have few or no calories, however they can be essential to the proper functioning of diverse cellular processes. Zinc, for example, is a co-factor in several proteins, in which is situated in a three-dimensional pocket with protein binding properties for signal transduction and enzymic function. The three-dimensional protein-zinc binding site has known linear amino acid sequences of cysteine and histidines. Zinc also interacts with lipid and nucleic acid structures. Free ionized zinc is tightly controlled as it participates with calcium for membrane efflux/influx potential wave signaling.

Minimum daily requirements of micronutrients have been published and most diets have ample supply of these essential micronutrients (vitamins and trace metals), though some noted common deficiencies can be found in the population at large, i.e., calcium, selenium and vitamin D (Shenkin 2006). Other instances of potential deficient dietary intake are in individuals with increased demand, or loss, and dietary intake of components that compete with specific micronutrients. Several micronutrients can improve the oxidative balance (vitamins A, C, folic acid and selenium) that potentially play roles in the formation of arterial sclerosis, cancer and in the decline of mental capacity in the aged. Despite a large amount of research, including phase III studies, there are no conclusive findings of specific micronutrients (above their minimum requirements) regarding their roles in prevention of these illnesses (Shenkin, 2006, Grober, 2016).

19.8 PLANT DERIVED MICRONUTRIENTS, PHYTOCHEMICALS AND MICRORNA

The concept of "eating your greens is good for you" is centuries old and incorporated in most world food traditions. Plant products are the major part of our diet. Much attention is given to the the macronutrients derived from plants like starches, proteins and oils, however the micronutrients and phytochemicals play key roles in our health. It is clear after a few decades into the "modern western diet", obesity, diabetes, cardiovascular, cancer and dementia have become more prevalent, and a concerted effort to change the food consumption habits could slow this trend. Micronutrients, mainly vitamins and essential minerals, have been investigated regarding health benefits and the results have been mixed. The non-essential micronutrients, phytochemicals specifically, hold some promise and pre-clinical studies are encouraging. Plant compounds have been administered for thousands of years for their medicinal properties, well documented in the Traditional Chinese Medicine and Ayurvedic Medicine literature. Aspirin is a good example of an active compound used for centuries for minor fevers, first as an extract isolated from willow tree bark, a practice going back to the Sumarians, 4000 BC, and is now one of the most commonly used medication, with its chemical structure identified as salicylic acid. Plant based anti-cancer drugs include vincristine and paclitaxel, isolated from Vinca rosea and pacific yew tree bark, Taxus brevifolia, respectively. Thousands of plant bioactive components can be identified from commonly consumed vegetables and fruits classified as phytochemicals, also considered as micronutrients.

Phytochemicals are grouped as phenolic acids, flavonoids, Lignans and Stilbenes. Multiple phytochemicals have been studied and unique pharmacological properties have been identified with more expected to be discovered, some with potential chemopreventive or anti-cancer properties. Polyphenols, for example, is a large class of phenolic acids readily isolated from coffee, tea, cocoa, grapes and other edible plants, that have anti-inflammatory, anti-oxidant, and pro-apoptotic effects. Thiols and sulfides found in garlic, onions and olives can decrease LDL and cholesterol. Flavanol consumption have been associated with lower colorectal cancer risks, and flavanols from cocoa improves endothelial function and lowered CHD risks in a 10-year study (nutrition.ucdavis.edu).

Human microRNAs, as ubiquitous modulators of gene function, provide a simple measure of biochemical function and regulation of molecular pathways. These molecular messengers or effectors are the nuts and bolts in the machinery of life functions leading to health or failing in illnesses, aging and cancer. How do the elements of micronutrients fit into these molecular pathways? Tea polyphenol EGCG alters a wide panel of miRNA in liver cancer cells in tissue culture, including miR-16, which down-regulates oncogene BCl2, increasing the apoptosis and death of these liver cancer cells. Resveratrol, a grape polyphenol, protects the endothelial cells in vessels from oxidative stress, an important mechanism for atherosclerosis, and regulates miR-21, amongst others. These specific miRs are closely modulating anti-inflammatory reactions in the endothelial and fibroblast cells (Bonnefont,2016).

Mirnas, as biomarkers in the study of nutrigenomics, are closely associated with functional operations of the cell in the presence of phytochemicals and other micronutrients (Rome, 2015). The stability of mirna of plant products has been shown after cooking to boiling temperatures and after ingestion and absorption through the gastro-intestinal tract. Dietary mirnas have been best studied in milk and few contributions to health in the infant were identified (Benmoussa, 2019). MicroRNA is one of many bioactive molecules in the maternal milk, among anti-microbial compounds, antibodies, growth factors and immune cells that benefits the infant. Maternal cells in the milk are found to intercalate with the infant gut cells forming microchimerism. Majority of milk derived mirnas modulates immune function in the infant, including the most prevalent mirna 148-a which down regulates DNA methyltransferase 1 (DNMT1), a regulator of the epigenome, and contributes to immune and growth functions. Interestingly cow's milk 148-a is identical to that of the human. Plant mirnas can be found in milk, mirna 168a and 156a, for example, affect adipose tissue function in the infant (Lukasik 2018). Plant mirna effects in humans represent the widely evident cross-kingdom gene regulation found in nature. In this context, plant mirna and phytochemicals can be classified as micronutrients. Mirna, tracked as a biomarker, may become a robust tool to link nutrition, metabolism, and gene expression to the study of diseases and used for dietary manipulations as a convenient therapeutic modality, thus providing a modern interpretation to the age-old applications of herb and traditional medicines.

19.9 FOOD DERIVED MICRORNAS: MARKERS FOR NUTRITION

Plant miRNA have multiple roles in plant development and adaptation to environmental stresses. Human mirna modulate DNA translation into proteins by messerger RNA by direct inhibition. Unlike plant miRNA, human mirna do not have exact complementarity to their corresponding mRNA, thus the inhibition can be partial and effect multiple mRNA. Mirna modulation has been found in every cellular function and disease processes, including cancer, diabetes, and inflammation. The ubiquity and stability of mirna both intra and extracellular, allow it to become markers of diverse metabolic functions and processes of malignant transformation. Zhang and colleagues, 2012, were the first group to demonstrate that plant miRNA can be absorbed from ingested rice and modulate lipid metabolism. Since then, dietary plant miRNAs in human sera and milk have been found and various downstream physiological effects were elucidated in humans (Wagner 2015, Xiao 2018). Mir 2911 from honeysuckle flower, consumed as tea, prepared after boiling in water, continues to be bioactive in its antiviral properties. Herbs are used in the treatment of several ailments, practiced in Traditional

Chinese and Ayurvedic Medicine. Despite the long history of practice and evidence of efficacy, many of the herb formula have not been tested using FDA standards of drug development and approval. For example, the active chemical in the plant product need to be characterized in its pharmacological properties and the dose administered need to be standardized. On the other hand, a single herb may contain dozens of active phytochemicals, which would be an enormous task to define their individual pharmacological properties. Over 10,000 phytochemicals have been isolated and studied (Jayaraman 2018). Plant miRNA in medicinal herbs, can assume the role of a biological marker to phytochemicals to dissect their physiological properties and their roles in therapy (Xie, 2016). Several phytochemicals have been studied pertaining to changes in human mirna after consumption. The flavonoid epigallocatechin-3-gallate (EGCG) has demonstrated significant anti-oxidant and anti-cancer activity. EGCG increases miR-16 and miR-210 in cancer cells in laboratory culture conditions and reduces growth rates in liver and prostate cancer cells by Bcl-2 apoptotic pathway and by blocking androgen receptors. Polyphenol from grape seed lowers the levels of mir-33 and 122 in hepatic cells and adipocytes with potential effects of lower deposition of lipids into adipocytes (Shrivastava, 2015). Nutrients and exercise can be closely monitored by measuring the different mirna profiles, serving as biomarkers for the interplay of insulin, glucose, and lipid in fat and muscle cells. These same mirna profile can display risk factors of related diseases in obesity and cardiovascular diseases (Arefhosseini 2014, Parr 2016).

The role of nutrition in our health is universally recognized. "Let food be thy medicine, thy medicine shall be your food" is a quote from Hippocrates and "He that takes medicine and neglects diet, wastes the skills of the physician" quoted from the Chinese folklore. The science of nutrition has a more recent history of molecular studies. Nutritional deficiency was first recognized by Casimir Funk and called it a lack of "vital amine" in chicken feed, causing a beriberi-like condition. Thiamine was isolated in 1926, later called vitamin B1, and confirmed that its deficiency leads to Beriberi in humans, condition affecting the heart and nervous system, (Mozaffarian 2018). In the 21st century, it is estimated that more people will die of diet related illnesses than of tobacco use. Component study of foods were able to outline the distinct contributions of macro and micro-nutrients. Plant based nutrients are the bulk of our foods and even today, major modern diseases in the form of diabetes and cardiovascular diseases can be prevented with diet emphasizing nutrients from plant sources. Application of nutrition sciences in weight reduction receives the most public attention and expenditures, however there is a caveat; weight and body mass index (BMI) alone may not reflect the entire picture of health. Absence of chronic diseases, longevity and quality of life are other measurable endpoints that are associated with good health. Rigorous clinical studies using these health endpoints require large number of volunteers and decades to complete. Intermediary endpoints such as biochemical blood tests can help clarify some of the health effects of nutrients. Study of plant mirna in foods associated with phyto-chemicals and their modulation of human mirnas have been promising in understanding nutrient effects in the intracellular molecular interactions. Plant and human mirnas have sequence complementarity (more than the few found) accounting for plant mirna exerting interference in our cell messenger RNA and other downstream effects. AI algorithms have found patterns of circulating DNA in liquid biopsies useful in diagnostics in cancer, and similar algorithms may recognize panels of plant mirna with specific metabolic pathways. These would challenge the concepts of cross-kingdom gene regulation versus evolutionary conserved gene functions.

19.10 CONCEPTS OF GOOD NUTRITION; IMPACT ON CANCER.

Studies on nutrition illustrate the complexities in achieving consensus and having complete confidence in describing the end-result of an intervention in complex biological systems as our bodies. Nutritional deficiency of a single biochemical element can cause multiple dysfunctions, often, hard to recognize and diagnose, requiring confirmation with biochemical tests. Dietary consumption of a single food component has numerous biochemical derivatives and the downstream effects on health are extremely difficult to measure in a reproducible manner. Despite these complexities of nutrition and health, current knowledge has established several dietary changes associated with lowering risks of specifiic chronic diseases. In this section, we will focus on the links between diet and cancer. The discussion will be limited to human phase III studies, i.e., randomized, double blind, controlled and prospective. Other research studies, pre-clinical and epidemiological studies, provide useful information to base theoretical considerations, proof of principles and design for phase III studies. The shortcomings of these pre-clinical studies have been mentioned before; i.e., controlled animal studies limit the number of variables and despite positive findings, they are not always reproducible in human studies. For example, anti-oxidant agents in reducing cancer risks. Retrospective epidemiological studies have yielded much information of dietary intake of specific components as fats, calcium, red meat, etc and effects on cardiovascular and malignant diseases, however, there are range of results including negative findings. Consensus can be approximated by comparing all studies in a meta-analysis, (Donaldson, 2004). Several studies have found that obesity is a consistent risk factor for higher breast cancer rates. Obesity is also associated with increased recurrences in treated breast cancer patients, (Ligibel 2017). Weight reduction diet and exercise in women with breast cancer have shown improvement in survival.

Colorectal cancer risks are associated with intake of red and processed meats, alcohol and lack of plant-based fiber. Lower recurrence rates have been found with individuals resected of early colorectal cancer adhering to few dietary criteria, increasing intake of fruits, vegetables, fish and poultry (Meyerhardt, 2007). This CALGB study group presented a more recent analysis of nut consumption which showed a dramatic decrease in recurrence and death events. The dearth of studies in other cancers, point to the difficulties in carrying out phase III studies where the detectable end-point differences will require a large study group, in the order of several thousand volunteers.

There is much talk surrounding some specific diets, the Mediterranean and the Paleo diets. The Mediterranean diet refers to the southern European diet, as in Greek foods, rich in olives, olive oil, fish, whole grains, nuts and salads. Mediterranean diet is associated with lower rates of cardiovascular diseases, diabetes, some cancers and neurodegerative diseases (Castro-Quezada 2014).

Paleo diet has received much attention and has gained many advocates. However sufficient scientific confirmation of health-related endpoints is still lacking. Living organisms have unimaginable creative ways and abilities to adapt to their environment, especially in modifying their diet to what the local environment is able to provide. What our ancestors ate and in what quantities determined our gene function and adaptation for an optimal body function, (Roess 2014). Thus, a diet of berries, nuts, vegetables, tubers, fruits and the occasional meat was the norm. The amounts of food were rarely above subsistence and occasionally abundant from seasonal harvest or successful hunt. Current research has concurred with this concept of fasting during lean times and abundant consumption during bountiful hunting and harvest seasons. Intermittent food deprivation coupled with exercise, lead to a leaner body weight and greater longevity coupled with lower rates of chronic diseases. Measurements of insulin growth factor (IGF1) show that lower levels generally correspond to longevity and lower risks of chronic diseases, see also section 18.5. The change into the modern Western diet places metabolic pressures on a genetic system acustomed to the paleolithic dietary regimens and is associated with the rise of the modern diseases, with aging, obesity and cancer. The modern man is surviving three times longer than the paleolithic man, thus the territory is uncharted when one takes the metabolic findings in the early adulthood from paleolithic diet and extrapolates them into our senior years. Adopting some of the dietary habits of our ancestors is an appealing solution to the modern diseases. Obesity among some ethnic groups can be clearly traced to inroads of the modern diet. Return to the older ethnic foods, can be an effective treatment of obesity and diabetes in these individuals (Jung, 2014). Colorectal cancer incidence has seen a dramatic rise in Asia in the last few decades. Dietary changes could be the main culprit, however, caution should be exercised prior to definite conclusions, since incidence may rise with improved endoscopic diagnosis (Arnorld, 2016). In addition, the global pattern of colorectal cancer follows an initial dramatic rise from approximately 15 cases annually/100,000 population, age adjusted, to 35 cases annually, peaking around 1990, then the incidence steadies into a plateau, and slight decrease past 2010. Longevity has risen in the last five decades and the incidence of age associated chronic diseases have increased. Change in our dietary habits has the potential to reverse these trends for obesity, cardiovascular diseases and for cancer.

Both the Mediterranean and Paleo diets stress the importance of whole fresh foods and avoidance of processed foods. Food additives for coloring, flavor enhancement, sweeteners and preservatives numbering in the several thousands have been approved by the FDA. They are likely culprits for some of the modern diseases when consumed in significant amounts (Jain 2015). Despite scientific review of several additives, olestra, acrylonitrile monomers (in plastic drink containers) and saccharin, just a few examples, showing significant health concerns, these food additives were able to pass the approval process, by the FDA. The FDA review and approval process goes forward, despite some of these food safety issues. In addition, FDA negative reviews for some of these food additives can be reversed by legal challenges (Noah 1997). The Delaney clause, amended in 1960, prohibits the use of any food substance found to be carcinogenic in humans or animals. Although the rule is succinct and clear, many food additives, despite some findings of carcinogenicity in experimental animals, have been approved. In some situations, what is considered carcinogenic varies according to the concentration of the substance and influenced by other co-factors in the environment. GRAS (generally recognized as safe), a designation by the FDA, are chemical substances that are exempt from review. GRAS include natural substances such as fruit extracts, and other compounds grandfathered in by prior usage in foods, ante-dating the review process. Several food additives raise concerns as potential carcinogens, including food coloring, nitrites, emulsifiers, aromatic hydrocarbons and heterocyclic amines (Fiolet, 2018). Increased consumption of processed red meat is associated with increased rates of colorectal cancer and increased intake of alcoholic beverages is associated with increase in breast cancers. Linkage between specific nutrients or processed foods and disease states are difficult to arrive by epidemiological studies due to multiple confounding factors. On the other hand, the link betwen childhood obesity and processed foods, especially drinks with sweeteners and fructose, snacks and fast foods are well established (Neto, 2017).

Caloric restriction and periodic fasting have become popular regimens for weight reduction and for health benefits. Longevity, lower rates of chronic diseases and cancer are among these benefits. These regimens mimic the paleolithic life-style in real-time, where the food supply was intermittent. Scientists are still studying the full extent of metabolic ramifications of these regimens. Among the metabolic changes, insulin growth factor decrease is intriguing in view of similar findings in Laron syndrome, an inherited defect in the human growth hormone receptor, section 16. Another consequence of fasting is a robust increase in autophagy. Autophagy is a common and necessary activity within the cells to recycle old proteins and other damaged organic molecules from oxidative radicals and optimize homeostasis in glucose, fats and amino-acids. Autophagy is important during fasting or during rise in energy requirements as in physical activity, counter balancing the activity of nutrient storage during food consumption. Autophagy and storage of excess glucose, aminoacids and fats are constant interactive processes that are integral to the metabolic balance and general homeostasis. Autophagy is the common pathway between diet, exercise and health, also discussed in the next chapter, 20.

CHAPTER 20

EXERCISE AND PHYSICAL ACTIVITIES

Humans have evolved over 2.5 million years to optimize their body functions for hunting and gathering foods. Only recently, farming and sedentary life style has taken hold. The human body requires physical activity for its best function. Physical activity has its obvious rewards, such as a muscular and fit physique, healthier bones and joints, greater alertness and more relaxed disposition. Improved brain function with physical exercise is not universally recognized. Physical exercise may be more important than brain games to ward off dementia. The feed-back from muscular movements, relayed by the brain and spinal-chord, activates the neural functions as well as production hormones such as endorphins, adrenaline, cortisol, neurotensins and myokines produced from muscle cells. In addition, physical activity improves the clearance of amyloid deposists, associated with dementia and Alzheimer's disease. Physical activity improves the function of macrophages and their phagocytic activity, and upregulates autophagy (Escobar 2018). Autophagy scavenges cell wastes and balances the optimal concentrations of the basic fuel and building blocks, glucose, fatty and amino-acids. Physical activity is then a pre-requisite for promoting housekeeping activities that are essential for cellular homeostasis. Autophagy recycles damaged and old proteins, and other tissue wastes that when accumulated can form amyloid plaques and other deleterious deposits in cells (Amm 2014). In addition, macrophage and neutrophil clearance of microbes is improved. Around microbial infections, there is increased amount of cellular debris and damaged proteins. Uncleared and accumulated waste can be found in all tissues, and form plaque like material, amyloid deposits, such as amyloidosis in lung parenchyma, in lymph nodes as in granulomatous lymphoid reactions, in the kidney as interstitial nephritis. Accumulated wastes increase ROS, leading to further molecular damage including damage to the genetic code. Mild to moderate exercise is the best cure for many of the chronic diseases such as cardiovascular diseases secondary to hardening of the arteries, type II diabetes, obesity, dementia and arthritis. In addition, exercise improves the overall immune function, lowering the effects of chronic infections. It is not entirely clear how physical activity improves most components of the immune system. Muscular activity activates the autophagy mechanisms that are basic in mobilizing the protein stores in the muscle. Autophagy within immune cells drives the phagocytic activity that is central in fighting and killing invasive microbes. Muscles are not usually thought of as metabolic organs, like the liver, but in fact, muscles are important in storing and mobilizing proteins, in modulating fat metabolism and in producing several hormones. The primary function of muscles, as we learned in school, is for locomotion. Yet, an organ which is primarily designed for movements, has a complex variety of other functions, inter-connecting with other organs in achieving body-wide homeostasis. For example, muscle activity modulates the storage and mobilization of amino-acids, protein building blocks, and coordinates with fat cells and liver cells to provide best balance between storage and mobilization of fats and glucose. Myokines and cytokines (interleukins 6,10 and others) produced in the muscle improve central nervous and immune system function, strengthen bones and promote hematopoiesis. In terms of cancer, exercise lowers the incidence of variety of cancers and lowers the risk of cancer recurrence and the development of metastatic disease. How does exercise produce all these beneficial health effects? We shall explore the physiological and molecular basis for cellular activity of myocytes.

20.1 SKELETAL MUSCLE: THE MASTER REGULATOR OF ENERGY BALANCE

The considerable muscle mass of 600 separate muscles, constituting nearly half of our body weight, perform multiple tasks besides efficient motor functions, such as glycogen and protein storage in coordination with fat metabolism in adypocytes and liver cells. Maintaining a constant supply of glycogen, precursor of glucose for our brain cells is a tall order, especially when the energy needs may vary with activities, which can increase by several fold. On the other hand, after meals, glycogen, fats and amino acid levels are in excess, storage is paramount in maintaining the blood levels in the desirable homeostatic levels, and at the same time, keeping reserves ready for lean times. In times of starvation, quite common for the gatherer hunter life-style, energy is extracted from liver and fat cell stores and, less appreciated, from the muscle glycogen and protein stores. Muscle activity coordinates much of the fuel management partly through multiple myokines ranging from lymphokine-like proteins, to adipokine modulators. Myokines stimulate brain-derived neurotrophic factors affecting adipose tissue, brain activity and immune function, (Kostrominova 2016, Schnyder 2015). On the molecular level, the mobilization of energy stores in the cells is accomplished by autophagy. Yoshinori Ohsumi was awarded 2016 Nobel prize for his work in the genes controlling autophagy in baker's yeast. Autophagy evolved in one-cell organisms with endocytosis, a form of "drinking" nutrients next to cell wall, to more developed forms of lysosomal vacuoles in processing the cell's own degraded molecules. Ohsumi advanced the science of autophagy, from over a century of works by other investigators like Metchnikoff and de Duve, who were also fascinated by the cell's ability for fight foreign invaders (phagocytosis) and the process food intake (cellular vesicular transport).

20.2 MUSCULAR ACTIVITY AND IMMUNE FUNCTION

"Young lad, go outside and take a walk, get some fresh air"

"Health is the vital principle of bliss, and exercise, of health." James Thomson

Exercise links to good health are believed world-wide and in diverse cultures. Life styles in the last century evolved to more sedentary activities, driving over walking, office jobs over manual work and passive entertainment over outdoor activites. Attitudes on physical activity changed our behavior favoring conforts around the "couch", especially in old age, to the point that physical activity, being the norm, is considered superfluous. The benefits are well documented in controlled studies regarding diverse bodily functions and amelioration of chronic diseases (McKinney 2016). How does physical activity lead to improved health and more specifically, what are the physiological and molecular changes? Let us first focus on the immune function.

The improvement of immune function measured in human volunteers and laboratory animals is wide ranging, from lymphokine and antibody responses, to cellular activities, as in phagocytosis, migration and cytotoxicity, (Terra 2012, Nieman 2019). Excessive exercise can expose the individual to higher susceptibility to infections due to a temporary downturn in the immune function.

What is fascinating about the subject of muscular activity and the proper functioning of the whole physical and molecular machinery, is the connection between the immune function and the nutritional metabolism, resulting in the proper maintenance of the molecular ecosystem, especially in the elderly, (Taylor, 2013). The next time you hear: "But, … I am too old to exercise", your response should be: "Yes, you are old, and absolutely not, that is why you need to exercise". How muscular activity helps the immune system, energy and nutrient metabolism can be explained by the molecular and physiologic activity of autophagy. Multiple molecular pathways are inter-connected with autophagy. The housekeeping and scavenging of waste products and "old" molecules, to recycling and supplying the basic fuel and new building materials for the cell are a few key functions of authophagy. One of the strong factors correlating with early death in the elderly is low muscle mass or sarcopenia. Regular physical activity amongst the elderly reverses some changes of immunosenescense.

Autophagy is the root mechanism of taking proteins, fats and sugars from cells (self eating) and releasing them into the blood stream or interstitial fluid (plasma) during fasting and periods of higher energy requirements. Autophagy takes place in vesicles associated with membranes, be it cell membrane, endoplasmic reticulum, nucleus or golgi body. The phagosomes are generated and promoted by several factors, including hypoxia, starvation, ROS, and by microbial products. Lysosomes perform similar functions, starting as single layer vesicles, gather deformed protein, lipids or gene fragments. Lysosome vesicles can discharge their content of gathered wastes to outside the cell by fusing with the cell membrane, or can grow in size, acquiring double layer membrane and sometimes fusing with autophagosome, (Sica 2015). When these functions are performed by immune cells, leukocytes or macrophages, they become an integral part of our immune capabilities. The importance of autophagy is further appreciated when put in terms of cell transport, waste clearance, metabolic homeostasis, cell renewal, recycling, immune function as well as apoptosis.

In order to answer our first question, how is physical activity necessary for normal autophagy, we need to again return to the muscles. Physical activity is one of the strongest up-regulatory signals for autophagy. Measurements in humans and animals support the benefits of physical activity in autophagy function in muscles and in other organs as the brain, (He 2012). Several of the genes and intermediate signaling proteins are upregulated for muscle protein degradation through autophagy and likely as result of increased myokines. The second major upregulator of autophagy is fasting. Nutritional research has revealed several health benefits of fasting including metabolic homeostasis, longevity, lower cancer, diabetes and obesity rates.

The metabolic pathways connecting diet, energy consumption and storage, re-cycling of old molecules and cellular wastes and immune activity are powered by the common engine of autophagy. This very under-recognized and ubiquitous activity performs cellular housekeeping thereby promotes longevity and good health in the aged. We can proclaim that diet and exercise are the two pillars of life and the molecular steps of autophagy, metabolic and ROS homeostasis, and immune surveillance completes the healthy life cycle, keeping the risks for molecular damage and mutations to a minimum.

20.3 EXERCISE FOR WASTE AND OXIDATIVE STRESS MANAGEMENT.

It is quite interesting that physical activity is at the center of our body's ability to rid itself of waste products. We are not just talking about large bowel and bladder function, but an overall ability to keep the balance of intake and output of products where unhealthy conditions associated with excess toxins and tissue waste products can accumulate, i.e., wastes on the molecular scale. We have compared our bodies as an ecosystem of trillions of cells surviving in an enclosed environment akin to our own planet, where environmental stresses and accumulation of wastes can cause havoc among the cellular inhabitants leading to health problems. Our environment is capable of self renewal, just as our bodies are able to rid wastes and regain homeostasis, mainly through autophagy.

How does exercise help elimination of waste products? Beginning with gut, not all food consumed is absorbed through the intestines, but eliminated from the gut. The liver excretes bulk of unwanted organic molecules into the duodenum in form of bile. Renal excretion, and sweat production

(to a lesser degree), eliminate much of the excess minerals, electrolytes and water. And lastly, at the cellular lever, autophagy is the main housekeeping and waste disposal mechanism. Sedentary life style is often associated with obesity and constipation along with multitude of health problems associated with dismotility of the large bowel: colon hypertrophy, diverticulosis, diverticulitis and ano-rectal diseases (Moses 1990). Exercise and physical activity will greatly improve both small bowel and large bowel motility, by stimulating the gut sympathetic and parasympathetic nerves to the bowel muscles. Decrease of large bowel transit time prevents of overgrowth of certain bowel microflora. In turn, this will alleviate one cause of chronic infection and the need to eliminate bacterial toxins. During exercise, renal function conserves and resorbs the free water filtration and the urine is then concentrated in salts, urea, ammonia and uric acid. Muscular activity elevates body temperature which is the stimulus for perspiration and sweating. After exercise, as the body fluids are replenished by oral intake, the kidneys will rebalance the osmotic load in the blood and excrete more water.
Exercise and physical activity improve renal function with increased glomerular filtration rates and improved excretion of some protein breakdown products. Exercise in chronic renal disease has also been found to improve renal function. The excretory function of sweat is minor compared to the kidneys except for sodium elimination. Sweat clears the hair follicles of excess debris and bacteria. Immune system function is remarkably improved in both cellular and humoral aspects, with an overall finding of reduced infections in individuals undergoing regular exercise. T-cell function, production of cytokines, oxidative burst in phagocytes and NK cells are increased with an associated down-regulation of toll-like receptors. Levels of immunoglobulins are increased as well as other measures of complement-humoral dependent cytolysis.

Excessive exercise and physical activity in the presence of extreme heat, water deprivation, or prolonged physical activity such as ultra-marathon can result in tissue injuries such as muscle breakdown, myoglobinuria, organ failure and immune suppression. Mild and temporary organ dysfunction can accompany moderate physical activity. The general rule of thumb is to increase physical activity on a gradual basis. In doubt or in cases of underlying illnesses, a physician should be consulted.

The fact that amyloid plaques and deposits in tissues are cleared by exercise, remain a fascinating process. These deposits are accumulation of proteinaceous debris, that are unique in different organs. As many as 30 different proteins may form amyloid fibrils which can line up into plaques. Other precursor components that contribute to these deposits are serum amyloid P component, apolipoprotein E, glycosaminoglycans, laminin and fibronectin. In the brain, it is associated with dementia, Alzheimer syndrome and several of the neuro-degerative syndromes. Among several causes of brain dysfunction in older age, is the malfunction of epoE and deposit of excess protein synuclein, also known as Lewy bodies (Jellinger 2018). In granulomatous disease, such as tuberculosis, the chronic inflammatory process deposits amyloid protein in several organs and can present as amyloidosis. Amyloidosis is also characterized by tissue accumulation of amyloid proteins from a variety of illnesses, including multiple myeloma and collagen vascular diseases.

How does exercise affect the clearance of these proteinaceous waste products? By improving the immune function where the clearance of amyloid is achieved by tipping the balance towards excretion of damaged proteins, preventing amyloid accumulation. Secondly, exercise diminishes oxidative stress and tips the balance of oxygen radicals and oxygen scavengers towards the preservation of normal protein and glycolipid structures. These mechanisms exist as basic ways that cells and tissues use to deal with input and output of absorbed ingested nutrients and environmental stesses. Autophagy participates in multiple functions, from metabolic balance of different nutrients to immune clearance of inflammatory residues. Autophagy has been found to be an important mechanism in clearance of amyloid deposits in the brain (Shin 2013). All tissues, from the brain to lymph nodes, possess powerful tissue macrophages and monocytes that perform the important function of engulfing and processing broken down lipoproteins, cell wastes from apoptosis or other inflammatory activities, i.e., autophagy in immune cells. Exercise is the necessary activity that enhances the normal clearance by the phagocytic mechanisms.

Exercise regulates the balance of oxygen radicals and prevents tissue damage from excess reactive radicals. Oxygen is essential to cellular function in generating energy, electron transfer in signal transduction, membrane transport, carbon transfer and generation of oxygen radicals. The byproducts of these activites are the free oxygen radicals in forms of superoxide, hydrogen peroxide, hydroxyl radical, aldehydes, peroxyls, epoxides and others, usually referred to as ROS (rective oxygen species). ROS are mostly generated in the mitochondria, but also produced in lysosomal vacuoles, ribosome and cell membranes. Excess ROS can cause many deleterious consequences such as DNA adducts with higher risk of gene mutations, increase in protein and lipid damage, apoptosis and senescense.

During active exercise and physical activity, the generation of ROS (reactive oxygen species) is increased, however the benefits last during the rest period, as the body remains more efficient in eliminating ROS. Exercise increases autophagy that clears the damaged and old cellular structures as a result of ROS but also regulates ROS by clearing defective mitochondria, a large source of ROS release.

CHAPTER 21

AGEING, WELL-BEING and CANCER

Well-being in the later years of life is truely valued. One can appreciate the wisdom learned and memories cherished from the past and anticipate good health in the golden years of the future. This goal has been sought throughout human history and is as coveted as the fountain of youth. Hopes for good health in the older years are challenged by the reality of increasing organ dysfunction and risks for familiar illnesses such as cancer and other chronic diseases of the aged. The fear of unexpected illness in old age resurfaces when a friend or family member becomes sick. Encouraging news are that the youth vitality and better state of health can be extended into older years. Ageing research benefited from efforts in cancer and molecular biology investigations, where new answers to the age-old senescense questions were a welcome by-product of the new discoveries. Most young individuals are disinterested in the aging question and find these issues irrelevant to their current daily lifes. The aging process, unknowingly to most, starts early. For example, endothelial arterial and brain plaques can be found in young individuals starting in their third decade, reported from autopsy series. Hayflick published his cell culture work in 1961 and demonstrated that normal adult cells have limited number of cell divisions, about 40-50, thereafter the cell dies, accounting for senescense. Paradoxically as the ageing cell reaches senescense, it is capable of morphing into a cancer cell, then becoming immortal. Research into cancer biology has yielded much understanding of the aging cell. These topics are relevant to the young, since some of these aging mechanisms are present in all young cells and the know how to slow senescense, are pertinent to the questions of cancer prevention.

Telomere is an elegant chromosomal mechanism regulating cellular aging. The telomere is a short segment of DNA that binds the loose ends of the DNA helix. Without telomeres, the DNA terminal bases become reactive and are at risk of translocation changes and mutations. As the cells undergo division and ageing, their telomeres shorten and will limit the ability to undergo further mitosis. Telomerase, an enzyme responsible for lengthening the telomere, is more active and present in higher quantities in the young tissues and in cancer cells. Modulating the telomerase function has been a keen interest for cancer and ageing research.

Multiple mutations and chromosomal changes are accumulated in old cells with potential deleterious consequences. Some of these deleterious effects will be minimized by DNA repair enzymes, and, if not repaired, it is eliminated by programmed cell death, or apoptosis. This in turn will under-populate tissues that perform vital functions at decreased capacity. Can these cells be retired and replaced by new ones? Nature has faced these questions in the event of physical injuries and tissues with higher rates of turn over. Several organisms can replace entire body parts, such as the salamander. In humans, some organs are capable of regeneration, the liver, skin, and bone marrow. Months after liver surgery, removal of several of the 8-segments, the liver will have regenerated its entire volume. This amazing replacement of large liver tissue can be seen in patients who had this procedure, by obtaining a CT scan. The skin, which is the largest organ in the body by weight, also has the ability to regenerate. Large areas of skin loss, after a burn or loss by trauma, can re-grow new skin. The new skin cells come from the remaining cells around the hair follicle. This process also allows the harvesting of partial thickness skin for grafting elsewhere in the body, in the treatment of burns and other areas of skin loss. Investigators from organ regeneration research will argue that many more organs are capable of regeneration in vitro, such as bladder over a dermal scaffolding, and muscles with proper nerve stimulation.

The turn-over rate of cells is extremely variable depending on the cell type. For example, the neurons in the brain, lasts your entire life without being replaced, while the red cell is replaced in 2-3 weeks. Other organs, lungs and kidneys, have a mixture of cells that are replaced with an intermediate time schedule of months to years. The renewing cells, known as the stem cells, are usually found in the vicinity, like the basal layer stem cells in the skin or gut lining. Some stem cells can originate in the bone marrow and arrive in tissues through the circulatory system. Stem cells can be toti-potential, like the embryonic stem cells, or further differentiated as the skin basal stem cells. Stem cells provide the "new" cells replacing the senescent cells and keeping tissues from aging. In addition, research in mice showed that rejuvenation of old under-performing tissue improves with elimination of senescent cells through drugs that enhance apoptosis. There are humoral components secreted by old cells, grouped as inflammatory proteins, that accelerate senescent tissue dysfuntion, on the other hand, young tissue humoral factors can rejuvenate old tissues, (Mahmoudi 2019).

Aging and cancer share the same molecular origins, beginning with DNA damage and mutations, (Silva 2019). Clearly the pathways diverge at some point, cell dysfunction and death from senescence on one road; accelerated growth or hyperplasia from cancer, on the other. As in cancer oncogenes, some specific genes mutations are more significant in ageing. The fact that these molecular events occur on a random basis, is not the entire issue that shapes our body function. There are many factors that increase or decrease the frequency of the random mutational events on the DNA. The crux is what can be done to minimize the mutational events, or how to reverse or minimize the effects of the mutations. These are not isolated events, but are common challenges for all living organisms. The DNA repair system has evolved, since the early days of life on Earth, into efficient protein enzymic machinery, capable of handling most of the assaults on the DNA structure,

ROS and radiation, for example. Nature is the great teacher, since through billions years of evolution, the molecular machinery has tried nearly all possible options, and as Darwin postulated elegantly, evolution determines the better choices of molecular pathways for living organisms. For example, plants and some animals have ways of avoiding cancer, and some animals outlive their peers. The answers are built into the genes and other molecular pathways, that on the whole are pre-determined and not derailed by random processes. This entire machinery and molecular "galaxies" can be explored for lessons on aging and cancer. Let us examine the relationship between DNA conservation and ageing.

21.1 SCIENCE OF AGEING; CURRENT UNDERSTANDING OF TISSUE DYSFUNCTION IN OLD AGE

The hallmarks of ageing hardly need description, as we can clearly notice the changes in ourselves with the passing of years and among our elderly family members and peers. The skin acquires wrinkles and tends to droop as elasticity is lost. The hair on our heads thins out, vision and hearing are not as acute, high blood pressure develops as our vessels harden and develop plaques. Our muscles lose tone and mass and our bones lose their strength and become demineralized, manifesting the characteristic posture of old age with back arching, forward bent know as kyphosis, and loss of stature. Our older tissues lose cells and function. Delving deeper into the nuts and bolts of aging, we must literally expand our focus into the microscopic dimensions, the cellular and molecular framework of these events. On this level, what are the changes that correspond to advancing age? We will outline several findings and connect these concepts with our subject at hand, cancer prevention and improvement of health, especially in the old age. Much of the research on cellular ageing has used animal models in mice, zebra fish, the worm C. elegans and in the unicellular yeast. Few key molecular pathways have been manipulated to prolong life in these experimental conditions, equivalent to human longevity of 130 years. Prolonging life-span in these animals and in the yeast models may not all translate directly to the human aging phenomenon. Though, some basic research findings may confirm or point to new hypotheses and molecular pathways. Several theories on ageing need to be considered with caution, as the conditions in older individuals, are more complex than a few variables studied in the well-controlled environment of experimental models. For example, a debate at the center of nutrition, ageing and cancer, is the concept of caloric restriction, leading to lean body weight, delaying ageing and is associated with better health and lower risks of cancer. Experiments in animals confirm this notion with the findings of lower insulin growth factor (IGF), lower BMI, lower blood sugars and fats, and increased autophagy. In human experiments, however, a consistent association of lifespan and BMI has not been found (Lorenzini 2014). Over 100 years ago, Rubner, proposed that animals with lower metabolic rates would live longer. Caloric dietary restriction was demonstrated to lower metabolism and body temperature and contribute to longevity (Heilbron 2003).

As the body tissues develop from the embryonic stages, the adult stem cells can differentiate into any cell types, while remaining in a quiescent state. The adult stem cells, contrasted to embryonic stem cells or induced pluripotent stem cells, are resident in their respective tissues, as in skin, bone marrow or muscles. As we age, these cells are slowly producing daughter cells and are re-populating tissues and providing functional renewal. This normal process of tissue renewal can slow the ageing process and contribute to longevity. There is one example illustrating one extreme of the aging spectrum, the congenital progeria, where aging is accelerated. Infants, with progeria, develop many hallmarks of octagenerians in only a few years. An inborn error in the LMNA gene responsible for a defect in the laminin A protein, which is associated with nuclear envelope defects. Progeria is also associated with defective stem cells and treatment with normal stem cells, in a mouse experiment, reversed some of the aging signs for a period of time. It is intriguing to see that, a pinpoint defect in a single protein in progeria can result in a complicated cascade of molecular changes resulting in accelerated aging. On the other end of the spectrum, groups of individuals with higher than normal longevity may have an abundance of stem cells or stem cells that are more capable in repopulating the aging tissues. Ageing has also been correlated with stem cell exhaustion in the bone marrow, melanocyte pool and other tissues. A recent study of centenarian blood cells revealed that in one individual, only two stem cells were renewing the entire white blood cell population. This finding confirms the relationship of ageing and stem cell exhaustion and demise.

On a molecular level, the telomere length is a curious association to cellular longevity. As mentioned in the beginning of this chapter, telomeres are DNA repeats that cap the ends of chromosome strands and play an important role in orientation during mitosis and avoiding the stickiness of the chromosome terminals and preventing attachment to other segments of the DNA. Short telomeres will activate apoptotic signals and prevent the completion of the mitotic process. In brief, short telomere will shorten the life of the cells and in turn, can accelerate ageing in tissues and organs. The telomeres can be lengthened by the enzyme telomerase, and its activity and telomere length are correlated with individuals with younger physiological age. Incidentally, cancer cells have found a way to lengthen telomeres, through telomerase.

Tissues and cells in aged individuals have greater numbers of DNA damage ranging from strand breaks, adducts, demethylation, mutations leading to mutagenic instability. Environmental stressors include naturally occurring oxygen reactive species, chemicals, carcinogens, radiation, and chronic inflammation that increase the incidence of DNA damage. The cellular DNA is quite active repairing itself, as the damaging hits occur at the rate of several thousands per day in a single cell. These damages and mutations can be passed on through the germ line to future generations and accumulated in the stem cells (Adams 2015). ROS (reactive oxygen species) generated in the cell are usually produced in the mitochondria, and in conditions of ROS excess, damage to protein, lipids and DNA occur by coupling of hydroxyl moieties. Mitochondrial DNA damage by ROS has generated interest as cause for aging and tumorigenesis, (Picard, 2013). ROS excess is common during substrate abundance as in excess food intake, obesity and diabetes. Longevity, in humans and in several animal models, has been associated with mild food deprivation. Food deprivation is also associated with lower rates of chronic diseases in old age including cancer. This topic is covered in chapter 20, Nutrition.

Two tissues that challenge the stem cell concept of ageing are the brain and the heart muscles, both of which have stable number of cells from infancy to death without apparent renewal from stem cells. Brain neurons are usually not subject to renewal, and the ones present as an adult have been established during our early infancy, when the brain cells stop multiplying. Neurons are the longest surviving cells in the body. The central nervous system is well protected within the cranium and our body has created special means to preserve its homeostasis, with the blood brain barrier, circulating cerebral spinal fluid and a complex network of micro-glial cells. The premature ageing of the brain can become the limiting factor in the length and quality of life.

The heart is composed of four muscle chambers, that pump blood to lungs and back and recirculating the blood to the rest of the body. The cardiac muscle cells are the stable work horse circulating blood through the maze of vessels from infancy to death, without rest nor replacement. This was the general knowledge up until 2009, when scientists through carbon-14 dating could identify 1% of new cardiomyocytes generated yearly in a robust young person and decreasing to 0.5% per year by the age of 50. Thus, at age 50 one still has half of the original heart cells present at infancy. This is still a remarkable feat. The turn-over of cells is very low which probably accounts for the low incidence of primary heart cancers. This fact is also interesting, knowing that brain cell turn-over is nearly non-existent and yet brain cancers do occur. The clue is that brain cancers arise from the supporting glial cells.

Returning to the question of DNA fidelity and ageing, how can we prevent DNA damage? The familiar themes of diet, exercise, methods in decreasing ROS stress, avoiding carcinogens and chronic inflammation are ways to decrease risk of DNA mutagenesis. To the point of ageing and longevity, protecting stem cell DNA is vital.

21.2 MORE ON STEM CELLS

Unlike the neurons in the brain and heart muscle cells, most cells in other organs, skin, gut, skeletal muscles, have turn over rates of few days to few years. The brain neurons fortunately last a life time for a good reason, as they are the repository of our memory. Teleologically, it is unclear why cardiac muscles have a low turn over rate. Skeletal muscles have a lifespan of 14-16 years, or shorter when injured or stressed in physical activity, and are renewed by local stem cells. Local stem cells are strategically placed in their privileged surroundings in their respective organs, surrounded by niche cells, which are important in the health and maintenance of the stem cells. Repopulation of senescent, or injured cells by stem cells is an ongoing activity that maintains the proper tissue function. How are stem cells maintained and kept from premature aging? How do stem cells provide the optimum rate in the generation of progenitor cells which differentiate into functioning young tissue cells. The niche cells coddling the stem cells are thought to play this important role, (Gattazzo 2014). Basically, longevity rests on the fertility and condition of the stem cells. The niche microenvironment drives such conditions. In this extracellular matrix surrounded by niche cells, the metabolic exchange, clearance of damaging ROS and damaged cellular components, interplay of cytokines and cell signaling proteins are kept in an optimum functioning state and favorable homeostasis. This allows stem cell dormancy when not called into new production of progenitor cells, and maintenance of steady state of pluripotency while few daughter progenitors are allowed to leave the niche and proceed to differentiation (Romito 2016). Stem cell dormancy and activation into active progenitor cells play important roles in aging and longevity. Niche microenvironment can modulate conditions responsible for malignant transformation of stem cells. Cancer stem cells have become a new model for tumorigenesis, metastatic behavior, tumor cell dormancy and therapeutic resistance (Aponte 2017). Niche cell protection can affect the aging of stem cells. A case in point are the stem cells in the human female ovary, reaching reproductive exhaustion or aging at menopause. This is not found in other mammals, where the reproductive age extends into relatively older age. In the male testis, the production of gametes continues into old age. It has been found that when post-menopausal ovary stem cells are isolated and grown in-vitro, they are able to reproduce gametes. This suggests that ovary niche cells are responsible for the functional behavior of the female germ stem cells.

Stem cells originate from a pool of pluripotent cells going back to the embryo, starting with one cell, the fertilized egg, divides into hundreds of new cells, as a round cluster, the morula, and able to grow into all the fetal tissues, starting with the primordial layers of ectoderm, mesoderm and endoderm. As the embryo matures, these cells become more differentiated onto the path to develop organs. For example, the hematopoietic cells develop from the mesoderm and populate the bone marrow and renew our blood cells. It is not clear when a cell has differentiated to the point that is incapable to reverse to a state that can divide indefinitely and change its basic function. We are learning more about this. For example, a protein factor that favor stemness, and another molecule that induces differentiation, interact to control the stem cell proliferation and differentiation. Fetal stem cells are capable of generating into any cells and adult stem cells have a degree of limitation as to the type and numbers of cells it can generate. There are signals that determine the fate of each stem cell from embryo to adulthood. In most adult organs, stem cells provide a steady supply of new young cells to replace aging cells. For example, red cells are renewed in 2-4 weeks, and the old red cells are destroyed by the spleen and by other phagocytic cells distributed in the liver, bone marrow, etc, called the reticuloendothelial system. In skin, the older cells are pushed to the surface in a matter of days and become flat, acellular and scaly as part of the outer keratin layer. The skin stem cells are located on the basal layer close to the capillaries and lymphatic channels. In the aged, the health of the stem cells will determine longevity. Stem cells are lost due to same forces that age the somatic cells.

Dormancy of stem cells in their niche, which are surrounded by mesenchymal cells, is a defense against the micro-environmental mutagenic factors, since mitotic activity exposes the DNA helix to molecular hits (Sottocornola, 2012). Dormant stem cells can extend availability of progenitor cells into older age. Activation of dormant stem cells into mitotic progenitor stages is associated with greater rate of deleterious mutations. Premature awakening of stem cells from the dormant state can lead to ageing, chronic diseases and cancer. Physiological recruitment of stem cells into tissue renewal by drawing some dormant cells into progenitor function, include conditions such as infection, tissue injury, and selective cell death within an organ from various causes. The concepts of healthy living and disease prevention, including cancer prevention, can be distilled into the simple ways of protecting our stem cells and stem cell dormancy.

Research in cloning and growing new organs, regeneration medicine or organogenesis, has changed the landscape in the field of stem cells, by finding new ways of reprogramming adult cells, such as skin, into pluripotent cells, called induced pluripotent cells (iPC). Induced pluripotent cells solves the problem of availability of stem cells, since embryonic tissue is limited. iPC has expanded the therapeutic potential of stems cells in treating various diseases such as Parkinson's, spinal-chord injuries, replacement of lost heart muscles, rejuvenating joints in arthritis or in athletic injuries. iPC studies with senescent cells have highlighted some of the important molecular pathways in aging, such as, nuclear membrane integrity and the role of lamin and progerin, mitochondria decline, chromatin and transcription factors, epigenetic histone and methylation units. These are factors, in addition to accumulation of DNA damage and mutations, as recognized by Medawar in 1952. The million-dollar question is then, can iPC reverse aging? The embryo is a product of two germ cells, coming from older stem cells (i.e. from parents), and could be thought of a natural way of inducing iPC and reversing aging albeit in a separate individual. Some obstacles encountered are that iPC induced from aged cells have lower yield and that aged cells carry greater number of mutations creating the same aging process in iPCs. On the other hand, aged fibroblasts have been reprogrammed into iPC with high degree of success, (Strassler, 2018). It is still a scientific mystery how a cellular transformation, induced or reprogrammed, can be achieved by a rather simplistic cellular perturbation. This perturbation comes in form of an electrical charge, chemical insult or small molecular transcriptional factors. Shinya Yamanaka reported, in 2006, four transcription factors, necessary for maintenance of stemness, that were key to iPC transformation. These factors were Oct4, Sox2, Klf4 and c-myc. In 2012, the Nobel Committee gave awards to John Gurdon and Yamanaka for "discovery that mature cells can be reprogrammed to become pluripotent". Fifty years earlier, Gurdon perfected the technique of nuclear transplantation to achieve pluripotency, a technique used later for cloning. Undoubtedly research in aging and iPC will lead to new molecular understanding of cellular transformation mechanisms. Imagine uncontrolled growth process in cancer being reprogrammed back to the differentiated cell growth patterns. This has been described experimentally using patient's cancer cells to induce iPC, and in a case of sarcoma iPC, the transformed sarcoma cells behaved as normal mesenchymal tissue, (Navarro, 2018).

Stem cell maintenance and longevity go hand in hand, and this relationship has been elucidated in studies on hydra, one of the primitive multicellular organisms in the phylum Cnidaria, which include jelly-fish. They are commonly found in fresh water, up to ten milimiters in length, and composed of three groups of cells, all permanently in the pluripotent stem cell stage. It can regenerate any portion of its body, foot, head and tentacles, and found to be "immortal". FoxO3 (Forkhead-Box Protein O) has been found to be the key gene regulating the stem cells longevity, and its corresponding proteins are transcription factors important in growth, stem cell maintenance, apoptosis and autophagy, (Tomczyk 2020). FoxO3 upregulation is associated with longevity in humans and also with lower incidence of chronic diseases. Autophagy, a downstream function of FoxO3, was key in promoting longevity.

Thus far we have followed the hypothesis that longevity and the biological events that support or lead to longevity are actors for good health in old age and preventive to cancer and chronic diseases. There are multiple factors; telomere activity, reactive oxidative species (ROS), epigenetic proteins and methylation, stem cells maintenance, autophagy and gene damage, all players in the ageing process. We postulate that one of the more important factors is gene mutation. How do we keep stem cells supplying our aging tissues with new cells? Is the the ageing process different in stem cells than in other tissues? The fact that humans can live up to and beyond 100 years, show that some stem cells do live longer and continue to be functional. Experimental models are able to manipulate several molecular pathways leading to longer organism survival. Niche micro-environment and dormancy could partially account for special ageing process in stem cells. DNA damage repair is primary mechanism in maintaining stem cell function into adulthood and avoiding cancer and chronic diseases (Vitale 2017).

21.3 LONGEVITY IS PROGRAMED IN THE GENES, OR DETERMINED BY ENVIRONMENT; NATURE OR NURTURE?

Longevity amongst mammals varies by body mass. Within same species, the life-span varies within a narrow range. Smaller mammals like rodents survive up to 24 months, have high fecundity, while larger animals live longer, having fewer offsprings with longer duration of maturation. Elephants and whales have longer infancy leading to longer growth period and larger body mass. Studies of centenarians have identified key genes linked to longer life.

Twin linkage studies show that genetic factors account for less than half of our longevity, (Martin 2007). Diet, physical activity, freedom from common infectious and chronic illnesses are factors attributed to the increase in average human life span, from 40 to 75 years, in the last two centuries. Human maximum life span (MLS) has not changed, stable at about 100-120 years. The average height and weight of humans, in the last few centuries, have increased with overall improved nutrition in infancy. This trend on body mass and the implications on aging, chronic diseases and cancer need to be contrasted to the more recent trends in obesity. Individually, longevity and lower risks of chronic diseases in the aged are correlated with lower body mass index (BMI), (Stenholm, 2017). These concepts agree with nutritional studies in diet restriction and improved autophagy, including genes correlated to longevity by genomic wide analysis, (Slagboom 2017). Muscle mass in the aged had stronger association with longevity than BMI. Metabolic signaling and nutrient processing regulate aging through interesting pathways. IGF1 is one common regulator that can explain the findings in Laron syndrome, caloric restriction and fasting. All three conditions result in low levels of IGF1 which influence other signaling pathways for glucose metabolism, as in Sirt1, AKT and of Fox0, or insulin receptor signaling AKT and mTOR. Other molecular pathways in aging are P16(INK4a), PARP (poly-ADP ribose polymerase) and DKC1, also known as dyskerin gene, key in telomerase maintenance. The chart outlining the genes and corresponding proteins, connected by the pathways controlling aging and longevity, would look like a celestial star diagram with hundreds of interconnecting lines, not yielding any further clarity. The take away lessons are that molecular pathways are redundant for any biological function and the routes with more converging pathways, as in autophagy and DNA repair, carry greater weight.

21.4 CHRONIC DISEASES AND AGEING

Chronic diseases in the aged are common and the mild forms are accepted as normal part of aging. These illnesses fit the general picture of tissue decay experienced by all organisms before death from old age. Even within a group of animals, longevity can vary by thousand-fold. Among mammals for example, shrew lives can be as short as 6 weeks, while whales can live up to 200 years. Several survival characteristics are determined by Darwinian selection by favoring the set of genes that are most efficient in achieving certain survival advantages. Evolutionary theory does not necessarily explain longevity, since most genetic modeling by selective pressures focus on reproductive functions. Several scientists have proposed other theories to explain the process of aging and longevity. Medawar in 1952, proposed that aging is due to dysfunction secondary to accumulated mutations and gene damage in the germ line and somatic cells. Today we know through molecular studies in stem cells and aging cells that other molecular events can contribute to aging. Telomerase dysfunction, transcription factor FOXO, nuclear membrane laminin abnormalities, and insulin growth factor I are some of the pathways affecting longevity, as seen so far, in the experimental context. Genetic instability and mutagenesis are well recognized pathways for oncogenesis, and less well recognized causes for chronic diseases and aging. Burnet in 1965, was one of the first investigators to link gene changes to chronic diseases associated with aging.

21.4.1 DEMENTIA

Dementia of old age, and other neural degerative diseases, including Alzheimer's, Parkinson's syndrome, Huntington and Lou Gehrig's (Amyotrophic Lateral Sclerosis) diseases, are associated with amyloid protein deposits, plaques and tangles around and within the neurons and glial cells. It is characterized by progressive loss of brain function, first presenting with short-term memory loss. The working definition of dementia is the progressive cognitive brain dysfunction that affects daily activities. The protenacious deposits are present in varying degrees, and direct causal relationship to dementia has not been well established, despite the strong association. One can develop dementia without amyloid plaques, and several forms and causes of dementia exist. There are several types of amyloid proteins and in some form of amyloidosis, specific diseases can increase its deposit into several tissues and not necessarily in the brain. These amyloid deposits are associated with pathological entities, such as myeloma, producing excess IgG immunoglobulins, chronic infections (tuberculosis) and inflammatory conditions like rheumatoid arthritis. Myeloid deposits in the heart can cause heart failure; in kidneys, resulting in glomerular disease and in the lungs, interstitial fibrosis. In the brain, the protein deposit amyloid Abeta2, is common, accumulated as breakdown product of apolipoprotein. The accumulation of waste products, specifically, deformed proteins aggregating into amyloid plaques, is a consequence of faulty clearance by autophagy (Uddin, 2018). This brings up the analogy of insufficient housekeeping function, on the cellular and molecular levels, in the brain and in other organs. Since the neurons are not renewed, and in fact, their longevity is required for memory and complex brain functions, the central nervous system cells are the most pampered cells in the body. The surrounding environment, provided by glial and other niche cells, is designed specifically to maintain a perfect homeostatic environment. In addition, cholesterol carrier apolipoprotein E plays important role in tau protein function in the neuronal microtubules and in the clearance of lipofuscin, both important players in brain amyloid deposits associated with aging and neurodegerative diseases. Autophagy in lysosomal vacuoles helped by the ubiquitin-proteosome system clears the intra-cellular deposits. Amyloid deposit can also occur in the extra-cellular, interstitial space, highlighting the importance of lymphatics in clearing the amyloid precursor proteins, especially in the brain, due to the blood-brain barrier. With the accumulation of perineural materials, neurotransmission can be affected.

The aging brain has well recognized progressive deficits in visual, hearing acuity and muscular reflexes and strength. This is contrasted to neurodegenerative diseases, more common in older age groups, secondary to interruption or decreased blood supply, such as strokes, or secondary to infections. In these cases of neurodegenerative diseases there is actual loss of neurons, the main functioning brain cells. In normal ageing, there is loss in the volume of gray and white matter, due loss of dendritic processes and glial cells, and to a lesser degree, neurons. This means that in the area of grey matter, there are losses of supporting glial cells and overall loss of myelinated portions of the neural cells. The slower or decreased brain function is resultant from slower dendritic or synaptic transmission of signals. Signaling through nerve fibers and across synapses depend on calcium influx, membrane electric potential, membrane ionic channels, and neuro-transmitter chemicals release. With ageing, these functions can be compromised, (Kumar 2007). Cognitive brain function loss with age is harder to define and understand. Dementia and Alzheimer's disease, by contrast, has been described as a predictable progressive cognitive and memory dysfunction associated with biochemical and histological changes. Despite a large volume of research in dementia, and several clinical drug trials, only one treatment has produced significant improvement and that is physical exercise. Five FDA approved drugs for treatment of Alzheimer's disease increases chemical intermediate acetylcholine and glutamate. Clinical benefits from these drugs are small. Physical activity improves autophagy, the housekeeping function in our tissues, especially in the brain. Exercise also reduces ROS excess and reduces the risks for other chronic illnesses of old age.

Brain senescense and associated dementia conditions can be explained by the same molecular changes common to cancer and aging, namely genetic damage and mutations. Genomics in neuroscience describe these findings as somatic brain mosaicism (Verheijen 2018). Autophagy, DNA repair and ROS balance are important modulators of intracellular mechanisms resulting in mutations. These intertwined molecular pathways, despite their complexities, are giving us important understanding into the pathogenesis of the major health problems of today and for the foreseeable future (chronic diseases of aging and cancer). In this context, cancer is no longer unique, as it shares common molecular footprints with other diseases of old age. In other words, we should ask, which spectra of mutations will lead to heart disease, dementia or cancer? In the brain, there is a low turn-over rate of neurons, which also begs the question that apoptosis of aging neurons is inhibited. Several investigators challenge the notion of absent or low turn over rates of neurons in the adult central nervous system, especially in the hippocampus. Findings show at least a low turnover rate after infancy. Strokes can cause significant loss of neurons in the central nervous system, and regeneration, neurogenesis, occur at variable rates and clinical recovery of cognition can correlate with neural stem cell activities around the areas of brain ischemic death (Rajkovic 2018).

21.4.2 CARDIOVASCULAR DISEASES

Major deaths and morbidities in cardiovascular illnesses are brought on by heart attacks and strokes, which are due to ischemia or oxygen deprivation caused by blockages in the arteries or platelet plugs from hypercoagulation. Important blood vessels at risk are the coronary arteries supplying the heart muscles and the branches of the carotid arteries supplying the brain. When critically interrupted with endovascular plaques, heart attack and stroke ensue. These blockages in the blood conduits simply look like sludge in old pipes with years of accumulated debris. But in fact, they are cellular defects in the endothelium, cells that line the arteries and veins. The accumulated sludge is made of glycolipids, cholesterol and defective proteins. High blood pressure, diabetes, high cholesterol and high lipid blood levels, obesity, smoking and chronic inflammation are major contributing factors for build-up of these vascular contrictions, known as arterial sclerosis. Other significant consequences are lower extremety ischemia, dementia, blindness and ischemic ulcers. Genome wide studies have identified genes associated with atherosclerosis and risk factors of high blood pressure, hyperlipidemia, and propensity for chronic inflammation (Stylianuo 2012). Control of high blood pressure, diabetes, and lowering blood cholesterol with drugs have decreased the prevalence of atherosclerosis and vascular thrombotic and embolic events. Nutritional changes can also be effective in preventing atherosclerosis by lowering lipid intake and by moderating diabetes. In addition, physical exercise decreases hypertension, hypercholesterolemia and hyperglycemia by activating muscle hormones, autophagy and modulating lipid and sugar metabolism (Martinet 2009).

21.4.3 DIABETES MELLITUS

This disease was recognized in Ancient Greece and Egypt, by the increased volume of urine, named after the Greek word diabetes, meaning siphon, or frequent urination. Mellitus was added later (Latin word for sweet or honey) by Thomas Willis, 1675, to differentiate from diabetes insipidous. Diabetic patients have elevated blood sugars, hyperglycemia, associated with several metabolic defects and cellular dysfunction that contribute to the hyperglycemic state and eventual multi-organ illnesses, as in hypertension, cardio-vascular disease, renal failure, neuropathy and blindness. A juvenile form, type I, presents in childhood, and is characterized by low insulin production and is a primary disease of the insulin producing Langerhan cells in the pancreas. Type II diabetes, the adult form, is characterized by obesity and cell membrane insensitivity to insulin. Clinical manifestations of diabetes are found in many tissues, in the form of arterial sclerosis and peripheral neuropathy. Other consequences are in the eye as retinopathy that lead to blindness and in the kidneys as glomerular sclerosis, that can lead to kidney failure, requiring dyalisis in the late stages. Small sensory nerves in the feet can fail, leading to numbness, pressure or traumatic sores and infections.

Diabetes, being a defect in the insulin secreting Langerhan cells and in the metabolism of sugar, can in fact represent a combination of many molecular missteps in the glucose metabolism. Just as in cancer, a conglomerate of simple and complex molecular and genetic changes, can lead to dramatic changes in cell behavior and function. In diabetics, the resulting cellular dysfunction accelarates the aging process. Insulin producing cells in the pancreas are lost in type I diabetes, through autoimmune T cell cytotoxicity. There are predisposing genes for several T cell antigens, including some HLA (human lymphocyte antigens), that are associated with type I diabetes (Mehers 2009). In type II diabetes, there are diverse genes that influence the production of insulin and tissue response to insulin. For example, the insulin receptor substrate (IRS-1) gene can be mutated in T2DM (type II diabetes mellitus). The melatonin receptor substrate (MTNR1beta) gene controls sleep cycle, and insulin release; Ankyrin 1, gene responsible for spherocytosis, modulates beta cells response to hypoglycemia; and growth factor receptor bound protein 14 (GRB14) gene, can affect insulin release through a tyrosine kinase receptor on various tissues, causing insulin resistance, (Brunetti, 2014). As we can see, there are dozens of proteins and pathways regulating glucose metabolism. Blood glucose concentration, its transport across cell membrane and glycolysis in the conversion to ATP are examples of steps controlled by specific genes and proteins that are at risk for alterations from DNA damage.

Obesity increases the risks for type II diabetes, and the clinical links include cardiovascular disease, hypertension, dementia and even cancer. The molecular basis for obesity and type II diabetes, down stream from the genetic changes, include the dopamine, adiponectin and leptin pathways. These hormones control appetite, satiety, and insulin responsiveness in tissues and in turn are regulated by diet and physical activity (Ruegsegger, 2017). The web of interconnectivity between molecular pathways, micro-environment homeostasis, and optimum cell function speaks to the common etiology and pathogenesis of chronic diseases and aging.

21.4.4 AUTO-IMMUNE DISEASES

Our immune system is designed to neutralize any invading organisms that penetrate our protective skin and aero-digestive mucosal surfaces. This system also participates in wound healing by marshaling several lymphokines, cell migration, neovascularization, clearance of deformed proteins and debris from injured cells, and elimination of transformed cancer cells. Foreign molecules are recognized and targeted for destruction and remodeling. When our own tissues are targeted as "foreign", or a loss of "self-tolerance", effector lymphocytes accumulate and begin the inflammatory reaction around these tissues, known as auto-immunity (Bolon 2012). The immediate tissue involved in this active immune reaction manifests itself with pain, swelling, and redness, the hallmarks of inflammation. There is an increase in vascularity and blood flow, with accumulation of inflammatory cells, discharging secretory products such as lymphokines, reactive oxygen products, and lysozymes. This active process is countered by cellular and humoral activity to slow the immune activity and return to a baseline homeostasis. In auto-immune diseases, this balance is lost, favoring immune reaction against specific normal tissue proteins.

When auto immune disease develops, usually in older age, tissues targeted can be specific or more diffuse, such as skin and kidney only as in scleroderma, or just joints as in rheumatoid arthritis. In other forms of autoimmune disease, multiple organs can be involved, as in lupus. The effects can be mild to severe. The autoimmune disease can be limited to a rash or mild proteinuria. More severe cases can present with skin desquamation or renal failure in cases of nephritis. As a group of diseases, is also referred to as collagen vascular diseases; Sjogren's disease involving the eyes, as in uveitis; or as scleroderma, lupus involving the skin and rheumatoid arthritis involving joints.

Genome wide studies point to genes in the MHC (major histocompatibility complex) region to be responsible for the autoimmune phenomena. These genes are templates for proteins, HLA (human lymphocyte antigens) and antigen presenting factors, that when malfunctioning, lead to immune reactivity against self-antigens and tissues (Rioux JD, 2005). Malfunction of antigen presentation to effector cells originate in the specific MHC genes that have undergone damage, mutations or epigenetic modifications.

Although some auto-immune diseases can present early in life, such as SLE (systemic lupus erythematosus), arthritis and thyroiditis, older age presents higher incidence of auto-antibodies associated with auto-immunity, (Vadasz 2013). Past infections or chronic infections increases the incidence of auto-antibodies. This may also be a sign of immune-senescense. Aging is associated with several changes that blunts the immune response, from decreased T-cell generation by thymic tissue, to antigen processing and stimulation of Treg , (Watad, 2017). Weakend immune response in the elderly should also lower the autoimmune reactions, unfortunately, this is not the case. Autoimmune illnesses are more common in women, another unexplained fact. In older age, the degraded cell proteins are more common and may be mistaken as foreign and generate auto-immune responses. Molecular mimicking, a strategy some microbes use to escape host immune resistence, induces host immune response with cross-reactions and turning on auto-immunity. For example, Epstein bar virus (EBV) infections can induce multiple sclerosis through mimicry of EBV nuclear antigen 1 and inducing the neural protein anotamin 2 (ANO2). In addition, normal response to infections and injuries are not properly turned off, leading to an activated immune response that can harm normal tissues, i.e., a dysfunctional immune tolerance. Herein, autophagy plays a central role by disposing worn out proteins, by properly initiating immune response in presenting antigens to effector cells and by modulating suppressor immunocytes in toning down the immune reaction and achieving a balanced immune tolerance.

21.4.5 CHRONIC INFLAMMATORY DISEASES

The current understanding of the microbiome has changed the perception of how our body deals with several of the common microorganisms, in and around our gut, bronchioles, mouth and skin. Whereas we previously thought our inner tissues were sterile, some of our body fluids, in the lung and peritoneal cavities, contain commensal organisms without eliciting the immune reaction as in an infectious process. Just as in the gut and on the skin, there are resident bacteria, fungi and viruses that actually benefit the surrounding cells by rejecting more virulent organisms. We no longer consider all microorganisms as invaders. The new concept of the microbiome allows the tolerance of "good" resident organisms, while rejecting others that can cause infections. Some infections, as in the gut, can be successfully brought under control, by using the good organisms in our microbiome. Prolonged antibiotic treatments will allow selective advantage to drug-resistant organisms that can alter the microbiome allowing troublesome infections. In addition, the microbiome provides beneficial byproducts such as short-chain lipids and some vitamins.

Most infections follow a typical course starting with prodrome, where the organisms multiply until reaching significant numbers to cause symptoms of fever, fatigue and other symptoms like cough, abdominal pain, diarrhea, muscle pain, and joint pain, depending on the organ system affected. The acute infection reaches a point of maximum immune mobilization of white cells, vascular blood flow, interstitial fluid overload, and destruction of the offending organisms, and then the inflammatory response recedes, by specific activation of immune inhibitory pathways. In chronic inflammatory response, there remains a smoldering degree of immune activity resulting in residual swelling and symptoms associated with infection or inflammation. The situation may vary from residual live organisms or residual debris from the acute phase, to immune dysfunction. This can be viewed as a stand-off between invaders and the home defenders. Some common scenarios are for example bronchitis in smokers, gum disease and periodontal plaques from lack of dental hygiene, inflammatory bowel disease, and others.

Chronic inflammatory conditions can also be caused by autoimmune diseases, in the absence of microbial contribution. When the condition is subclinical, usually asymptomatic, diagnosis can be difficult and suspected in cases of non-specific symptoms of fatigue and unease. Blood test of ESR (erythrocyte sedimentation rate) and CRP (C reactive protein) are usually elevated and a carefull physical exam can reveal findings of localized inflammation. Chronic inflammation increases ROS (reactive oxygen species) and tilts the balance towards ROS excess, which can contribute to DNA damage and accelerated the aging process.

Chronic inflammation is found in obesity. Adipocytes (fat cells) are both increased in numbers and in size in obesity. Adipocytes are sources of inflammatory factors like IL6 and TNF. CRP produced by liver cells in presence of chronic inflammation is also increased. Metabolic endotoxemia, associated with the gut microbiome, can induce insulin-resistance, commonly found in obesity associated type II diabetes. Obesity and diabetes increase the risks for other chronic diseases, cardiovascular and cancer. Experiments in mice showed appropriate microbiome transplants can cause weight gain or reduction. In humans, higher Firmicutes to Bacteroidetes ratio in the microbiome can induce weight reduction and is associated with weight reduction measures including by surgical alterations of the gut (Tseng, 2019).

As the chronic inflammatory conditions are ameliorated, immune competence is improved and risks of diseases of ageing and cancer are lowered. Minimizing chronic inflammation, decreasing ROS excess and protecting DNA from stresses can slow cellular aging. In addition, circulating damaged DNA can be a source of chronic inflammation, a feedback loop commonly found in the elderly, as in autoimmune conditions (Ioannidou, 2016).

21.4.6 CANCER

Cancer is closely associated aging and shares many of the basic molecular dysfunction of chronic diseases. Most of us, however, do not consider cancer as a chronic disease, since at a first glance, the tumor is there or not. From a molecular standpoint, the progression of cancer from a relatively normal cell is a continuum over several years or decades. With modern oncological treatments, many cancers can be maintained for many years in check, without complete eradication. Moreover, the molecular basis for cancer inception and growth, namely gene damage and mutations into oncogenes, is the very platform we need to understand for prevention strategies. We are indebted to the research funds and resources directed at curing cancer which also pushed ahead the field of molecular biology. DNA oxidative damaging events are surprisingly frequent, in the order of 10,000 per cell daily. These single damaging events on the chromosome, if not fixed, result in mutations during mitosis. Both gene damages and mutations are modulated by the cellular microenvironment and homeostatic mechanisms affected by our daily activities in diet, exercise and exposure to pollutants. Although most of us think that a doctor's office visit and check up is the most important factor in our health, current research will point to the equally or more important consequences from actions in our daily activities, as the main contributors to our health. These steps in cancer prevention, elaborated in this book, will change our attitudes toward the importance of daily activities that impact directly on our health, ageing and chronic diseases.

21.4.7 COMMON CAUSES OF CHRONIC DISEASES AND COMMON PREVENTION STRATEGIES

Pursuing the story of cancer prevention has led us to the root causes of cancer. Under the surface, the cancer picture is more complex and shares common molecular origins with other diseases of older age, otherwise known as chronic diseases. As we age, our underlying molecular structures are suffering damaging blows and acquiring temporary or permanent gene, protein and lipid structural changes. The silver lining in this otherwise inevitable saga of aging, is that few housekeeping measures can improve the outlook on all these fronts, prevent chronic diseases, including cancer, and improve the overall health and well-being, while, at the same prolonging our aging years, (Li, 2020).

The complex cancer story reflects the very intricate secrets of life, from cell growth and replication to apoptosis or programmed cell death and renewal. The stability of our organic molecules is constantly under pressure and the threat of gene mutations are ever present. Gene mutations are at the root cause of cancer. Gene mutations, damages and epigenetic changes will slow immune activity, disrupt wound healing, alter lipid storage and recycling of injured proteins. In turn, as part of this aging process, chronic diseases can set in.

The common prevention strategies for cancer, chronic diseases and aging with grace (so to speak) are to prevent minute molecular damages in our cells. Optimizing function of the inner machinery (maintaining homeostasis) and improving the DNA repair mechanisms are good starting points. There are dozens more mechanisms contributing to or alleviating aging and genetic damage or stress. The molecular pathways or mechanisms are intertwined, redundant and wide reaching. The totality of the organic molecules, cellular structures, their functions and energy transfers, can be viewed as a closed system through molecular ecology, following the laws of thermodynamics and physiological principles of homeostasis or allostasis (Perez-Ortin 2019). The ecological mantra of living clean, eat healthy and exercise seems too obvious and simplistic. Our molecular microenvironment is inextricably linked to the ambient environment, which is under stresses of pollution, human activities, destruction of natural habitats and climate change. Likewise, our cellular microenvironment needs special care to maintain homeostasis and avoid molecular stresses. Enviromental harmful agents such as tobacco, radiation, toxic chemicals, food additives can pollute our internal microenvironment, alter the homeostasis and increase ROS radicals. (More on molecular ecology, chapter 22)

The common strategies are simple and fit the common-sense approaches. Avoid potential carcinogens in the environment, including pollutants and microbes in the air and water, consume fewer processed foods and more fruits, roots, nuts and vegetables, and keep up with physical activity, especially in the older years. These life-style measures from our own initiative should be complemented by yearly consultation with your doctor who can monitor your progress with blood tests (liquid biopsy) and screening exams. Advances in molecular biology allow insight into these molecular pathways and create a score card in how we are taking care of our own microenvironment. A to do list will be reviewed. Just as our outdoor environment is able to recover, when given the chance, our own cellular molecular environment will achieve homeostasis with few simple steps.

21.5 INCREASE LONGEVITY, SAME AS REVERSING AGEING?

Average life span has doubled from 40 years in 1900 to what it is today. One could credit nutrition, clean water and improved healthcare as major factors in this remarkable improvement in human longevity. The decrease of deaths from early XX century from infections, as in pneumonia and cholera, has allowed many more citizens to reach beyond their 5th and 6th decades of life, (Bunker 2001). Lives saved in infancy and young adulthood will eventually extend longevity figures. Treatment of hypertension, diabetes, and obesity has lowered the risk of death in cardiovascular diseases, which in turn contributed to the gains in longevity since the 1950's. Health improvement interventions, no matter how small, can contribute to longevity. For example, the replacement of cataracts with implanted lenses, is performed nearly a million times yearly in the U.S. There is a significant improvement in vision and quality of life with an estimated 6 months increase in longevity.

Without a specific cause of death, like illnesses or trauma, and without specific causes of chronic diseases, the determinants of longevity will mirror the factors that slow or prevent aging. These factors are the exactly what we have outlined in the present discussions.

21.5.1 REPLACING OLD BODY PARTS: HELPFUL IN OLD AGE?

Let us reverse our focus from the cellular and molecular and look at the bigger picture, the organs in the body like the analogy of fixing and maintaining a complex mechanical machine. Will replacing a body part keep your machine working better? Will a hip replacement make you feel renewed? If walking is limited by an arthritic hip joint or a joint damaged by sports or trauma, hip replacement can take away the pain in the joint and allow greater mobility. Despite some of the risks of the procedure, and residual post-operative problems such as pain, a functional new hip is a plus. Can a series of body part replacements approach a new functional person? A rhetorical question usually met with a negative answer, except a few exceptions, perhaps. Will a patch work replacement prolong life and meet the criteria of well-being for the long term in your senior years? Facial plastic surgery will make you look and possibly feel younger, organ transplant will prolong your life when a vital organ fails. Dental health should be emphasized as it contributes to adequate nutrition in the elderly as well as minimizing chronic infections in the oral cavity.

Just as for a car that you favor and want to extend its driving years, good maintenance is still best strategy and will extend the life of several components. Similarly, for an aging body regular maintenance and housekeeping activity are required for disease prevention. The housekeeping chores discussed for cancer prevention are the same routines one would carry out for extending organ function in the aged, or reversal of ageing. Caring for our bodies as fine-tuned engines, from the organ-system viewpoint, one is well atuned to the need for maintenance activities. From a cellular and molecular viewpoint, the health housekeeping needs are just as important but not as obvious nor as pressing. As we can show how the advances in molecular medicine can impact our daily lives, and illustrate the steps needed to maintain molecular homeostasis in the cell, everyone will be adopting these routines of cancer and chronic diseases prevention, thereby translating their every day living into improved healthy living, especially in older age.

21.5.2 ROLE OF STEM CELL HEALTH IN THE AGED; THE GUT MODEL.

Most organs are regenerated by resident stem cells that are situated in the basal tissue layers, such as in skin, gut, and various glands. In the gut for example, the mucosal cells are repopulated every 5 days. The old cells are shed into the lumen of the gut and new ones are generated by the stem cells at the basal layer of the intestinal crypts and slowly migrate up the crypts to the luminal surface. On the surface, lining the lumen, these cells interact with the enteric juices and the microbiome. In the gut lumen, the sulcus entericus flows by, mixed with ingested food and secreted digestive juices, and closer to the gut lining cells, the mucous layer gives a more complex dimension to the microbiome flora. Aided by our normal gut flora, the gut cells perform an incredible job in keeping unwanted foreign materials out and absorbing the needed fluids and nutrients. With a plethora of microorganisms in the surface of the gut, it is incredible that chronic inflammation is not problematic. In addition to the clusters of immune cells in the gut mucosa, the mucous goblet cells produce a protective mucous that provide a balance in the interface with microbes, friends and foes, without undue amount of inflammatory reaction. When excessive inflammation occurs, surface ulcers can develop, as well as diarrheal state, an over-growth of some organisms and decreased transit time. Ulcers and cell disruptions are healed at a rapid rate. The growth response is regulated by the rate of stem cell proliferation. In old age, there is a thinning of gut mucosa and shortening of the gut villi, the projections and folding in the gut surface and an over-all reduction of gut cells. In turn, both nutrient absorption and interface with the gut microbes can be disrupted.

How do we preserve our stem cells healthy which can then happily replace the loss of old cells? The answer repeats the same theme of proper nutrition, exercise, maintaining the necessary homeostasis, avoiding built up of waste products. For the gut, for example, attention to the normal protective gut commensal flora, is another key factor. A prolonged course of antibiotic intake for an infection, can lead to overgrowth of invasive and opportunistic bacteria, such as C difficile, that can cause lethal gut infections. Probiotic bacteria and food additives have been promoted, that in many instances can "settle down" the gut function and prevent diarrhea or constipation. Another factor is the homeostatic mechanisms between the stem cells and their protective niche cells. In the gut, the mucosal stem cells are in contact with the immune cells, mucosal goblet cells, several hormone producing endocrine cells, and the muscular cells that are responsible for motility and peristalsis. All these cells participate in the stem cell niche, the surrounding supporting cells, that modulate stem cell health and reproduction (Ullah, 2018). In turn, gut health is critical in old age as the senescent gut can be a major source of chronic inflammation. Stem cell health in the aged may be one of the most important contributors to the elderly's well being. How do you simply measure stem cell condition, when there are diverse types of progenitor cells and niche tissues? Geromirs, microRNAs closely associated with stem cell function and molecular pathways, can be used as biomarkers that can give a microscopic view of these cellular interactions, (Ugalde 2011).

Therapy with stem cells have been used in trials for spinal chord injury, heart failure, diabetes and cartilage growth. The gold standard for stem cell therapy is of course, bone marrow transplantation, from both autologous and allogeneic source of cells. The stem cells can be collected from bone marrow aspiration, or from peripheral blood using pheresis. With new sources of stem cells, namely iPC, the range of potential therapies can be expanded, (Martin 2017).

21.5.3 ELONGATING TELOMERES

Telomere, a DNA segment of repeats TTTAGGG, located at the end of chromosomes, can be lengthened by the enzyme telomerase. In cancer cells and in normal in young cells, the telomeres are longer. When telomere length becomes short, then instead of cell division, apoptosis occurs and cell death results. Experimentally, telomeres have been lengthened by activating telomerase. In animal experiments, insertion of the gene segment TERT, which controls the functional protein telomerase, can activate telomerase to increase the length of telomeres. TERT is active in embryonic growth stages and silenced in adult somatic cells. Telomeres are long in stem cells, although the oocyte telomere starts short until fertilization and then the embryo cells quickly activate TERT. There are drugs that may activate or inhibit telomerase activity, which can be used for anti-aging or cancer treatment purposes. Telomerase activity, telomere length and age of cells are found to be associated with each other. Youth, physical activity, diet rich in plant sources, life style associated with lower ROS excess and lower mutagenic activity are also correlated with increased telomerase activity. Molecular interactions in the regulation of telomerase activity have been studied in the context of cancer therapies, and more recently, as anti-aging compounds, (Saretski, 2016). Several anti-aging agents are available in the marketplace. In some, the active ingredient is an extract of the plant, Astragalus membraneceus, and in one mouse study, the drug did not lengthen the telomeres, though some animals lived longer. As in many drugs purified from natural plant products, the beneficial effects may be obtained by consuming the plant parts in the natural form. In fact, numerous plants and vegetables contain high activity of telomerase, especially in the parts with active growth such as flower buds, shoots, seeds and young roots. There are minimal differences between plant and mammalian telomerase and the telomere TTTAGGG tandem repeats are similar in humans and plants, reflecting the importance of telomere function and conservation through evolution. The fundamental question is whether ingested plant telomerase and associated activators, can activate human telomerase. There are also multiple inhibitors of telomerase, with potential anti-cancer effects, some for example, can bind to telomeres. The telomere is the focal point of longevity, cancer transformation and death, and not surprisingly, the genetic clockwork for telomere is also the focal point for other promoter genes responsible for the basic control of these functions such as the Wnt, PTEN, P53 and NFK-B genes.

Elizabeth Blackburn and colleagues Jack Szostak and Carol Greider were awarded the Nobel Prize for their work in telomeres and telomerase in 2009. Aging research and rejuvenation work focused on this short segment DNA and some promising steps were achieved. For example, when RNA coding for TERT was introduced into cells, telomere lengthening was achieved and allowed cells to live longer.

21.5.4 MICRORNA MODULATION IN AGEING

MicroRNA modulates DNA function by inhibiting messenger RNA translation of proteins. It is intrically involved in all DNA transcriptional activities, and serves as another intermediary regulating step to all normal and pathological cellular conditions. In aging there is a profound change in miRNA profiles, mostly to the lower spectrum and possibly explaining the findings of protein excess within old cells. Specific mirna are associated with stem cell aging (Watanabe 2018). When serum factors from younger animal is given to the older, known as parabiosis, the older animal is found to behave younger including finding several measures of cell senescense being reversed. In mice, administration with a cocktail of mirna can reverse aging studied by several molecular endpoints (Kim 2017). MiR 17-5p, part of miR 17–92 cluster, participates in cMyc cell growth promotion, and repressed by P53, associated with apoptosis. MiR 17-5p levels are found 4-fold lower in senescent tissues. When administered in mice, these animals were found to live longer by 16%.

There is also intriguing new research on relationship of some specific miRNA and telomerase. Mir-1207-5p and mir-1266 supress hTERT, the reverse transcriptase gene for telomerase which in turn will limit cell survival.

CHAPTER 22

MOLECULAR ECOLOGY AND CANCER PREVENTION. OTHER NEW PARADIGMS?

Scientific studies of nature events, whether using physics, mathematics, chemistry or biology, all share some common elements. Scientific observations and experiments show certain patterns and findings confirming prescribed laws or behaviors and by using deductive logic, new theories and predictions can be formulated into new hypotheses. Hence, the new events can be viewed through the lens of proven theories and then use new tools to probe new frontiers that may prove to revise the old science into new paradigms. Some of the methodologies and technologies developed in one discipline can be applied to great advantage in a different field of study. For example, statistical analysis developed in mathematics can be used in medical studies. The design of a study to test a hypothesis in complex and diverse biological systems is best structured using statistics in order to achieve reliability and validity. A simple tool used in shoe repair can be applied in the surgical science, redesigned as the Bethune rib cutter. In cancer prevention, as the medical sciences progress from the cellular to the molecular framework, our understanding of malignant diseases evolves to driver oncogenes from the organ-based cell classification of tumors. The sub-cellular organelles and molecular view of biological functions take on the new and previously unrecognized roles in the behavior of cancers. New theories and paradigm from related disciplines can usher new understanding of biological events, where the interaction of these molecular units are examined under the theories of evolution, ecological diversity and environmental sciences reveal new insights into our state of health and illnesses.

Molecular ecology is a perfect example of separate disciplines coming together creating a new paradigm. Molecular ecology approaches the landscape of our internal organs and systems as a composite of diverse molecules interacting as an ecosystem. The definition of molecular ecology, attributed to Paul Weiss, is the following: "Continuum of biological interactions between the molecular, cellular, organismal levels to the environment", (Lambert 1995). Molecular epidemiology is often used in the understanding of cancer pathogenesis (Greenwald 2009), and more recent references to molecular ecology, encompasses the entire field of epidemiology, genomics and molecular interactions. In oncology, the study of cancer, molecular ecology examines the process through the lens of growth dynamics of cancer cell populations (diverse clones), (Maley 2017).

Environmental factors in tumorigenesis include exposure to carcinogens, in which the interface is through the skin, lungs or digestive tract. Essentially all what we do within earth's environment in terms of food consumption, breathing the atmosphere, and drinking out of the connected body of waters, contributes to our environmental exposure. Climate change and environmental pollutants are common areas of concern and create new pertubations in our molecular milieu and in time aggravating current illnesses or creating new pathologies. Destructive storms, contamination of drinking water with industrial by-products, micro-plastics and decrease in air quality, all impact our inner body molecular ecology. The impact on different life-forms are dramatic as we see loss of species and sheer numbers of living creatures, due progressive shrinkage and degradation of our habitat. What has raised concern on our environment as result of global warming, illustrates the fact that we have reached the limits of what our environment can tolerate. These alarm bells should also make us pay closer attention to our own intra-cellular environment. Alarm bells ring for our molecular ecology as well, in the form of increased rates of cancer, obesity, chronic illnesses including dementia, diabetes and cardiovascular diseases. The population older than 60 years is the largest growing sector. In the elderly population, we find that the intra-cellular molecular ecology is stressed to the point that homeostasis becomes difficult to maintain. Younger individuals are not immune to these problems. There is increase in cancer risks in the younger population, previously only seen in the young with germ line inherited onco-genes. Our own internal environment has undergone significant changes. Stresses on a cellular level can be summed up by looking at levels of ROS and the corresponding intracellular coping mechanisms. Molecular ecology frames the gene and other molecular damages from cellular micro-environment stresses as pertubations in the cell and how each molecular unit affect each other. These ecological pertubations in the molecular units form the basis of aging, cancer and other chronic diseases. For example, in this molecular ecology paradigm views molecular pathways as systems, like the ROS coping system of proteostasis (Korovila 2017). Modeling the myriad of biological interactions to few simple cellular pathways is the scientific methodology to approach more complex issues in molecular ecology. Molecular homeostasis exists for all life-forms and deviations will generate excess ROS. Proteins depend on its 3-dimensional structure for optimal function, and ROS increases the process of protein aging, deformation and denaturation, which in turn is renewed by the process of proteostasis involving proteasomes, endocytosis and autophagy. Deficient states in proteostasis result in emphysema, asthma and COPD in the lungs, fatty liver, cirrhosis in the liver, and in neural degenerative diseases. Cumulative effects of ROS over time and inssuficient proteostasis contributes to aging, and increased risks of cancer and of chronic diseases. The perfect storm formed by the conditions of older population, atmospheric and water contaminants, additives in food processing, and global warming may cause havoc in our cellular coping mechanisms and result in higher rates of illnesses and cancer. Today we must include another major factor during our current pandemic, that of infectious agents as the covid-sars-2, affecting a significant fraction of the world population. Near term and chronic effects of covid on our molecular ecology are still being studied (more on chapter 23).

Increase in atmospheric CO2 gases in the last few decades from 305 parts per million (ppm) to currently 410 ppm is ascribed to human activity, and in some situations, indoor concentrations can be found much higher in the 1,000 ppm range. Tissue rise in CO2 is associated with acidity and theorized to contribute to oncogenesis by mitochondrial dysfunction and increased oxidative radicals. Lung cancer in smokers can potentially be induced by the increase in local tissue CO2, in addition to several carcinogens in the tobacco smoke. Can ambient CO2 have a direct effect in the future cancer risks?

The Warburg effect, described by Otto Warburg in 1924, shows that cancer cells prefer the glycolytic pathway for glucose metabolism, instead of aerobic phosphorylation, producing far fewer ATP, the energy transmitting molecule, a rather inneficient process. The glycolytic pathway makes cancer tissues more acidic. Acidic environment leads to activation of lysozymes and genes favoring metastatic disease (Kato 2013). Increased tissue CO2 may slow the Warburg effect and lactate production and drive aerobic oxidation. The driver of Warburg effect, though inefficient, is a faster reaction and more suitable for cancer growth requirements, (Epstein 2017). Even today, Warburg effect is referenced as the rationale for treatment, such as starvation or low-sugar diets, and even, the use of TPN (total parenteral nutrition) in malnourished cancer patients. These nutritional based treatments have not proven to be effective as cancer therapies.

Globocan report of worldwide cancer statistics, 2012, showed increased incidence and death rates from several common cancers, including breast, colorectal and lung, associated with colder climate. An exception was cervical cancer, where the distribution of HPV is more prevalent in countries near the tropics such as India and Mozambique. Experimental cancers in mice grew faster in colder temperatures, and lymphocyte cytotoxicity against cancer cells was found to be temperature dependent, greater at body temperature 37 C as opposed to room temperature of 24 C. Voskarides collected genomic data on populations in cold and high- altitude regions and concluded that some genes were selected for climatic adaptation, however, rendered a distinct disadvantage in cancer development, refered as genetic pleitropism (Voskarides 2017). Thus far, we do not have observable evidence of cancer incidence changes due to global warming and climate change, except an increase of skin cancers from increased outdoor activities. Theorectically, increases in other cancers are expected, due to ROS excess in warmer temperatures (shown in animals) and due to increase in microbial diseases (Paital 2016).

Genomic studies of tumors have gathered thousands of mutated genes with some interesting clustering by different statistical algorithms. Many of these oncogenes are common and recognized amongst lung, colorectal and melanoma, such as Ras, Myc, P53 and Braf. Thousand other oncogenes are less common and their corresponding proto-oncogene are not well characterized. The first task is to compile all the mutated genes, then to figure out their significance, (Ding 2018). The classification of all these oncogenes into driver and passenger genes is one system of classification that is consistent with molecular ecology. We have seen by histopathological and cell surface markers that wide clonal diversity develops within a tumor driven by genetic instability. The oncogenes with greater "fitness" or survival advantage will result in higher growth rates and gene dominance as the driver mutation. Passenger mutations, which are the bulk of mutated genes found, are considered passive "hitchhikers". Although their significance is not clear, their role has yet to appear in this complex micro-environment of special niches, (McFarland 2017). The tumor oncogene spectrum can be explored for therapeutic advantage by neutralizing specific targets that are over-expressed.

22.1 QUANTUM BIOLOGY OF CANCER. A NEW PARADIGM?

Physicists are known to formulate mathematical equations that describe universally any event in nature, specified by certain given variables. Not surprisingly, physicists think that is appropriate to apply the same formulations to living processes. Niels Bohr in 1932 made several proposals in his lecture, Light and Life, that alluded to a molecular basis of life and these predictions inspired scientists like Delbruck and Watson in contributing to field of molecular biology and genetics. Schroedinger wrote “What is Life: The physical aspect of the living cell” in 1944 and discussed aspects of quantum physics and thermodynamics in biological systems. Quantum physics, in contrast to the classical Newtonian physics, shows the duality of matter and energy, of particles and waves, and explains the quantum units of photon in the nano- meter dimension. There are no contradictions between quantum and classical physics, since the dimensions wherein the laws apply are separated by a billion-fold, just as the laws in astrophysics governing blackholes are applicable here on earth, once those dimensions are reached.

The dimensions of molecular interactions within our cells are in the nanometer scale, meaning that the biology of molecules fits into the dimensions of quantum mechanics (Waring 2018). The concepts of quantum coherence, tunneling and entanglement may shed new light in many biological processes (McFadden 2018). Tunneling explains how an electron traverses a barrier, when analysed as a wave form. Normally, the electron as a particle would be stopped by the same barrier. Tunneling can explain enzyme function, which catalyzes the binding of two molecules, overcoming energy barrier, and achieving exchange of electron into lower energy states. Entanglement between two molecules demonstrate the coordination of two or more of their respective electrons into a superimposed state, according to their spins and Pauli exclusion principle. The quantum view contrasted to our own classical concepts of life is illustrated by Schroedinger’s cat model, simultaneous in a state of being alive and dead, when placed into a quantum black box. Entanglement accounts for migratory bird's ability to sense the interaction between the eye chromophobe molecular spin and the earth's magnetic field. Quantum coherence shows how electron can be transported through a lattice structure with higher efficiency than expected and coherence among these electrons illustrates the marvel of photosynthesis and mitochondrial ATP generation.

Quite possibly, the cell has taken advantage of quantum mechanics in a sophisticated degree, to the point that physicists study photosynthesis looking for ways to solve the quantum computing problem. Quantum computing takes advantage of the third state of quantum superposition to increase speed and alternate pathways of computing. Currently, absolute low temperatures are required for quantum computers, while in photosynthesis similar work is accomplished at higher temperatures. Many scientists think the cell, being a wet and warm bag of organic molecules, is incapable of yielding any fine physical measuments. On the other hand, within the cell, the molecular movements and interactions seemingly chaotic and random, follow the principles of quantum physics, performing miraculous life changes, through signal transduction, fine-tuning of protein synthesis, membrane transport and nerve conduction. These are a few examples that belie any doubts on the significance of living molecular functions at the quantum level.

What about our cancer question; how does quantum biology explain uncontrolled cell growth or provide a different platform for switching off uncontrolled growth? The National Cancer Institute (NCI) in 2008 initiated a program (Physical Science-Oncology Network) looking for novel ways to solve the cancer question. Through this Network scientists could employ some of the tools developed in physicics, super-computing, and chemical engineering (Zahir, 2008). As part of this NCI initiative, many more scientists are looking at cancer as the next big unsolved physical-biological problem. Novel approaches from a sub-atomic viewpoint have been explored.

A common DNA mutation is associated with proton tunneling in the tautameric forms of Adenosine-Thimine/Cytosine-Guanine bonds (Brovarets 2018). The "proton sharing" state in the A-T bonds, for example, also represent a on-off switch for oncogene function. The off-position functions like many of the gene silencing techniques in molecular genetics, such as methylation or sex gene expression in fish. Several apoptosis genes play a crucial role in cancer growth, i.e., when early in oncogenesis, in the suppressed state driving growth, or later in clinically established malignancies, apoptosis is enhanced by therapeutic modulators. Molecular signals interact with several genes that determine whether the cancer cell lives or dies. The P53 gene or the mutated oncogene counterpart, for example, could demonstrate this duality. Clinically, advanced tumors are characterized by clonal diversity, including clones that show high degree of necrosis. Could this proton-transfer "switch" play a role in P53 function where within the same cancer, some cells apoptosis genes, while "on position", can achieve completion of cell death, while in others (heterogeneity of tumors), apoptosis will be inhibited, held in the "off position"? Are there new molecular pathways that capitalize on this newly recognized tautameric switch? Biochemically, several small molecules, such as protoporphyrins, are capable to "switch" P53 gene into a pro-apoptotic pathway. Can these dual gene functions be studied as quantum entanglement and find simpler ways of switching P53 apoptotic function to the on-position in the cancer cell, even in the mutated or oncogene P53? The Schroedinger cat paradox, alive or dead in the quantum world, describes the reality in cancer clonal heterogeneity perfectly. Within the cancer, the cells can live or die, depending on their oncogene quantum entanglement state. Curing cancer can then be realized by shifting the balance of the entanglement switch in the oncogene towards apoptosis.

23

FUTURE PERSPECTIVES AND THE PANDEMIC OF 2020.

How to exploit the common molecular threads connecting cancer, chronic diseases and ageing.

Throughout human history, the description of our medical knowledge and diseases reflected our understanding of nature in general. In the ancient world, the five elements, wood, water, fire, earth and metal, were the scientific basis to describe bodily interactions and diseases (traditional Chinese medicine, 475-221 BC) and Hippocrates, (c460-370 BC), who wrote about the four humours that corresponded to air, water, fire and earth.

Advances in science occur during periods of political, social and economic stability as in the Reinassance, and during the first industrial revolution, as examples in the Western World. Similar examples can be found in Mesopotamia, Egypt and China. The study of cancer, oncology, rose from necessity, as the incidence of cancers increased with the aging population. Cancer research advanced quite rapidly, benefited from the explosion of new findings in physics, electron microscopy, biochemical engineering, computer technology, molecular cell biology, and immunology. Looking back several decades, the cancer puzzle seems nearly solved, yet cancer incidence and mortality are reaching new heights and will likely be responsible for one of the highest death rates this century, worldwide. We have also pointed out the common molecular insults in cancer as in other chronic diseases of old age and indeed aging itself. As the confluence of many of these diseases come together in older age, the consequences are clear with higher degree of dysfunction and deaths. Molecular medicine will find new cures and already determined some of the common molecular basis for these apparently different illnesses and inevitable degradation of aging. The successes have been gratifying as in the treatment of Hodgkin's lymphoma, testicular cancer, mole pregnancies, and cures from targeted biologics and immunotherapies. Medical advances have been impressive and give the notion that in most illnesses, science will eventually find the solution.

On the other hand, the cancer problem seems to grow relentlessly. The projected numbers for cancer are to rise in the order of 70% in most parts of the world, in the next 20 years. In China, for example, lung cancer will be the most common malignancy, affecting both smokers and non-smokers. In the USA, lung cancer of the type not associated with tobacco, the adenocarcinoma instead of squamous carcinoma, is on the rise, as well as tumors found in the younger age group as in rectal cancer and GE junction cancers. Air and drinking water qualities are of concern in many counties in the U.S. (Jagai, 2017). Our ambient environment has a significant impact in our inner microenvironment inside and outside our cells. The cumulative impact of persistent organic pollutants can be captured by exposomes and ultimately impacting the genome (Patel 2016). Capturing accurate data is essential for any scientific pursuit. Today, Medical Sciences are studying cellular functions and diseases on the molecular dimensions that will lead to understanding medicine through new clinical mechanisms and with confirmation or revision of accepted hypotheses. Since the origin of living organisms on this planet, nature has been a platform for constant unintentional experiments on inummerable molecular events involving nearly infinite number of organisms. Becoming aware of these "experiments in nature", the "complete history of biology", scientists would find treasure trove of "new information" to guide current research and project future directions in disease paradigms and development of new therapies.

Humans are living longer, and babies born today, have a remarkable life expectancy, estimated at 100 years. Yet, the diseases of old age are expected to become more prevalent, not only because of the demographics of population over 60 years of age, but also because of an increase in rates of cancer, dementia, obesity and diabetes. Some obvious changes in our environment can be implicated. Cancer Research Council, UK, estimated that cancer incidence will increase worldwide, by 68%, from 2012-2030. This is based on current estimates and projection of population demographics (cancerresearch.uk.org). In the US, CDC (Centers for Disease Control) has forecasted an absolute increase of 24% from 2010-2020, mainly based on population increase, and an actual decrease in rates of cancer deaths, although an absolute increase of 15% amongst men (cdc.gov/cancer/dcpc). The increase in cancer numbers are mainly a result of graying of the population, as the group over 65 years of age will triple, worldwide, by 2050, as the entire population will actually reach 9.7 billion people. The rate of some cancers, per 100,000 individuals, is increasing. Lung cancers will increase in some countries, as in China and Indonesia, due to increased tobacco smoking. In the U.S. lung cancers have decreased by 36% in the last twenty years due to lower tobacco use. Thyroid cancers have increased, in the U.S., probably from increased use of imaging tests and aggressive surgical interventions. Changing rates of cancer can give clues to new factors in the environment or diet contributing to carcinogenesis. Melanoma and skin cancers are increasing 5% yearly. The increase is due to increased sun exposure, ozone thining, and greater outdoor activity with warmer climate. Global warming will affect world population health by disrupting food production, by forcing migration and by stressing government and health resources. Aside from greater outdoor activities and sun exposure, and economic disruptions, warming temperatures effects on health and aging will be one of the unknown factors to be studied. Variations in cancer incidences due to climate differences are difficult to determine. For example, comparing cancer incidence in the areas of the world with higher latitudes and more temperate climate to more equatorial locations and tropical climates is confounded by differences in income, ethnicity and rates of infectious diseases. Climate change, a manifestation of environmental stresses, including excess carbon emissions, will affect our health, in ways that are difficult to predict.

Prevention need to be the main weapon in the cancer fight and key areas have been pointed out by Thun (Thun 2010); decreasing tobacco smoking, obesity, diabetes and common infections. In addition to the cancer burden, chronic diseases of older age, cardiovascular diseases, diabetes, dementia, arthritis and others, are all growing burdens and threats to the health of the aged. The silver lining on these dire forecasts, that could compromise the quality of life in our older age, is that all these diseases could be grouped together for some common prevention measures. The molecular insights into cancer development, namely gene mutation and DNA damage, are common to other chronic diseases and to the process of ageing itself. The prevention measures of diet modification, exercise, avoidance of agents that can increase DNA damage, minimize excess oxygen reactive species (ROS), and clearance of intracellular waste products, can potentially yield the beneficial results for all three major health problems: cancer, chronic diseases and aging.

What is in store for the future? The cancer story looks hopeful in the U.S., for example, overall death rate from colorectal cancer (CRC) has decreased, from colonoscopic screening and the wide use of NSAIDS (non-steroidal anti-inflammatory drugs). There are potential pitfalls, as in CRC, there is a definite increase in rectal cancers in the young (Stoffel 2015). The increase of lung cancers in non-smokers can be an impetus to find the contributing air pollutants and effect change, as in eliminanting lead base fuels, for example (Samet 2009). The increase in GE (gastro-esophageal) junction cancers is also unexplained (Quante 2013). Could there be environmental or dietary agents responsible for new increase in cancers? Potentially toxic agents are plausible factors as both global environment and our own cellular environment are under stress and exposed to multiple changes.

For each of these examples, one could find other biological factors such as underlying mutations for CRC in the young, and acid-reflux for GE junction cancers. Multiple causative factors are usually the rule.

Where will science take us? The study of molecular biology spurred by cancer research has yielded numerous advances which will eventually translate into improved health gains. At the same time, the smart cellular phone and the internet have changed our daily lives remarkably. MRI imaging, minimally invasive surgery, robotics, artificial intelligence and gene testing have changed the routine health assessment. Yet, our patient-doctor interaction has changed little. Electronic medical records (EMR), rather than paper charts are more pervasive. How will medicine assess and treat cancer ten years hence? Genomics will tell us some of the early molecular signals for irreversible oncogenic transformation. We will also have better options in giving these transformed cells the signals to commit programmed cell death or apoptosis. In fact, this is the pathway that organisms, in nature, use to avoid cancers. Plants have more vigorous pathways in apoptosis, thus preventing cancers. Naked rat moles and elephants have much lower rates of cancers than expected. Amongst humans, we have examples of "cancer resistance" as in heavy smokers free of cancers and nonagenarians living in good health free of malignancies. We will discover new unique molecular pathways, possibly, tumor suppressor genes, that either eliminates the early cancer cell or stops the oncogenic progression. For several decades, immune rejection of tumors was well worked out in laboratory animals, however, in humans, tumor induced immunesuppression was difficult to overcome until the recent work with check-point inhibitors. Stem cell studies showed few molecular switches to turn adult cells into induced pluripotent stem cells, i.e., "turning back the clock", that potentially can be used in cancer treatment. There may well be molecular switch that turns off cell division and proliferation, in a selective manner, which could then "turn-off" the cancer propensity to grow and metastasize.

Advances in science will lessen the cancer burden in society. Yet, much can be accomplished today with the current tools. Cancer prevention is one of these tools that has been woefully underused. Much attention has publisized the benefits of new diagnostic techniques and treatments. Nevertheless, majority of cancers dealt by the oncology doctors are at a late stage with inherent low cure rates. By the time of diagnosis, the tumor has been growing for a decade or more. Cancer prevention engages the cancer at the cellular and molecular levels, prior to becoming entrenched into fabric of our micro-environment.

Cancer prevention needs to become front and center in the healthcare billing in our old age and will become "prime time" and cost-effective. Where 50% of cancers can be prevented today, in a decade we should see vastly more cancers prevented and decrease in both incidence and death rates from cancer worldwide. Everyone's genome can be deciphered, for prices that are constantly falling, and searched for all common and some rare oncogenes and associated mutations. In addition, molecular markers can be measured on a yearly basis to monitor diet, physical activity and exposure (exposome) to potential carcinogens. Certain miR (microRNA) can reveal our bodies molecular eco-health, proper balance of nutrients, immune competence, activity of our DNA repair enzymes, and balance of reactive species. Plant and animal microRNA will reveal the nutrient benefits for a particular disease and become key to direct our dietary intake. There will numerous agents and serum molecules that will become biomarkers to monitor diet, and dietary additives, gut microbiome and exposure to carcinogens.

23.1. PANDEMIC OF 2020

Infectious diseases were the main cause of death throughout history until the last century, with notable epidemics caused by bubonic plague, small pox to cholera. The influenza pandemic of 1918, infected 500 million people, a third of the world population, then, and causing up to 50 million deaths. By the mid century, antibiotics and vaccines have limited the impact of "pestilence" and epidemiologists moved their focus to cardiovascular diseases and cancer. Though the "common flu" has a yearly resurgence, affecting 35 million in the US with 34,000 deaths in 2019-20 season, most individuals and physicians are able to accommodate this disease with the usual precautions of vaccination in the fall, extra rest and symptomatic treatment.

The corona RNA virus of covid-19 pandemic has, by mid-year 2020, infected 5.5 million of the world inhabitants and responsible for 350,000 deaths, outpacing other recent pandemics, from SARS, MERS and Ebola viruses. The rapid spread, death rates of 3%, wide differences in clinical responses from the absence of symptoms to rapid respiratory insufficiency, cytokine storm, multiple organ failure and Kawasaki syndrome in the young, have set this pandemic apart from other wide spread infections. The death rates for 2020 from covid-19 will surpass that of chronic diseases such as cancer and cardiovascular diseases, combined. The impact of this pandemic on our health, economic well being, and social interactions, will reach deep into our communities, and wide around the world, disrupting trade and straining political relationships. Most of us will focus on the task at hand, of sustaining our family daily needs. The need to understand the larger picture, our role in this highly connected society, is still very relevant. How can this pandemic be prevented or mitigated and how can one protect our loved ones and fellow citizens, especially the aged and frail, from getting ill? This corona virus, and future pandemics, demonstrate the need to understand molecular ecology about ourselves and about organisms around us. The discussion in previous chapters regarding molecular and precise medicine becomes very relevant in understanding how the virus affects our bodies, sickening a wide spectrum of our cells, and how our own immune system plays the major defensive role.

When sheltering at home orders were issued by the Health department, City and State governments, instructions were given for wearing masks, hand washing and physical distancing, in order to diminish or stop the virus human to human transmission and prevent infections. The individual with covid-19 symptoms should be tested for the virus and persons with positive results should be quarantined for 10-14 days and until tested negative. Despite these measures, the virus can still reach our mucous cells in the nose, mouth and eyes. In the end, the "buck" stops with your immune defense system. How ill you become after covid-19 infection or after any microbial infection depends on how your immune system is able to limit its growth and spread from portal of entry to becoming systemic and wide spread. Our natural ability to survive a pandemic while others sadly succumb to the infection was recognized even prior to the concept of immunity, dating to 430 BC, ascribed to the Greek Thucydides, who described persons who cared for plague victims without getting sick themselves. The physician Al-Razi, 9th century, wrote of lasting immunity in persons exposed to small pox and measles. The practice of variolation dates several hundreds of years in China, Africa and India prior to Edward Jenner development of the small pox vaccine, 1798, a safer, more effective and reproducible treatment than prior forms of variolation. In the past three centuries, prior to effective vaccines to several infectious diseases, the concept of herd immunity and "acclimation" have been described and used by epidemilogists. In the flu pandemic of 1918, the death rates were higher in two age groups, 15-30 years and over 60 years. The individuals of ages 30-60 years were found to have partial immunity from exposure to prior flu pandemics. Children younger than 15 years were also spared, similar to the present covid-19 pandemic (to be discussed later). In 19th century, New Orleans was afflicted by repeated yellow fever epidemics. As a result, a special class of individuals, the "acclimated" persons, who had natural immunity to the disease, were treated with special privilege (Olivarius, 2020). As in the past, the concept of natural immunity can be misused, especially in a vacuum of scientific data. In the USA, without a national consensus on public health best practices, the youth has shown some disregard to physical distancing and more reliance on "herd immunity", even to the point of wanting to be exposed to covid-19, believing in the common misconception: "it's just the flu". In Sweden, the national consensus relied heavily on the benefits of "herd immunity". At this point, scientists are still undecided on the question of the coexistence of immunity and active virus carrier condition, and the risk of becoming a "super spreader".

The importance of the immune system is central to our health. We have discussed the subject of tumor immunology, as the immune system interfaces with cancer, chronic diseases, and aging in the context disease prevention and molecular biology. In the context of pandemics, the immune system plays a central role not only for the individual at risk but for the population at large, as well. The health-conscious public have focused much attention on the immune system and "boosting immunity" has become synonymous to improvement of health (Macedo, 2019). The lay press and dietary supplement industry are replete with advice and products to improve your immune system with no oversight from the FDA, i.e. free from the requirements of safety, toxicity and efficacy testing (Dietary Supplement Health and Education Act, 1994). Advances in molecular biology bring new understanding to the interaction of the immune system with many aspects of diseases and health, including several new findings with respect to the current pandemic.

When the covid-19 viruses enter your body, most commonly through the nasal-oral route, they have to gain access into your cells to replicate. Three group of cells are more susceptible to virus entry, associated with ACE 2 (angiotensin converting enzyme 2) receptors and other surface proteins: nasal goblet secretory, type II pneumocytes in the lung alveoli and intestinal absorptive enterocytes. New viral RNAs are replicated in the cytoplasm along with capsid proteins forming thousand new virions, that can be released causing rapidly increasing magnitude of illness. The symptoms can develop in the first few days with fever, sore throat, runny nose and cough which are common manifestations of the flu and then can progress to shortness of breath, pneumonia like picture with collapse of lung air cells and bronchioles. At this point, other organs can fail associated with cytokine storm or direct invasion by viruses. At the organ failure stage, the death rate is over 50%. There are several steps in progression of the infection where the covid can be vulnerable to the immune anti-viral armamentarium. While in the extracellular compartment, antibodies, opsonins, complement, and phagocytic cells like dentritic and NK cells, can attack the virus through recognition of spike or capsid proteins. The adaptive immunity (acquired) can be primed by prior infections, exposures to microbes or by vaccines. Innate immunity deals with new foreign molecules derived from invasive organisms such as toxins, lipopolysaccharides (LPS), microbial associated lipoproteins or pathogen-associated molecular patterns (PAMPs) recognized by pattern recognition receptors (PRR), where the new foreign epitopes are quickly presented by DS (dendritic cells) to activate T and B lymphocytes, producing effector and cytotoxic T cells and production of more antibodies by B cells. At the cell surface there are protein ligands that facilitate immobilization of the virus and destruction by phagocytic cells and activated T lymphocytes. Once inside the cell, the virus can be isolated in endosomes and destroyed by xenophagy, a form of autophagy. In the cytosol the viral protein or nuclear material can activate STING (stimulator of interferon genes) which in turn can initiate the production of multiple cytokines (Prompetchara, 2020). It has been reported that the eye conjunctiva can be a site of virus entry, as is confirmed for some other type of viruses. Facial and eye shields are worn by frontline hospital personnel in care of covid-19 patients for protection. In some patient series reports, conjunctivitis has been reported under 5% prevalence. There are sparse ACE2 receptors in the conjunctiva and viral isolates from the eye or tears has been uncommon, even with persons with known covid infection (Sun 2020). Eye protection with goggles or face shields is advised, since the eyes can be a portal of entry, with secondary transmission to the nasopharynx via lacrimal ducts or by touching and rubbing the eyes.

23.1.1 CYTOKINE STORM

Cytokine storm is one of the most severe consequences of covid-19 infections. The patient, suffering from cytokine storm, requires intensive care, often with ventilator support, infusion of intravenous fluids due to diffuse tissue edema, pharmacologic treatment for low cardiovascular pressures, and progressive dysfunction of kineys and liver develops. The recovery is slow and risk for death is over 50%, and higher in the elderly. This response to overwhelming infection is not uncommon, seen with bacterial, fungal and other viral illnesses, as in severe influenza and SARS. The underlying pathogenesis of the cytokine storm in covid-19 is the presence of excessive high numbers of virions replicated and released, associated with toxic viral foreign proteins, eliciting a burst of cytokine production. The cytokine storm is led by production of interferon, followed by TNF, interleukins, chemokines that help fight the virus by further activating both the cellular and humoral immune arms. The systemic reaction in the patient starts with fever, chills, muscle and joint aches, and can progress to mental depression, leaky vessels leading to swelling, lower blood pressure (shock), and intravascular coagulation (disseminated intravascular coagulation, DIC).

The severity of the illness correlates with the higher level of cytokines and usually with number of microbes and their release of toxins (LPS for gram negative bacteria, coagulants, neurotoxins by Botulinum, etc). In some patients, the high level of cytokines is dis-proportionate to the number of viruses and occasionally even in the absence of viruses. The evolution of the storm can occur slowly over days or quickly over few hours. Localized bacterial infection, for example, causes a localized swelling, redness and pain and can be easily treated by antibiotics and sometimes surgical drainage. The immune reaction walls off the infected area, and the cytokine release is localized, only to become more systemic or "blood poisoning" if the the infection escapes the local immune defense, spills into the blood circulation and microbes continue to multiply. Other form of cytokine storm can arise as a complication of immunotherapy for cancer, pancreatitis, Castleman's disease, and others non-infectious etiologies. Among cytokine hyperinflammatory conditions from influenza and corona viruses, the spectrum of severity can vary and indeed the amount and blend of cytokines can differ. For example, when the cytokine is primarily IL1 or IL6, treatment with targeted neutralizing antibodies or receptor antagonists, can yield dramatic improvements.

The entire pathophysiology of cytokine storm needs many more studies (Tisoncik 2012). As the etiologies of cytokine storm are multiple, the progression of the body overwhelming response to several cytokines is not well understood. The cytokine storm, due to immunotherapies, have been unpredictable. Several treatments have been studied, and some found with partially successful responses. Remdesivir, an adenosine analogue and inhibitor of RNA virus replication through blockage of RNA dependent polymerase, has shown approximately 30% response in survival improvement when given in the ICU setting. Convalescent plasma, containing antiviral antibodies and when given at the appropriate time can prevent entry of the virus into cells. Protease inhibitors, Lopinavir and Ritonavir, may slow the release of viruses. Interferon, pegylated IFN alpha2a, can boost the innate immunity when given prior to the peak of cytokine storm (Nile 2020). Steroids, namely dexamethasone, given during during the pulmonary phase of the disease, was found to improve survival, reported by University of Oxford. Some patients, given steroids early in the course of the cytokine storm, have remarkable responses, hence supporting the hypothesis that the high cytokine release is a hyperallergic response rather than elicited by high number of viruses.

23.1.2. KAWASAKI DISEASE IN CHILDREN AND COVID-19

Kawasaki disease was described over 50 years ago, affecting mostly children under 5 years of age, presenting with fever, mucocutaneous swelling and inflammation, pain and redness of the distal extremities. These findings were caused by vasculitis of small and medium caliber arterioles, and sometimes associatiated with intravascular coagulation, anemia, and interestingly thrombocytosis. The higher incidence in Japan and other countries in Asia signals genetic predisposition in Asian ethnicities even when diagnosed in Western countries. The seasonal presentation pointed to a viral infectious etiology, probably a RNA virus (Rowley 2018). Several fold increase in incidence during the Covid-19 pandemic, points to the viral pathogenesis, and in fact 80% of Kawasaki disease during this pandemic were found in children with the positive corona virus PCR test or antibody test. Most children recover with anticoagulation therapy and IVIG (intravenous immunoglobulin), however up to 20% can develop coronary artery aneurysms. Sometimes the disease can start with mild symptoms and findings causing a delay in diagnosis.

Post-infectious vasculitis is uncommon, found mainly in adults (Belizna 2009), which makes Kawasaki disease even more intriguing. The pathogenesis appears to be similar in all infection associated vasculitides. The vasculitis is an inflammatory process, not involving direct infection in the endothelial cells of the vessels, but a reaction towards deposition of "super antigen" antibody complexes. Other possibilities include the generation of auto-antibodies, or delayed activation of lymphocytes homing to the endothelial cells and releasing local cytokines. Severe sequelae occur when intracranial or carotid artery branches are involved and when coronary artery aneurysms develop.

23.1.3. ASYMPTOMATIC COVID-19 CARRIERS AND SUPER-SPREADERS

Covid-19 pandemic reached the world population with more speed and penetration compared to recent SARS, MERS and EBOLA epidemics. The transmission rate or contagiousness depend on several factors including virion viability in ambient aerosol droplets, invasiveness into aerodigestive tract cells, replication rates and number of virions expelled into the ambient air through breathing, speech and coughing and onto surfaces through fecal oral route. The time period of virion shedding while ill or without symptoms can increase the human to human transmission rate. The high rate of asymptomatic carriers, in some groups higher than 50% of total numbers infected, leads to the difficult task of identifiying the subjects and prevention of further transmissions. Some investigators downplay the existence of asymptomatic spreaders, saying that most will show haziness of lung fields on CT scan and that the "asymptomatic" individuals will eventually develop symptoms when studied in detail. Nevertheless, significant number of young individuals continue to interact at work and play, capable of spreading covid-19 without having fever, cough or other flu-like symptoms.

In significant number of hosts the covid-19 does not elicit much immune activity, nor cell death after virion replication. These individuals do not develop signs of illness. There are countless different viruses that co-exist in and around our cells without causing disease. They are part of our microbiome. It is unusual for a new virus, responsible for a pandemic with significant death rates and at the same time, be found in large proportion of individuals in co-existence mode, in other words, as asymptomatic carriers. How can one's immunity geared to fight, be "tamed" by this new corona-virus? Studies in general healthy individuals with a wide age range found around 16% of individuals to be carriers of influenza viruses and yet to be asymptomatic. Children and young adults outnumbered older individuals in the category of no symptoms, and mild symptoms increased among older young adults (Leung 2015). Significant number of asymptomatic individuals carried more than one type of viruses. A simple explanation is that the virus, through rapid mutations, explore different molecular pathways to survive in the animal kingdom despite well developed means of defenses. In bats, for example, a common natural reservoir of coronaviruses, many of which do not infect humans, have a serine-358 replacement in the STING protein (activation of interferon genes). As a result, bats do not reject or get ill from these viruses. In humans, children or older individuals with prior exposures to coronaviruses, through adaptive immunity, have immunoglobulins that can partially protect against covid-19, allowing a much milder infection and a low-grade infection without symptoms of "flu" illness. Intra-cellular viral genome and proteins can be held isolated in endosomes, continue to replicate at limited capacity and extruded, without causing cellular harm or significant reaction. There is much to be learned from the present covid-19 pandemic.

23.1.4 MOLECULAR IMMUNOLOGY AND MOLECULAR EPIDEMIOLOGY OF COVID-19 PANDEMIC

Molecular advances in medicine has changed dramatically how we approach and evaluate diseases as we have seen in cancer, cancer prevention, chronic diseases and aging. Employing genomics and proteinomics, cellular functions are understood as molecular interactions and more diseases have more in common than what was seen from the anatomical point of view in terms of symptomatology and clinical findings. Immune defenses, crucial to how our bodies react to the new virus SARS CoV-2, can be more clearly understood through molecular pathways. In conditions with known molecular imbalance, as in diabetes, obesity, heart disease, emphysema, cancer and old age, the covid-19 infections are more severe. Molecular biology helps us to understand the interface of our environmental co-habitants with our cells in a new light. Genomics of microbial and viral DNA and RNA can measure the totality of germs in our tissue fluids. The number of viruses in our body is in the order of 380 trillion, ten times more than the number of bacteria or cells (Riley 2018). Each person has their own microbiome and virome that could potentially cause disease as in appendicitis or a perforated bowel, but mostly, they protect us from more virulent invaders as in antibiotic resistant bacteria or new mutant viruses. Each type of virus has a narrow range of host and cells it infects. Among coronaviruses, the vertebrate hosts range from bats, ferrets to domesticated farm animals, cows, horses, pigs, dogs and cats. Within each host, the types of cells affected depend on the attachment proteins on the virus capsule. Thus, the epidemiology of each virus infecting humans can be traced to the virion molecules and to the hosts proteins on the cell surface and cytoplasm. Zoonotic viral transmission, animals to humans, is a major concern. Influenza, West Nile, Rabies are common and there is risk of new ones, as in covid-19 to cause a major pandemic. Endemic human viruses as in influenza or commensal viruses in our virome can also undergo mutations or evolve to become more virulent. However, unlike zoonotic viruses, more virulent human viruses evolved from like viruses that has left some imprint in our collective adaptive immunity, thus unlikely to cause devastating illnesses or epidemics. Worlwide cooperation is required for systematic surveillance for any new potential infectious agents, in animal and in humans, that include reporting, digital media, big data analysis, artificial intelligence and molecular genomics of pathogens (Bedford 2019, Houlihan 2019). For example, early in 2020 pandemic, in a few hospital pneumonias thought to be due to influenza, the new SARS CoV-2 was actually isolated. New zoonotic viruses can spread as human to human transmissions at low numbers, going undetected until becoming a major outbreak, unless systematic testing is in place.

Covid-19 or SARS-CoV-2 infection has many similarities to SARS-CoV-1, responsible for the pandemic of 2003. Both are Beta-coronavirus, positive stranded RNA, with capsid spike proteins, that can bind to ACE2 (angiotensin converting enzyme 2). ACE2 is present on nasopharyngeal cileated cell surfaces, lung cells and enterocytes. These cells, first to be infected, explain the pathophysiology of covid-19 with flu like symptoms and progression to breathing difficulties (respiratory insufficiency), diarrhea, and eventually cytokine storm. There are similarities in the two SARS-coV illnesses, and some clear differences. SARS pandemic of 2003 had higher death rate, around 10%, but only infected 8,000 individuals around the world with 700 deaths. Vaccine was under development when the virus vanished two years later. Six months into the pandemic, SARS-CoV-2 is clearly more highly transmissible with over 7 million people infected and causing approximately 3% mortality rate. The high transmissibility can be explained by the high rate of asymptomatic carriers who continue to come into multiple contacts, often among workers around essential businesses. The asymptomatic super-spreaders are thought to have infection of the nasopharynx only, stage I only. Stage II being viruses infecting the upper airways, associated with cough and fever while in Stage III the virus has reached the lung cells, causing respiratory alveoli collapse and lung consolidation. A sensitized adaptive immunity, i.e., prior exposure to other corona viruses, can hold the infection in check to stage I only. Since the virus require intracellular entry to replicate its RNA, our defenses mount several ways of neutralizing the virus prior to cell entry. In the nasal passages, the virus suspended in aerosol droplets will be filtered and trapped, preventing further travel into the air bronchioles or lung cells. Here it is met by antibodies, especially IgA, opsonized, phagocytosed by monocytes and dendritic cells, which will process the antigens and present to lymphocytes in the process of activation and recruitment. Antibodies are directed towards the viral capsule glycoproteins, especially the spike proteins in coronaviruses, RBD (receptor binding domain) region for ACE2, preventing its entry into cells (Shang 2020). Once the virus attaches to the host cell surface, several proteases allow fusion of capsid membrane to cell membrane and the viral RNA is then transferred into the cytosol. Most investigators think that the viral genome including remnants of its capsid are enveloped by endocytosis into endosomes. At this stage, the viral RNA can still be destroyed, by hydrolytic enzymes, or the viral genome can multiply within the endosomes or at nearby ER (endoplasmic reticulum) along with synthesis of corresponding viral proteins. Depending on the viral activity, new virions can be extruded out of the cell without cell death, or the viral contents are replicated at a degree that causes cell lysis and death. The intracellular innate immunity includes activation of interferons and autophagy. Viruses including covid-19 have learned to inhibit the autophagy/phagocytic process through production of proteins (nsp6, p4b, p5). This learning process is another description of evolution through mutations and selection pressured by host defenses. On the hand, enhancing autophagy directed at viruses, xenophagy, could prevent a more severe illness by destroying the intracellular viral genome and associated proteins (Carmona-Gutierrez, 2020). In addition, autophagy can limit the inflammatory process, not only by limiting the viral load, but also by digesting excess cytokine and their precursors.

The warfare between viruses and hosts on the molecular level, sparring in the domain of immune defenses and autophagy, will have winners and losers. As we learn more about the role of key molecules engaged in how viruses gain advantage in the cell entry process in order to reach the host machinery for protein synthesis, microRNAs of viral and host origin stand out as important players. Early in the development of life forms, bacteria acquired defenses against phages (viruses), and likewise, phages used siRNA (small inhibitory RNA) to gain advantage in introducing its genome into the host's (Daveau 2010). One of this defense systems, involves CRISPR/Cas mechanisms to destroy viral RNA or DNA segments. Taking advantage of this trick developed by bacteria, CRISPR/Cas has revolutionized gene editing in laboratories and now in human cells. In the current pandemic, SARS-CoV-2 miRNA and corresponding human miRNA have been mapped and they play dinstinct roles in determining the coronavirus success in infecting humans and in the severity of illness (Bruscella 2017, Liu 2020). For example, human miR 4661-3p targets the spike protein gene on covid-19, while several virus miRNAs, i.e., MD2-5p and MR147-3p, target hosts mechanisms of apoptosis and immune recognition.

Current understanding of the molecular aspects of immune response will revolutionize development of new treatments and vaccines for viruses capable of reaching thousands to millions in the population as in the covid-19 pandemic. Genomic measurement of covid-positive individuals, genomic epidemiology, cytokine proteonomics, host and viral mirna profiles, viral genome and protein measurements are a few new technologies that can generate new treatment strategies (Bedford 2019).

Despite these newer anti-viral approaches, success in limiting the pandemic has been mixed, with some countries suffering fewer transmission and deaths compared to others, while in others, including the U.S., the numbers of infections are still rising. Isolating infected individuals, physical distancing, use of face masks and other methods of mitigation are effective, however ultimately anti-viral drugs and vaccine are needed to rescue us out of this pandemic. Herd immunity is the ultimate goal, and viral persistence in immune carriers may be one achiles heel, and frequent mutations causing immune escape will be problematic as is true with influenza infections. Effective and safe vaccines have minimized the impact of dozens of common infectious illnesses, and for SARS-Cov-2 a vaccine will make a difference for society to function by allowing larger numbers of people to congregate. Traditional vaccines are based on antibody response to proteoglycan epitopes located on the viral capsule. The process requires culture of attenuated viruses, isolating parts of the viral proteins and packaging these antigens (sometimes whole virus) into a vaccine given by injection or intranasal route. Attenuated virus can occasionaly cause disease after vaccination. A new method is to use mRNA as the vaccine, not dependent on growth of viruses or synthesis of viral proteins. One form of mRNA covid-19 vaccine is into human trials stage of development.

Anti-viral medicines or molecules that inhibit viral replication can be effective in viral illnesses. The ideal drug is one that is affordable, with no side effects and that can be taken early with the onset of symptoms and be effective in preventing the more serious form of the viral illness. For the current SARS-CoV-2 pandemic few drugs are being tested. Remdesivir shortened the recovery period 11 vs 15 days (compared to placebo) and resulted in fewer deaths 7.1% vs 11.9% in a randomized trial (Beigel 2020). Remdesivir is a nucleotide analogue, that inhibits the viral polymerase, and was used effectively against Ebola. Other anti-virals: lopinavir/ritonavir (protease inhibitor used for HIV) and ribavirin (guanosine analogue, inhibits RNA polymerase, modulates interferon) are undergoing trials.

23.1.5. BOOSTING IMMUNITY DURING THE PANDEMIC

Strong immunity, nearly synonymous to good health, will help fight off the covid-19 infection and avoid the more severe lung infection, cytokine storm and death. Health recommendations abound, during this pandemic, in how to boost your immunity. We have framed immunity in the contex of cancer prevention, how your immunity can prevent cancer and how it fights off established cancers. The strategies to maintain our inner environment homeostasis will in the end prevent cancer, avert chronic diseases, delay systemic decline in aging and most important of all, keep the immune system ready to respond and vigilant. Most commercially driven websites mention diet, fruits, vitamins, antioxidants, probiotics, minerals and vitamin C, specifically, as the most recommended supplements to improve your immune system (Macedo 2019). Vaccines was only ranked 27th on this study. Surveys show over 50% of Americans take one or more supplements or CAM (complementary and alternative medicines) to "boost immunity and health". CAM has a global market worth 133 billion USD, and paradoxically, individuals using CAM are associated with a decrease in the use of vaccines.

Immune dysfunction from aging, immunosenescense, is the commonest condition suffering adverse outcomes from the coronavirus pandemic. About 80% of deaths from covid-19 are among men over the age of 65. Older women are a third less affected than men. African-Americans, Native American, and individuals of Hispanic and Asian descent suffered the higher death rates in this pandemic. The confounding factors of social-economic income and education has not been controlled in these epidemiological data. Others at risk are cancer, collagen vascular diseases, diabetes and cardiopulmonary patients including ones with hypertension and chronic obstructive lung disease (COPD). Older individuals have slower antibody response, thymic involution, deficient antigen presentation by dendritic cells and fewer and less cytotoxic T cells. The ability to tone down the cytokine response and numbers of T suppressor cells are deficient, associated with increased low-grade inflammation, inflamm-aging (Aiello,2019). Aged individuals often are found with nutritional deficiencies, specifically micronutrients such as zinc, selenium, vitamins D and C. These elements can be tested and replaced. Other possible helpful dietary additions are PUFA, polyunsaturated fatty acids, like 3-omega fatty acids, pro-biotics and tea EGCG, epigallocatechin 3-gallate (Wu 2018). Exercise and brief fasting periods can improve immune function through activation of autophagy. Sufficient rest and sleep as well as a happy disposition, i.e., decreasing stresses are life style maneuvers that improve overall health and immunity as found in many studies in neuroimmunology.

Cancer is recognized by our immune system as a foreign cell, and tumor antigens do provoke an immune response. Undoubtedly many cancers are stopped by immune rejection. Some cancers are able to escape immunesurveillance through immune blockade or immune tolerance. Viral infections are stopped and rejected by immune defenses, innate and adaptive, and the covid-19 is dealt in a similar manner, by each individual immune response. The unique aspects of this coronavirus relative to SARS-CoV-1 and MERS are due to the immune response to the different epitopes, proteins and microRNA unique to SARS-Cov-2. The unique clinical aspects are its high transmissibility (R0 2.5 vs 1.7 and <1 for SARS and MERS), cytokine storm (also seen in the severe acute respiratory syndrome in the previous corona pandemic), and Kawasaki syndrome in kids. We are still learning more about the respiratory involvement, associated cytokine storm and multiple organ failure, the main causes of death. For covid-19 bilateral lung involvement is higher than in SARS, where unilateral lung involvement was more common. Cancer, with associated high genetic instability, is able to probe the weaknesses in the immune defense, through high numbers of mutations. Likewise, viruses, including covid-19, devise multiple ways to gain advantage over the immune defenses. Viruses adaptation is due to the high mutation rate, as they do not have a nucleotide repair system. For example, viruses can manipulate the recognition molecules (MHC, major histocompatibility complex) used by our immune system to initiate rejection of a "non-self" molecule or cell. The high transmissibility of SARS-CoV-2 compared to previous coronavirus pandemic can be explained by its ability to co-exist within asymptomatic or minimal-symptomatic individuals who continue to transmit the virus.

Cancer molecular biology ushered in several new paradigms, envisioning cancer as a condition with altered molecular pathways, stemming from genome mutational changes. The molecular basis of cancer transformation, share similar molecular changes with other conditions such as chronic diseases and aging, namely gene mutations and stresses on other cell molecules, proteins and lipids. We have also learned that cells have multiple pathways to cope with these stresses on the molecular level and well prepared to cope with other disruptions that include invading infectious agents, trauma and wound healing. Molecular pathways underlying immunity are closely intertwined with other cellular functions supporting metabolism, growth, autophagy, trans-membrane signaling, oxidative balance, that in the end maintain intra-cellular homeostasis. From this molecular overview of immunity, akin to health maintenance at the cellular level, the proper way to improve and boost immunity, is to follow the many strategies outlined for cancer prevention. Immune competence, hence, could be amenable to short-term boosting or up-regulation, however, the more prudent strategy is to maintain and optimize the molecular homeostasis that garantees healthy functioning of the entire molecular ecology of our cells, especially the function of immunity (Marques, 2018).

24

CALL TO ACTION: A PERSONAL GUIDE

We have outlined the scope of cancer as one of the chronic diseases limiting our well-being and sometimes our lives and how it is intertwined with the normal process of ageing. Currently, we intervene medically when the tumor announces its presence by symptoms, by a lump, or found incidentaly by imaging or diagnostic tests. These tumors are usually larger than we hoped and growing for years since their inception, with a decade or more without any signs or symptoms. It is often not detectable by routine tests. By intervening early in the tumor development, treatments will be more successful and less drastic in terms of side effects, such as a radical surgical procedure. Cancer prevention measures will do away with conditions that facilitate tumor growth and if tumor does continue to grow, it can be detected much sooner than later, by targeted approaches. We have covered most of these topics separately, in several prior chapters. Below, we summarize the steps for check-up and simple self-initiated measures.

1. How early should we begin some of these prevention measures? As early and as young as you become aware of these major health problems. At the same time, this awareness provides a major opportunity to significantly improve our health. These small steps one can adopt, help our internal ecosystem to stay the course of homeostasis. These steps, when embraced, become our new daily habits and pathways for good health. We hope that your parents, or the adults in the family, are encouraging their infants, children

or young adults to follow good advices and habits they can adopt. These habits start with foods with fewer additives, fewer processed foods and beverages with no sugars, corn syrup, artificial coloring or sweeteners. Avoid exposure to tobacco smoke or other air pollutants like engine exhaust fumes. The proliferation of leaf blowers has also become a significant air pollutant, with dust, bacteria and much more blown into the air, becoming an easy conduit into your lungs. As an example, these leaf blowers can be avoided. Most garden surface leaves and dust can be swept and kept locally as compost material. Atmospheric hazards include living near busy highway, with high levels of combustible exhaust, or near factories with release of chemicals into the air. These latter examples may be more difficult to avoid. Clean water source has become an issue in many cities in the U.S. due to old water pipes, and storage facilities. Home water filtration systems can provide some protection. Prolonged sun exposures, to the point of skin burns can increase the risks of skin cancer later in life, however moderate exposures are beneficial in terms of vitamin D generation and eye development. Regular exercises and physical activity increase the cardiovascular and pulmonary reserve development of the young body and increase the waste clearance housekeeping activities of autophagy. Other steps of monitoring some molecular markers are introduced in your 4th to 5th decades of life or if there is a strong family history of cancer.

2. When should I consult my doctor regarding cancer prevention? It is never too early to ask your doctor about cancer prevention. Here are some pointers on information to have at hand to help assess your cancer risks. Most families do not discuss their own history of family members that had cancer. Some may think the information may burden the young. Fair enough, but a record should be kept and discussed among the relatives, and if there are more than two loved ones that had cancer, in the first and second degrees, i.e., immediate

family, and cousins, aunts, grandparents, then this information could alter cancer risks. Most cancer screening guidelines start in the forties and fifties. In the abscense of increased family risks, once you complete your 40th birthday, it is a good time to consider a time-out for cancer prevention. If there is significant family history of cancer then a consultation between and 30th and 40th birthdates is suggested regarding your risks for cancer. Risk assessment goes beyond your inherited risks, and include work-place and home environment exposures, diet, daily habits and physical activity. The criteria for gene testing are changing rapidly with the falling costs of genomic technology and increasing capability of computing, artificial intelligence and accumulated clinical experience.

3. What can I do for myself to decrease my risks for developing cancer? Good news! There is much one can do to lessen your own risks for cancer and the benefits will also improve your overall health and longevity. Let us just talk about diet and exercise for now. Our collective attitude for both diet and exercise is that they are optional. Like the New Year's resolution that is made but more difficult to follow through, a few months later. Hopefully one will have an attitude adjustment after the science is understood, especially after reading the information in several of the previous chapters. What you can do for yourself, in improving your dietary habits, and adhere to an exercise program, are as important as the medications and instructions on a prescription from your doctor. Using the analogy again, that your body has an ecosystem (molecular microenvironment) similar to our planet's ecosystem, what you put into your body and what you are able to clean up, "is what you are". Both can reach a saturation point, but the pristine balance can be restored and needs care. Much what we eat and drink are processed, containing extra additives and preservatives, that even in minute quantities, over time accumulate to the point

of causing toxic stresses and carcinogenesis. Let us mention some common daily choices we can make: oatmeal instead of packaged breakfast cereal or for lunch fresh salad, nuts and stir-fried vegetables with small portions of meat instead of potato chips, soda and bologna meat sandwich. These choices, which can be adapted to any one's taste, can make a difference when added over months and years. Much of the fruits, vegetables and meats are stored over long periods, after then nourishing ingredients are lost or altered. Obesity is now common, even among children, which was not seen prior to 1950's. Keeping away from "junk foods" is part of the solution. Physical activity has not been recognized for its importance in placing the muscles as a metabolic organ and as a modulator of cellular waste management. These points are even more important to the health of the older individuals. For your children, these daily habits can be made routine and natural (as breathing in and breathing out), and they will find confort in following the good practices into their adulthood. Vegetarian diet is probably healthier than diets with high calories, fats and meat. However, one does not need to be a purist about the diet; consuming junk food from time to time is not (super) harmful, just as eating red meat in moderation, a class II carcinogen by WHO. Occasional intake may not significantly increase risks of colon cancer (best to consume with some vegetables). Although we highlighted that we have seen the ecological systems of our planet and of our body reach their limits, there is resilience and junk foods or any stresses to a manageable degree is acceptable. The sensible guidelines are that food consumption should include plenty of fresh foods, especially fruits, nuts and vegetables. If your weight, controlled by height, is above the normal range, then cut down on calories and fats and increase your physical activity.

In the future, we may know which vegetable, root, nuts or fruits will be best for ameliorating a particular illness or will be key to reducing a particular cancer risk, by their specific phytochemical or microRNA content. Before then, it is best to widen the variety of fresh plant products you consume. The emphasis should also be on fresh, since perishable products, usually travel long distances, and are kept stored for weeks prior to reaching the consumer. Tending to your own garden can be a partial solution; you will be surprised as to how many edible or fruiting plants one can grow in limited land spaces or in planters. Personally, I find quite relaxing in caring for my tomatoes, beans and cucumbers. Small bushes of blue berries and raspberries can be ornamental as well as providing some seasonal treats.

4. If these self-help prevention measures are as simple as outlined, why very few people are signing up? Much have been written on life-style changes and resolutions not realized, however, let us try another nudge. A common inertia factor is how busy we are and how can we allocate more time in our day. Few little steps will get us doing the right thing. First, prioritize your schedule. Your health should rank up there. Furthermore, a busy and stressful life-style can lead to fatigue and subtle health problems. The right diet and exercise will make you more relaxed, in better health, tolerate more stress and perform well at your work. Secondly, a healthy diet that includes more greens and less animal products is more sustainable for the earth's future.

   Adding physical activity to your busy schedule seems difficult for most, and here group pressure or finding a partner really helps. Join a team, club or group; whether be sports, dance, walking, cycling, bird-watching or walking your pet; you will be rewarded for the physical activity and outdoor atmosphere. One could convince the group at work to exercise together, taking 30 minutes out of your work team busy schedule, could in the end increase work productivity, group creativity and morale. In fact, some of these strategies have been adopted in the work place resulting in health benefits and productivity gains.

Fatigue and stress are common realities that make us put off taking up any chores, most of all a very needed bit of exercise. Mental exhaustion and depression are almost synonymous to our daily routines of life. Often there are organic underpinnings, such as vitamin and micronutrient deficiency, especially vitamin D, sleep deprivation, and lack of physical activity. Indeed, physical activity is necessary for our daily routine and the best cure for the blues and blahs. Fresh air among woods and gardens, social interactions are also good antidotes to depression. Loneliness among the elderly can be another big health problem that can be solved by social interactions and physical activity.

The pandemic of 2020 has changed our lives drastically and underlined the importance of good health and immunity. Despite many other practical concerns, pursuit of work, societal interactions, entertainment and ease of travel, will be resoved in the end, collectively.

5. What can the doctor do for me to lessen my risks of getting cancer? After getting your past medical history, including family and dietary history, the doctor will assess the need for screening tests. Cancer screening is discussed in Chapter 7. The need for gene testing will be considered. Soon genomic testing will be routine, where all 3,000 genes will be known for each person. Any genetic mutations will be reavealed, not only the inherited ones but also newly acquired somatic mutations. In the meantime, targeted gene testing will be evaluated for the individual with higher risks according to

family history. Tumor markers, imaging tests, and more futuristic markers for optimal diet, physical activity, exposures to potential carcinogens and DNA stresses other than mutations will also be assayed, depending on personal risks of certain tumors. Health maintenance doctor visits on yearly basis should include a cancer prevention component (ideally as part of heart and geriatric health).

6. Any disavantages to gene and biomarker testing? Yes, testing without appropriate indications is called "shotgun approach", and the potential damage is in the false positive test results and miss-interpretation of the tests. For example, an elevated CEA (carcinoembryonic antigen) use as blood test in the follow-up of resected colon or other GI cancers, may be due to liver dysfunction or recent alcohol intake and not from tumor regrowth. Gene testing depends on the lab, and on the specific methodology used. Tandy-Connor (2018) found 40% rate of false positives among results from direct to consumer marketed kits. Interpretation of the gene test results depends on the clinical history and variants of uncertain significance. Epigenetic changes, and proteinomics may also become part of the screening armamentarium. Harm may result from potential invasive tests recommended as follow-up to the screening and diagnostic investigations. Inexpensive screening tests can be used, false positive results can be verified, in addition, false negative tests can partly be salvaged by using overlapping tests and paying close attention to risk assessment.

7. I am in my fifties, and I understand my risks for cancer are higher; what can I do for cancer prevention? The median age for presentation for most cancers is the age of 55 and in this age group standard screening protocols for the common cancers are recommended. Inheritable cancer risk needs proper genetic testing prior to the fifth decade of life. Older individuals with possible inherited oncogene should also have genetic testing. In addition,

yearly physical exam and health maintenance doctor's consultation is mandatory, for age 50 and older. In addition to blood tests for blood count, chemistry, lipid panel, liver and kidney function tests, your doctor will also include tests, specific for certain cancers, and others that can clue into your risks for molecular dysfunction. These tests include markers of chronic inflammation (CRP and sed rate), tumor markers for epithelial tumors (CEA, CA 125 and 19-9, AFP, PSA), and selected microRNA panel. The latter two tests are not agreed upon by all doctors. Tumor markers are not FDA approved for screening, however, judicious use of tumor markers creates a cost-effective screening strategy. The interpretation of these results needs a high index of clinical awareness of the patient's cancer risks. A positive tumor marker test in the screening setting are worked up in a different algorithm than in the surveillance setting. For example, a repeat abnormal test is ordered to check for possible laboratory error, imaging tests can be considered and no invasive tests are ordered unless the evidence is compelling as in several progressively rising values of tumor markers and positive imaging tests. These tests may show a state of molecular balance that may benefit for adjustsments in diet or physical activity level (Dufresne 2018).

8. Any new preventive measures, relevant in the near future?

Genomic tests:

Protooncogene mutations, SNP and some epigenetic changes can be revealed in genomic testing. Cancer genes carried in the germ line can be detected in blood tests using the chromosomes of white cells (liquid biopsy). The inherited cancer genes can be identified in this manner. Acquired mutations in the somatic cells, new mutations you acquired during your life-time, may not be detectable by a liquid biopsy. The somatic cells subjected to the molecular stresses leading to mutations could be measured by obtaining direct samples or links to these affected somatic cells. Exposure to chemicals, ROS, radiation, inflammation, extreme conditions in temperature, hypoxia, nutrient excess or deprivation can leave traces in the exposome and their significance can be better understood, as in tests of the epigenome. Significant ROS adducts and amyloid deposits can be measured in red cells, potentially reflecting carcinogenic exposure and increased risk for DNA mutations. The lead time of early diagnosis can be as long as 20 years with a caveat of 20% rate of false positives by some estimates. Cancer prevention and risk assessment for cancers is a novel field, with some notable exceptions. Papanicolau smears for cervical cancer, endoscopies for upper and lower gastrointestinal cancer, mammograms and other screening protocols all have proven efficacy and known rates of false negative and false positives. All new tests incorporated into the cancer prevention strategies, will improve the accuracy, sensitivity and specificity of the overall early detection efforts. False positives can be compensated by obtaining other non-invasive confirmatory tests.

Biomarkers:

There are several tumor markers that are used in the diagnosis and surveillance of cancers. Early oncogene activity disrupts some proteins or receptors that can be detected. MicroRNAs can reflect gene translation activity including mutated oncogenes. Early and established cancers have unique miRNA profiles. The ideal miRNA panel monitors your cancer risks and detects any early diversion from the molecular balance conducive to reducing the genetic hits and mutations and simultaneously enhancing the DNA repair/autophagy systems. In addition, this miRNA profile will also diagnose early cancers. This is a tall order, and the panel may require a list of dozens miRNA, and interpretation of results will require a robust clinical experience and computerized algorithms. We are approaching these goals and there are panels that will yield diagnosis and risks for 8 separate cancers and clues to some important molecular pathways (Song 2017). Tumor markers in terms of proteoglycans or cDNA (complimentary DNA) can be utilized for diagnostics and surveillance.

The ideal surveillance test is to measure the state of homeostasis in our cells and of the few important molecular functional pathways. From these key measurement points and with known reference to one's genome, risks for cancers and other illnesses can be calculated. For example, immunity is one important gauge that is central to states of cellular basic functions and homeostasis.

Liquid biopsy for early detection of cancer or cancer risks is a hot topic or research, and the better tests will emerge from on going investigations.

9. How can a doctor with cancer prevention expertise help in addition to my family doctor? Your doctor is the best person to guide you through any of your medical problems, as the professional that knows you best. You do not expect one doctor to have all the answers, thus in some cases one can ask the input of a consultant with a particular expertise. In terms of a guide to monitor and minimize your cancer risks, this book can be referenced for some basic information, scientific background and further sources. Cancer specialists with interest in cancer prevention can be consulted. Currently, there are no standards in training clinicians for cancer prevention. There are agreed criteria in screening for breast, colon and prostate cancers, just a few examples. These criteria were developed for the average risk individual, however, over half of the population have higher risks in one or another category. Advising the individual requires personalizing the risks

and finding the appropriate prevention strategies. The best strategy is to rely on your personal doctor to guide you in making your health management decisions and consider all expert advices as second opinions.

25

SUMMARY

Understanding cancer and how to prevent is a complex and intricate subject and not to be avoided or shunned into denial since we are all susceptible to the environmental factors enhancing the risks of developing an unwanted tumor or other chronic illnesses. Inherited factors are important and may not be evident or phenotypically expressed in our immediate family members. We can summarize and simplify the subject by drawing some universal facts and science theories that all nature events follow. A favorable environment for the well-being of human-kind is rapidly changing with our climate, with ongoing atmosphere and water pollution. Our bodies have fascinated scientists since ancient history from anatomical through cellular and now molecular framework of comprehension. Molecular basis of life, humans included, have been shaped over millions of years and perfected with Darwinian selection to succeed in a chosen environment. The modern life-style, rapidly changing not solely driven by technology, is generating a wide mismatch between our genes, modeled in the last thousands of years, and battered in the current stresses of ecological changes in the atmosphere, bodies of water and foods. Our daily activity would not be recognized by the hunter-gatherer generation. The modern man is living longer and has a larger stature. The environmental stresses from pandemic to air and water pollution and food sources transformed by industrial processing, translate into seemingly different types of illnesses, infections, chronic diseases, cancer and the inevitable deteorating conditions of senescense. An ageing population will also increase the risks for more severe illnesses in general. From the molecular basis, all these illnesses have the same basic dysfunction of molecular pathways that maintain our cellular integrity and closely interdependent function of trillion of cells in our body.

Preventing cancer is the same as keeping your health in good shape, especially in the older individuals. Molecular biology, genetics and ecology can guide us to effective preventive measures for all these illnesses of older age. As we have seen, the young can fall ill from these same diseases, which are preventable. In addition, some of the more important preventive measures are not high-tech like genomics or immune-therapy, but as simple as diet modification and exercise. Our intracellular molecular environment is kept in a state of homeostasis by acquiring necessary nutrients and clearing old proteins and waste products facilitated by physical activity and autophagy.

Your personalized cancer prevention plans will have your risks for various common cancers monitored with biological markers that will reflect your molecular make-up in your genes and proteins, refered in the scientific terms of genome, epigenome, proteome and exposome. These precise medical techniques can also be applied to larger group of individuals and to society at large and indeed will be necessary to cope with the large cancer burden in the future. Humans have changed this world for better or worse, the reality depending on the observer, but from a practical point of view, humans are living longer and gained in stature. Scientific capabilities have been unparalleled. We are able to understand living organisms to the molecular level as well reaching out to galaxies many light-years away. On a high note, we can use the science know how and technology to improve our health and hopefully our planet.

INDEX

A – C

D -F

G – I

J – L

M – O

P – R

S – U

V – Z

Further Reading and References

Chapter 1. Introduction.

Michael Morange: A History of Molecular Biology. Harvard University Press, 1998.

Chapter 2. Magnitude of the Disease. The killer disease of the XXI century, despite the pandemic of 2020.

Mariatto AB, Yabroff KR, Shao Y: Projection of the cost of cancer care in the U.S. JNCI 1573, 2011.

Rahib L, Smith BD, Aizemborough R et al: Projecting cancer incidence and deaths to 2030: The unexpected burden of thyroid, liver, pancreas cancers in the U.S. Cancer Res 24: 1-9, 2014.

Chapter 3. What is cancer and what is cancer prevention?

Bhatt A: Evolution of clinical research: A history before and beyond James Lind. Perspect Clin Res 1:6-10, 2010.

Hadju SI: A note from history: Landmark in history of cancer. Cancer 117: 1097-1102, 2010.

Pray LA: The discovery of DNA structure and function: Watson and Crick. Nature Education 1:100, 2008.

Chapter 4. Cancer Risk Assessment; you can reduce your risk score and prevent cancer.

Bailey MH, Tokheim C, Porta-Pardo E, et al: Comprehensive characterization of cancer driver genes and mutations. Cell 173:371-85, 2018.

Begg K, Tavassoli M: Biomarkers towards personalized therapy in cancer. Drug Target Review, on line posting, 2017.

Cervelli T, Borghini A, Galli A, Andreassi MG: DNA damage and repair in atherosclerosis: current insights and future perspectives. Int J Mol Sci 13:16929-44, 2012.

Eyers H, Kahn R, Robertson RM, et al: Preventing cancer, cardiovascular disease and diabetes. Circulation 109:3244-55, 2004.

Fagny M, Platig J, Quackenbush J, et al: Nongenic cancer-risk SNPs affect oncogenes, tumor suppressor genes and immune function. Br J Cancer 122: 569-77, 2020.

Fujii T, Shimade K, Nakai J, et al: MicroRNAs in smoking-related carcinogenesis: biomarkers, functions, and therapy. J Clin Med 98: doi 3390, 2018.

Heitzer E, Perakis S, Geizl JB, et al: The potential of liquid biopsies for the early detection of cancer. NPJ Precision Oncol 1:36, 2017.

Howell A, Anderson AS, Clarke RB, et al: Risk determination and prevention of breast cancer. Breast Cancer Res 16: 446-465, 2014.

Huang K, Mashi RJ, Ding L, et al: Pathogenic germline variants in 10,389 adult cancers. Cell doi 10.1016, 2018.

Knudson AF: Two genetic hits (more or less) to cancer. Nature Rev Ca 1: 157-62, 2001.

Li X, Blount PL, Vaughan TL, Reid BJ: Application of biomarkers in cancer risk assessment: evaluation from stochastic clonal evolutionary dynamic system optimization point of view. PLOS doi 10.1371, 2011.

Malcovati L, Galli A, Travaglino A, et al: Clinical significance of somatic mutations in unexplained blood cytopenia. Blood 129:3371-8, 2017.

Martincorena I, Fowler JC, Wabik A, et al: Somatic mutant clones colonize the human esophagus with age. Science 362:911-7, 2018.

Nakagawa H, Fujita M: Whole genome sequencing analysis for cancer genomics and precision medicine. Cancer Sci 109: 513-22, 2018.

Price KS, Svenson A, King E: Inherited cancer in the age of next-generation sequencing. Biol Res Nurs doi 10.1177, 2018.

Sanchez-Vega F, Mina M, Armenia J, et al: Oncogenic signaling pathways in The Cancer Genome Atlas. Cell 173:321-37, 2018.

Suwinski P, Ong C, Ong HS, et al: Advancing personalized medicine through the application of whole genome exome sequencing and big data analytics. Front Genetics: doi 10.3389, 2019.

The Breast Cancer Association Consortium: Commonly studied single-nucleotide polymorphism and breast cancer. J Natl Cancer Inst 98: 1382-96, 2006

Tomasetti, Vogelstein: Variation in cancer risk among tissues can be explained by the number of stem cell divisions. Science 6217:78-81, 2015.

Walcott FL, Patel J, Lubet R, et al: Hereditary cancer syndromes as model systems for chemopreventive agent development. Sem Oncol 43: 134-45, 2016.

Weitzel JN, Blazer KR, MacDonald DJ, et al: Genetics, genomics and cancer risk assessment. CA Cancer J Clin 61:327-59, 2011.

Yamashita S, Kishino T, Takashi T, et al: Genetic and epigenetic alterations in cell tissues have differential impacts on cancer risk among tissues. PNAS 115:1328-33, 2018.

Chapter 5. How does cancer prevention leads to good health, longevity and prevents chronic diseases?

Basile KJ, Johnson ME, Xia Q, Grant SFA: Genetic susceptibility to type 2 diabetes and obesity: Follow-up of findings from genome wide association studies. International J Endocrinol 2014: id769671, 13 pages.

Chakarov S, Petkova R, Russef GC, Zhelev N: DNA damage and mutation. Types of DNA damage. Biodiscovery 11:1, 2014.

Lakhani CM, Tierny BT, Yang J, Patel CJ, et al: Repurposing large health insurance claims data to estimate genetic and environmental contributions in 560 phenotypes. Nat Genetics 51:327-34, 2019.

Loomans-Kropp HA, Umar A: Cancer prevention and screening: The next step in the era of precision medicine. NPJ Precis Oncol 3:3, 2019. E 10.1038.

Pignolo RJ: Exceptional human longevity. Mayo Clin Proc 94:110-24, 2019.

Preker AS, Adeyi OO, Lapetra MG, et al: Health care expenditures associated with pollution: exploratory methods and findings. Ann Global Health 82: 711-21, 2016.

Chapter 6. The Science of Cancer Prevention

Baggerly CA, Cuomo RE, French CB et al: Sunlight and Vitamin D: necessary for public health. J Am Coll Nutr 34: 359-64, 2015.

Begum R: A decade of genome medicine: toward precision medicine. Genome Med 11:13, 2019.

Brennan P, Wild CP: Genetics of cancer and new era of cancer prevention. PLOS Genetics doi 10.1371, 2015.

Bruchner BL, Jamail IS: Disruption of homeostasis induced signaling and crosstalk in the carcinogenesis paradigm. Epistemology of the origin of cancer. 4open 2: 6, 2019.

Chu DZJ, Hussey MA, Alberts DS, et al: Colorectal cancer pilot study: importance of intraluminal lesions. Clin Colorect Cancer 10: 310-16,2011.

Cordain L, Eaton SB, SebastianA, et al: Origins and evolution of the western diet: Health implications for the 21sy century. Am J Clin Nutrition, 2005

Davies KJA: Adaptive homeostasis. Mol Aspects Med 49:1-7, 2016.

Ding L, Bailey MH, Getz G, et al: Perspective on oncogenic processes at the end of the beginning of cancer genomics. Cell 173: 305-20, 2018.

Friedl P, Alexander S: Cancer invasion and the microenvironment: Plasticity and reciprocity. Cell 147:992-1009, 2011.

Gleason M, Bishop NC, Stensel DJ: The anti-inflammatory effects of exercise: Mechanisms and implications for the prevention and treatment of disease. Nat Rev Immunol 11:1-10, 2011.

Golemis EA, Scheet P, Beck TN, et al: Molecular mechanisms of the preventable causes of cancer in the US. Genes & Development 32: 868-902, 2018.

Gotzsche PC, Jorgensen KJ: screening for breast cancer with mammography. Cochrane Database Syst Rev 4: doi 10.1002, 2013.

Helvie MA, Bevers TB: Screening mammography for average-risk women: The controversy and NCCN's position. JNCCN 16: 1398-1404, 2018.

Jalal S, Earley JN, Turchi JJ: DNA repair: From genome maintenance to biomarker and therapeutic targets. Clin Cancer Res 17: 6973-84, 2011.

Keith R, Miller YE: Lung cancer chemoprevention: current status and future prospects. Nat Rev Clin Oncol 10:334-43, 2013.

Khan J, Wei JS, Ringner M, et al: Classification and diagnostic prediction of cancers using gene microarray expression profiling and Artificial Neural Network. Nat Med 7: 673-9, 2001.

Kobrunner SHH, Hacker A, Sedlacek S: Advantages and disadvantages of mammographic screening. Breast Care (Basel) 6: 199-207, 2011.

Lappe JM, Gustafson DT, Davies KM, et al: Vitamin D and calcium supplementation reduces cancer risk: results of a randomized trial. Am J Clin Nutr 85: 1586-91, 2007

Liberti MV, Locasale JW: The Warburg effect: how does it benefit the cancer cell? Trends Biochem Sci41:211-8, 2016.

Luo D, Gilbert LA, Shokat M: A bounty of new challenging targets in oncology for chemical discovery. Biochem 58:3328-30, 2019.

Miller AB, Wall C, Baines CJ et al: Twenty-five year follow up for breast cancer incidence and mortality of the Canadian National Breast Screening Study: Randomized screening trial. BMJ 348: 366, 2014; PMID 24519768.

Mocellin S, Pilati P, Briarava M, et al: Breast cancer chemoprevention: a network meta-analysis of randomized controlled trials. JNCI J Natl Cancer Inst 108: doi 10.1093, 2016.

Mucci LA, Hjelmborg JB, Harris JR, et al: Familial risks and hereditability of cancers among twins in Nordic countries. JAMA 353:61-8, 2016.

Nagler RH, Fowler EF, Marino NM, et al: The evolution of mammography controversy in the new media: A content analysis of four publicized screening recommendations, 2009-2016. Women's Health Issues 29: 87-95, 2019.

Peek RM: Prevention of gastric cancer: When is treatment of H pylori warranted? Therap Adv Gastroenterol 1:19-31, 2008.

Riggs BL, Hartmann LC: Selective estrogen receptor modulators – Mechanism of action and clinical applications. NEJM 348: 618-629, 2003.

Smart CR: Highlights of the evidence of benefit for women aged 40-49 years for the 14-year follow-up of the breast cancer detection demonstration project. Cancer 1994.

Srivastava S, Ghosh S, Kagan J: The making of a PreCancer Atlas: Promises, challenges and opportunities. Trends Cancer 4: 523-6, 2018.

Torday JS: Homeostasis as mechanism of evolution. Biology 4:573-90, 2015.

Tutuncuoglu B, Krogan NJ: mapping genetic interactions in cancer. Genome Med 11, 2019.

USPSTF: Screening for breast cancer: U.S. Preventive Services Task Force recommendation statement. Ann Int Med 151: 716-26, 2009.

Chapter 7. Cancer Screening and Early Diagnosis.

Lung:

Abeele DR, Adams AM, Berg CD et al: Reduced lung cancer mortality with low dose computed tomography screening. N Engl J Med 2011, 365:395-409.

Omenn GS, Goodwin GE, Thorquist, et al: Effects of a combination of beta carotene and vitamin A on lung cancer and cardiovascular disease. N Eng J Med 1996, 334:1150-5.

Planchard D, Besse B: Lung cancer in never-smokers. Eur Respir J 45:1214-7, 2015.

Wikoff WR, Hunash S, DeFelice B, et al: Diacetyspermine is a novel pre-diagnostic serum biomarker for non-small cell lung cancer and is additive performance with pro-surfactant protein B. J Clin Oncol 33: 3880-6, 2015.

Breast:

Keating NL, Pace LE: New guidelines for breast cancer screening in US women. JAMA 314: 1569-71, 2015.

Kopans DB: Arguments against screening mammography continues to be based on faulty science. Oncologist 19:107-12, 2014.

Seely JM, Ahassan T: Screening for breast cancer in 2018. Curr Oncol 25: s115-24, 2018.

Wai ES, D'yachkova Y, Olivoto IA, et al: Comparison of 1-year versus 2-year intervals for women undergoing screening mammography. Brit J Cancer 92:961-66, 2005.

Welch HG, Prorok PC, O'Malley AJ, et al: Breast cancer tumor size, overdiagnosis, and mammography screening effectiveness. N Engl J Med 325:1434-47, 2016.

Zambito DP, Jiang Z, Wu H, et al: Identifying a highly-aggressive DCIS sub-group by studying intra-individual heterogeneity among invasive breast cancers patients. PLOS doi 10.1371, 2014.

Colorectal:

Chu DZJ, Giacco G, Martin RG: Significance of synchronous carcinoma and polyps in colon and rectum. Cancer 57:445-50, 1986.

Tinmouth J, Vella EG, Baxter NN, et al: Colorectal screening for the average populations: evidence summary. Can J Gastroenterol Hepatol doi 2878149, 2016.

Liver:

Sherman M et al: Screening for hepatocellular carcinoma: Rationale for the American Association for the studies of liver diseases. Hepatology 56:793-5, 2012

Cervix, Ovary and Endometrium:

Buys SS, Partridge E, Black A, et al: Effect of Screening on Ovarian Mortality, PLCO. JAMA 305: 2295-2303, 2011.

Mitra A, MacIntire DA, Marchesi JR, et al: Vaginal microbiota, Human Papillova Virus infection and intra-epithelial neoplasia: What do we know and where do we go next? Microbiome 4:58, 2016.

Schlichte MJ, Guidry J, Grant-Kels J: Current cervical carcinoma screening guidelines. J Clin Med 4:918-32, 2015.

Prostate:

Andreole GI, Crawford ED, Grubb RL et al: Mortality results from a randomized prostace-cancer screening trial. N Engl J Med 2009, 360: 1310-9.

Azgomi SH, Hafshejani AM, Ghonchech M, et al: Incidence and mortality of prostate cancer and their relationship with the human development index worldwide. Prostate Int 4: 118-24, 2016

Schroder FH, Hugosson J, Roobol MJ, et al: Screening and prostate cancer mortality in a randomized European study. N Engl J Med 360: 1320-8, 2009.

Violette PD, Saad F: Chemoprevention of prostate cancer: myths and realities. JABFM 25:111-9, 2012

Chapter 8. Cancer Vaccines and Immunotherapy

Esshar, Z: From the mouse cage to human therapy: a personal perspective in the emergence of T-bodies/CAR T-cells. Hum Gen Ther 25:773-8, 2014.

Garland SM, Kjaer SK, Monoz N, et al: Impact and effectiveness of the quadrivalent HPV vaccine: a systematic review of 10 years real-world experience. Clin Infect Dis, epub, 2016.

Jandhyala SM, Talukdar R, Subramanyam C, et al: Role of normal gut microbiota. World J Gastroenterol 27:8787-8803, 2015.

Jenkins RW, Barbie DA, Flaherty KT: Mechanism of resistance to immune check-point inhibitors. Brit J Cancer 118: 9-16, 2018.

Mantovani A, Sica A: Macrophages, innate immunity and cancer. Curr Opinion Immunol 22: 231-7, 2010.

McCarthy EF: The toxins of William B Coley and the treatment of bone and soft tissue sarcomas. Iowa Orthop J 26:154-9, 2006.

Mellman I, Coukos G, Dranoff G: Cancer immunotherapy comes of age. Nature 480: 480-9, 2011.

Mohajeri MH, La Fata G, Steinert RE: Relationship between the gut microbiome and brain function. Nutr Rev 76:481-96, 2018.

Parish CR: Cancer Immunotherapy: The past, the present and the future. Immunol Cell Biol 81:106-13, 2003.

Peterson CT, Sharma V, Elmen L, Peterson SN: Immune homeostasis, dysbiosis and therapeutic modulation of the gut microbiota. Clin Exp Immunol 179:363-77, 2014.

Qu C, Chen T, Fan C et al: Efficaccy of neonatal HBV vaccination on liver cancer and other diseases over 30 years follow up of Qidong hepatitis B intervention study: a cluster controlled randomized trial. PLOS Med, epub 1001774, 2014.

Ren J, Zhao Y: Advancing chimeric antigen receptor T cell therapy with CRISPR/Cas9. Prot Cell 8: 634-43, 2017.

Rosenbaum L: Tragedy, perseverance and chance: the story of CAR-T therapy. NEJM 377: 1313-5, 2017.

Van der Stergen SJ, Hamleh M, Sadelain M: The pharmacology of second-generation chimeric antigen receptors. Nature Rev 14: 499, 2015.

Wirth TC, Kuhnel F: Targeting neo-antigens; Dawn of a new era in cancer immunotherapy? Front Immunol 2017, published online.

Zhan T, Rintdorff N, Betge J, et al: CRISPR- CAS9 for cancer research and therapy. Sem Cancer Biol, 2018, on line.

Chapter 9. Common Cancers

Skin

Balch CM, Urist MM, Karakousis CP, et al: Efficaccy of 2 cm surgical margins for intermediate thickness melanomas (1-4mm). Ann Surg: 218:262-7, 1993.

Balch CM: Detection of melanoma metastases with the sentinel node biopsy: The legacy of Donald L. Morton MD (1934-2014). Clin Exp Metastasis. 2018.

Batra S, Kelley LC: Predictors of extensive subclinical spread in nonmelanoma skin cancer treated with Mohs micrographic surgery. Arch Dermatol 138: 1043-51, 2002.

Garland CF, Garland FC, Gorham ED, et al: Role of vitamin D in cancer prevention. Am J Public Health 96:252-61, 2006.

Griewank KG, Scolyer RA, Thompson JF, et al: Genetic alterations and personalized medicine in melanoma. J Natl Cancer Inst 106: djt 104, 2014

Handley WS: The pathology of melanotic growths in relation to their operative treatment. Lancet 1:927-33, 1907.

Reichrath J, Numberg B: Cutaneous vitamin D synthesis versus skin cancer development. J Dermatoendocrinol 1: 253-61, 2009.

Saraya M, Glanz K, Briss PA, et al: Interventions to reduce skin cancers by reducing exposure to UV radiation. Am J Prev Med 27:424-66, 2004.

Thompson JF: Updated ASCO/SSO guidelines on sentinel lymph node biopsy in melanoma: Addressing fundamental clinical questions. ASCO Post 2018.

Breast

Anampa J, Makower D, Sparano JA: Progress in adjuvant chemotherapy for breast cancer: an overview. BMC Med 13:195, 2015.

Corso G, Veronesi P, Sachini V: The Veronesi quadrantectomy: historical overview. Ecancermedicalscience 11:743, 2017.

Karagiamis GS, Goswami S, Jones JG, et al: Signature of breast cancer metastasis at a glance. J Cell Sci 129:1751-8, 2016.

Momenimovahed Z, Salehinyia H: Epidemiological characteristics of and risk factors for breast cancer in the world. Breast Cancer 11:151-64, 2019.

Welch HG, Prorok PC, O'Malley AJ: Breast cancer tumor size, overdiagnosis and effectivenesss of mammographic screening. NEJM 365:15, 2016.

Colorectal

Chu DZJ, Giacco G, Martin RG, VF Guinee VF: The significance of synchronous carcinoma and polyps in the colon and rectum. Cancer 57:445-50, 1986.

Matsuda T, Yamashita K, Hasegawa H, et al: Recent updates in the surgical treatment of colorectal cancer. AG Surg doi 10.1002, 2:129-36, 2018.

Mattar M, Frankel P, Chu DZJ, et al: Clinicopathologic significance of synchronous and metachronous adenomas in colorectal cancer. Clin Colorectal Cancer 5:274-8, 2005.

Stintzing S: Recent advances in understanding colorectal cancer. F1000Res 7:1528, doi 10.12688, 2018.

Gynecologic Cancers

Cramer DW, Vitonis AF, Terry KL, et al: The association between Talc use and ovarian cancer. Epidemiology 27:334-46, 2016.

Committee Opinion No 620. Salpingectomy for ovarian cancer prevention. Obstet Gynecol 125: 279-81, 2015.

George SHL, Garcia R, Slomovitz BM: Ovarian cancer: the fallopian tube as site of origin and opportunities for prevention. Front Oncol 6:108, 2016.

Schenberg T, Mitchell G: Bilateral prophylactic salpingectomy as a prevention strategy for women at high risk of ovary cancers: a mini review. Frontiers Oncol 4:21, 2014.

Schiffman M: HPV testing in the prevention of cervical cancer. JNCI 103: 368-83, 2011.

Prostate

Bill-Axelson A, et al: Radical Prostatectomy or watchful waiting in early prostate cancer. N Engl J Med 370:932-42, 2014.

Irshad S, Bansal M, Castillo-Martin M, et al: A molecular signature predictive for indolent prostate cancer. Sci Transl Med 5: 221ra21, 2013.

Miah S, Catto J: BPH and prostate cancer risk. Indian J Urol 30:214-8, 2014.

Liver

Mehanen B, Lubrano J, Duvoux C, et al: Liver transplantation versus liver resection for hepatocellular carcinoma in intention to treat: An attempt to perform an ideal meta-analysis. Liver Transp 23: doi 1o.1002, 2017.

Singal AJ, Pillai A, Tiro J: Early detection, curative treatment, and survival rates in hepatocellular cancer surveillance in patients with cirrhosis; a meta-analysis. PLOS Med: 10.1371, 2014, epubC

Westbrook RH, Dusheiko G: Natural history of hepatitis C. J Hepatol 61, s58-s68, 2014.

Zhu Z, Dai Z and Zhou D: Biomarkers in early hepatocellular carcinoma. Biormarker Res 1:10, 2013.

Hematogenous Cancers

Arber DA, Orazi A, Hasserjian R, et al: The 2016 revision of the WHO classification of myeloid neoplasms and acute leukemias. Blood 127: 2391-2405, 2016.

Coller BS: Blood at 70: Its roots in the history of hematology and its birth. Blood 126:2548-60, 2015.

Mao L: Notch mutation: multiple faces in human malignancies. Cancer Prev Res 8:doi 10.1158, 2015.

Norwell PC: Discovery of the Philadelphia chromosome: a personal perspective. J Clin Invest 117:2033-5,2017.

Pandita A, Ramados P, Pondel A, et al: Differential expression of miRNAs in acute myelogenous leukemia quantified by Nextgen wequencing of whole blood samples. PLos 14: e0213078, 2019.

Kidney and Bladder

Barrisford GW, Singer EB, Rosner IL, et al: Familian renal cancer: Molecular genetics and surgical management. Int J Surg Oncol doi 658767, 2011.

Bellmont J, Orsle A, Leow JJ, et al: Bladder cancer: ESMO practice guidelines. Ann Oncol 25, suppl 3: 40-8, 2014.

Lindgrem D, Ericksson P, Krawczyj J, et al: Cell type specific gene programs of the normal human nephron define kidney cancer subtypes. Cell Reports 20:1476-89, 2017.

Bony and Soft Tissue Sarcoma

Barr FG, Zhang BP: The impact of genetics on sarcoma diagnosis: An evolving science. J Clin Cancer Res. Doi 10.1158, 2006.

Borden EC, Baker LH, Bell RS, et al: Soft tissue sarcoma in adults. Clin Cancer Res 9: 2003.

Burmingham Z, Hashibe M, Spector L, et al: The epidemiology of sarcoma. Clin Sarcoma Res 2:14, 2012.

Pancreatic

Bartolini I, Bencini L, Risalti M: Current management of pancreatic neuroendocrine tumors. Gastroenterol Res Pract id 9647247, 2018.

Zhang Q, Zeng L, Chen Y, et al: Pancreatic cancer epidemiology, detection and management. Gastroenterol Res Pract id 8962321, 2016.

Thyroid

Abdullah MI, Junit SM, Ng KL, et al: Papillary thyroid cancer: genetic alterations and molecular biomarker investigations. Int J Med 16:450-60, 2019.

Fisher SB, Perrier ND: The incidental thyroid nodule. CA Cancer J Clin 68: doi 10.3322, 2018.

Gambardella G, Patrone R, Di Capua F, et al: The role of prophylactic central compartment lymph node dissection in elderly patients with differentiated thyroid cancers. BMC Surg 18:110, 2019.

Jegerlehner S, Bulliard J, Aujesky D, et al: Overdiagnosis and overtreatment of thyroid cancer: A population-based temporal trend study. Plos One 12: e0179387, 2017.

Pstrag N, Ziemnicka D, Bluyssen H, Wesofy J: Thyroid cancers of follicular origin in a genomic light. Mol Cancer 17: 116, 2018.

Shih SR, Jan S, Chen KY, et al: Computerized cytological features for papillary thyroid cancer diagnosis. Cancers 11:1645, 2019.

Chapter 10. Unusual Cancers

Among immunesuppressed patients

Chapman JR: Cancer in transplant recepients. Cold Spring Harbor Med Perspect 2013.

Noonan AM, Pfeiffer RM, Dorgan JF, et al: Cancer attributable mortality among solid organ transplant recepients in the US, 1987-2014. Cancer doi 10.1002, 2019.

Rangwalla S, Tsai KY: Role of the Immune system in skin cancer. Brit J Dermatol 165:953-65, 2011.

Chronic Wounds

Antonio N, Behrndtz MLB, Ward LC, et al: Wound inflammatory response exhacerbates growth of pre-neoplastic cells and progression to cancer. EMBO J 34: 2219-36, 2015.

Cvetanovich A, Filipove S, Zivkovic N et al: Tumor infiltrating lymphocytes and breast cancer. De Gruyter doi 10.1515, 2016.

Indolent versus Aggressive Behavior

Dias-Camara DA, Mambelli LI, Porcachia AS: Advances and challenges in cancer stem cells reprogramming using pluripotent stem cell technologies. J Cancer 7:2296-2303, 2016.

Neophytou C, Boutsikos P, Papageorgis P: Molecular mechanisms and emerging therapeutic targets of Tripple-negative breast cancer metastasis. Front Oncol 8:31, 2018.

Brain Cancers

Brennan CW, Verhaak RG, Mckenna A et al: The somatic genomic landscape of glioblastoma. Cell 155:462-77, 2013.

Lamburn G, O'Carroll MJ: Brain tumors: Rise in GBM incidence in England 1995-2015 suggests an adverse environmental or life style factors. J Envir Public Health 2018.

Mansouri A, Karanchamdani J, Das S: Molecular genetics of secondary Glioblastoma multiforme. Chapter 2, Glioblastoma, ed De Vleeschouwer S, 2017.

The Cancer Genome Atlas Network: Comprehensive, integrative genomic analysis of diffuse lower-grade gliomas. N Engl J Med 372:2481-98, 2015.

Pediatric Cancers

Begemann M, Waszak SM, Kurth I, et al: Germline GRP161 mutations predispose to pediatric medulloblastoma. J Clin Oncol 38:43-59, 2020.

Gilheeny SW, Kieran MW: Differences in molecular genetics between pediatric and adult malignant astrocytoma. Future Oncol 8:549-58, 2012.

Kuhlen M, Taeubner J, Bokhardt A: Family-based germline sequencing in children with cancer. Oncogene 38: 1361-80, 2019.

Lu C, Zhang J, Nagahawatte P et al: J Invest Dermatol 135:816-23, 2015.

Vogelstein B, Papadopoulos N, Velculescu VE: Cancer genome landscape. Science 339:1546-58, 2013.

Lung Cancer in non-smokers

Bivona TG, Doebele RC: A framework for understanding and targeting residual disease in oncogene driven solid cancer. Nat Med 22: 472-8, 2015.

Sarnet JM, Tang EA, Boffetta P, et al: Lung cancer in never smokers. Clinical epidemiology and environmental risk factors. Clin Cancer Res 15: 5626-45, 2009.

Zhou F, Zhou C: Lung cancer in never-smokers – The East-Asian experience. Transl Lung Cancer Res 7: 450-65, 2018.

Kaposi's Sarcoma and Cutaneous Lymphoma

Dourmishev LA, Dourmishev AL, Palmeri D, et al: Molecular genetics of Kaposi's Sarcoma-associated herpesvirus (Human Herpesvirus 8) epidemiology and pathogenesis. Microbiol Mol Biol Rev 67: 175-212, 2003.

Fugii K: New therapies and immunological findings in cutaneous T-cell lymphoma. Frontiers in Oncol doi 10.3389, 2018.

Trophoblastic Tumors of Pregnancy

Sawiki JA: Fetal microchimerism and cancer. Cancer Res doi 10.1158/0008-5472, 2008.

Seckl MJ, Sebine NJ, Fisher RA, et al: Gestational trophoblastic disease. ESMO clinical practice guidelines. Ann Oncol 24:39-58, 2013.

Sunami R, Komno M, Tegaya H: Migration of microchimeric fetal cells into maternal circulation before placenta formation. J Chimerism 1:66-8, 2010.

Chapter 11. Cancer Survivors

Golemis EA, Scheet P, Hopkins N, et al: Molecular mechanisms of the preventable causes of cancer in the United States. Genes Development doi 2018.

Linde N, Flueger G, Aguirre-Ghiso JA: The relationship between dormant cancer cells and their microenvironment. Adv Cancer Res 1332:45-71, 2016.

Lochhead P, Chan AT, Hishihara R, et al: Etiologic field effect: reappraisal of the field effect concept in cancer predisposition and progression. Modern Path 28: 14-29, 2015.

Pecmezi DW, Demark-Wahnefried W: Updated evidence in support of diet and exercise interventions in cancer survivors. Acta Oncol 50:167-78, 2011.

Thomas F, donnadieu E, Ujvari B, et al: Is adaptive therapy natural? PLOS Biol doi 2018.

Chapter 12. Psychosocial Aspects

Adler NE, Page AEK, ed. Cancer Care for the whole patient. Meeting Psychosocial health needs. Natl Academies Press, 2008.

Gullett NP, Mazurak v, Hebber G et al: Nutritional intervention for cancer induced cachexia. Curr Probl Cancer 35:58-90, 2011.

Kubler-Ross E: On death and dying. Simon and Schuster, 1997.

Kubler-Ross, E: On death and dying: What the dying has to teach doctors, nurses, clergy and their own families. Scribner, 2014.

Penet MF, Zaver B: Cancer cachexia, recent advances and future directions. Cancer J 21:117-22, 2015.

Chapter 13. Genetics of Cancer

LaDuca H, Polley EC, Yussuf A, et al: A clinical guide to hereditary cancer panel testing: evaluation of gene-specific cancer associations and sensitivity of genetic testing criteria in a cohort of 165,000 high-risk patients. Genetic Med 2019.

Malone ER, Oliva M, Siu LL, et al: Molecular profiling for precision cancer therapies. Genome Med 12: 8, 2020.

Merker JD, Oxanrd GR, Compton C et al: Circulating tumor DNA analysis in patients with cancer. ASCO and CAP joint review. J Clin Oncol 16: 1631-41, 2018.

Olivier M, Goldgar DE, Sodha N et al: Li-Fraumeni and related syndromes: Correlation between tumor type, family structure and TP53 genotype. Cancer Res 65: 6643-50, 2003.

Price KS, Svenson A, King E: Inherited cancer in the age of next-generation sequencing. Biol Res Nurs doi 10.1177, 2018.

Rehm HL, Berg JS, Brooks LD, et al: ClinGen – The Clinical Genome Resource. N Engl J Med 372: 2235-42, 2015.

Romero-Arias JR, Santiago GR, Hernandez JXV, et al: Model for breast cancer diversity and spatial heterogeneity. Biorxiv doi 10.110/276725, 2018.

Testa U, Pelosi E, Castelli G: Colorectal Cancer: Genetic abnormalities, tumor progression, tumor heterogeneity, clonal evolution and tumor-initiating cells. Med Sci 6:31, 2018.

Vogelstein B, Papadopoulus N, Velculescu VE, et al: Cancer genome landscapes. Science 339: 1548-58, 2013.

Wild CP: Exposome: Concept to utility. Int J Epidemiol 41: 24-32, 2012

BRCA

Janavicius R: Founder BRCA1/2 mutations in Europe. Implications on breast and ovaryan cancer prevention and control. EPMA J 1:397-412,2010.

King MC, Levy-Lahad E, Lahad A: Population-based screening for BRCA1 and BRCA2. JAMA 312:1091-2, 2014.

Rebbeck TR et al: Risk of breast cancer after bilateral oophorectomies in BRCA1 mutation carriers. JNCI 91:1475-1479 ,1999.

Skol AD, Sasaki MM, Onel K: The genetics of breast cancer risk in the post-genome era: thoughts on study design to move past BRCA and towards clinical relevance. Breast Cancer Res 18: 99 DOI 10.1186, 2016.

Polyposis Syndromes

Bertario L, Russo A, Radice P, et al: Genotype and phenotype factors as determinants for rectal stump cancer in patients with familial adenomatous polyposis. Ann Surg 231:538-43, 2000.

References:

Bonner MP: Gastrointestinal inherited polyposis syndromes. Med Path 16:259-65, 2003

Calva D, Howe JR: Harmatomatous polyposis syndrome. Surg Clin North Am 88:779- ,2008.

Vassen HFA: Review article: Lynch Syndrome (Hereditary Non-Polyposis Colon Cancer) AP&T 26:113-26, 2007.

Li-Fraumeni Syndrome

Sorrell AD, Espenschied CR, Culver JZ, et al: TP53 testing and Li-Fraumeni syndrome: Current status of clinical application and future directions. Mol Diagn Ther 17:31-47, 2013.

Multiple Endocrine Neoplasia

Thaker RV: Multiple endocrine neoplasia type 1 (MEN1) and type 4 (MEN4). Mol Cell Endocrinol 386: 2-15, 2014.

Zhao JQ, Chen ZJ, Qi XP: Molecular Diagnosis and comprehensive treatment of MEA 2. Hereditary Cancer Clinical Practice 13:5, 2015.

Gene Testing

Attimos PG, Barthlemy P, Awada A: Molecular biology in Medical Oncology. Discovery Medicine 92, 2014.

Cohen JD, Li L, Wang Y, et al: Detection and localization of surgically resectable cancers with a multi-analyte blood test. Science doi 10.1126, 2018.

Rodriguez H, Pennington SR: Revolutionizing precision oncology through collaborative proteogenomics and data sharing. Cell 173:535-9, 2018.

Weitzel JN, Blazer KR, MacDonald DJ, et al: Genetics, genomics and cancer risk assessment; state of the art and future directions in the era of personalized medicine. CA Cancer J Clin 61: 327-59, 2011.

Tubbs A, Nussenzweig A: Endogenous DNA damage as a source of genomic instability in cancer. Cell doi 10.1016, 2017.

Metastasis

Blomberg OS, Spagnuolo L, Visser KE: Immune regulation of metastasis: mechanistic insights and therapeutic opportunities. Dis Models Mech doi 10.1242, 2018.

Pachmayr E, Treose C, Stein N: Underlying mechanisms for distant metastasis Molecular biology. Viceral Med 33:11-20, 2017

Psaila B, Lyden D: The metastatic niche: Adapting the foreign soil. Nat Rev Cancer 9:285-93, 2009

Chapter 14. Molecular Medicine

Bhattacharya A, Ziebarth JD, Cui Y: SomamiR: a database for somatic mutations impacting microRNA function in cancer. Nucleic Acids Res 41: D977-2, 2013.

Brennan P, Wild CP: genomics of cancer and a new era for cancer prevention. PLOS Genetics, 2015.

History of Human Genome Project, Science 291:1195, issue Feb 2001.

Gagan J, Van Allen EM: Next generation sequencing to guide cancer therapy. Genom Med 7:80, 2015.

Kensler TW, Spira E, Garber JE, et al: Transformation of cancer prevention through precision medicine and molecular immune-oncology. Cancer Prev Res 9: 2-10, 2016.

Li SC, Tashiki LML, Kabeer MH, et al: Cancer genomics research at crossroads: Realizing the changing genetic landscape as intratumoral spatial and temporal heterogeneity becomes a confounding factor. Cancer Cell International 14:115, 2014

Tomasetti C, Manchionni L, Nowak MA, et al: Only three driver gene mutations are required for the development of lung and colorectal cancers. PNAS 112: 118-23, 2015.

Yeo J, Crawford EL, Zhang X, et al: A lung cancer risk classifier comprising genome maintenance genes measured in normal bronchial epithelial cells. BMC Cancer 17:301 doi, 2017.

Chapter 15. Environmental Risks

Bagnardi V, Rota M, Boteri E, et al: Light alcolhol comsumption and cancer: a meta-analysis. Ann Oncol 24: 301-8, 2013.

Boffetta P, Nyberg F: Contribution of environmental factors to cancer risk. Brit Med Bull 68;71-94, 2003.

Eskola M, Elliot CT, Hajslova J, et al: Towards a dietary-exposome assessment of chemicals in food: An update on the chronic health risks for the European consumer. Crit Rev Food Sci Nutrit doi 10.1080, 2019.

Fiolet T, Srour S, Touvier M: Consumption of ultra-processed foods and cancer risk. BMJ 360: k322, 2018.

Gorlach A, Dimova EY, Petry A, et al: Reactive oxygen species, nutrition, hypoxia and diseases. Redox Biol 6:272-85, 2015.

Jia W, Pua HH, Li QJ, el al: Autophagy regulates endoplasmic reticulum homeostasis and calcium mobilization in T lymphocytes. J Immunol 186: 1564-74, 2011.

Miller GW, Jones DP: The nature of nurture: redefining the definition of the exposome. Toxicol Sci 137:1-2, 2013Ma Q: Advances in mechanisms of antioxidation. Discovery Med 2014.

Malarkey DE, Hoenerhoff M, Maor RR: Carcinogenesis: mechanisms and manifestations. Handbook of Toxicology Pathology, Chapter 5, 107-46, 2013.

Maynard S, Schurman SH, Harboe C, et al: Base excision repair of DNA oxidative damage in association in cancer and aging. Carcinogenesis 30:2-10, 2009.

Ratna A, Mandrekar P: Alcohol and cancer: Mechanisms and Therapies. Biomol 61, doi 10.3390, 2017

Samoylenko A, Hossain JA, Mennerich D: Nutritional countermeasures targeting reactive oxygen species in cancer. Antioxid Redox Signal 19: 2157- 9, 2013. Sciacca S, Conti GO: Mutagens and carcinogens in drinking water. Mediterr J Nutr Metab 2: 157-62, 2009.

Sugimura T: Nutrition and dietary carcinogens. Carcinogenesis 21: 387-95, 2000.

Vrijens K, Bollati V, Nawrot TS: MicroRNAs as potential signatures of environmental exposure and effect: a systematic review. Environ Health Perspect 123, 2015, doi 10.1289.

Wild CP: Complementing the genome with an exposome. Cancer Epidemiol Biomarker Prev 14:1847, 2005

Chapter 16. Why Plants do not develop cancer.

Albuquerque TAF, do Val LD, Magalhaes JP: From humans to hydra: patterns of cancer across the tree of life. Biol Rev 93: doi 10.1111, 2018.

Aktipis CA, Boddy AM, Jansen C, et al: Cancer across the tree of life: cooperation and cheating in multi-cellularity. Phil Trans Royal Soc B, Biol Sci. doi 10.1098, 2015.

Doonan JH, Sablowski R: Walls around tumours. Why plants do not develop cancers. Nature Rev Cancer 10:794-802, 2010.

Gelvin SB: Agrobacterium-mediated plant transformation. Microbiol Mol Biol Rev 67:16-37, 2003.

Gomez MAQ: Identification of novel oncogenes through data integration and comparative genomic analysis between humans and plants. Ghent University, Faculty of Biosciences, PhD dissertation, 2011.

Gravot A, Richard G, Lime T, et al: Hypoxia response in Arabidopsis roots infected by Plasmadiasphora Brassicae supports the development of clubroot. BMC Plant Biol 16: 251, 2016.

Hansen G: Evidence for Agrobacterium-induced apoptosis in maize cells. MPMI 13: 649-57, 2000.

Hassan M, Watari H, AbuAlmaatari A, et al: Apoptosis and molecular targeting therapy in cancer. Biomed Res Int 2014, doi 150845.

Kekistalo J, Bergquist G, Gardestrom P: Cellular timetable of autumn senescense. Plant Physiol 139: 1635-48, 2005.

Lacroix B, Citovsky V: Crown gall tumors. Elsevier, 2013.

Mauchiline TH, Malone JG: Life in earth – The root microbiome to the rescue? Curr Opin Microbiol 37: 23-28, 2017

Petrov V, Hille J, Roeber BM, et al: ROS-mediated abiotic stress-induced programmed cell death in plants. Front Plant Sci 6: 69-98, 2015.

Reape TJ, Molony EM, McCabe PF: Programmed cell death in plants: distinguishing between different modes. J Exp Botany 59: 435-44, 2008.

Chapter 17. MicroRNA and Human Cancers.

Ahmed FE, Amed NC, Vos PW, et al: Dignostic MicroRNA markers to screen for sporadic human colon cancer in blood. Cancer Genom Proteonom 9: 179-192, 2012.

Backes C, Fehlmann T, Kern F, et al: miRCarta: a central repository for collecting miRna candidates. Nucleic Acids Res 46: D160-7, 2018.

Bhat SA, Hassan T, et al: MicroRnas and its emerging role in breast cancer diagnostic marker. Adv Biomarker Sci Tech 1: 1-8, 2019.

Braga EA, Fridman MV, Morozov SG, et al: Molecular mechanisms in clear cell renal cell carcinoma: Role of mirnas. Front Genet e 10.3389, 2019.

Chen B, et al: Emerging microrna biomarker for colorectal cancer diagnosis and prognosis. Royal Soc Biol e 10.1098, 2019.

Chen L, Gibbons DL, Goswami S, et al: Metastasis is regulated via microRNA-200/ZEB1 axis control of tumor cell PD-L1 expression and intratumoral immunosuppression. Nat Commun 5:5241, 2015.

Eamens A, Wang MB, Smith NA, et al: RNA silencing in plants: yesterday, today and tomorrow. Plant Physiol 147:456-68, 2008.

Dufresne S, Rebillard A, Friedenreich CM, et al: Review of physical activity and circulating miRNA expression: Implications in cancer risk and progression. Cancer Epidemiol 27: doi 1055-9965, 2018. Eamens A, Wang MB, Smith NA, et al: RNA silencing in plants: yesterday, today and tomorrow. Plant Physiol 147:456-68, 2008.

Eamens A, Wang MB, Smith NA, et al: RNA silencing in plants: yesterday, today and tomorrow. Plant Physiol 147:456-68, 2008.

Filipow S: Front Genet e 10.3389, 2019.

Gougelet A, Colnot S: MicroRNA-feedback loop as a key modulator of liver tumorigenesis and inflammation. World J Gastroenterol 19:440-4, 2013.

Guo S: Dove Press e 10.2147, 2018.

Hamam R, Hamam D, Alsaleh KA, et al: Circulating mircroRNAs in breast cancer. Cell Death Dis 8: e3045, 2017.

Jeong KS, Zhou J, Griffin S, et al: MicroRNA changes in firefighters. J Occup Envir Med 60: 469-74, 2018.

Link A: World J Gastroenterol 24:3313-29, 2018.

Liu S, Weiner HC: Control of the gut microbiome by fecal mircroRNA. Microb Cell 3:176-7, 2016.

Segura MF, Greenwald HS, Hanniford D, et al: MicroRNA and cutaneous melanoma: from discovery to prognosis and therapy. Carcinogenesis 2012.

Urabe F: Clin Cancer Res e10.1158, 2019.

Viennois E, Chassaing B, Tahsin A, et al: Host derived microRNAs can indicate gut microbiota healthiness and ability to induce inflammation. Theranostics 9: 4542-7, 2019.

Yang X: Int J Biol Sci 15:1712-22, 2019.

Zheng H, Zhang N, Zhao R, et al: Plasma mirnas as diagnostic and prognostic biomarkers for ovarian cancer. PLOS one 8: e77853, 2013.

Plant MicroRNA and Human Cancer

Arteaga-Vasquez M, Caballera-Perez J, Ville-Calzada J: A family of microRNAs present in plants and animals. Plant Cell doi 10.1105,2006.

Bellato M, Marchi DD, Gualtieri C, et al: A bioinformatics approach to explore microRNA as tools to bridge pathways between plants and animals. Front Plant Sci 10: 1535, 2019.

Cabrera J, Barcala M, Garcia A, et al: Differentially expressed small RNA in Arabidopsis galls formed by Meloidogynes javanica. New Phytologist 209: 1625-40, 2016.

Li Z, Xu R, Li N: MicroRNAs from plants to animals, do they define a new messenger for communication. Nutrition and Metabolism 15:68, 2018.

Lin Q, Ma L, Lin Z, et al: Targeting microRNAs: a new active mechanism of natural compounds. Oncotarget 8: 15961-70, 2017.

Palaez P, Sanchez F: Small RNA in plant defenses responses during bacteria and virus interactions. Similarities and differences. Front Plant Sci 4:343, 2013.

Yang BF, Lu XT, Wang ZG: MicroRNAs and apoptosis: implications in the molecular therapy of human diseases. CEPP (Clin Exp Pharma Physiol) doi 10.1111, 2009. Yuan C, Steer CJ, Subramanian S: Host-microRNA-microbiota interaction in colorectal cancer. Genes 10: 270, 2019.

Zhang L, Hou D, Chan X, et al: Exogenous plant MIR 168a specifically targets mammalian LDLRP1: evidence of cross-kingdom regulation by microRNA. Cell Res 22: 107-26, 2012.

Chapter 18. Nature's Solution to Cancer

Caulin AF, Maley CC: Peto's Paradox: evolution's prescription for cancer prevention. Trends Ecol Evol 26: 175-82, 2011.

Gorbunova V, Scluanov A, Zhang Z, et al: Comparative genetics of longevity and cancer: Insights found in long-lived rodents. Nat Rev Genet 15: 531-40, 2014.

Lanou AJ, Svenson B: Reduced cancer risk in vegetarians. Cancer Manag Res 3: 1-8, 2011.

Lewis KN, Soifer I, Melamud E, et al: Unraveling the message: insights into comparative genomics of the naked more-rat. Mamm Genome 27:259-78, 2016

Nunney L: Commentary: Multistage model ofcarcinogenesis, Peto's paradox and evolution. Int J Epidemiol 45: 649-53, 2016.

Laron's and Down's Syndromes

Baier SR et al, 2014: MicroRNAs are absorbed in biologically meaningful amounts from nutritionally relavant doses of cow milk and affect gene expression in peripheral blood mononuclear cells, HEK-293 kidney cell cultures, and mouse livers. J Nutr 144:1495-500.

Bartel B, Bartel DP: MicroRNAs: At the Root of Plant development? Plant Physiol 132:709-17, 2003

Elshimali Y, Saba H: Down Syndrome, molecular genetics of clinical findings. J Genom Proteom 6, 2012 (pub on line).

Janecka A, Rzepa MK, Biasaga B: Clinical and molecular features of Laron Syndrome, a genetic disorder protective from cancer. In Vivo 35:354-81, 2016.

Key TJ, Schatzkin A, Willet WC, et al: Diet, nutrition and the prevention of cancer. Pub Health Nutr 7: 187-200, 2004.

Kong YW, Ferland-McCullough D, Jackson JT, Bushell M: MicroRNAs in cancer management. Lancet Oncol 13: e249, 2012.

Longo VD, Finch CE: Evolutionary medicine: From dwarf model systems to healthy centenarians. Science 299: 1342-6, 2003.

Witwer KW, Hirschi KD, 2014: Transfer and functional consequences of dietary microRNAs in vertebrates: concepts in search of corroboration. Bioessays 36:394-406.

Xavier AC, Ge Y, Taub JW: Down Syndrome and malignancies: a unique clinical relationship. J Mol Diagn 11: 371-80, 2009.

Zhang L, et al, 2012: Exogenous plant MIR168a specifically targets mammalian LDLRA P1: evidence of cross-kingdom regulation by microRNA. Cell Res 22:107-26.

Centenarians

Serbezov D, Balabanski L, Lladjidekan S: Genomics of longevity: Recent insights from research on centenarians. Biotech biotech equip 32 (6): 2018.

Chapter 19. Nutrition

Brown AE, Walker M: Genetics of insulin resistance and the metabolic syndrome. Curr Cardiol Rep 18:75-88, 2016.

Chassaing B, Koren O, Goodrich JK, et al: Dietary emulsifiers impact the mouse gut microbiota promoting colitis and metabolic syndrome. Nature 519:92-6, 2015.

Conlon M, Bird AR: The impact of diet and lifestyle on gut microbiota and human health. Nutrients 7:17-44, 2015.

Devaraj S, Hemarajta R, Versalovic J: The human gut microbiome and body metabolism: Implications for obesity and diabetes. Clinical Chem 59:617-28, 2013.

Hunter P: We are what we eat: the link between diet, evolution and non-genetic inheritance. EMBO rep 9:413-5, 2008.

Mozaffarian D: Dietary and policy priorities for cardiovascular disease, diabetes and obesity. Circulation 133:187-225, 2016.

Poore GD, Kopylova E, Knight R: Microbiome analysis of blood and tissues suggest cancer diagnostic approach. Nature doi 10.1038, 2020.

Rosenberg E, Rosenberg IZ: Microbes drive evolution of animals and plants: the hologenome concept. mBio 7: 1-15, 2016.

Schnorr SL, Sankaranayranyan K, Lewis CM, et al: Insights into human evolution from ancient to contemporary microbiome studies. Curr Opin Genet Develop 41: 14-26, 2016.

Singh RK, Chang HW, Yan D, et al: Influence of diet on the gut microbiome and implications for human health. J Transl Med 15: 73-90, 2017.

Schulze MB, Gonzalez MAM, Fung TT, et al: Food dietary patterns and prevention of chronic diseases. BMJ 361, doi 10.11361, 2018.

Skerrett PJ, Willet WC: Essentials of healthy eating: a guide. J Midwifery Womens Health 55:492-501, 2010.

Tuso PJ, Ismail MH, Ha BP, et al: Nutritional update for physicians: plant-based diets. Perm J 17: 61-66, 2013.

Youssef A, Aboalola D, Han VKM: Roles of Insulin-like growth factors in mesenchymal stem cell niche. Stem Cells Int doi 9453108, 2017.

Nutritional Defficiencies

Barennes H, Khouanhauan S, Rene JP: Beriberi (thiamine deficiency) and high infant mortality in Northern Laos. PLOS doi 10.1371, 2015.

Beardin AE, Stover PJ: Insights into metabolic mechanisms underlying folate-responsive neural tube defects: a minireview. Birth defects Res A Clin Mol Teratol 85:274-84, 2009.

Liu T, Howard RM, Mancini AJ, et al: Kwashiorkor in the US. Arch Dermatol 137:630-6, 2001.

Micronutrients and Phytochemicals

Benmoussa A, Provost P: Milk microRNAs in health and disease. Comp Rev Food Sci Food Safety 18: doi 10.1111, 2019.

Bonnefont-Rousselot D: Revesratrol and cardiovascular diseases. Nutrients 8:250, 2016.

Garcia-Segura L, Perez-Andrade M, Miranda-Rios J: Emerging role of Mirnas in gene regulation by nutrients. Nutrigenet Nutrigenomics 6: 16-31, 2013.

Grober U, Holzhaur P, Kisters K, et al: Micronutrients in oncological interventions. Nutrients 8: 361, 2016.

Lukasik A, Brzozowska I, Zielenkiewicz P, et al: Detection of plant mirnas abundance in human breast milk. Int J Mol Sci 19:17, 2018.

Rome S: Use of mirna in biofluids as biomarker for dietary and lifestyle interventional studies. Genes Nutrition 10: 33, 2015.

Shenkin A: Micronutrients in health and disease. Postgrad Med 82:359-67, 2006.

Food derived MicroRNAs

Arefhosseini SR, Mamaeghani ME, Mohammadi S: MicroRNA regulation by nutrients. The new ray of hope in obesity related lipid and glucose metabolic disorders. Metabol Synd 4:158, 2014

Jayraman KS: Phytochemicals database raises hopes for herbal drugs. Nature India doi 10.1038, 2018.

Mozaffarian D, Rosenberg I, Uauy R: History of modern nutrition science. BMJ 361, doi 10.1136, 2018.

Parr EB, Camera DM, Burke LM, et al: Circulating microrna responses between low and high responders to a 16-week diet and exercise weight loss intervention. PLOS one, on line 152545, 2016.

Shrivastava SK, Arora S, Averett C, et al: Modulation of micrornas by phytochemicals in cancer: Underlying mechanisms and translational significance. Biomed Res Internatl 2015, article 848710.

Wagner AE, Piegholdt S, Ferraro M, et al: Food derived micrornas. Food Function 6: 714-8, 2015.

Xie W, Weng A, Melzig MF: MicroRNA as new bioactive components of medicinal plants. Planta Med 82: 1153-62, 2016.

Xiao J, Feng S, Wang X, et al: Identification of exosome-like nanoparticles derived microRNA for 11 edible fruits and vegetables. Peer J doi 10.7717, 2018.

Zhang I, Hou D, Zhang CY, et al: Exogenous plant MIR 168a specifically targets mammalian LDLRAP1: evidence of cross-kingdom regulation by microRNA. Cell Res 22: 107-26, 2012.

Designing nutrition for cancer prevention

Arnold M, Sierra MS, Laveisanne M, et al: Global patterns and trends in colorectal cancer incidence and mortality. Gut doi 10.1136, 2016.

Castro-Quezada I, Roman-Vinas B, Serra-Majen L: Mediterranean diet and nutritional adequacy: a review. Nutrients 6: 231-48, 2014.

Donaldson MS: Nutrition and cancer. Review of the evidence for an anti-cancer diet. Nurtrition J 3:19, 2004.

Fiolet T, Srour B, Selem M, et al: Consumption of ultra-processed foods and cancer risk: results fron NutriNet-Sante cohort. BMJ 360: doi 10.1136, 2018.

Jain A, Mathur P: Evaluating hazards posed by additives in food. Curr Nutr Res Food Sci 3: doi: 10.12944, 2015.

Jung SJ, Park SH, Choi EK, et al: Beneficial effects of traditional Korean diets on hypertensive and T2 diabetic patients. J Medicinal Food 17: doi 10.1089, 2014.

Ligibel JA, Barry WT, Alfano C, et al: Randomized phase III trial evaluating the role of weight loss in adjuvant treatment of overweight and obese women with early breast cancer. NRJ Breast Cancer 3: 37, 2017.

Meyerhardt JA, Niedzwieki D, Hollis D, et al: Association of dietary patterns to cancer recurrence and survival in patients with stage III colon cancer. JAMA 298: 754-64, 2007

Neto HAP, Ausina P, Gomez LS, et al: Effects of food additives on immune cells as contributor to body weight gain and immune-mediated metabolic dysregulation. Front Immunol doi 10.3389, 2017.

Noah L: Legal aspects of food additive approval process. Natl Academies Press, 1997.

Roess B: Evolutionary eating: a critical evaluation of Paleo diet. http://scholarship.depauw.edu/studentresearch. 2014.

Chapter 20. Exercise and Physical Activity

Amm I, Sommer T, Wolf DH: Protein quality control and elimination of waste: the ubiquitin-proteosome system. Biochim Biophys Acta 1843: 182-96, 2014.

Dungey M et al: Inflammatory factor and excise in chronic kidney disease. Int J Endocrinol, 2013.

Escobar KA, cole NH, VanDusseldorp TA, et al: Autophagy and aging: maintaining the proteome through exercise and caloric restriction. Aging Cell 18: doi 10.1111, 2018.

Gleeson M: Immune function in sport and exercise. J applied physiol 103:693, 2007.

He C, Sumpter R, Levine B: Exercise induces autophagy in peripheral tissues and in the brain. Autophagy 8: 1548-51, 2012.

Jellinger KA, Korczyn AD: Are dementia with Lewy bodies and Parkinson's dementia the same diseases? BMC medicine 16:34, 2018.

Kostrominova TY: Role of myokines in the maintenance of whole-body metabolic homeostasis. Minerva Endocrinol 41:403-20, 2016.

Marnett LJ: Oxyradicals and DNA damage. Carcinogenesis 21:361-70, 2000.

McKinney J, Lithwick DJ, Morrison BN, et al: Health benefits of physical activity and cardiorespiratory fitness. BCMJ 58:131-7, 2016.

Moses FM: The effect of exercise on the gastrointestinal tract. Sports Med 9:159-72, 1990.

Nieman DC, Wentz LM: The compelling link between physical activity and the body's defense system. J Sport Health Sci 8: 201-17, 2019.

Poortmans JR, Vendrestreten: Kidney function during exercise in healthy and diseased humans. Sports Med 18: 419, 1994.

Schneider CD, Oliveira AR: Oxygen free radicals and exercise: mechanisms of synthesis and adaptation to the physical training. Rev Bras Med Esporte 10:314-8, 2004.

Schnyder S, Handschin C: Skeletal muscle as an endocrine organ: PGC-1alpha, myokines and exercise. Bone 80:115-25, 2015.

Shin JY, Park HJ, Kim HN, et al: Mesenchymal stem cells enhance autophagy and increases clearance of B-amyloid in Alzheimer's disease models. Autophagy 10:32-44, 2013.

Sica V, Galluzzi L, San Pedro JMB, et al: Organelle-specific initiation of autophagy. Mol Cell 59:522-39, 2015.

Taylor D: Physical activity is medicine for older adults. Postgrad Med J 90:26-32, 2014.

Terra R, da Silva SAG, Pinto VS, et al: Effect of system: Response, adaptation and cell signaling. Rev Bras Med Esporte 18, 2012

Chapter 21. Ageing, Well Being and Cancer.

Aponte PM, Caicedo A: Stemness in Cancer: stem cells, cancer stem cells and their microenvironment. Stem Cell Int doi 10.1155, 2017.

Gattazzo F, Urciuolo A, Bonaldo P: Extracellular matrix: A dynamic environment for stem cell niche. Biophys Biochim Acta 1840: 2506- 19,2014.

Heilbronn LK, Ravussin E: Caloric restriction and aging: Review of the literature and implication in human studies. Am J Clin Nutrition 78:361-9, 2003.

Mahmoudi S, Xu L, Brenet A: Turning back time with emerging rejuvenation strategies. Nature Cell Biol doi 10.1038, 2019.

Navarro AM, Susanto E, Falk A, et al: Modeling cancer using patient-derived induced pluripotent stem cells to understand development of childhood malignancies. Nature Cell Death Disc 4: 7, 2018.

Romito A, Cobellis G: Pluripotent stem cells: Current understanding and future directions. Stem Cell Int: 9451492, 20 pages, 2016.

Silva PFL, Schumacher B: DNA damage responses in ageing. Open Biol doi 10.1098, 2019.

Sottocornola R, Celso C: Dormancy in the stem cell niche. Stem cell Res Ther 5:10, 2012.

Strassler ET, Aalto-Setala K, Kiahmer M, et al: Age is relative-Impact of donor age on induced pluripotent stem cell-derived cell functionality. Front Cardiovasc Res doi 10, 1139, 2018.

Tomczyk S, Suknovik N, Galliot B, et al: Deficient autophagy in epithelial stem cells drives aging in the fresh water cnidaria Hydra. Stem Cells Regen 147: doi 10.10.1242, 2020.

Vitale I, Manic G, DeMaria R, et al: DNA damage in stem cells. Molecular Cell 66: doi 10.1016, 2017.

Longevity

Martin GM, Bergman A, Barzilai N: Genetic determinants of human span and life span: Progress and new opportunities. PLoS Genetics 3: e0030215, 2007.

Slagboom PE, Berg N, Deelen J: Phenome and genome-based studies into human ageing and longevity: an overview. Biochim Biophys Acta doi 10.1016, 2017.

Stentholm S, Head J, Aalto V, et al: Body mass index as a predictor of healthy and disease-free life expectancy between ages 50 and 75: a multicohort study. Int J Obesity 41:769-75, 2017.

Chronic diseases and aging

Bolon B: Molecular and cellular mechanisms of auto-immune diseases. Toxicol Path 40: 2012.

Brunetti A, Chiefari E, Foti D: Recent advances in molecular genetics of type II diabetes mellitus. World J Diabetes 5: 128-40, 2014.

Burnett M: Somatic mutation and chronic disease. Brit J Med: 332-41, 1965.

Charleswort B: Fisher, Medawar and Hamilton and the evolution of aging. Genetics 156: 927-31, 2000.

Ioannidou A, Goulielmaki E, Garinis GA: DNA damage: from chronic inflammation to age-related deterioration. Front Genet 25: doi 10.3369, 2016.

Kumar A, Foster TC: Neurophysiology of old neurons and synapses. Chapter 10 in: Brain ageing: Models, methods and mechanisms. Riddle DR, editor; CRC press, Boca Raton, 2007.

Martinet W, De Meyer GRY: Autophagy in atherosclerosis. Circ Res 104:304-17, 2009.

Mehers KL, Gillespie KM: Genetic basis of type I diabetes. BMB 88: 115-29, 2009.

Rajkovic O, Potjewyd G, Pinteaux E: Regenerative medicine therapies targeting neuroinflammation after stroke. Frontiers Neurol 9; 2018.

Rioux JD, Abbas AK: Paths to understanding the genetic basis of autoimmune disease. Nature 435: 584-9, 2005.

Ruegsegger GN: Running from disease: Molecular mechanisms associating dopamine and leptin signaling in the brain with physical inactivity, obesity, and type 2 diabetes. Front Endocrinol doi 10.3389, 2017.

Stylianuo IM, Bauer RC, Reilly MP, et al: Genetic basis of atherosclerosis: Insights from mice and humans. Cir Res 110:337-52, 2012.

Tseng CH, Wu CY: The gut microbiome in obesity. J Formosan Med Ass 118: s3-9, 2019.

Uddin MS, Stachowiak AA, Momin A: Autophagy and Alzheimer's disease. Front Aging Neurosci doi 10.3389, 2018.

Vadasz Z, Haj T, Kessel A: Age-related autoimmunity. BMC Med 11:94, 2013.

Verheijen BM, Vermulst M, van Leeuwen FW: Somatic neuron mutations during aging and neurodegeneration. Acta Neuropathol 135: 811-26, 2018.

Watad A, Bragazzi NL, Ahmed M, et al: Autoimmunity in the elderly: Insights from basic science and clinics. Gerontology 65:525-32, 2017.

Prevention Strategies, Reverse Aging

Adams PD, Jasper H, Rudolph K: Age-induced stem cell mutations as drivers for disease and cancer. Cell Stem cell 16:601-12, 2015.

Bunker JP: The role of medical care in contributing to health improvements within societies. Int J Epidemiol 30:1260-3, 2001.

Finch CE: Evolution of the human lifespan and diseases of aging: Roles of infection, inflammation and nutrition. PNAS 107:1718-24, 2010.

Kim JH, Lee BR, Choi ES, et: Reverse expression of aging-associated molecules through transfection of microRNA to aged mice. Mol Ther Nucleic Acids 6:106-15, 2017.

Li Y, Schoufour J, Wang DD et al: Healthy life style and life expectancy free of cancer, cardiovascular disease and type 2 diabetes: prospective cohort study. BMJ 368: 16669, 2020.

Lorenzini A: How much should we weigh for a healthy and longer life span? Frontiers Endocrinol 5:121, 2014.

Martin U: Therapeutic applications of pluripotent stem cells: challenges and risks. Front Med 4: 229, 2017.

Perez-Ortin JE, Tordera V, Chavez S: Homeostasis is the Central Dogma of molecular biology. RNA Biol doi 10.1080, 2019.

Picard M, Turnbull DM: Linking the metabolic state and mitochondrial DNA in chronic disease, health and aging. Diabetes 62: 672-8, 2013.

Saretski G, Walter M: Therapeutic targeting of telomerase. Genes (Basel) 7: 39-70, 2016.

Ullah M, Sun Z: Stem cell longevity and anti-aging genes: a double-edged sword – job of life extension. Stem Cell Res Ther 9:3, 2018, doin10/1186.

Ugalde AP, Espanol Y, Lopez-Otin C: Micromanaging aging with microrna. J Nucleus 2:499-55, 2011.

Watanabe K, Ikuno Y, Kakeya Y et al: Functional similarities of microRNAs across different types of tissue stem cells in aging. BMC Inflam Regen 38: 9, 2018.

Chapter 22. Molecular Ecology, Quantum Oncology

Brovarets OO, Tsiupa KS, Hovorun DM: Novel pathway for mutagenic tautomerization of classical A-T DNA base pairs via sequential proton transfer through quasi-orthogonal transition states: A QM/QTAIM investigation. PLOS doi 10.1371, 2018.

Ding L, Bailey MW, Porta-Pardo E, et al: Perspective on oncogenic process at end of the beginning of cancer genomics. Cell 173:305-20, 2018.

Epstein T, Gatenby RA, Brown JS: The Warburg effect as an adaptation of cancer cells to rapid fluctuations in energy demand. PLOS one doi 10.1371, 2017.

Greenwald P, Dunn BK: Landmarks in the history of cancer epidemiology. Cancer Res 69: 2151-62, 2009.

Kato Y, Ozawa S, Miyamoto C, et al: Acidic extracellular microenvironment and cancer. Cancer Cell Int 13:89-97, 2013.

Korovila I, Hugo M, Castro JP, et al: Proteostasis, oxidative stress and aging. Redox Biol 13:550-67m 2017.

Lambert D: Invited commentary. N Zealand J Ecol 19: 93-6, 1995.

Maley CC, Aktipis A, Graham TA, et al: Classifying the evolutionary and ecological features of neoplasms. Nature Rev Cancer doi 10.1038, 2017.

McFadden J, Al-Khalili J: The origins of quantum biology. Proc Royal Soc A doi 10.1098, 2018.

McFarland CD, Yaglom JA, Wojitkowiak JW, et al: The damaging effect of passenger mutations on cancer progression. Cancer Res 77:4763-72, 2017.

Paital B, Panda SK, Hadi AK et al: Longevity in animals under ROS stress and disease susceptibility to global warming. World J Biol Chem 7: 110-17, 2016.

Voskarides K: Conbination of 247 genomic-wide association studies reveal high cancer risk as result of evolutionary adaptations. Mol Biol Evolution doi 10.1093, 2017.

Waring S: Quantum biology: a scientific revolution on understanding of biological systems. Biol Syst Open Access 7: doi 10.4172, 2018.

Zahir N: The NCI physical sciences-oncology network. Trends in Cancer doi 10.1016, 2018.

Chapter 23. Future Perspectives, Pandemic of 2020

Jagai JS, Messer LC, Rappazzo KM, et al: County-level cumulative environmental quality associated with cancer incidence. Cancer 2017, doi 10. 1002.

Patel CJ: Analytical complexities in detection of gene variant by environment exposure interaction in high-throuput genomic and exposomic research. Curr Environ Health Rep 2016 d, 64-72, doi 10.1007.

Quante M, Abrams JA, Wang TC: Rapid rise of gastroesophageal junction tumors: Is inflammation in the gastric cardia the underwater iceberg? Gastroenterol 145: 708-13,2013.

Samet JM, Tang EA, Boffeta P, et al: Lung cancer in never-smokers: clinical epidemiology and environmental risk factors. Clin Cancer Res 15:3526-45, 2009.

Stoffel EM: Colorectal cancer in the young adult: opportunities for prevention. J Clin Oncol 35:3525-7, 2015.

Thun MJ, DeLancey JO, Center MM, et al: The global burden of cancer: priorities for prevention. Carcinogenesis 31:100-10, 2010.

Pandemic 2020

Bedford J, Farrar J, Nkengasong J, et al: A new twenty-first century science for effective epidemic response. Nature 575: 130-6, 2019.

Beigel JH, Tomashek KM, Mehta KA, et al: Remdesivir for the treatment of Covid-19 NEJM doi 10.1056, 2020.

Belizna C, Hamidou MA, Shoenfeld Y, et al: Infections and vasculitis. Rheumatol 48: 475-82, 2009.

Bruscella P, Bottii S, Trabucchi M, et al: Viruses and miRNAs: More friends than foes. Front Microbiol doi 10.3389, 2017.

Carmona-Gutierrez D, Bauer MA, Madeo F, et al: Digesting the crisis: autophagy and coronaviruses. Microbial Cell 7: 119-28, 2020.

Daveau H, Ganeau JE, Moineau S: CRISPR/Cas system and its role in phage-bacteria interaction. Ann Rev Microbiol 64:475-93, 2010.

Houlihan CF, Whitworth JAG: Outbreak science: Recent progress in the detection and response to outbreaks of infectious diseases. Clin Med 19:140-4, 2019.

Leung NHL, Xu C, Cowling BJ, et al: The fraction of influenza virus infections that are asymptomatic. Epidemiology 26: 862-72, 2015.

Liu Z, Wang J, Liu X, et al: Implications of the virus-encoded miRNA and host miRNA in the pathogenicity of SARS-CoV-2. arXiv 2004.04874, 2020.

Macedo AC, De Faria AOV, Ghazzi P: Boosting the immune system, from science to myth: Analysis the infosphere with google. Front Med 6: 165, 2019.

Nile SH, Nile A, Kai G, et al: Covid-19: Pathogenesis, cytokine storm and therapeutic potential of interferons. Cytokine Growth Factor Rev, doi 10.1016, 2020.

Olivarius K: The dangerous history of immune privilege. NY Times, 4/12/2020, Opinion page.

Prompetchara E, Ketloy C, Palaga T: Immune responses in covid-19 and potential vaccines. Asian Pacif J Allergy Immunol doi 10.12932, 2020.

Riley LW, Blanton R: Advances in molecular epidemiology of infectious diseases. Microbiol Spectr 6: doi 10.1128, 2018.

Rowley AH, Shulman ST: The epidemiology and pathogenesis of Kawasaki disease. Front Pediatr doi 10.3369, 2018.

Shang J, Wan Y, Li F et al: Cell entry mechanisms of SARS-CoV2. PNAS 117:11727-34, 2020.

Sun C, Wang Y, Liu G, Liu Z: Role of the eye in transmitting human coronavirus. Front Pub Health doi 10:3389, 2020.

Tisoncik JR, Korth MJ, Katze MG et al: Into the eye of the cytokine storm. Microbiol Mol Biol Rev 76:16-32, 2012.

Boosting Immunity

Aiello A, Frazaneh F, Accardi G: Immunosenescense and its hallmarks: How to oppose aging strategically? Front Immunol 2019.

Macedo AC, Vilela de Faria AO, Gezzi D: Boosting the immune system, from science to myth. Analysis the infosfere with google. Front Med 6: 165, 2019.

Marques RE, Marques PE, Texeira MM, et al: Exploring the homeostatic and sensory roles of the immune system. Front Immunol 7: 125, 2018.

Wu D, Lewis ED, Meydani N, et al: Nutritional modulation of immune function: analysis of evidence, mechanism and clinical relevance. Front Immunol 9: 3160, 2018.

Chapter 24. Call to Action, a guide.

Dufresne S, Rebillard A, Friedenreich CM, et al: Review of physical activity and circulating miRNA expression: Implication in cancer risk and progression. Cancer Epidemiol 27: doi 1055-9965,2018.

Song T, Liang Y, Cao Z, et al: Computational analysis of specific microRNA biomarkers for non-invasive early cancer detection. Biomed Res Int soi 10.1155/4680650, 2017.

Tandy-Connor S, Guiltinan J, Krempeley M, et al: False-positive results released in direct-to-consumer genetic tests highlights the importance of clinical confirmation in the appropriate care of patients. Genetics Med 2018, doi.